THE LOCUST YEARS

The Story of the
Fourth French Republic

1946–1958

FRANK GILES

Carroll & Graf Publishers, Inc.
New York

Published by arrangement with Reed Consumer Books, London

First Carroll & Graf edition June 1994

Carroll & Graf Publishers, Inc.
260 Fifth Avenue
New York, NY 10001

Library of Congress Cataloging-in-Publication Data

Giles, Frank.
    The locust years : the story of the Fourth Republic, 1946–1958 /
Frank Giles.
        p.   cm.
    ISBN 0-7867-0056-4 : $26.95
    1. France—Politics and government—1945–1958. 2. Monnet,
Jean, 1888– —Influence. 3. Gaulle, Charles de, 1890–1970—
Influence. I. Title.
DC404.G53   1994
944.082—dc20   94-4673
                                                                  CIP

Manufactured in the United States of America

For Kitty

'And I will restore to you the years
that the locust hath eaten . . .'

The Book of Joel 2:25

'Oui, la France se relèvera.'

General de Gaulle, London, 26 June 1940

'The Fourth French Republic was arguably the most successful
of all French Republics, except that it failed.'

R.E.M. Irving, *The First Indochina War* (1975)

Contents

Illustrations

1. The Champs-Elysées on Liberation Day.
2. De Gaulle leaves Notre-Dame after a service of thanksgiving.
3. Georges Bidault and Ho Chi Minh.
4. Recording the results of the national referendum, 13 October 1946.
5. Strike at the Renault factory, May 1947.
6. Parisians queue for a bus.
7. Violence in the coalfields, October 1948.
8. Robert Schuman presents his government to Vincent Auriol.
9. Jean Monnet.
10. Antoine Pinay.
11. Dien Bien Phu.
12. Public anguish in Paris at the news from Indochina.
13. Pierre Mendès-France.
14. Pierre Poujade.
15. General Massu.
16. The mob in Algiers storm the government offices.
17. The 'Committee of Public Safety'.
18. De Gaulle at his press conference, 19 May 1958.
19. The 'Republican' demonstration against De Gaulle, 28 May 1958.
20. President Coty greets General de Gaulle at the Elysée.
21. De Gaulle at the Arc de Triomphe, 8 January 1959.

Photo credits: Nos. 1 and 12, Magnum Photos Limited; 2, 3, 5, 8, 9, 10, 11, 14, 15, 16, 17, 18, 19, 20 and 21, The Hulton Picture Company; 4, 6 and 7, *Illustrated London News*; 13, Camera Press.

The map on p.55, reprinted from *The First Indochina War* by R.E.M. Irving, is reproduced by permission of Croom Helm Ltd.

Preface

The first, and not the simplest, task of anyone writing about the Fourth French Republic is to define its time-span – when it was born and when it expired.

One possible birthday is 21 October 1945, when the French people, finally freed of the last remnants of German occupation, voted in a national referendum to kill off the preceding, Third, Republic and replace it with another régime. Another way of looking at it is to say that the Fourth Republic effectively came into existence on 13 October 1946. On that day, in a national referendum, the electorate approved by a narrow majority the second draft of a new Constitution, a first draft having been rejected by an earlier referendum on 5 May 1946. A third version would be to say that the new Republic did not begin to function in all its attributes until 20 January 1947, when with the election of Vincent Auriol as its first President, the new régime was equipped with the last of its component parts.

At the other end of the span, the Fourth Republic was to all intents and purposes put to sleep on 1 June 1958, when under the threat of civil war General de Gaulle, having been asked by President Coty to form a government, became Prime Minister with the task of drawing up a new Constitution to replace the one accepted in October 1946. That new Constitution was approved, by a massive majority, in a referendum on 28 September 1958. But the Fifth Republic did not formally begin its life, and therefore the Fourth was not clinically dead, until 8 January 1959, when General de Gaulle, as newly elected President, took over from René Coty, the second and last President of the Fourth Republic.

Whatever chronology is favoured, I have tried to tell the story of France from the moment of the Liberation in 1944 to the upheaval which in 1958 brought de Gaulle back to power. I have drawn upon many published and some unpublished sources and have benefited from numerous conversations with those – French, British, American, Belgian – who were involved in one way or another with developments in France and its domestic and foreign policies during these twelve years.

My special thanks are due to Professor Douglas Johnson, Emeritus Professor of French History at the University of London, who read the entire text and made many expert and valuable comments. Mr Munir Benjenk, who lived in Paris for many of the Fourth Republic's troubled years, also read the complete typescript and suggested corrections and emendations. M. Robert Rothschild, formerly Belgian Ambassador in Paris and London, who was *directeur de cabinet* to Belgium's Foreign Minister, Paul-Henri Spaak, in the 1950s, read some of the text, and so did Sir Brooks Richards, who in his distinguished diplomatic career has served two spells at the British Embassy in Paris. Mrs Susan-Mary Alsop, a former Paris resident, also read several chapters. While acknowledging my debt to these helpful critics, I remain responsible for everything I have written.

Among those who have spent time and trouble supplying me with information are: M. Maurice Aicardi, Mme Jacques de Beaumarchais, M. Bérard-Quélin, M. L'Ambassadeur Geoffroi de Courcel, M. Jacques Chaban-Delmas, M. Michel Debré, M. Maurice Faure, M. Jacques de Folin, M. André Fontaine (Editor of *Le Monde*), M. Olivier Guichard, M. l'Ambassadeur Robert Gillet, M. Claude Kemoularia. M. Jean Laloi, M. l'Ambassadeur Emmanuel de Margerie, the late Général Jean-Louis de Rougemont and Mme de Rougemont, M. Maurice Schumann, Lord Gladwyn (Gladwyn Jebb), Lord Plowden, Sir Frank Roberts, Mr Douglas Dillon, Mr Matthew Looram and Mr Richard Holbrook. In the *Times* office in Paris, Phil Jacobson and Nora Harper were extremely helpful. I want to thank all of these, and still greater is my debt to my old friend M. Vincent Labouret, who has been unsparing with his advice, wisdom and Parisian hospitality. During the Paris researches, Claude and Marguerite Labouret were also generous hosts, and so were Sir Ewen and Lady Fergusson, who preside with such distinction over the splendours of the British Embassy.

I must also express thanks for their helpfulness and courtesy to the staffs of the following libraries: the London Library, Chatham House (Royal Institute of International Affairs), the

Institut Français de Londres, the Taylorian Institute, Oxford, the Bibliothèque Nationale, Paris, and the Library of Congress, Washington DC.

One source which I have used throughout has been my own despatches (what an old-fashioned ring that word has in the parlance of modern journalism) to *The Times* in London. I was the assistant correspondent in the *Times* office in Paris from May 1947 to December 1949, and chief correspondent there from February 1953 to December 1960. I therefore had a ringside seat at many of the events described in this book, and over the years filed hundreds of thousands of words to the paper about French affairs.

While this long experience is no guarantee of what the Collect for Whit Sunday calls 'a right judgement in all things', it has certainly helped in the task of describing the developments I witnessed. Because this is not a personal memoir but an attempt at an historical record, I have made only a few references to my own contributions to the *Times* file, but inevitably they, and my own memories, have played their part, for better or for worse, in shaping and presenting the narrative, and trying to impart the flavour of what life in France during those years was really like.

One special acknowledgement I must make, and that is done with a heavy heart. The book was first commissioned by Barley Alison, a director at Secker & Warburg and the master-mind behind her own illustrious imprint, the Alison Press. I had known Barley in Paris after the war, when she was serving in the British Embassy. Her interest in and knowledge of French affairs was considerable, and it therefore gave me pleasure and confidence when she said she would take the book under her wing. 'You could start', she wrote, 'with the Liberation of Paris if you felt like it and end with de Gaulle's takeover.' That is just what I have done. Alas, Barley saw only the first few draft chapters, which I am glad to say she liked. On 28 May 1989, she died suddenly.

Dan Franklin, the publisher of Secker & Warburg, then took over the book, and his constant encouragement has been of great help. I also owe a lot to Steve Cox, who brought impressive expertise to the editing of the text. For the index, I was fortunate to secure the services of that prince of craftsmen, Mr Douglas Matthews, of the London Library.

F.G.

Prelude

On 4 April 1954, Joseph Laniel, the Prime Minister of France (or President of the Council, as he was called under the Fourth Republic; in this book, the person holding this office will for convenience be described as Prime Minister), accompanied by René Pleven, the Minister of National Defence, attended a special mass, held at the church of St Louis des Invalides, for those who had been killed in the Indochinese war, then more than seven years old. A few weeks previously, the Vietminh, Ho Chi Minh's army, had laid siege to Dien Bien Phu, the entrenched camp in Northern Vietnam which the French High Command had decided – against the strong advice of the General Staff in Paris – to make the centre of its efforts to control the north of the country. Since then, just as the generals in Paris had warned, things had been going badly for the camp's 10,000 defenders. The Vietminh had them pinned down in the hollow where their superiors had so unwisely chosen to base them. Heroic though their resistance was, it was becoming unpleasantly clear that only an intervention by the American air force could avert a French disaster.

Not that French opinion generally seemed, at that stage, to be much moved by the prospect. The Indochinese war had never impinged upon popular imagination. It was a long way away. No conscripts were ever sent there. There were other things, nearer to home, to think about. In particular, there was the plan for a European Defence Community (EDC), a device thought up by the French themselves for allowing the rearming of Germany without creating the dangers of an independent *Wehrmacht* and a German General Staff. For all its ingenuity, the plan had met with some strong opposition since its promulgation two years earlier. This was especially true in the Army, where anxieties over careers and a mistrust of the traditional enemy mingled with fears that the French Army, as part of this new hybrid, might become an emasculated and inglorious imitation of its former self.

Alphonse Juin, the only living Marshal of France, had made himself the spokesman for these fears. A few days before Laniel and Pleven sallied forth to honour the fallen of Indochina, the Marshal, who never hesitated to call a spade a spade and did not mind who heard him doing it, had made a particularly mordant attack, at a dinner for serving and reserve officers, on the EDC. He was especially bitter about the Laniel government's unwillingness to listen to his earlier warnings, delivered only a few days previously: 'I am not going to say Mass twice for deaf men,' he said insultingly.[1] No government worthy of the name could accept this, even from a Marshal of France. Laniel called a Cabinet meeting, at which it was decided (despite the reservations of some ministers) to relieve Juin of his functions as military adviser to the government and Vice-President of the High Council for National Defence. He was left only with his international post as Commander-in-Chief of NATO forces in central Europe.

A few days after this punishment was promulgated, General de Gaulle, who since his resignation as head of the first post-war pro- visional government eight years earlier had kept up an intermittent verbal assault on the men and machinery of the Fourth Republic, was asked at a press conference what he would have done if, as head of the government, he had been thus confronted by a general officer. With a sublime lack of modesty he replied: 'I was France, the State, the government. I spoke in the name of France. I was the independence and the sovereignty of France. That moreover was why, finally, everyone obeyed me.'[2]

From St Louis des Invalides, on that early spring morning in 1954, the Prime Minister and Minister for National Defence went to the Arc de Triomphe where, at the tomb of the Unknown Soldier, nearly all Parisian patriotic ceremonies tend to terminate. A large crowd of ex-servicemen – one of the most powerful and vociferous pressure groups in France – awaited them. This crowd booed and jeered. Gaullist groups distributed pamphlets with, on one side, the legend, 'Today Juin is sacked, tomorrow will de Gaulle be arrested?' and on the other side, 'Will Juin be replaced by von Stülpnagel?' (Commander-in-Chief of the German forces of Occu- pation in France, 1942–4). Laniel was molested, and only with difficulty was he escorted to the car of the Chief of Staff. Pleven was struck in the face by a senior officer. The attendant forces of police showed a noticeable lack of interest in maintaining and restoring order.

Commenting on this deplorable scene the next day, Hubert Beuve-Méry, the editor of *Le Monde*, wrote: 'A danger is reborn which is the logical consequence of inertia and political incompetence. Dictatorships are born from the impotence and disorder of democracies.' Beuve-Méry was not alone in harbouring these sentiments. A year later François Mauriac, the gloomy and prophetic Catholic intellectual, writer, novelist and pamphleteer whose views were simultaneously admired and abhorred, according to the standpoint of those reading them, wrote of 'these last sad years' that 'the great burgeoning of hope which the Liberation caused to spring from the soil of our downtrodden country has wilted, its branches leafless and already dead.'[3] Yet that rowdy episode at the Arc de Triomphe occurred less than eight years after French voters, with their approval by referendum of a new Constitution, had brought into being the Fourth French Republic, successor to the largely discredited Third Republic. Though this referendum was a half-hearted affair, with one-third of the electorate abstaining and nearly one-third voting against, it was the culmination of a long process of discussion and compromise.

Mauriac had been right to speak of the hopes which accompanied the Liberation of France in 1944. To those emerging from their time of trial then, the years of defeat and despair were over. A brighter future seemed to beckon, so people hoped, in which pre-war scandals, maladministration, political intrigue, party strife, and what men of the Left saw as the uncontrolled power of big business would have no part. So what had gone wrong? What had happened to the noble vision of a fairer, more united and better ordered France? Had that vision been, in fact, no more than a pipe-dream; was the reality represented by the bitterness and contempt of the crowd at the Arc de Triomphe?

CHAPTER 1

The General Comes and Goes

It was hardly surprising that the Liberation of Paris in late August 1944 was marked with scenes of wild and patriotic enthusiasm. General de Gaulle, parading down the Champs Elysées and proceeding to Notre Dame for a thanksgiving ceremony, was the central and acclaimed figure (just as, a few months earlier, Marshal Pétain, paying his only visit to German-occupied Paris, was given a rapturous welcome by the crowds, for whom his uniform and Marshal's badges of rank were the first reminder of French military dignity they had seen for nearly four years). But at Notre Dame there was trouble. Shots rang out, bullets ricocheted off the walls, people threw themselves to the ground, the service had to be cut short. Accounts differ about the source of the shooting. One historian[1] quotes the innocent theory, advanced by some of those present, that the culprits were the pigeons within the Cathedral; disturbed in their lofty nests by the commotion below, they flew about, according to this account, with a great flapping of wings, whereupon the armed escort opened fire. The General's immediate reaction, expressed in a letter to his wife the day after, was to dismiss the shooting as an example of over-excitement – 'The first shot was the signal for general and promiscuous firing'.[2] But in his memoirs, written ten years later, he took a more sinister view. By that time, he had decided that the trouble was caused by the Communists, wishing to perpetuate the maintenance of revolutionary power and the continued functioning of the (largely Communist-dominated) local Committees of Liberation.[3]

Already de Gaulle, never one to welcome power sharing, had demonstrated his reservations towards the Resistance – i.e. the internal anti-German and anti-Vichy organisations. On the way down the Champs Elysées, he had been accompanied by the members of the National Council of the Resistance (CNR), the supreme body of the internal Resistance of which Georges Bidault, the future foreign minister, was President. At a certain point, Bidault, a small, somewhat feline, and certainly not military figure, broke ranks and moved forward to march level with the towering de Gaulle. The latter was not having this. '*Monsieur, un peu en arrière, s'il vous plaît*,' he ordered.[4] It was not the only rebuke for the wretched Bidault. 'There are two things which exasperate de Gaulle,' he said in his sardonic way some time later, 'two things which he can't abide: the Allies and the Resistance.'[5]

The previous day, de Gaulle, as head of the provisional government, had been formally received at the Paris Hôtel de Ville. As President of the CNR, Bidault asked him 'solemnly to proclaim the Republic'. 'The Republic has never ceased to exist,' retorted the General. 'Free France, Fighting France, the French Committee of National Liberation [the precursor in Algiers of the provisional government] have all in turn embodied it. Vichy always was and remains null and void. I am the President of the government of the Republic. Why should I proclaim the Republic now?'[6] And off he went, back to his office at the War Ministry in the Rue St Dominique, which he had chosen as his headquarters in order to emphasise the continuity of the real, legitimate France in comparison with the transitory and now defunct Vichy regime. It was in these offices that Clemenceau had installed himself in 1917, and here that in the summer of 1940 de Gaulle had performed for a couple of weeks the duties of Under-Secretary of State in the doomed Reynaud government, the last to rule France before defeat and the onset of the Vichy régime.

The Fourth Republic, the subject of this book, did not formally see the light of day until the autumn of 1946, when the second of two national referenda on a new Constitution brought it into being. The two years between the Liberation and that date were a transitional period, a kind of constitutional no-man's-land. Despite de Gaulle's assertion about the continuity of the Republic, the Third Republic, initiated in 1875, had in effect committed suicide in July 1940 when, in the bitter hour of defeat by Hitler's Germany, the Senate and the Chamber of Deputies, sitting together, had voted full powers to Marshal Pétain. The rival government of General de Gaulle, which began its existence in Algiers in 1943, transferring to Paris as soon as the liberation of the capital made it possible to do so, was at first no more than a provisional administration, unrecognised at that stage by either the British or American governments. But at least this provisional arrangement had made it possible for de Gaulle to take steps to thwart both the Anglo-American plans to impose Allied military government upon liberated France and the intentions, real or suspected, of the Communist-dominated element of the Resistance to seize power. In the first months of 1944 decisions were taken and proclaimed in Algiers which asserted the responsibilities in liberated France of the Committee of National Liberation, and appointed special commissioners (*commissaires de la République*) to take charge of administration in the liberated regions. By these same decisions, the targets for social and economic policy were also defined.

With the war still unfinished, German armies fighting on French soil and French prisoners-of-war still in captivity, to establish new, democratically elected institutions was impossible. But already in 1943, in Algiers, de Gaulle, seeking to strengthen his position vis-à-vis London and Washington by building up his own legitimacy, had introduced representatives of the traditional parties, including the Communists, into the National Council of the Resistance. He was before long to begin complaining about the encroachments of these parties onto ground where they had, according to him, no business to be. But it was he who had first breathed new life into them, and he had done so precisely to enhance his own authority in face of the possible pretensions of the internal Resistance.

If the General appeared suspicious of and ungenerous to the Resistance, it was because he was determined that there must be no rival to the central authority of the State which it was his purpose to rebuild. For the first few months after the Liberation, it was inevitable that the newly installed authorities had in many cases to share power with the Communist-dominated militia and the local liberation committees in much of southern France. But from the start, the General left no doubt as to who was to be master. On 28 August 1944 he summoned the members of the CNR and told them they would be absorbed into the Consultative Assembly, the nearest thing to parliament possible at that time of continuing war. At the same time, he ordered the Forces Françaises de l'Intérieur (FFI) to be dissolved and its men transferred to the order of battle of the regular French Army, where they could continue the fight against the Germans.

Early in September, de Gaulle announced the formation of the first provisional government for liberated France. Its members, if they were not all Gaullists (the term, as a political label, had not yet become part of ordinary usage), all shared to a greater or lesser degree the hopes and objectives of the post-Liberation days. De Gaulle's appointments were a shrewd mixture of Resistance representatives, new to the field of national politics, such as Bidault; pre-war party politicians, such as Pierre Mendès-France; and a number of non-political figures. They comprised two Communists, four Socialists, three Mouvement Républicain Populaire (MRP) – the newly constituted Christian Democrat type of Catholic party, which brought the confessional element into the government for the first time in the history of Republican France – three Radicals, one 'Moderate' (right-wing) and nine apolitical men.

In view of his later fulminations against the political parties of the Fourth Republic for the way in which Ministries were formed according to the principle of everyone having a fair share of the cake (*'dosage'*, in French political jargon), the degree to which de Gaulle applied the very same principles is remarkable. But then he was trying to build a government of real national unity, however fragile that unity might be below the surface. The Provisional Consultative Assembly also reflected the same balance of forces as between the internal and external Resistance, as well as containing sixty of the members from the Assembly elected in 1936 who had voted against Pétain in July 1940.

If the General, in the interests of re-establishing firm central authority, was intent on cutting the Resistance down to size, that did not detract from the intense impact of the ideas and aspirations of the men and women who had fought in its ranks and who now, in an upsurge of hope and optimism, were like people emerging from darkness into light. In this first radiant dawn of the Liberation, there was no doubt – or if there was, the doubters kept a prudent silence – about the widespread wish to turn the page on the past and open a new one. The prevailing note, sounded most insistently in the programme of the CNR, was for a greater role for the State in the management of the economy and the nationalisation of a large part of the country's productive capacity. In many respects, the CNR's ideas were an enlargement of the policies of the Socialist-led, Communist-backed Popular Front of the Thirties, policies which had been derided and opposed at the time by the Right. Now that Right had been (temporarily) silenced, discredited by its support of Vichy. Instead, the Left, a broad spectrum running from the MRP through the Socialists to the Communists, fortified with the moral authority of the Resistance, had become the guardian of the national interest.

Even *Le Figaro*, not normally associated with left-wing ideology, looked forward to 'harmonising the freedom of the individual, which is more necessary and more sacred than ever, with the collective organisation of society, made inevitable by the conditions of modern life'.[7] *Combat*, the new newspaper which had Albert Camus as its leader writer and represented more than any other publication the purest spirit of the Resistance, proclaimed in its first issue (21 August 1944) that 'We shall have achieved only a tiny part of our task if the French Republic of tomorrow becomes strictly dependent, like the Third Republic, upon the power of money . . . The liberation of Paris is only one step in the liberation of France . . . and here we must read the word liberation in its broadest sense.' The paper's standing slogan was *'de la Résistance à la Révolution'*. François Mauriac, typically lyrical, was even more starry-eyed. In an article with the title 'Towards a humanist socialism', he wrote:

> That the great mass of the French people has rediscovered their pride in their country, no one today can deny. The bourgeoisie, taken as a whole, is resigned to the inevitable. There are no longer on the left enough 'non-patriots' [i.e. Muscovite Communists], and the Right no longer numbers enough inflexible opponents to legal revolution for the political elements in the country to group themselves, as formerly they did, around these two antagonistic poles. Hence the possibility of a vast gathering of the French people, whom the Resistance has already brought together.

Read today, such words reveal a level of naïveté and clouded judgement that strains credulity. But this is using hindsight. In 1944, great numbers of French people really did think and hope like this. The CNR charter, though socialistic in spirit, was not a revolutionary programme. If anything, it could be likened to a more radical version of the New Deal. As far as it was what a writer in *Le Monde* called a collection of wishes rather than a real programme of reforms,[8] it commanded a wide measure of support. De Gaulle spoke for all who shared these hopes when, in Lille at the end of September 1944, he outlined the objectives which France needed to reach: 'State control over the management of riches shared in common, security and dignity guaranteed to each worker.' He waxed lyrical over the prospects offered by *dirigisme* and a State-controlled economy: 'We want it to be the State which, for the benefit of all, spearheads the economic effort of the entire nation and acts in such a way as to improve the life of each French man and woman.' It was almost as though he was revealing himself as a closet Socialist.

But then Socialism, in its updated form of '*Travaillisme*', became a fashionable will-o'-the-wisp, enthusiastically pursued by the veteran Socialist leader Léon Blum, who returned from a German con- centration camp in April 1945. In his first speech to his party colleagues after he got back to France, he boldly claimed that 'Socialism is the meeting point . . . of all the great currents now sweeping across France, Europe and the whole world . . . Economic liberalism is dead.' However mistaken he turned out to be in the long run, his confident assertion in 1945 seemed to be well supported by developments in France. Months before Blum was again breathing the air of freedom and before the country was finally rid of the German invader, a new economic and social structure was going up. At the end of September 1944, the northern coal-mines were nationalised, followed four months later by the Renault factories. Before the end of 1945, the aeronautical industry had been nationalised and Air France created as a national airline. The Bank of France and the four biggest deposit banks passed under the control of the State, as did the whole credit system. Over the same period (December 1944–October 1945) a social security scheme obligatory for all wage-earners – the French equivalent to Beveridge – was established by ordinance (although delays and difficulties meant that this did not become fully comprehensive until as late as 1967).

All these reforms and innovations derived more or less directly from the ideas of the Resistance and the programme of the CNR. *Dirigiste* in flavour, they embraced the obligation to ensure that French destinies should never again be allowed to pass into the hands of 'the trusts' (large private concerns) that had contributed – as popular legend had it – to France's downfall and disgrace in 1940. Yet although the various nationalisation bills were voted by large majorities in the Consultative Assembly – the disorganised and depressed state of the Right contributed to this result – the Communists did not altogether approve of these nationalisations.

Their role in the Resistance and careful fostering of their reputation as the guardians of Republican virtues were court cards in their hand, but that did not mean they accepted the rules of the new card game. 'We are in favour of revolution, tomorrow,' explained Maurice Thorez, the Communist leader (who returned to France in November 1944 from the Soviet Union, whither he had fled, a deserter from the French Army, in 1939). 'Meanwhile today we want the capitalist régime to function according to its own laws, which must be left intact. We are not going to help the capitalist régime to reform itself.'[9]

This piece of higher pragmatism did not deter the Communists, once the nationalisation programme had got under way, from systematically infiltrating the staffs, above all the senior posts, of the newly nationalised concerns. A good example of this process can be found in the activities of Charles Tillon, who was the Communist minister in charge of the aircraft industry for the first two years after the Liberation. Directly the Gnôme-et-Rhône plant and other well-known aircraft construction factories were nationalised, a Communist was appointed director-general, flanked by five directors, also Communists. The head of the personnel department and his staff, all Communists, were responsible for recruitment. Most of the technicians who had served the private company were dismissed, the number of such posts raised from 232 to 396, and all of them were filled with Communists or fellow-travellers.[10] Recruitment advertisements were placed only in *L'Humanité* and three other Communist or Communist-sympathising newspapers. Pressure was exerted on heads of department and, through them, on the work-force to join the Confédération Générale du Travail (CGT), the Communist-dominated union. Dues collected by joint workers' and management committees, intended by law to be used for social purposes, were deflected to subsidise a Communist propaganda sheet. These details only emerged three years later, long after the Communists had left the government, but they serve to show how the post-Liberation upheavals were used by the Communists to build up their power and prestige. Some of the more acute observers were conscious from an early stage of what was going on. At the Socialist Congress of September 1946, André Philip, a prominent Socialist, complained of the way in which the Communists were 'using nationalised industries (for example the mines) in order to achieve their party's domination of the very structure of the State'.[11]

Whether or not these post-war reforms constituted a new French Revolution, and if so, whether they should be placed to the credit of the Fourth Republic, are nice points. Though the Third Republic was effectively dead, the Fourth did not exist, in any constitutional sense, in 1944 and 1945. Non-existent entities cannot be apportioned anything, either praise or blame. And there is also the question of what makes a revolution, how great must the upheaval be to gain the title? Years later, Raymond Aron, the journalist, sociologist and scholar, said to de Gaulle, who by then had withdrawn from the political scene, that French people from time to time make a revolution but never reforms, to which the General replied: 'They only make reforms on the occasion of a revolution.'[12] In his immodest way, he always considered himself to be the only revolutionary in France. If his claim is in any way tenable, then history must accord him at least some of the credit for driving through the reforming ideas which originated in the Resistance. None was to prove more significant for the future of post-war France than the creation (the work principally of Michel Debré, a future prime minister of the Fifth Republic) of the Ecole Nationale d'Administration, the forcing ground for clever French diplomatists and civil servants, and an antidote, as it were, to the Ecole Libre des Sciences Politiques ('Sciences Po'), with its traditional views of history and its embodiment of economic liberalism. Equally important, and equally to the credit of de Gaulle, was the creation of the Commissariat Général au Plan, in other words the Monnet Plan which, under the inspired leadership of Jean Monnet, was to plan and direct the 'modernisation and equipment of metropolitan and overseas France'. The decree which brought the Plan into existence was passed, without parliament ever being consulted, in early January 1946. Not bad going, it might be thought, for a country whose economy had been smashed by war and occupation, part of whose territory was still occupied by the enemy, whose prisoners-of-war did not begin to return home until the spring of 1945, whose yearnings for national unity were constantly being challenged by the trials of collaborators and men of Vichy, and numerous of whose senior civil servants had to be dismissed because of their service under Pétain.

The incidence and effects of *l'épuration* – meaning, in this context, the process of punishing and removing from their posts all those who could be proved to have voluntarily collaborated with the Germans or been the willing servants of the Vichy régime – were important elements in post-Liberation France. Those who suffered under it, and their families, were often provided with a sense of grievance, as equally were many Resistants and non-collaborators who felt that retribution had not gone far enough. For years to come, stories were propagated (mostly by disgruntled Vichy sympathisers) that the Resistance movement, led and encouraged by the Communists among them, had prior to the Liberation indulged in an orgy of summary vengeance. Certainly something of the sort went on. Rough justice, the paying off of old scores, personal vendettas were all the more or less inevitable sequel to the years of occupation and different attitudes towards it. The military tribunals of the FFI, the self-appointed courts-martial and the *tribunaux populaires* carried out their own unofficial form of *épuration*, estimated years later by Robert Aron to have led to between 30,000 and 40,000 summary executions. Subsequent findings, notably an inquiry by the Comité d'Histoire de la Deuxième Guerre Mondiale,[13] put the figure far lower: about 9,000 summary executions, most of them the work of the Resistance before the Allied landings, plus 767 death sentences carried out later as a result of trials under the law. Many of those concerned probably deserved their punishment, some perhaps did not. But inevitably the *épuration*, which ought to have been a great national act of self-healing, too often assumed, or at least was suspected of assuming, a political colour. With the coming of the Cold War two years later, these stories of 'Communist justice' took on added emphasis and commanded wider credence.

Various courts were established by the provisional government to deal with cases of collaboration. Because their jurisdiction was necessarily retrospective, they could not help being seen as courts of exception. As well as the special Cours de Justice, they included the civic courts concerned with alleged offences of *indignité nationale* – for example, membership of the Vichy militia and anti-Jewish organisations or other bodies in favour of collaboration. There were also departmental committees which examined cases of economic collaboration, including the making of illicit profits. Finally, the High Court was set up for trials of members of the Vichy government. The juries for this were drawn partly from a list of pre-war parliamentarians, partly from a list of Resistants. This provision, and the four-member juries for the special courts, in whose choosing the local liberation committees had, at least to begin with, a large hand, invited the criticism that the aggrieved had been authorised to judge the aggressors.

As the result of this official *épuration*, up to the end of 1948 just over 160,000 cases were examined, of which 45 per cent ended in acquittal, 25 per cent in *dégradation nationale*,* 16 per cent in prison or detention, 8 per cent in forced labour, and 4 per cent in death sentences (7,037, of which 4,397 were *in absentia*).[14] By comparison, 400,000 cases of collaboration were heard in Belgium, 110,000 in the Netherlands, and 90,000 in Norway, far less populous countries. According to one modern historian, 'as a painful epilogue to the civil war which had raged since 1940, the *épuration* in France was moderate, much more so than in Belgium, Holland, Norway and Denmark'.[15]

In addition to the judicial process, an administrative purge in each government department created its own problems, as experienced officials were relieved of their posts, to be replaced with others with a more estimable war record but fewer, or sometimes no, qualifications (see p. 43). But even this process was limited. As de Gaulle declared in July 1944, it was out of the question to 'sweep aside' the great majority of civil servants. Two months later, he was back on the same theme, emphasising France's need of 'all her children' in the work of national reconstruction.

The General's own judgement on the *épuration*, summarised years later in his war memoirs, was that 'the work of justice was carried out as impartially as it was humanly possible to do in the midst of passions aroused. The judgements were rare which had subsequently to be recognised as ill-founded.'[16] This rather bland generalisation takes no account of the controversy stirred up, at the time and later, by the course of *épuration*. Much of it came from the ranks of the demoralised and discredited Right, intent upon accusing the Resistance, and first and foremost the Communists, of betraying the cause of justice for political and vengeful ends. Such arguments had some foundation. Delays and irregularities did characterise some of the *épuration* process: the Laval trial before the High Court (October 1945) was a gruesome farce, with some of the (political) jury threatening the accused in open court with the firing

---

* This was the punishment for those convicted of *indignité nationale*. It involved deprivation, for varying periods, of civil and political rights and a ban on wearing decorations or entering certain professions.

squad. De Gaulle, appealed to, chose not to stay or remit the death sentence, despite the fact that Laval had tried at the last moment to poison himself and had to be almost dragged to face the firing squad. Nor did these objections come only from the Right. None was more energetic than François Mauriac, in his *Figaro* articles, in arguing the case for clemency, above all for writers accused of collaboration. On the other hand, the administrative purge of ministries and the civil service was seen by many as being too lenient; in an opinion poll of December 1944, 65 per cent thought it insufficient.

If there is anything more devastating for the morale and unity of a nation than civil war, it is the aftermath to civil war. The gallantry of the Resistance, its hopes for the future, forged as they were in the comradeship of danger and sacrifice, could not offset the fact that the men and women of the Resistance were a small minority compared with the 'silent and massive acquiescence'[17] of the rest of the population in the Vichy régime. Unlike the First World War, from which the country emerged grievously stricken but victorious and united, all French people having undergone the same experiences and sufferings, the 1940–44 time of trial divided France into different families, ranging from the heroes of the Resistance or the Free French forces to the unashamed apologists for a new, Nazi-inspired order in Europe. In between these two extremes stood a great mass of ordinary French men and women, neither Resistants nor collaborators, silent and often unhappy witnesses to the condition to which destiny and human failings had reduced their proud and ancient nation.

In such circumstances, it was one thing to talk about and hope for national unity and something quite different to realise it. In the period immediately after the Liberation, aspirations naturally tended to soar above the level of ordinary mortal values, notably in the longing for a more efficient State and a fairer society. De Gaulle himself, in his memoirs, set the scene for this sought-after resurgence when he wrote that ever since the collapse of Napoleon and the First Empire France had been living 'in a chronic state of infirmity, insecurity and acrimony'. The 1918 victory had revived morale, but only until the 1940 defeat, when 'the soul of France died a little more'. So many disasters, he observed, had inflicted terrible wounds upon national unity. All fifteen régimes supervening since 1789, 'each in turn installed by revolution or *coup d'état*', had been swept away by catastrophes, leaving 'ineffaceable divisions' behind them.[18]

This gloomy interpretation of recent French history (which fails notably to accord the tribute due to the Third Republic for its many remarkable achievements) contrasts with the tone of de Gaulle himself, as head of the provisional government after the war, when in numerous speeches and broadcasts he emphasised the blossoming of a new sense of national unity. Speaking to the first meeting of the Consultative Assembly in the Luxembourg Palace on 9 November 1944, for example, he said that it was 'inevitable and desirable' that different tendencies in public opinion should be expressed, but added that 'there is no reason to doubt that when the vital interests of France are involved, all will be able to recreate the same admirable unanimity which enabled them to stand up to the oppressor and the arms of the invader'.[19] He must have known that this was rhetoric, that the 'admirable unanimity', so far as it had existed, had been in favour of accepting, however reluctantly, Vichy and defeat. He was no doubt trying, as he had a right and duty to do, to raise morale and inspire his countrymen with the urge to create a new society. But read today, these speeches, for all their warning note about the hard road ahead, seem to have pitched expectations impossibly high. Given the long record of 'ineffaceable divisions', given the strains imposed by occupation and resistance (or non-resistance) to it, given that *épuration* was bound to reopen as many old wounds as it healed, it was not very likely that sweetness and light were going, suddenly and miraculously, to prevail. One answer thus already suggests itself to the question of what went wrong with post-Liberation hopes: noble and visionary though they were, they had no more reality than a dream which, like most dreams, dies at the opening day.

At least the broadly based nature of de Gaulle's first post-Liberation government preserved the appearance of unity, however much the underlying facts might belie it. Not that the general public paid much attention. It was too preoccupied, that first winter of Liberation and partial peace, trying to keep warm and feed itself. 'Parisians are colder than they have been any other winter of the war,' reported Janet Flanner in January 1945; 'they are hungrier than they have been any other winter of the war.'[20] Two months later, she noted that 'the great disappointment to the man in the street and the woman in the kitchen was that de Gaulle [in his important speech to the Assembly, outlining his plans for the future of France] did not say a word about butter'. The last time there was an issue of rationed butter had been the previous Christmas Eve.

People were resentful and critical, to say the least. Meanwhile the apparently uncontrollable, or at least uncontrolled, black market seemed to make a mockery of all those bright hopes of justice and efficiency and incorruptibility. Never an easy or docile people to govern, the French public's natural tendency to grumble about the way it is being ruled and the men doing the ruling received a powerful impetus in this post-Liberation era – indeed, for a long time to come – in the shape of mismanagement of the distribution and supply of food. To an average family, and on a day-to-day basis, this is what mattered far more than the debates in the Assembly or the efforts at Constitution-making. The British people, it has been said, is less interested in the equality of man than in the inequality of horses. Similarly for the French, the prospects for their midday meal could be said to loom larger than their concern with the notion of fairness or, for that matter, liberty or fraternity.

Among the *chansonniers* whose traditional displays of irreverence nothing could impede, a favourite song had the punning title of '*Sans beurre et sans brioches*'.* But for the time being de Gaulle, despite his avoidance of the subject of butter, was above criticism or reproach. Many of the traditional élites, the disgruntled Right, the impenitent Vichyites, were by definition not Gaullists, but because of their fear of the Communists they chose not to train their sights upon the General. This was not true of his ministers or of the system over which he presided. They were fair game for the grumbles and complaints, nurtured in this instance by some well justified grievances, which are the normal product of a free society. As for the Resistance vision – myth does not seem too strong a word for it – its fading was strikingly confirmed in January 1945. Then, an attempt to fuse together all the elements of the Resistance into one broad movement failed entirely. Had it succeeded, the way would have been open for the Communists to rule the roost. The non-Communists, the Socialists in particular, saw the trap and refused to walk into it. The Resistance, composed of so many disparate elements, had never been a single, united

---

* The pun is upon the words used to describe Pierre du Terrail de Bayard, a brave captain in the Italian wars of Charles VIII, Louis XII and François 1er, known as '*le chevalier sans peur et sans reproche*'.

organisation. Now the failure of this post-Liberation attempt to give it the appearance of unity was the first major political setback for the Communists. It was the beginning of the process which, as political realities began to displace headier ideas, would increasingly isolate the Communist party, pushing it to its natural place on the extreme Left and leaving the field clear for a new non-Communist and increasingly anti-Communist grouping of the Centre–Left. An essential part of that grouping was the Catholic MRP which, as a new, post-war phenomenon, could not in any degree be held responsible for the defeat of 1940 or for Vichy.

But if this was an immense advantage, the very nature of the new party, occupying the centre of the political spectrum, provided its rivals, particularly the Communists in their search for left-wing unity, with a permanent opportunity for making trouble and stirring up old quarrels. Nothing marked more clearly the return to pre-war political party games than the highly effective Communist efforts, in the early months of 1945, to make common cause with the Socialists on *laïcité*, the historic quarrel between clericalism and anti-clericalism, expressed in its most acute political form in the issue of state aid to Church schools. This was a nearly infallible way of uniting the divided Left (for naturally the Socialists were anti-clerical) and discomforting the MRP. '*Laïcité* was the hidden reef that wrecked the proposal for a French Labour party – the foresight of a few Resisters and [Socialist] leaders could not overcome the determination of the [Socialist] militants to stand by their old creed and flag.'[21] Thus the Communists, the self-styled defenders of Republican virtues against the bourgeoisie and the priests, were left for the whole period of the Fourth Republic with an unblemished record (for what it was worth) of proclaiming and fighting for *laïcité*. Had things been otherwise, had Socialists and MRP been able to send the old war horse back to its stable or put it out to grass for ever, the history of post-war France would read very differently.

The municipal elections of April–May 1945, the first post-war political test, saw the Communist party dominating the Left, the Radicals and Moderates declining, and the MRP making what seemed to be a breakthrough, despite the scurrilous attacks to which it was subjected – '*MRP=Mensonge, Réaction, Perfidie*' was one example. The Communists repeated their success at the October 1945 general elections to the Constituent Assembly – i.e.

the parliament which was to prepare a new Constitution. These elections, at which 77 per cent of those qualified to vote did so (including women for the first time), marked the emergence for the time being of the Communist party (26.1 per cent of votes cast) as France's leading party.

They also provided for two potential majorities. The Communists, with 160 seats, the MRP, with 152, and the Socialists, with 142, between them accounted for three-quarters of the votes cast and over 80 per cent of the seats in the new Assembly. A tripartite coalition was not only numerically possible but would reflect the will of the electorate. Alternatively, the Communists and Socialists enjoyed an absolute majority in the Chamber and could have formed a new Popular Front, dominated by the Communists who this time (unlike the Popular Front of 1936, which they supported while remaining outside the government) would have assumed a dominant role in the Ministry. At no other time was France closer (in theory) to becoming a 'popular democracy'. But the theory remained theory. It did so partly because of the MRP's successes. Although second to the Communists in terms of votes won, it established itself in October 1945 as the unchallenged centre party. This was something of an optical illusion. In fact, the party's greatest electoral victories were in Brittany, Normandy and Alsace, all former conservative and clerical bastions. In Paris also, its candidates attracted the bulk of the conservative vote. Already, despite its genuinely 'liberal' and Resistance core, it had become the temporary rallying point for the forces of the Right. Nonetheless because of the position this enabled it to carve out for itself upon the political chess board, it could exert an influence and play a role which meant not only that its opposition to a new Popular Front was a permanent factor but that throughout the course of the Fourth Republic no government could be formed without its participation or at least support.

Even more important as an obstacle in the path leading to a Popular Front was the attitude of the Socialists. Hardening their hearts and blocking their ears to the Communist siren song of left-wing unity and the defence of the working class, they decided that it was impossible to govern the country without the MRP. The Communists were stymied. But this did not mean that they could be discounted. Like the Caucus Race in *Alice in Wonderland*, where all did well and all received prizes, all three major parties could, and did, claim to have won the October elections. Whatever the future might hold, whatever the changes wrought and hopes raised by the Resistance and the Liberation, these elections marked the return to the centre of the stage of the political parties. It was not a prospect to please the austere autocrat in the Rue St Dominique. Three months earlier, one of his ministers had asked him why he had not chosen the constituency system as the electoral law (instead of proportional representation) and then, by supporting the candidate in each constituency that stood in his name, he could be sure of getting a majority in the Assembly favourable to his ideas about the new Constitution. 'When are you going to understand', replied the General testily, 'that my ambition is never to be the leader of a majority?'[22]

This professed indifference to politics contrasts strangely with de Gaulle's unwillingness or inability to go for the hard option when presented with it. Long before the elections, in January 1945, he had taken a decision which was to have important and unfortunate consequences for the economic and social development of post-war France. Faced with the choice between two, widely differing, financial policies, one of them favoured by his Minister of Finance, René Pleven, the other by his Minister for Economic Affairs, Pierre Mendès-France, he chose the former and thus gave the green light to the inflation which was already gathering pace. De Gaulle was emphatically no expert in economic affairs, though there is no certain proof that he ever uttered the legendary words 'the baggage train will follow on' (*l'intendance suivra*, a military expression implying that he could not be concerned with economic or administrative detail, which would look after itself). Mendès-France was such an expert, and before the Liberation, while still in Algiers as Commissioner for Finance in the provisional government, had prepared a plan for austerity and monetary reform, designed to freeze wages and prices and paralyse the black market and the illicit gains of wartime profiteers by an obligatory exchange of notes. Post-war Belgium had chosen such a policy. But in Paris, once the provisional government was installed, Mendès-France found not only his plan opposed by most of its members but large and inflationary wage increases already granted. The counter-view, represented by Pleven and the Ministry of Finance, was based on the thought that France had already endured five long years of suffering and should not be asked to accept further sacrifices, particularly monetary ones. By mid-January 1945, Mendès-France, despairing of getting his views accepted, resigned.

In his letter of resignation to de Gaulle,[23] he recalled that the only two monetary measures to be taken so far were the launch of a loan ('only a prestige success') and the confiscation of illicit profits ('which should have been preceded by an inventory of fortunes'). Too much of this sort of thing, he claimed, had been seen between the wars; 'the lack of courage and imagination in public finances was an essential cause, just as great as mistaken military doctrines, of defeat in 1940.' The price and wage spiral could only be stopped 'if the government, by means of courageous decisions which will strike public opinion, at last provides evidence of its resolve to break the inflationary cycle.' The choice was between a voluntary application of the brakes, or accepting an indefinite devaluation of the franc. 'Mon Général', the letter ended, 'I appeal to you, to your inflexibility, to all the reasons for which the French have confidence in you, to take the measures necessary for public salvation.'

It was a good letter, a strong letter, an 18-page letter. De Gaulle asked the two protagonists, Pleven and Mendès-France, to come the following Sunday to his official residence in the Bois de Boulogne to argue the matter out. Pleven, solid, phlegmatic, resistant to flights of fancy or high-falutin' ideas, spoke for twenty minutes. Mendès-France, a man of passionate convictions and unstoppable eloquence, held forth for more than two hours. The General's reported comment on the encounter was that he would never again allow anyone to talk to him for nearly three hours about economic affairs.[24] He did persuade Mendès-France to withdraw his resignation and Pleven to make a few concessions, but two months later prices were still chasing wages, and Mendès-France pressed for a calling-in and exchange of bank-notes. Pleven resisted, pointing to the difficulties and uncertainties of such an operation. 'To all the different forms of rationing, I am not going to add another, that of money,' he said.

Looking back down the years, it is easy to argue that in 1945 de Gaulle backed the wrong horse. Mendès-France's letter proved prophetic. The Fourth Republic was to bear the burden of inflation for most of its troubled life. Yet at the time de Gaulle's choice was easy to understand. Most of his professional advisers took the Pleven, rather than the Mendès, line. Mendès-France's ideas, for all their brilliance and originality, failed to take account of certain

French characteristics, one of which was and is a rooted objection to 'fiscal inquisition' – for that is what would have been involved in tracking down, as Mendès-France would have done, the recipients of the some 600 billions of notes spent by the Germans under the occupation. Nor was it any coincidence, or example of party politicking, that Mendès-France got such meagre support within the government. No one was more opposed to his ideas than the Communists, who accused him, to adapt a famous phrase from British politics, of trying to devalue 'the franc in your pocket'. Only de Gaulle, with his assured position as the emblem of national integrity and his supposed disregard for popular opinion and party warfare, could have overridden the opposition and come down on Mendès-France's side. Why he went the way he did must remain largely speculation. The best guess is that as well as listening to professional advice, he calculated that acceptance of the Mendès-France view would have meant his staking his whole reputation, all his authority, all his mystique, upon the result, and this at a time when he was preoccupied with issues that for him took priority over everything – fighting the Germans, fighting the British and Americans, fighting for France's international position . . . Compared with these operations, monetary reform seemed small beer indeed. Better to go with the Pleven approach, which would leave his hands free for other and greater tasks. Mendès-France resigned for a second and final time and, apart from one brief flicker of limelight after de Gaulle's resignation in 1946, disappeared from the forefront of the political stage for some years. Describing the episode in his memoirs much later, de Gaulle explained that 'if I did not adopt that policy that Mendès-France put forward, I in no way ruled out making it my own one day, when circumstances had changed'.[25]

Circumstances did change, but in a way that, far from steering de Gaulle on to another economic tack, caused him to remove his hand from the tiller altogether. For 1945 saw him engaged not only in trying to restore France's position in the world but also in initiating the process which would equip her with new political institutions – i.e. providing her with a new Constitution. This rapidly brought him into conflict with the Constituent Assembly elected in October 1945.

To begin with, things went his own way. The popular consultation in October had been more than just voting for an Assembly. It also involved a national referendum, in which two questions were asked: should the Assembly to be elected be a Constituent Assembly, and should its powers be limited to seven months' duration, during which time it was to confine itself to voting the budget, enacting major structural reforms, and preparing a Constitution to be submitted to a further referendum? Replying No to the first question would mean, in effect, reinstating the Third Republic; No to the second question that the Assembly would be completely sovereign, in which case the Communists would be likely to have the greatest influence. No wonder that de Gaulle called loudly for a Yes–Yes result. He had no wish to see an omnipotent Assembly nor – though his position was intermittently rather more ambiguous here – a return to the Third Republic.

His attitude provoked opposition within the Consultative Assembly. The Left, led by the Communists, attacked the whole idea of a referendum as smelling of a plebiscite. French politics, because of their revolutionary origins, are imbued far more than their British counterpart with a strong sense of the past. 'To think of politics in terms of history is a psychological peculiarity of the French.'[26] It was completely predictable that de Gaulle should be compared with Napoleon III, who nearly a century previously had used the weapon of the plebiscite to win power. The General defended himself easily enough, but his referendum proposals stirred up all sorts of dark suspicions, and not only among the Communists, that he was really working towards a régime where the government would be largely independent of control by the elected parliament. In the end however, he got his *Oui–Oui*: over 96 per cent of those voting rejected a return to the Third Republic ('Well, this time it's really dead,' he observed, with evident satisfaction),[27] and 66.3 per cent said Yes to the second question.

So far, so good. But there was now an elected Assembly, with the government partially responsible to it, and charged with the task of preparing a new Constitution. Squalls were bound to come, and come they did. The first crisis of the newly installed parliamentary régime began immediately the curtain rose. De Gaulle, as head of the provisional government, tendered that government's resignation to the Assembly. It voted unanimously, bar one vote, for his renomination, with the task of forming a new government. Two days later (15 November 1945) Thorez, as head of the largest party, went to see de Gaulle and asked him to bestow one of the key ministries – either Interior or Defence or Foreign Affairs – on the Communists. De Gaulle refused. Thorez took offence, complaining publicly that the General had impugned the patriotism and war record of the Communist party. De Gaulle denied he had done any such thing, renewed his invitation to the Communists to join the government, but reserved to himself the right to choose ministers. Thorez maintained his demands. The General, threatening to resign without actually doing so, placed his commission in the hands of the President of the Assembly and went on the air to tell the public that he could in no way give the Communists any of the three posts they were asking for, posts which determined foreign policy – namely 'diplomacy which expresses it, the Army which supports it, the police which protects it'. Whatever de Gaulle may have known or suspected up to then about the Communists' ambitions and Muscovite affiliations, this was the first time he came into the open with his thoughts about their role. As he wrote later in his memoirs, he was not prepared, as the world threatened to divide into two power blocs and the shadows of the Cold War grew darker, to compromise the French policy (i.e. his policy) of holding a balance between the two great post-war powers, the US and the USSR.

The next day, 18 November, this General who held politics and politicians in such contempt showed that he was no mean hand at playing the game himself. He sent what looked very like an ultimatum to the President of the Assembly, asking that body to confirm or cancel the mandate (to form a government) it had entrusted to him. When the Assembly met on the 19th, the scenes round the Palais Bourbon recalled earlier, pre-war, days of tension and disorders. Large numbers of troops were deployed and police check-points established. Despite the indignation of the Communist orators within, all passed off peaceably however. The Assembly, by a large majority, invited the General to resume the task of forming a government. This he did, giving four posts to the Communists (National Economy, Labour, Industrial Production and Armaments – this last appointment meaning that the party got its hands on at least one part of the defence system). Thorez was made one of four ministers of State (a more influential position than it sounds in English). Once again, the Assembly gave de Gaulle its unanimous approval.

The 'crisis' had lasted seventeen days and de Gaulle had apparently emerged victorious. In fact, he had had to accept, in a way completely at odds with his own philosophy, the exigencies of the Assembly and the parties. Not only had the motion approved required the General to resume negotiations for the formation of a tripartite government (Communist, Socialist, MRP), but another, Socialist-inspired, motion had spoken of this mandate as 'imperative'. In other words, it was the Assembly and the parties who had emerged as the decision-takers, who had laid down in advance the composition of the new government. The wonder was that de Gaulle accepted a mandate couched in these terms. A few years later, he told Maurice Schumann that it was because he had had 'pity on this country'. But the auguries were not good, and very soon worse was to befall.

The main task of the Constituent Assembly, as its name suggested, was to prepare a Constitution for the Fourth Republic. Its Constitutional Committee immediately set to work and in three weeks had arrived at a draft which would have reduced the position of a future President of the Republic to that of a mere puppet, with fewer powers than those enjoyed even by the largely impotent President of the Third Republic. Even more unacceptable to the General was the answer given to him when he enquired about the progress of the Committee's work. Its rapporteur, an MRP deputy who had been one of his ministers in the post-Liberation government, explained that as he, de Gaulle, had not been elected a member of the Constituent Assembly, he had no business with the Committee's affairs.[28] 'To attempt, under such conditions', he wrote in the memoirs, 'to pursue my goals in this crucial area as in all other respects would be to invite impotence and insult.'[29]

From now on, a collision course was unavoidable. The General felt increasingly ill at ease in parliament: 'Seated at the front of the hemicycle [the ministerial front bench in the semicircular chamber] I felt the heavy gaze of 600 MPs converging on me, and I experienced, almost physically, the weight of a general malaise.' On the last day of 1945, in the budget debate in the Assembly, a Socialist amendment was tabled, calling for a 20 per cent cut in military expenditure. It was, in part, a Socialist ruse to outflank the Communists, including the Communist Minister for Armaments, who vigorously defended his budget. For de Gaulle, who was his own Minister of Defence, this was an unacceptable insult. He went to the hated Chamber on the afternoon of New Year's Day 1946 and read the deputies a stern lecture: 'If you do not take account of the absolute need for authority, dignity and governmental responsibility, you are heading for a situation where, sooner or later, I predict you will bitterly regret having taken the road you will have taken.' He also added that this would doubtless be the last time he would address the Chamber, a remark which strangely went almost unnoticed. In fact, as he later recorded, he left the Palais Bourbon that evening having made up his mind to step down. So as not to appear too precipitate, he then went off with his family on holiday to the Côte d'Azur. On his return, he began telling his staff and certain ministers of his decision. (To one of them, the elder statesman of the MRP, he said: 'The one thing that I forbid after my departure, and I request you to make this known to M. Bidault, is that neither you nor M. Bidault should become head of the government.' He had of course no right to forbid anything which might happen after he had gone.) Then, on Sunday morning, 20 January, he summoned all the ministers to the Rue St Dominique where, in uniform and looking grave and tired, he told them that he was resigning. There is some conflict of evidence about what he said, none whatever about the fact that having spoken briefly he left the room. One account has him deploring the party system but explaining that he had no means of getting rid of it except by dictatorship, 'which I don't want and which, no doubt, would end badly.' Another, possibly more accurate, makes no mention of the dictatorship remark, but confirms his refusal to work within the party system.

In his resignation letter to the President (Speaker) of the National Assembly, de Gaulle asserted that his task was finished, and gave rather too rosy an account of the progress made towards recovery and reconstruction. These formalities completed, he and Madame de Gaulle went to a rented government-owned property, a former royal hunting lodge, at Marly, near Paris, where two days later, seated on a packing case containing his papers, he told an Agence-France Presse reporter: 'It's like Longwood here.'*

To the French people, the news came as a shock, in the sense of something unexpected. One observer wrote that 'The General does not come well out of it and disillusion is close at hand.'[30] Another says de Gaulle's departure 'left French morale in a state of empty gloom . . . the past fortnight has obviously been the worst since the war ended.'[31] Yet contemporary opinion polls show a diversity

* Longwood was the name of the house on St Helena where Napoleon spent his final exile.

of views: the resignation left 40 per cent discontented, 32 per cent satisfied, 28 per cent indifferent; 41 per cent felt de Gaulle had done a good job, 36 per cent thought otherwise, 23 per cent had no view. Another question about how people would vote if de Gaulle became head of a new party yielded the result: for him 31 per cent, against 46 per cent, don't know 23 per cent. There was a widespread feeling that he had given an over-optimistic view of the situation in France. Rationing – of food, clothes, petrol – was in full force and was to remain so for a long time to come, and those who could not or would not afford black-market prices were often hard pushed to make do.

What does not seem to have been seen clearly at the time were the institutional issues underlying de Gaulle's resignation. He stood for a strong executive power not totally dependent, indeed as little dependent as possible, upon the parties in the Assembly. The opposing view, held by the Socialists, Communists and some Radicals, was that the government should result from inter-party agreements in parliament; where that agreement could not be established, there could be no government. The wonder is that so few people seem to have realised that once the October 1945 elections had created a Chamber where Communists, Socialists and MRP shared power, it was virtually impossible that de Gaulle and 'the system' could work together. As he himself had told the Chamber, with brutal frankness, 'There are two conceptions. They are not reconcilable. Do people want a government that governs, or do they want an all-powerful Assembly?' It was all very well for him to tell the Council of Ministers (Cabinet), after the elections that 'I am not sure that the best calculation for you [i.e. the three parties] is to separate yourselves from the national interest', but this begged the question of who was best qualified to define the national interest. Even his way of running a Cabinet meeting grated. It was, according to one of the ministers, 'forbidden to take notes, to smoke before the General had lit his cigarette, to question him . . .'[32] Jacques Dumaine probably made the best analysis when he wrote (in his diary for 21 January): 'A military man can never adapt himself completely to the business of politics . . . although General de Gaulle has shown himself to be an astute politician, he remains too much of a soldier to accept the perpetual life of compromise which is the lot of a man in public life.'[33]

A final point is that in 1946 de Gaulle had not learnt, as he was to do later on, the art of 'massaging' the politicians and the parties. In 1958, once he had been re-established legally in power as the result of events in Algeria, he played his hand skilfully and with tact vis-à-vis the parties, so that before long he was able to fashion the Fifth Republic according to his own liking. Admittedly, the circumstances were different. In 1958 the parties – or most of them – had had, because of the demonstrable inability of the government to control or influence developments, the shock of their lives. They were in a mood, those of them who had voted de Gaulle back to power, to cause no trouble. In 1945–6 the reverse was true. Even so, had the General sought through tact and persuasion, instead of scorn and hostility, to promote his constitutional ideas, the story might have been a different one. Or possibly not. Perhaps the collision course was inevitable. Compromise on matters of principle was never the General's forte.

CHAPTER 2

A Difficult Birth, and an Unwelcome Christening Present

Charles de Gaulle's memoirs, like those of many men and women who have played an active and sometimes contentious public role, are at once an essay in self-justification and a nostalgic reordering of the facts of history (they are also a literary *tour de force*). Thus he wrote, about the period immediately following his resignation, that 'the mass of French people retreated into sadness . . . Everyone, whatever his view, had the basic feeling that the General had taken away with him something primordial, something permanent, something necessary, that he incarnated history in a way that the party régime could not do.'[1] This was the way he wanted to see things, but as the figures quoted on p. 27 suggest, it was a very partial account of the way things were. De Gaulle's postbag did contain, it is true, many letters of regret and admiration. In fact, his departure in 1946 was much less deplored and caused less bafflement than his resignation as President in 1969, on the improbable issue of French regionalisation. And if he believed, as there is strong evidence to suggest he did, that within a very short space of time the political parties, driven by popular pressure, would be asking him to return on his own terms, then he was deluding himself.

It took only two days after that Sunday when de Gaulle strode out of the War Ministry for the three dominating parties to agree upon a new government and its leader. The process was not without its difficulties, and certainly would not have gone so quickly if fears of a move by de Gaulle had not prevailed. First of all the Communists, as the largest party, claimed the premiership for Maurice Thorez. The MRP having blocked that one, the Communists tried to make common cause with the Socialists. The latter were not to be drawn into a new Popular Front alone with the Communists. They had already, after the October 1945 elections, rejected that temptation, and were not going to yield to it now. The MRP's agreement was needed, they said – in other words, a renewal of the tripartism which had emerged from the autumn elections. This left the ball at the feet of the MRP. They were in a dilemma. As the party of loyalty to de Gaulle, they could have cashed in on his prestige by going into opposition, but this would have meant leaving a Communist–Socialist government in power (assuming that Socialist reservations could have been overcome). American loans were an indispensable condition of French recovery. It was improbable that an American government would lend money to a Marxist régime in France – a point reinforced by a senior general on the General Staff, who warned the President of the MRP, Maurice Schumann, of the likely reactions in Washington to a French government headed by Maurice Thorez.[2] Already the approach of the Cold War was influencing the French internal scene. The MRP therefore decided to renew the tripartite arrangement. A charter was drawn up, full of brave sentiments and moral commitments to good behaviour between the parties, who undertook to avoid 'oral or written arguments of an offensive and injurious nature'. The President of the Constituent Assembly, Félix Gouin, an unassuming, scholarly Socialist, reluctantly allowed himself to be chosen as head of the government and, like de Gaulle before him, *de facto* head of State. Between him and his predecessor there could scarcely have been a greater contrast. A man from the south who had been a deputy for twenty-two of the pre-war years, Gouin had joined de Gaulle in London and later, in Algiers, became President of the Consultative Assembly. *Combat* complained of his 'apologetic airs; he can foresee how unpopular he is going to be and he doubts his own capacities.'[3] Gouin was, it is true, a modest man, but this was too harsh. Blum had the greatest regard for him and he had been a good Speaker. But he was not of heroic stature, and was the first to admit it.

The tripartite protocol was of course a farce. It is hardly credible that knowing politicians like Bidault or Thorez or Vincent Auriol, the veteran Socialist who, a year later, was to be elected the first President of the Fourth Republic, could have believed in the pledges it contained. But tripartism, for all its unreality, provided the necessary framework for the transitional period between de Gaulle and the formal establishment of the Fourth Republic. Most of 1946 was spent by the parties and politicians in Constitution-making, of one sort or another. But already, long before the process was complete, certain political bad habits were becoming established in a way that was to pre-empt the yet-to-be-born Constitution. Thus Gouin made it quite clear from the start that he did not intend to pick his own ministers. To the leaders of the three parties in the coalition, he said, in effect, 'Here are the jobs I propose giving to your party, now go away and choose the people to fill them.' Ministers would therefore be beholden for their appointment not to the Prime Minister but to the choice of their own party caucuses. Already, long before any constitutional text was drafted, the power of the executive had been weakened and that of the Assembly and parties reinforced.

The tripartite 'good behaviour' contract had said nothing about the Constitution. That was to remain the business of the Constituent Assembly and its Constitutional Committee, not of the government. The October referendum had effectively buried the corpse of the Third Republic. Fashioning its successor was to prove a much more difficult task, involving the rejection of a first draft by a national referendum, another round of general elections to a second Constituent Assembly, and finally, a year after the interment of the Third Republic, narrow acceptance of a new draft by a second referendum.

The forty-two-member Constitutional Committee of the Assembly began its work in December 1945. On 19 April 1946 the Assembly approved the resulting draft by 309 votes (mostly Communists and Socialists) to 249 (MRP, Radicals and Right). In the discussions leading up to this decision, tripartism, so far as anyone interpreted the word as meaning a broad measure of agreement between the three main post-war parties, was revealed as the sham it always was.

The two left-wing parties – Communists and Socialists – who formed a majority in the Committee approached Constitution-making heavily under the influence of French revolutionary history. They looked to the *régime d'Assemblée*, with a single, all-powerful Chamber, to withstand attacks upon 'Republican liberty' – attacks which in 1946 could be thought to include the possibility of a strike from de Gaulle. They therefore made common cause in favour of a single Chamber, the supremacy of the parliamentary majority and a President of the Republic with minimum power. The MRP (whose electorate, it must be recalled, included large numbers of those traditional right-wing supporters who would have voted for right-wing parties had the latter not, for the time being, faded into the background) did their best to resist what seemed, given the overall Communist–Socialist majority, to be an invitation to 'popular democracy'. If the Left feared the perceived intentions of de Gaulle, the influence of the moneyed classes and the erosion of the people's rights, the Right (including in this context the MRP) feared the establishment of a Communist-dominated régime.

Throughout the first part of 1946, to the general indifference of the public, arguments about uni-cameralism and bi-cameralism continued to fill the committee rooms of the Assembly. The MRP failed to win any important concessions and considered, but decided against, withdrawing from the coalition. Finally, the draft Constitution, as approved, was rejected by a majority of those voting in a national referendum held on 5 May 1946 – almost exactly one year after the end of the war in Europe. 10.5 million votes were cast against the draft, 9.4 million in its favour. It was the first time in French political history that the electorate had responded to a referendum with a negative answer. It was also, in one respect, an indication – not overwhelming, but clear enough – that most French people did not accept the Communist–Socialist model of a single Chamber possessed of almost limitless power. In another, and more important respect, it was a straight political setback for the Communists. An opinion poll showed that half the 'No' votes had been prompted by a dislike of Communism, compared with 22 per cent who found the text a bad one and 10 per cent who were governed by party loyalties. Anti-Communism, which in the Fourth Republic was to provide such a powerful lubricant to the political machine, was thus seen to be the strongest element in this unexpected rejection of a Constitution which had been approved by a comfortable majority of the Constituent Assembly. As a leading Socialist, Daniel Mayer, wrote in his party newspaper, 'the Communist association of [a vote in favour of the draft Constitution] and *Thorez au pouvoir* is . . . to some extent responsible for the result.'[4]

The Communists could however qualify their dismay with the outcome of the elections for the second Constituent Assembly, held on 2 June 1946. They actually increased their share of the vote, compared with the previous October (26.4 as against 26.1 per cent). The MRP reaped their reward for having led the 'No' lobby, increasing their percentage from 25.6 to 28.2 per cent, a result which edged the Communists out of the role of leading party. The Socialists lost ground, and the Radicals – the mainstay of pre-war Republican governments – began their long journey back from their post-Liberation wilderness. Because tripartism still existed – Bidault, despite de Gaulle's earlier strictures against him, formed a government from the same coalition which had preceded the elections – the Right–Left divide was not as dramatically apparent as it might have been. But a significant shift in popular opinion had taken place, the most important aspect of which was that a sizeable number of Socialist supporters had defied the party and voted '*Non*' in the referendum. Their action marked another stage in the impending rupture between Communists and Socialists which was to prevail for many years to come.

General de Gaulle, by then installed in his modest country home at Colombey-les-Deux-Eglises in eastern France, had played no part in the referendum campaign. In June, as work was beginning in the new Constituent Assembly on a second constitutional draft, he broke his silence with a speech at Bayeux, on the second anniversary of his return to France. In it, he formulated his ideas with great lucidity, ideas which were to remain constant until they were translated into reality in the 1958 Constitution for the Fifth Republic. In pouring rain, and heard by large and enthusiastic crowds, he laid down the principles upon which he considered France should be governed: two Chambers, separation of powers, ministerial responsibility, a federal system for the former French empire, to be called the French Union, and above all a President of the Republic equipped with real, strong, powers. 'Executive power should proceed from the Chief of State, whose position is above the parties, and who is elected by a college which includes parliament but is much larger, so that the President of the Republic is at the same time President of the French Union.'[5] The President's tasks, according to de Gaulle, would be to appoint ministers, above all the prime minister, to promulgate laws and decrees, to serve as an umpire who stands above political events and, finally, 'if the country [*patrie*] should be in danger, [the President] has the duty to become the guarantor of national independence'.

This last phrase evoked accusations of Bonapartism from many critics. In fact, despite his authoritarian ways, there is no evidence that at any time in his remarkable career did de Gaulle harbour thoughts of dictatorship, even though he had ample reason to know how difficult it is to govern the French people democratically. What he had in mind in 1946, as in 1958, was the shambles of 1940 and how to avoid a repetition. In reality, the Bayeux manifesto had nothing anti-democratic about it; it did not even envisage, in the precise meaning of the words, a presidential system. But in 1946 it had two things against it: the imperious personality of the General and the strong suspicion that in defining the powers of the President he was thinking of himself; and the fact that the speech was made only five months after his own abrupt resignation, and only six years after the establishment of the absolutist Vichy régime.

The Bayeux speech had the effect of causing the MRP, champions of the 'No' lobby in the recent referendum, to seek to shape the second draft in such a way as to meet some of the General's points. They did make progress over the status of the President of the Republic and the reintroduction of the principle of a second Chamber – even though the latter would have much less legislative scope compared with the Third Republic's Senate. But de Gaulle's conception of the powers with which the executive needed to be equipped remained completely at odds with that of the Left – and indeed of many deputies who did not sail under that flag. This counter-view to the General's ideas was that in a democracy the people express their will through the operation of the elected parties, not through some godlike figure from on high with the power to appoint governments and dissolve parliament. The difference was irreconcilable. The MRP, which sent its emissaries to Colombey to try to sell the amended constitutional text, came away with a flea in its ear. Publicly, de Gaulle made known his total rejection of the new text in a speech at the end of September at Epinal. It contained one of his early public references to the coming of the Cold War and the incipient clash between the USSR and the USA, and included the words, 'We shall only resolve the enormous problems of the present and the future under the leadership of a just and strong State.'

One particular aspect of Constitution-making revealed ambiguities which were to have a crucial effect upon the future of the Fourth Republic. This concerned the French Union, the new name given to the French colonial empire. In the draft rejected by the May referendum, the inhabitants of the empire were promised full equality with French citizens. The empire, transformed into a union, was to be based on free consent. This apparently generous provision was left vague as to its application and exact meaning. In particular, there was no indication whether it allowed for, or implied, the right of secession. While this draft seemed to mark a conscious effort to move away from the old idea of assimilation towards federal or semi-federal forms, it stopped short of saying so. It was thus broadly in keeping with the conclusions of the conference held in 1944 at Brazzaville, under the auspices of the provisional government. This meeting, notable because it was attended only by officials and administrators and not by representatives of the indigenous populations, ruled out any idea of colonial self-government. 'The formation of independent governments in the colonies, even in the distant future, cannot be contemplated': this was how those at Brazzaville saw the future. To make sure there was no doubt, they added that 'the political authority of France is to be exercised with precision and rigour over all the territory of her empire.'

It was not easy to reconcile this stern edict with de Gaulle's apparently liberal words at Brazzaville: 'In French Africa, as in other territories where men live under our flag, there will be no progress . . . if men cannot raise themselves little by little to a level where they are capable of taking part in the management of their own affairs . . . it is the duty of France to act so that this is so.'[6] De Gaulle was later to forget these words, but in the post-Liberation period a series of reforms was enacted affecting the overseas territories, including the abolition of forced labour and the extension to those territories of the Republican principles of the mother country. Nevertheless the question remained unresolved as to whether all this was to lead to emancipation or to assimilation under another name.

The second Constituent Assembly, where the Communists and Socialists no longer had an absolute majority, modified even this tentative approach to decolonisation. Although the preamble to the new draft rejected colonial rule based on arbitrary power, all reference to free consent disappeared. Right-wing and Radical voices, more numerous in the new Assembly, spoke out against the dangers of the empire disintegrating or, as Edouard Herriot, the influential Radical elder statesman, put it, of France becoming the 'colony of her colonies'. Bidault, as Prime Minister, played a predominant role here. Faced with the difficulty of the Assembly in reaching any agreement on this part of the Constitution, he chose implicitly to engage the future of his government upon his concept of what the French Union was to be, namely a rigid, centralised structure in which Paris would call the tune, while French settlers in the overseas departments and protectorates would preserve their own status and privileges. Like many of his compatriots at the time, Bidault, a former professor of history, was temperamentally and morally incapable of accepting, even of envisaging, any yielding up of French sovereignty anywhere. For him, what had been shown on pre-war atlases as French territory all over the world must continue to figure as such.

In the prevailing mood, it was less surprising than it might seem today that the Socialist Colonial Minister (Ministre de la France d'Outre-Mer), Marius Moutet, shared this thinking. Up to a point, it was a victory for the Right in the Constituent Assembly and for the colonial and commercial lobbies, but above all it was a contradiction in terms which was certain to cause trouble in the future. While the preamble to the Constitution spoke of France's wish to lead the peoples for whom she was responsible to the freedom to administer themselves and to manage their own affairs democratically, it also outlined the shape of the French Union in a way that made it clear that there was no question of consulting those 'peoples', who were therefore to have no choice: 'France with its overseas peoples creates a Union based on equality of rights and duties, without distinction of race or religion.' The same thought appeared again in chapter VIII of the Constitution, on the organisation of the Union. This certainly seemed to reject assimilation, but did not proceed from there to admit the principle of federation. If independence for the units of the French empire was inadmissible and assimilation impracticable, what remained? The Constitution left the question in the air. And it did so for the simple reason that 'nearly all French political leaders behaved as though nothing had changed since the war in the traditional French attitude on colonial questions'.[7]

The outcome of the debates on the future constitutional arrangements for the French Union was the subject of a strange bargain between Bidault and Thorez: the former undertook to win approval for a new statute for the civil service, a cherished ambition of the Communists, if the latter would sanction the proposed, partly contradictory, provisions for the French Union. On Bidault's list of priorities, the civil service was something that was well worth staking in return for the shining prize of overseas France.

Political calculations apart, Bidault was imbued with the idea that the greatness of France was bound up with her role as an imperial power. Later on, as the Algerian drama developed, he moved steadily, where North African policy was concerned, towards the right and the extreme right. But in 1946 his attitude was by no means singular or exaggerated. It was representative of a widespread refusal or inability to admit that the colonial era was drawing to a close. Writing in June 1946 in *Le Monde*, Beuve-Méry noted perceptively that neither public opinion nor the government was paying sufficient attention to what was going on in the component parts of the former French empire. The old French policy of assimilation, he pointed out, was increasingly unreal. Up to a point, the new Constitution recognised this, proclaiming that the French Union was to be composed of nations and peoples pooling their efforts and resources so as to develop their respective civilisations, and announcing the prospect of autonomy. But neither explicitly nor implicitly was there any reference to what, in British parlance, would be called dominion status, nor to the possibility that one day French sovereignty might cease to be the golden rule.

On the contrary, most of French opinion regarded the French Union (when it gave any thought to the matter) as a form of continuation of the colonial empire. Nothing illustrates this more strongly than what secondary school books in use under the Fourth Republic had to say about the nature of the Union. Successive generations of French children were taught that 'it is her overseas territories which confer on France her rank as a great power' and that 'European France is a medium-sized power, with overseas France she is a great power, the French Union.'[8] This trend of thought, so widely inculcated and professed, exerted an immense influence on French attitudes towards colonial questions, and goes far to explain why the retreat from empire was so traumatic an experience for the Fourth Republic, leading finally to its collapse.

Along with this notion of imperial status and its significance for France went another, even more sacred one, whose origins were rooted in the Revolution itself and embodied one of the fundamental principles of French public law: the inalienability of the national heritage, the unity and indivisibility of the Republic. Eight years later, on the outbreak of the Algerian rebellion, François Mitterrand, then the Minister of the Interior, not a man whose name could possibly be associated with colonial lobbies, formulated this theory in triumphalist terms: 'From Flanders to the Congo, there is one law, one single nation, one single Parliament. This is the

Constitution and it is our will.' The French Union sections of the
1946 Constitution may have been frequently obscure, but they
reflected clearly enough this cardinal belief.

On 13 October 1946, the Fourth Republic came formally into
existence, when a second national referendum yielded a majority
favourable to the new draft Constitution. (The birth pangs of the
Republic were not in fact finally over until the election, in January
1947, of Vincent Auriol as its first President.) The result was hardly a
vote of confidence in the future. Only 67.4 per cent of the electorate
had chosen to vote, of whom just over 9 million (36.1 per cent) were
in favour of the new draft, nearly 7.8 million (31.3 per cent) against.
Apathy, indifference or plain hostility characterised for the most
part the public response. The new text established two Chambers
and by comparison with the first, rejected, draft increased the
President's powers. But it still left effective responsibility in the
hands of the National Assembly. Its authors – the Constitutional
Committee and the Constituent Assembly itself – were not, most
of them, particularly proud of their work. It bore all the marks of a
compromise and thus gave no one complete satisfaction. An MRP
spokesman, trying to make the best of an unsatisfactory situation,
referred to the art of the possible. Mauriac, in *Le Figaro*, was
less mealy-mouthed: 'So many years lost,' he wrote, 'simply to
arrive at this patching together, this re-upholstering.' Hardly had
the echoes of the referendum died away, than public figures such
as Mendès-France were calling for its revision.

Because so many people, de Gaulle foremost among them, were
to blame institutional weakness for the shortcomings of the Fourth
Republic, it is important to appreciate the mood and atmosphere
in which the Constitution was drawn up. The first, May, referendum and the ensuing general election in June had shown that
there was a majority in the country opposed to Communist and
Socialist ideas, specifically to the notion of the *régime d'Assemblée*.
But it was only a small one, and much of it was motivated by
straightforward anti-Communism. Nevertheless that still left the
old antagonisms and ideologies of Right and Left, themselves the
legacy of history, unsoftened. Both groupings were inspired by
fear – the Left's of dictatorship of men (one man especially), the
Right's of the dictatorship of parties (one party in particular).
Memories of how the second Chamber – the Senate of the Third
Republic – obstructed the programme of Léon Blum's Popular

Front in the Thirties weighed heavily. Thus in the Assembly and its Constitutional Committee the margin for compromise was minimal, and this was reflected in the obscurity of much of the wording of the Constitution as finally adopted. Had there been no de Gaulle to make the Bayeux and Epinal speeches, things would obviously have been different. As it was, 'the ghost of Charles de Gaulle haunts the Constituent Assembly as the Comte de Chambord haunted that of 1870.'9*

Inevitably, comparisons were made between the beginnings of the Third and Fourth Republics. Both came into existence by the narrowest of margins. Both were the result, directly or indirectly, of defeats inflicted by Germany on France. Nobody, in 1875 or 1946, seemed to think that the prospects were very brilliant. Yet there were two important differences. The first, noted by André Siegfried, was that 'the elaboration of the [1946] Constitution was carried out by the parties. . . . Before the war, the parties were, for the most part, weak . . . with little influence on their members . . . They became highly rigid and disciplined after the war . . . endowed with powers which . . . were exercised without direct responsibility vis-à-vis the electorate.'10 The second difference was that the Third Republic was so rich that it easily paid the bill, levied after the Franco-Prussian war, for German reparations. The Fourth was so poor that it had to beseech the US government (as Britain had to do) for credits.

The Gouin government despatched Léon Blum to Washington – he had never before been to America – as a result of which the US agreed to write off most of the French debt and extended further credits, in return for an undertaking that France would abandon its pre-war protective trade policies. No other formal conditions were levied, but the unspoken thought, which had so much influenced the decision of the MRP not to allow a Marxist coalition to assume power after de Gaulle's retirement at the beginning of the year, was that the presence of the Communists was a questionable element at a time when American–Russian tensions were constantly increasing. Blum himself formulated the problem

* The Comte de Chambord was the Bourbon descendant who, according to his monarchist supporters, should rightly have become Henry V after the collapse of Napoleon III's empire. He might have done so, had he not made it a condition that the Tricolour should be replaced with the white flag of the Bourbons.

in somewhat different, but still prophetic, terms when he spoke of 'those two great parties [Communists and Socialists] whose simultaneous presence in government is at once indispensable and impossible'. Here was the nub: if the Left–Right divide could be thought of in British terms, providing an alternating government and 'loyal' opposition, then the imperfections of the Constitution would not have come to matter so much. But as every anti-Communist (including most Socialists) knew, things were and could not be as simple as this. The Communists, an essential part of any left-wing coalition, had shown, in the Resistance, their devotion to the French *patrie*; the trouble was that they had a second *patrie* to the east. In the event of international trouble, which *patrie* would come first?

Disquieting though these geopolitical questions might be, there were other, more immediate, pressures on the governments that ruled France in 1946. Hardly had the Washington loan agreements been signed in May, than the Communist-dominated trade union, the Confédération Générale du Travail (CGT), pressed for an across-the-board wage increase of 25 per cent. Whatever the political motives – the move was made on the eve of the June general election – the claim had some sound economic reasons. In April 1946, weekly wages (with social transfers) stood at an index figure of 443 (100 in 1938), while the cost of living was at 700. By October, the gap had widened further. Distress and discontent were real and widespread. Bidault, the new Prime Minister, decided to call an economic conference to be attended by representatives of industrial and agricultural unions, employers and the government (shades of Edward Heath and his attempts, during his premiership in the early Seventies, to get agreements between similar organisations in Britain). The employers backed union claims, pressing for their part for an unfreezing of industrial prices. They had little to fear, as they saw it, from inflation, indeed much to gain, for it would mean increasing revenues (on paper) with which to finance reconstruction. Politically, the other parties in the coalition felt disinclined to let the Communists make all the running. The agreement reached by the Bidault government in October confirmed wage increases in excess of 25 per cent, and industrial and agricultural prices soon followed; by the end of the year they had increased by an average of 50 per cent. Rail fares rose by 15 per cent, a ticket on the Paris Métro went up from 2 to 5 francs. Thus the inflationary cycle was given another vicious twist. Not until December did the government succeeding Bidault's, under the premiership of Léon Blum, try to stop the stampede by imposing a 5 per cent price reduction. By then it was too late. Years later, two distinguished and disinterested economists gave it as their view that the outcome of the 1946 conference on wages and prices represented the worst mistake in the economic and financial field since the Liberation.[11]

The complexities of putting together a new Constitution were not the only preoccupations of 1946. They were not even the principal one. An opinion poll taken in October showed that 46 per cent of those questioned knew about the 'wine scandal' (described below), compared with 24 per cent who were interested in the constitutional debate. Here was another example of how the wish for innovation, born of the Resistance, could not efface old habits and traditions. The Third Republic had had its fair share of scandals, involving corruption and monkey business in high places. As is the way with French scandals, they were seldom cleared up, either by judicial or parliamentary inquiry, but that did not stop the public, titillated by saturation coverage in the popular press, from deriving much enjoyable shock and horror from the 'facts' presented to it. The period preceding the establishment of the Fourth Republic was no different. In some respects indeed the search for and revelations of a good scandal received extra emphasis, for 1946 was a time of shortages and rationing, especially of food and wine. Any allegations of improprieties or administrative incompetence in this sector could be guaranteed to evoke a wide and indignant response. It was calculated that as many as 4 million people were black marketeers in one form or another. From this jungle of corruption and malpractice, real or suspected, sprang the 'wine scandal' which became public in the summer of 1946.*

Like most affairs in France, its details are complex. In essence, it concerned the disappearance of large quantities of wine imported by the Ministry of Food from Algeria, and destined for the French consumer, who because of shortages in domestic production was limited to a (theoretical) ration of two litres a month. Suspicion fell upon Pierre Malafosse, the civil servant who was head of the

* Much of the following account is based on the relevant chapter in G. Elgey, *Histoire de la IVe République*, vol. I, *La République des illusions* (Paris, Fayard, 1965), pp. 172–91.

drinks directorate at the Ministry of Food, and he was sacked from his post. This man, a prominent Socialist with a fine Resistance record, was friendly with Gaston Defferre, later to become one of the leading figures in the Socialist party and Mayor of Marseilles for many years. Defferre, in turn, had close personal and party links with Félix Gouin, the Prime Minister who succeeded de Gaulle and who now, late in 1946, was Deputy Prime Minister in the Bidault government. He interceded with the Minister of Food, Yves Farge, to see Malafosse.

Farge, a near-Communist who was also notable in the Resistance, above all in Lyon, was on bad personal terms with Gouin. Nevertheless he saw Malafosse. The interview, far from leading to the latter's reinstatement, resulted in Farge, an ebullient ex-journalist from the south, prone to exaggeration and self-advancement, ordering an inquiry into the drinks directorate. This showed, beyond doubt, that all was not well. The forty members of its staff who were working there at the moment of the Liberation were all sacked, to be replaced with former prisoners-of-war with few if any qualifications. No proper records or accounts had been kept. Farge decided first to take the matter to the courts, and second to make the most of his own role as the discoverer of the fraud. Malafosse protested his innocence, Defferre's friendship was revealed and rumours that he had been involved in shady dealings over the derequisition of a steamer began to circulate, Gouin's name was dragged in, notably by Farge, and so were some names of his staff. By this time (October) the referendum on the second constitutional draft was approaching, to be followed by a general election. The press had a field day, delivering with each issue more and more juicy 'details', and not just about the missing Algerian wine. There were also allegations of an enormous wine shipment to Belgium, another shipment to Switzerland of which only one-third was actually delivered, and phantom vessels plying clandestinely between Algeria and France.

There was a row at the Council of Ministers between Farge and Gouin. An official telephone tapper alleged that Gouin, in a telephone call, had demanded the payment of millions of francs,*

---

* These were the old, 'light' francs. In 1960, after de Gaulle's return to power, the 'heavy' franc was introduced by the simple expedient of chopping a nought off the face value of coins and notes.

in return for authorising the sale of wine. Gouin, for his part, suggested that the Communist party, seeking to discredit the Socialists at election time, might be behind Farge's campaign. It was a splendid, a full-sized, a top-quality scandal and it ran for years. A parliamentary committee of inquiry produced a report of 1,779 pages, various courts handed down various judgements. Yet nothing was ever definitively proved, certainly not against the hapless Gouin. The president of the parliamentary committee, when finally it reported, went so far as to say that most of the frauds they had been looking into had had no effect upon the supply of wine for current consumption. Fraud there almost certainly was. At some time, somewhere and by someone, some wine seems to have been improperly deflected from its intended market. But lack of adequate statistics made it impossible to say when, where, how much and who profited. Farge, whatever political motives were imputed to him, may well have been acting in good faith. The Ministry of Food was certainly in need of a cleansing operation. But for all the ferocity of his campaign against the black market, it cannot be said that he succeeded.

This seedy affair was nonetheless instructive. Firstly it showed that in this post-war period, the quality of ministerial staffs was not always what it should be. The Appeal Court of the Seine department, while finding Gouin blameless, passed some critical remarks about his official entourage which, it said, included proven collaborators as well as suspicious characters. The truth is – and it is one which had an important bearing on the development of post-Liberation France – that appointment to posts in the administration, the nationalised industries and party organisations was often not based upon qualifications or suitability but upon wartime record. (Even this criterion was not foolproof. A member of Gouin's staff was found to be, instead of a Resistant, a supporter of wartime Franco–German collaboration.) *Epuration* – the trial of collaborators and Vichyites – had removed numerous experienced men from the public service (see p. 14), and in their place had come others who were not really fitted, indeed, sometimes were not fitted at all, for the job. The head of Gouin's private office, a Marseille lawyer, confessed that he knew nothing about administration. There was a strong Marseille flavour to the business transacted within this office, just as there was a whiff of Algiers in the office of Gouin's *directeur de cabinet*, a French-Algerian who in pre-war times had been director of Algerian hospitals. In another judgement, a Seine court pointed out apropos of Malafosse, the director of the drinks division, that 'brilliant qualities cannot take the place of experience slowly acquired by officials who reach the highest posts by means of lengthy intellectual and moral preparation'. These findings and observations may not have thrown much light upon the wine scandal, but they revealed, in a manner that could not fail to be disquieting, that something was not right with the way in which the country was being administered.

A second consequence of the wine scandal was more deep-seated and, in the long run, unhealthy. French people are notoriously suspicious and scornful of those who try to govern them. This is partly the result of an excess of individualism, partly the historic popular conception of 'Them' and 'Us' – on the one hand the unseen but omnipotent State and its workings, and on the other the struggles of the ordinary man or woman to defend his or her personal patch of independence and self-interest. No one put it better than Harold Laski, the British Labour party intellectual who in July 1948 attended the French Socialist party's national congress in Paris, and sent a friendly and humorous message of greeting to President Vincent Auriol, himself a Socialist. It read: 'The *Fronde* [a powerful body of opposition to the throne during the minority of Louis XIV] is a political and social movement of the 17th century which, to please socialists, has been carried over into the 20th century so as to protect the people against the possibility of being governed.'[12] The wine scandal, with its allegations against ministers, parliamentarians, officials, its insinuations that there was something rotten within the machinery of State, its implications that, as usual, it was the ordinary citizen who was being diddled out of his modest rights, in this case to a glass or two of wine – the wine scandal did a great deal, even before the new Constitution took effect, to stoke up the always latent fires of anti-parliamentarianism. No matter that nothing was proven. Mud, if thrown sufficiently hard and widely, is bound to stick somewhere. It stuck, for example, to Félix Gouin, whose political career and prospects were effectively ruined. He might, but for the scandal, have been chosen as the first President of the Republic.

But if the 'them' and 'us' division thus received fresh emphasis, no one could claim that the French people were being left without a voice in the choice of who should govern them. Following two general elections to two Constituent Assemblies and two constitutional referenda, they were now (November 1946) summoned to the polls once more to elect a National Assembly. Not surprisingly, abstention was on the high side (22 per cent). The result re-emphasised the hardening of French opinion into two blocs, with the MRP regaining some of its lost ground, the Socialists continuing their previous slide, and the Communists, their support growing in response to the spread of anti-Communism, increasing both their share of seats in the National Assembly and in their percentage of the total vote. They thus regained their place as the leading party, but the Left as a whole – Communists and Socialists – again failed to win a majority in the Chamber. Tripartism, never a substantial fabric, had now worn so thin as to become transparent. Neither Thorez nor Bidault succeeded in their bid for the premiership. The only solution, a temporary one to carry the country through to the presidential election in January, was a minority, one-party, Socialist government. Léon Blum consented to lead it.

So the last stage in the work of institutional construction was reached. At the Palace of Versailles, on 16 January 1947, on a cold clear day, the Socialist Vincent Auriol, aged sixty-two, was elected the first President of the Fourth Republic by the newly elected members of both Chambers, the National Assembly and the upper house, the Council of the Republic. Much bargaining between the parties having taken place before the voting began, it took only one ballot to choose Auriol, who was supported by Communists and Socialists, a few others, and by eleven African deputies, imported by special plane by the resourceful Jules Moch, Socialist Minister of the Interior. With an escort of military motor-cyclists, the new President drove to the Elysée Palace to begin his seven years of service. De Gaulle, talking to his secretary about the presidential election, said that the journey from Versailles to Paris took place amidst general indifference – 'Not a flag, not a cheer, not a lifting of hats, nothing . . . the silence of the sea'.[13] Other, less mocking, witnesses spoke of cheers, flag waving, at least in Paris itself, a fringe of people lining the streets.

Auriol himself, in one of the first entries in the voluminous diary he was to keep throughout his presidency, writes of crowds all the way. But even his natural elation was qualified by the circumstances and the environment. In contrast to the cheers of the crowd, the Elysée seemed to him a sad place. 'This Republic, which was so uncompromising, high-minded and fraternal under the occupation,' he wrote, with a fine disregard for chronology, 'has been born in the throes of labour pains.' Before going to bed that night, he read the reports of prefects on the situation in the country. 'My heart was torn apart, as if I were hearing the poignant psalm of David: "Out of the depths have I cried unto thee." Those who are deaf to this anguished appeal of France are lacking in reverence.'[14]

In many respects, the infant Republic was lucky to have such a man to guide its faltering steps. His father had been a baker in a small town near Toulouse. Graduating in law and philosophy from the University of Toulouse, the young Vincent joined the Bar, was elected a Socialist deputy in 1914, became a specialist in economic and financial affairs, and in 1936 was appointed Minister of Finance in Léon Blum's Popular Front government. He voted against the Pétain régime on 10 July 1940, was placed under house arrest, later escaped and joined General de Gaulle in Algiers. After the Liberation, he served as one of de Gaulle's ministers, and in 1946 became President (Speaker) of the Constituent Assembly in succession to Gouin. Speaking with a strong southern accent, stout, with a left eye that disconcertingly resembled a poached egg (the result of a childhood accident with a revolver), 'Tauriol', as he was often called (a southern-type elision between the 't' of Vincent and the 'a' of Auriol), was a patriotic, experienced, loyal and firmly anti-Communist Socialist, very much a parliamentarian of the old school. His election was in effect and to a large degree a signal that, new Constitution notwithstanding, the clock had been turned back to Third Republic time.

Auriol had considerable charm, and was not above mocking himself. At the time of the visit to Paris in 1948 of Princess Elizabeth, the future Queen of England, she said something to him about her English accent in French. '*Cherre Prangcesse*,' he replied in his rich Toulouse twang, '*regarrdez le miang*.' As President of a deeply divided nation, he was acutely conscious of his responsibilities and managed, at times in the face of some criticism, to make the presidency a good deal more influential than the Constitution had intended. He was naturally as aware as any thinking Frenchman, indeed with a good deal more reason a good deal more aware, of the brooding presence in the background of General de Gaulle, and the way in which he tried, unsuccessfully, to make peace with the first of the Free Frenchmen presents a rather touching (and sometimes naïve) picture of a thoroughly decent man. Only two days after his election, 'Tauriol' sent a handsome message to de Gaulle at Colombey, paying tribute to him for his war-time role and inviting him and Mme de Gaulle to a family house-warming party in the private apartments in the Elysée. 'Whatever our differences over the Constitution,' the President told his emissaries to say, 'I rely on his advice and would like him to come to see me often.'

De Gaulle sent a polite message back but refused the invitation because, he said, his visits to Paris always created a fuss. The real reason was his refusal to have anything to do with 'the system', though in addition to that, the thought of the de Gaulles and the Auriols having a party together at the Elysée is at once comic and improbable. But Auriol made two more unsuccessful attempts to get the General to the Elysée, the second being on the occasion, in May, of a presidential dinner for Winston Churchill, in Paris to receive the Médaille Militaire. With reason, Auriol was upset at this discourtesy, and noted in his diary: 'I wonder if I am going to continue to receive refusals of this kind.'

The President's first duty, after his election, was to appoint a new government, Blum's minority government having resigned. He drew up a list of questions on home and foreign affairs for discussion with the political parties. 'Indochinese policy' was one of them. This was a christening present the newly born Republic could have done without.

The Indochinese empire, the jewel in France's imperial crown, had been consolidated in the early years of the Third Republic into five elements: the French-protected kingdoms of Laos and Cambodia and the three territories (*kys*) of Vietnam – Tonkin in the north, Annam in the centre (these were also protectorates) and Cochinchina in the south, which was a colony. After the fall of France in 1940, all these had remained under Vichy's rule, an arrangement agreed with the Japanese after their establishment of control over South-East Asia. Then on 9 March 1945 the

Japanese, alarmed by what seemed to be a surge of Resistance sentiment among the French in Indochina, swept aside this administration and supported the Emperor of Annam, Bao Dai, in his proclamation of the end of the French protectorate and of the independence of Vietnam. Five months later, bombed and atom-bombed into submission, Japan surrendered, and into the vacuum thus created in Vietnam stepped the Vietminh.

This was one of the anti-Japanese resistance groups founded in 1941 by a fervently Communist schoolteacher who had spent some years in France, China and the Soviet Union. His name was Nguyen Ai Quoc, later to be more famously known as Ho Chi Minh ('He Who Enlightens'). By ruthless methods the Vietminh had secured a strong position in Tonkin. In view of the later American intervention in Vietnam against the Communists, it is ironic to think that in the early and middle 1940s the Vietminh, in its conflict with both Vichy and the Japanese, had the support of both the Kuomintang Chinese and the US, neither of whom wanted to see French colonial rule restored in Indochina.

The first two things Ho Chi Minh and his followers did after the Japanese surrender were to declare themselves to be a 'National Liberation Committee' and then to persuade Bao Dai to abdicate and join in proclaiming the 'Democratic Republic of Vietnam'.[15] Crafty Ho knew the value in peasant politics of continuity, and the hereditary Emperor of Annam represented that element. Bao Dai, by now an ordinary citizen, was appointed 'Principal Counsellor' to the embryo government.

Bao Dai, often portrayed in the Paris press as a playboy and opportunist, was in fact far more prescient than he was ever given credit for. On 20 August 1945, after the Japanese surrender and just before his own abdication, he sent a message to de Gaulle, as head of the provisional French government, in which he warned that the only way to safeguard French interests and the French cultural heritage in Indochina 'is by frank and open recognition of the independence of Vietnam and by renouncing any idea of re-establishing French authority here under whatever form'.[16] There was no answer from Paris.

A small number of informed and far-sighted Frenchmen also realised the need to recognise changed circumstances. In March 1945, Pierre Messmer, French liaison officer in the Far East, later to become a minister in Fourth Republican governments (and a prime minister under the Fifth), reported from his base in Calcutta that the Vietminh, though of Communist inspiration, was the only body with which to do realistic business. Some months later, when next in Paris, he found his report had been left unread and pigeon-holed.[17] The episode typifies what in the future was to befall much of the information flowing – or not flowing – between Indochina and Paris. Accurate knowledge about Indochinese affairs was not easily come by in Paris, where few people knew or cared to know much about the dimensions of nationalist movements in French possessions overseas.

In March 1945, soon after the Japanese coup, the Ministry for Overseas France published a statement of intent, foreseeing an eventual Indochinese federation consisting of Laos, Cambodia, Tonkin, Annam and Cochinchina. It would have a French-nominated governor-general, who would appoint indigenous or French ministers. As originally conceived, this policy may have seemed to its authors to be reasonably liberal and forward-looking. By foreseeing a new federal-type state, it certainly appeared to break with the old, centralised colonial system. But by the time it was promulgated, the Vietnamese nationalists had proclaimed independence, which made the document seem distinctly old-fashioned. It was in fact rather less liberal than some of the reforms earlier introduced by the Vichy administrators. It was also a long way from Messmer's views. As for General de Gaulle, he seems to have been less concerned with internal developments in Indochina than with the need to uphold French prestige and status. Before anything else could happen, he insisted, French authority must first be re-established. At present (summer 1945) there was nothing to be done. France had no troops ready to be despatched to Indochina. At the Potsdam conference, to which France was not invited, it was decided for the time being to partition Indochina, the Chinese receiving the Japanese surrender in the north, the British in the south.

Meanwhile, de Gaulle chose two men to reimpose the French presence as soon as this was possible. He appointed General Philippe Leclerc Commander-in-Chief in Indochina and Admiral Thierry d'Argenlieu the High Commissioner there. They made an odd pair. Leclerc was a superb professional soldier and a vivid personality, whose military exploits had made him the best-known and most popular of all the officers fighting in the name of Free France. D'Argenlieu, by contrast, was by vocation a Carmelite monk, who had joined the Free French Navy, risen to Admiral's rank but had become, by the end of the war, almost unknown to a wider public. Jacques Dumaine wrote that 'his tight lips, his cold yet intense gaze and the unctuous way in which he rubs his hands together are surely the outward signs of a monkish Machiavellianism.'[18] A member of his staff thought he had 'the most brilliant mind of the twelfth century'.[19]

Although popular legend has come to identify Leclerc with liberal ideas about the future of the empire and of Indochina in particular, and the Admiral with exactly the opposite views, the matter is more complicated than that. In 1945, it was Leclerc who was thinking in terms of military reconquest and the maintenance of empire, while d'Argenlieu was contemplating the vision of independence. At the end of December 1945, after less than three months in Saigon, he was talking about how the colonial régime was destined to disappear, and warning de Gaulle against acting too late and thus forfeiting advantage.[20]

Before long, however, the two men had exchanged positions. Leclerc came to appreciate that while re-establishment of French authority in the south was desirable and feasible, to do the same in the north, the seat and source of nationalist power, required negotiations with Ho Chi Minh. For his part, d'Argenlieu eventually set his face against any such negotiations. He refused to go to Hanoi, and instead concerned himself principally with restoring colonial rule in Cochinchina and purging all those French officials who had collaborated with Vichy. Thus the final paradox lay in Leclerc, the military commander, becoming convinced of the need for a political solution, while d'Argenlieu, in whose hands rested the political authority, was unable or unwilling to envisage anything save the reimposition of French rule. One possible explanation for his change of heart was de Gaulle's resignation on 21 January 1946. With his person and influence removed from the head of French affairs, to such an ardent Gaullist as the Admiral the conception of a French 'Commonwealth' must at once have looked less practical or attractive.

The British soon relinquished their role in the south, having thrown their weight (in a way not intended by the Potsdam decision-makers) completely behind Leclerc's intentions to reassert control there.* By February 1946, the latter was able to announce that Cochinchina and south Vietnam had been 'completely pacified'.[21] But in the north, Ho Chi Minh, after the Japanese surrender, had established a *de facto* government that was not going to go away. No one saw this more clearly than Jean Sainteny, the French representative in Hanoi, who worked at getting on to good terms with Ho Chi Minh. Leclerc and he, in the absence of d'Argenlieu who had temporarily returned to Paris to promote his policies, entered into negotiations, authorised by the Gouin government, with Hanoi. The result was an agreement signed on 6 March. Ho Chi Minh, in his eagerness to get rid of the undisciplined Chinese army of occupation, was ready to make concessions, notably that French forces should relieve the Chinese in the north and establish a military presence for five years. In return, the French would recognise the Republic of Vietnam as part of an Indochinese federation, itself to be part of the French Union. The unity of the three *kys* – Tonkin, Annam and Cochinchina – a vital point in Ho's drive for total independence for all Indochina, was left to be decided by a referendum of the local populations.

On the face of it, this agreement promised well. It seemed to hold out the prospect that France might be the first of the major European

---

* It is not within the scope of this book to tell the story of British operations in Indochina in 1945–6. Because the British force, under Major-General Douglas Gracey, arriving in Saigon in September 1945, appeared to do all it could to ensure the suppression of the Vietnamese revolutionary movement and the reimposition of French rule, it can be argued that Britain helped in some degree to make inevitable what turned out to be twenty-eight years of war, first between France and Vietnamese nationalism, and then between the US and the Vietminh.

This view takes no account of the situation facing Gracey at the time. He had initially only 600 troops with which to disarm 50,000 Japanese and maintain law and order. Saigon, where Vietnamese revolutionary control was almost totally deficient because of rivalries and disputes between the various sects, was in a state of chaos. Gracey found it necessary to call upon Japanese troops (who were supposed to be prisoners-of-war) to restore order. This meant fighting against the Vietnamese revolutionaries. By mid-October, with the arrival of more and more French troops, Leclerc had succeeded in re-establishing French rule in Saigon, which he would have had great difficulty in doing had the revolutionaries been left unchallenged. British troops began to be withdrawn, the last leaving in March 1946. It is easy to say that Gracey exceeded his instructions, which were not to become involved in the internal affairs of Indochina; more difficult to be certain about what in the circumstances he should have done.

colonial powers to move towards decolonisation. But such optimism disregarded two factors. First, there were interested parties both in Saigon and Paris who disliked the very idea of negotiating with the Vietminh. Principal among them was d'Argenlieu, who expressed his feelings to General Etienne Valluy, his deputy: 'I am amazed, General, that is the only word I can use, amazed that France's leaders prefer negotiations to action when we have such a magnificent expeditionary force in Indochina.'[22] Although he did with one voice give provisional approval to the 6 March agreement and consented to meet Ho Chi Minh on board a French warship, with another he sought to persuade Marius Moutet, the Minister for Overseas France, that the right course was to create, in defiance of the agreement, an independent Cochinchinese Republic. In Paris, Moutet, a weak minister uncertain of his own mind, gave encouragement to this idea.[23] His governmental colleague Georges Bidault, Foreign Minister under Gouin and soon to become Prime Minister himself, suffered from no such weakness: he was not, and never was to be, in a decolonising mood.

Second, the 6 March agreement, though it appeared to buy time for both France and the Vietminh, in fact left unanswered several crucial questions. It avoided, indeed appeared to rule out, the principle of independence; and it left vague the true relationship between the proposed Indochinese federation and the as yet unborn French Union. Leclerc saw clearly enough the possibility that such a loosely worded document might be the subject of prevarication. In his report to Paris, he insisted on the loyal implementation of the agreement, even if the dreaded word independence had to be written into it.

This is exactly what did not happen. Realising that the best way of denying the Vietminh their future hold over the whole of Vietnam was to create a *fait accompli* in the former colony of Cochinchina, d'Argenlieu, backed by powerful business and colonial interests, encouraged its secession. In June, an 'autonomous Republic of Cochinchina' was proclaimed by d'Argenlieu and a puppet government installed, without the Gouin government demurring. Ho Chi Minh learnt the news in the aeroplane taking him to Paris for the conference at Fontainebleau which was to give flesh to the bones of the March agreement. He nearly turned back but decided in spite of everything to go on, still hopeful that he could win the goal of Indochinese independence with French consent and without having to fight for it.

His optimism proved groundless. The Fontainebleau conference broke down, partly on differences over Cochinchina, partly on the issue of independence, but above all because the French side, rightly or wrongly, lost any confidence they ever had in the good faith of Ho Chi Minh. A letter from Leclerc to Maurice Schumann, President of the MRP, played its part here.[24] In it, not only did he intemperately declare that France had already won the war in Indochina but he also warned that Ho was a great enemy of France and that no concessions should be made to him. Leclerc was a man generally of liberal ideas, not an old-school colonialist, so his views in this context carried weight. That they were contradictory with his earlier attitude was proof of the extreme complexity of the Indochinese situation. It would be just as wrong to attribute a monopoly of consistently 'good' judgement to Leclerc as it would be to debit d'Argenlieu with unerringly 'bad' ideas.

Schumann showed the letter to Bidault, by now Prime Minister, who was not slow, in his instructions to the French negotiating team at Fontainebleau, to hearken to its advice. The head of that team, a founder member of the MRP, a close friend of Bidault's, and a man with former business interests in Indochina, would also have found it easy to accept that Ho Chi Minh was a man not to be trusted. From now on, therefore, the drift to war quickened. While the Fontainebleau conference was still sitting, d'Argenlieu in Indochina, without getting the prior approval of his government, called a conference there to discuss the future of the Indochinese federation and Cochinchina's position within it. This is just what the conference at Fontainebleau was supposed to be discussing. Evidently the bad faith of which Ho Chi Minh was suspected was not all on his side.

Nonetheless, though Fontainebleau finished negatively, Ho signed an agreement with Moutet which left the doors open. Whether he did this to buy time, or was gambling on a stronger Communist influence in Paris after the next general election, or whether he genuinely wanted to avert war, is hardly relevant. The momentum of events was already unstoppable. A press campaign developed in Paris against any prospect of abandoning parts of the French Union. The Leftist press, on the other hand, was generally sympathetic to the Vietnamese cause, attacking d'Argenlieu and demanding his recall. But even here, the picture was blurred. The Communists, still part of the government, had not yet marked out their opposition to the course of events in Indochina. Once they had passed into opposition, and with the coming of the Cold War, the tone of their dissent became sharp and shrill. But after the signing of the agreement of 6 March 1946, Thorez had told a pro-French Vietnamese politician that he, Thorez, was not anxious to see the Tricolour hauled down in Indochina.[25] If Thorez thought like this, it is likely that numerous Communist voters thought the same, at least at that time. In any event, it would have needed a strong and resolute government to take the decision to defy right-wing pressures and recall d'Argenlieu. This is just what was lacking. Instead, there was a divided coalition, headed by Bidault, a hard-liner where French Union affairs were concerned. D'Argenlieu remained for the time being at his post, unrebuked.

On 23 November 1946, after clashes and incidents in Haiphong, the port for Hanoi, and a typical display by the French authorities in Hanoi, Haiphong and Saigon of contradictory orders and actions, the cruiser *Suffren* bombarded the Vietnamese quarter in Haiphong and French troops were sent in to clear it. In a massive effort to show the Vietnamese who was master, French tanks, artillery and aircraft were all deployed. Vietnamese casualties amounted, according to French estimates, to 6,000 dead. The Vietnamese put their own figure at nearly 20,000. When the news reached Paris, Bidault's government backed the military action; before it was mounted, he had authorised the use of artillery. In vain did Sainteny, using his good relationship with Ho Chi Minh, try by diplomatic methods to arrest the dire march of events. There was a last-minute glimmer of hope when Léon Blum replaced Bidault as head of the government in Paris. On 15 December Ho sent him a message, suggesting that everything should go back to what it was before the Haiphong bombardment. This message did not reach Paris until 26 December. Allegedly, it was held up in Saigon by members of d'Argenlieu's staff, though one of them has absolutely denied this. What is certain is that it got to Blum too late: just as the French hard-liners were in the ascendant, so the Vietminh were preparing to strike, by now convinced that the French were not only resolved against any recognition of the Vietnamese Republic but were set on the military reconquest of the whole of Tonkin. The formidable General Giap, the Vietminh's military commander, went on the offensive in Hanoi on 19 December 1946 against French

property and persons, and about forty people were killed. French forces responded and by the following night were in control of the city centre. Ho Chi Minh and his staff took to the countryside. Seven and a half years of war had begun – nearly four times that span, if the American war against the Vietnamese Communists is counted.

The news hit Paris, where people were far more preoccupied with the daily struggle to exist than with the obscure Fontainebleau negotiations and their aftermath, like a bombshell. 'Ho Chi Minh shows his true colours,' ran a Radical newspaper's headline; the MRP's official paper had: 'Vietminh unleashes hostilities against France'. Blum, the old Socialist and humanitarian, was grievously perplexed. He had written only a few weeks earlier, in his Socialist paper *Le Populaire*, that independence for Vietnam was the only solution. Now he told the National Assembly that the old colonial system was over and done with, and added that negotiations would be resumed once order had been re-established. It seemed a harmless and reasonable formula, but in fact it would ring out like a death-knell throughout the years of the Fourth Republic. Military victory first, negotiations later may have sounded sweet to ears which in recent times had heard too much of humiliation and defeat, but it was to lock France into long, cruel and expensive wars, first in Indochina, then in North Africa, from which she derived no benefit whatever.

Along with Blum's stance went the conviction, accepted by the greater part of French opinion, that the Vietminh, by their attack on Hanoi, had placed themselves beyond the pale. The events of Hanoi effaced any doubts about the French assault on Haiphong, details of which had in any case been played down in the French press. Blum despatched Moutet to Indochina to appraise the situation on the spot, and the Minister was horrified by what he saw and learnt in Hanoi, where d'Argenlieu showed him photographs of the corpses of women and children mutilated by the Vietminh. Moutet considered that the attack on 19 December, carried out when the Vietminh were still talking about negotiations, fully justified a military response; the Vietminh were not to be trusted. 'Once the army has re-established order, it will again be possible to look at political problems'[26] – the Blum formula in other words.

In the years to come, and as the Cold War developed, the French struggle in Indochina could be represented and justified as a battle for Western, democratic, values against the common enemy. But even in those opening stages, the alleged inadmissibility of Ho Chi Minh and the Vietminh as valid interlocutors was as strong a factor in the formation of French policy as the resolve not to suffer any more humiliating retreats. As d'Argenlieu put it publicly in early January 1947: 'It is from now on impossible for us to deal with Ho Chi Minh . . . We will find other people in this country with whom we can deal, who will doubtless be nationalists also, but those other ones [i.e. the Vietminh] have disqualified themselves.'[27] In a decolonising context, this refusal to negotiate with someone because his views and actions were repugnant was not, of course, specifically a French syndrome. Britain made the same mistake with Kenyatta in Kenya, Makarios in Cyprus. But at least British governments came to accept the inevitable and to change their policies. The men once regarded as arch-fiends thus became in time, and with different treatment, responsible and respected statesmen.

French governments, on the other hand, were at no time sufficiently strong or united to effect such a change. Nor did they appear to want to. Only the Communists, and some back-bench Socialists, stood for a resumption of negotiations with Ho Chi Minh, and even the Communists, as Thorez had shown, wanted to preserve the link with France. Two months later, in March 1947, the Communist party's central committee voted in favour of withholding military credits for the pursuit of military operations. This was the beginning of the series of events which was to culminate, in May, in the eviction of the Communists from the government. Whatever their motives, however marked the sophistry with which they argued that it was possible to oppose the government's Indochinese policies and yet remain a part of it, the Communist attitude on Indochina, viewed through the binoculars of history, can now be seen to have been more perspicacious and realistic than that of the other parties. In 1947, of course, it did not look like that at all. As the Cold War gathered strength, the very fact that the Communists stood for a resumption of negotiations with Ho Chi Minh was sufficient in itself to condemn that policy.

This was one of the dramas and the tragedies of the Fourth Republic. It may have seemed appropriate for Auriol, in the Cabinet, to appeal 'in a voice choked with real emotion' to Thorez to remind his friends of patriotism and of the sacrifices made in common for the Liberation of France. He was equally reflecting ministerial opinion when he pointed out that it was the Vietminh who had attacked at Hanoi and that to withhold defence credits would be to 'hand over our compatriots held hostage there to massacre'.[28] But this strength of feeling cannot obscure the fact that France drifted into war without a realistic reckoning of the likely consequences and without adequate exploration of the prospects for a negotiated settlement. It was to be a drift into defeat and humiliation.

Such a judgement is not just easy hindsight. Leclerc, who had resigned his command in July 1946 (his place was taken by the bellicose Valluy), was persuaded by a sorely troubled Léon Blum to return to Indochina in early 1947, on a brief inspection tour. Despite his continuing mistrust of Ho Chi Minh, expressed before the Fontainebleau conference, he reported that while it was necessary to build up French military strength, anti-Communism would be a useless lever so long as the problem of nationalism was not solved. 'In 1947,' he wrote, 'France will no longer put down by force a grouping of 24 million inhabitants which is assuming unity and in which there exists a xenophobic and perhaps a national ideal. . . . The main problem from now on is political.'[29] Leclerc (who was killed in an air crash in Africa a few months later) seems to have been periodically of more than one mind, but his view on Indochina, as the war began to take hold, was unequivocal: he told Maurice Schumann early in 1947 that wars could no longer be won by military means alone.[30]

So there were people in France who could grasp the wider issues and point to the higher national interest. They included, certainly as time went on, many rank-and-file Socialists. But they, and those who thought like them, were not strong or determined enough to withstand the pressures of the reconquest lobby, consisting of most of the MRP (despite its generally liberal outlook) and the representatives, in and out of parliament, of colonial interests. Socialist ministers, above all Moutet, are specially to be criticised for the compliance and lethargy with which they went along with the actions on the ground of such fire-eating personalities as d'Argenlieu or General Valluy, the Commander-in-Chief in succession to Leclerc, who did all they could, often in the absence of firm directives from Paris, to ensure that French rule should be restored to the whole country. It was Moutet who said, in a speech in the National Assembly on 18 March 1946, that 'What I reprove Admiral d'Argenlieu for is not that he did not follow the directives of the government. I reproach him for having anticipated them.'

Almost three years later, a Socialist, Oreste Rosenfeld, said in the Assembly of the French Union that 'the great responsibility of the government of M. Georges Bidault and M. Maurice Thorez was not to have the authority to prevent Admiral d'Argenlieu from following a policy contrary to that of the French government.'[31] This stricture makes insufficient allowance for the mood prevailing at the time. The feeling that France had done enough retreating and should now stand firm was deeply rooted. If the politicians, notably the Socialist ministers, took the wrong road in Indochina in 1945–6 – and General de Gaulle, as head of the first provisional government, must also bear a share of the blame – they were only reflecting the state of mind of the greater part of the nation. It scarcely matters today, now that the passions of the time are only memories, who was responsible for the breakdown at Fontainebleau or what sparked the outbreak of hostilities on the ground. There is certainly a case for arguing that a chance for avoiding war was missed in 1946.* But there can be no escaping the fact that the respective aims of Paris and Hanoi were irreconcilable. French policy was woolly, the ruling coalition riven by differences, the pro-consuls on the ground prone to take matters into their own hands. But one thing is clear. No French government in 1946, even one including the Communists, was ready to concede Ho Chi Minh's ultimate aims for Vietnam: complete unity and independence, even within the notional framework of the French Union. The Vietminh attack at Hanoi on 19 December 1946 was the final point of no return. Compared with the arcane Fontainebleau negotiations, which never aroused much public interest, the killing of French people inevitably gave rise to strong feelings in France that this was not the time to be thinking about doing a deal, least of all with those who were responsible for the killing.

As the new Constitution came into effect, and as the Indochinese war began to make its first demands upon French military and financial resources, the public in the capital showed its longing to escape from worries and shortages by packing into the Paris nightclubs, where the young Yves Montand, beginning his career as a singer of working men's songs, was the idol of the crowd. A foreign observer wrote: 'For the past two months, there has been a climate of indubitable and growing malaise in Paris, and perhaps all over Europe, as if the French people, or all European people, expected something to happen or worse, expected nothing to happen.'[32] At least where the French were concerned these worst expectations were not fulfilled. 1947 was to see happenings of a kind to satisfy the most confirmed seekers or fearers of something new.

* It is put most eloquently by Sainteny in his book *Histoire d'une paix manquée* (Paris, Amiot-Dumont, 1953).

CHAPTER 3

A Brush with Civil War

The French Communist party, founded in 1920 when it split from the Socialists, was devoted, like its counterparts in other countries, to achieving power by whatever means seemed appropriate at the time. Inconsistencies, sudden changes of the party line in keeping with Moscow's directives, were no problem, such was the force of discipline and hierarchy within the ranks. If at one moment in the Thirties social democracy, not Fascism, was the ultimate enemy of the working class, so be it. If, at the next, collaboration with those very Socialists seemed to be the road to power (as it did seem at the time of the Popular Front), again so be it. Such violent zigzags were decided at the top, without tiresome discussion among the rank and file. Thus on the outbreak of war in 1939 the Communist party line was impeccably anti-Nazi, its deputies voted unanimously in favour of the defence budget, and those of military age rejoined their regiments. This did not last long. As a sequel to the signing of the German–Soviet pact, the line in Moscow changed. From then on until Hitler's invasion of the USSR, the war became, according to Soviet and French Communist doctrine, one of capitalist imperialism, in line with Lenin's theory of 'revolutionary defeatism', launched at the beginning of the First World War. The party was proscribed by the French government and its newspapers obliged to publish secretly. Maurice Thorez, the party leader (known grandiloquently as *Le Fils du Peuple*, a ghosted autobiography with that title having been published before the war), deserted from the French Army and fled to Moscow, where he spent the rest of the war. After the French defeat in 1940 and German occupation, the Communist line was firmly anti-Vichy but no less anti-war and anti-British. 'De Gaulle', declared the secretly published *L'Humanité*, 'is English capitalism. Pétain, Doriot, Laval is German–French capitalism.' But pacifism remained the party directive; there was no call to undermine or fight against the occupying power (although some Communist Resistance networks were established during this period, the work of individuals, Armenian immigrant workers among them).

The German attack on Russia must have come as a relief to many French Communists. From now on, resisting the Germans was a patriotic duty. Suddenly the 'mercenaries of the City of London' had become 'our gallant British allies'. There is no doubt about the contribution of the Communists to the Resistance. While party claims that under the occupation 75,000 supporters had been shot will not stand up, it is quite possible that this number died in one way or another as the result of occupation. One of the most moving letters written by a member of the Resistance about to be shot by the Germans came from Gabriel Péri, a former journalist on *L'Humanité*. He was one of those who began organising resistance before the German attack on Russia and was taken by the Gestapo, who offered to spare him if he reneged. He refused, and the night before his execution wrote: 'May my friends know that all my life I have remained faithful to the ideal; may my companions know that I am going to die so that France may live . . . Adieu and *vive la France*.'[1] In the same letter, he wrote of Communism preparing the way for *'les lendemains qui chantent'** – in other words, Communism, the patriotic, Resistance-inspired faith, was the key to the future.

Fighting the Germans was not only patriotic but also another, and highly marketable, way of advancing revolutionary aims. The same metamorphosis occurred in other Communist parties, inviting suspicions among the wary. In Britain, Lord Swinton, head of the wartime Security Executive, voiced these in a sporting metaphor: 'The Communist game is still the same, but it is being played on a much better wicket.'[2] For the French Communists, their new line had the added attraction of enabling them to penetrate and appeal to sections of the population, such as the peasants and the trade unions, which had hitherto proved immune to the charms of Communism. Best of all, the party was as a result allowed, was indeed invited, into the inner sanctums of power. De Gaulle, who already in Algiers had given official status to the Communist party,

* 'The joyous future' would be an approximate translation.

accorded it two posts in the post-Liberation government and the following year (1945), while refusing to hand over any of the three key portfolios demanded by Thorez (see p. 24), increased their representation in the government by five appointments, including the economic strongholds of National Economy, Industrial Production and Labour.

For years after, the traditional right wing and *haute bourgeoisie* claimed – and some circles continue to claim – that de Gaulle betrayed the national interest by thus opening the gates to the enemy. What he was doing, of course, was to seek to win the cooperation of the working class in the work of rebuilding the economy. He said as much in his memoirs, where he wrote that it was impossible to exclude the Communists 'when the very substance of France would be seriously compromised if the whole people were not brought to the task [of reconstruction]. Not that I had any illusions as to the party's "loyalty" . . . I knew it aimed at seizing total power.'[3] At least, he added, 'So long as I was in office, not a single strike occurred.' He said in 1955: 'If I hadn't been in Paris [at and after its Liberation] there would have been a Communist government, not immediately, there would have been a National Front government . . . then France would have lost her independence and French people their memories of Freedom.'[4]

That was how it seemed to many people at the time and later. 'The Communists', noted Jacques Dumaine in his diary in January 1946, after de Gaulle's withdrawal, 'are already preparing in secret the setting up of a totalitarian regime . . . there will be a gradual transition from three to two parties, with the ideal attained when only one party remains.'[5] This may well have been the case, but what is equally true is that the Communists at this period were against violent action. Even de Gaulle himself, while not doubting the long-term aims of the party, did not consider them dangerous; 'reeds painted to resemble iron' he called them contemptuously. Most French historians today consider that, however potent the means at their disposal, the Communists were not interested in undermining the authority of the State which de Gaulle, in 1944, was in process of re-establishing. On the contrary, the party saw its duty and interest for the time being as helping to build up national unity around de Gaulle, thus contributing to the eventual defeat of Nazi Germany, while at the same time increasing its own authority and influence at every level. 'We must hold national unity dearer than what we ourselves cherish,' wrote Thorez in September 1944 from Moscow.[6] In other words, the class struggle, the overthrow of the bourgeoisie and all the other aims of classic Communism were, at least temporarily, to be set on one side. With Thorez still absent, this line was not always congenial to all the party. De Gaulle's decision in the autumn of 1944 first to dissolve the internal Resistance forces (FFI) and integrate them with the regular Army, and then to dissolve the 'patriotic militias', Communist-dominated bodies which in some areas had arrogated to themselves the powers of the central government, did not go unchallenged. Jacques Duclos, in Thorez's absence acting head of the party – a short, plump man from the Pyrenees with a capacity for parliamentary invective which was to cause many a scene at the Palais Bourbon in the years to come – protested against what he called a conspiracy against the Republic. His opposition to de Gaulle never wavered. But once Thorez was back in control – he returned from Moscow at the end of November – the line was redefined in language that could have issued from the lips of the General himself. 'The local and departmental Liberation committees', Thorez told the party central committee, 'must not usurp the functions of municipal and departmental administrations, any more than the National Council of the Resistance is a substitute for the government.'

De Gaulle had certainly calculated correctly in thinking that Thorez's return was desirable in the national interest. In his memoirs, he explains how the Communist leader contributed towards the work of national restoration, 'while doing his best for the interests of Communism'. Other contemporary eye-witnesses record that Thorez, a burly, red-faced man capable of considerable charm (the American Senator Vandenberg, seeing his beaming face at an official Paris luncheon-table in May 1946, kept inanely repeating: 'How can such a healthy man be a Communist?'[7]), played a conciliator's role within the government. Duff Cooper, the British Ambassador, who could not be suspected of left-wing tendencies, also thought Thorez had 'great charm' and, far from deploring de Gaulle's attitude, considered it 'very sensible' of him to include the Communists in his government.[8]

During this time when they were enjoying the fruits of office, the Communists adopted some impeccably orthodox views, urging the need for a strong Army and for greater productive efforts by the workers. When nationalist riots broke out in Algeria in May 1945, the party condemned them as 'a fascist conspiracy' and declared that 'France is and ought to remain a great African power'. (This line was soon to be abandoned in favour of one supporting nationalist movements wherever they surfaced.) Even Communist support for Ho Chi Minh was presented as the vision of a future Vietnam within the framework of a loosely structured French Union.

These arguments were largely tactical. The Communists knew that any attempt in France to seize power by force would be withstood by American and British forces, still physically on French soil. The only way forward was to win popular support by championing popular causes (such as patriotism), fostering the unity of the Left, and building up the conditions which in the end would result in a Communist-led parliamentary majority. As Thorez put it some time after his return, 'the union of working-class and republican forces is the sure foundation of democracy . . . the French workers' party which we wish to create by the fusion of Communists and Socialists would be a guide towards this democracy, *nouvelle et populaire*.'[9]

A description has already been given of how the Communists used the Constitution-making procedure in 1945–6 as a means of drawing the Socialists into their net. Their plans very nearly succeeded, but in the referendum on the first, Communist- and Socialist-inspired, Constitution, 600,000 Socialist voters failed to cleave to the party line, and that text was rejected. From then on Communist hopes of securing parliamentary control became increasingly unrealistic. Partly this was due to the courageous refusal of the Socialist leaders – Blum, Auriol, Gouin – to play the Communist game, despite the pressures within Socialist ranks for working-class unity. No one was more inclined to apply those pressures than Guy Mollet, who in September 1946 became Secretary-General of the party. A young schoolteacher (English was his subject) from Arras with Marxist views and a fine Resistance record, in the Fifties he was to become Prime Minister and lead France into the Suez fiasco. His militancy nearly saved the Communists from eviction from government in May 1947, the most important development in post-Liberation history.

Events which followed quickly upon Auriol's entry into the Elysée showed that tripartism, for long an artificial device, was at last melting away. Increasingly the Communists were isolated within the government – over Indochina, over the brutal suppression of an uprising in Madagascar, over wage restraint. Meanwhile in the world beyond, the announcement of the Truman Doctrine presaged the splitting of Europe into two blocs. One dramatic incident emphasised the widening gap between the Communists and the other parties. In March 1947, while other members of the National Assembly rose to their feet in a gesture of solidarity with the expeditionary corps in Indochina, the Communist members and above all the Communist Minister for National Defence (the party had at last succeeded in getting its hands on this lever of power, even if its margins of influence had been much reduced) remained seated, despite the exhortations of his fellow ministers. 'If you go on like this,' Gouin said prophetically to Thorez, 'things are going to break up.'[10]

Vincent Auriol's first act after assuming the presidency had been to appoint a new Prime Minister, Léon Blum having presented the resignation of his minority Socialist government. Auriol's choice was Paul Ramadier, a cultivated, hard-working, moderate Socialist, wounded in the First World War, a Resistant in the Second. He had been a disastrously incompetent Minister of Food after the Liberation (though every holder of that unenviable post had been more or less of a disaster). With his buttoned boots and white goatee beard, he could have been a caricature of a Third Republic politician. He enlarged the tripartite formula by putting together a multi-party coalition, consisting of Socialists, Communists, MRP, Radicals and Independents (and including incidentally a future President of the Fifth Republic, the young François Mitterrand). No common thread united this political rag-bag. There were disagreements on almost everything – food policy, further nationalisations, national defence, the Franco-British treaty of Dunkirk which was in the making. But of all the dissentients, none was more out of step than the Communists. Auriol, whose diary is full of reports from various sources about Communist plans and intentions, noted on 29 January that they were up to their double-faced tricks again: 'They belong to the government while preparing for its failure and downfall.'

Once the Truman Doctrine had been announced, it certainly began to look as though the Communists were out to make trouble. In the Council of Ministers in mid-March, Thorez complained that the US wanted to carry out a world policy based on the ideology of free enterprise, despite the risk of dividing the world into two hostile blocs. Denouncing world ideological policies was a piece of cheek, coming from a confirmed Stalinist like Thorez (even if he did speak, as Auriol noted, 'in a calm voice'). But there was something in what he said: two blocs were forming, and French adhesion to the Western one received a powerful impetus from the breakdown of the long-running four-power conference in Moscow, when not only did the prospects for coexistence between the 'Western and Soviet systems receive a severe setback, but France failed humiliatingly to win Soviet support for some of her positions on Germany and the Saar. From that moment on, the idea of France holding the balance between East and West was in practice at an end.

These foreign influences certainly played an important part in the drama which led to Communist exclusion from the government. There had already been a menacing episode in March, when the central committee of the Communist party had voted to withhold military credits for Indochina, a decision defended by Thorez in the Council of Ministers on the grounds that the party (which had voted for Ramadier's original programme) could not agree with the government's Indochinese policy. Despite this, Thorez added, he did not think these difficulties justified a government crisis. He was saying in effect that a party was under no obligation to subscribe to all the policies of the government to which it belonged. This questionable proposition was inspired, where the Communists were concerned, by the hope that Bidault, at the Moscow conference, would somehow maintain the French position of halfway-house between the Eastern and Western blocs and gain Soviet support for French views on the future of Germany. If the Communists were to leave the government, it would be the end of those hopes.

The surprising thing was that Thorez's line was accepted more or less without demur by the other ministers; Ramadier even went so far as to thank him 'for the support he had contributed in difficult circumstances'. The explanation is that the other parties in the coalition, prompted by Bidault from Moscow, also wanted to avoid a government crisis so long as any hope survived of a satisfactory outcome for France of the four-power conference.

Once that hope had expired, the realities of the political situation in Paris became clearer. Ramadier, by no means a rabid anti-Communist, had by the end of April become increasingly doubtful about the possibility of continuing to include Communist ministers in a government many of whose policies they consistently opposed. Already in March, the Communists had been dismissed from the Belgian government, and in May the same thing was to happen in Italy. The Truman Doctrine, and the girding up for the Cold War which it heralded, had marked a momentous change in the international climate.

But it was on a domestic issue that the break finally came. A strike at the Renault factory on the outskirts of Paris against the rising cost of living was the occasion. It was begun by Trotskyite elements, who called for an increase in basic wages. To begin with, the Communist-dominated CGT opposed the strike, thus loyally sticking to the government line of wage and price control. But as the movement spread, and as Socialist and MRP newspapers mischievously gloated over the CGT's discomfiture, so the CGT and the Communists made a 180-degree turn and came out in support of the strikers. From a Communist point of view, it was hardly possible, whatever the political consequences, to do otherwise if the party was to maintain its position as defender of working-class interests. Ramadier, thought Thorez, would either have to agree the wage increases (thus torpedoing the government's wage and price policy) or resign; it was inconceivable that he would try to govern without and against the Communists.

Thorez had miscalculated. Ramadier, encouraged by Auriol, was resolved to stand firm. At the Council of Ministers on 1 May, he argued that a general increase in salaries would be disastrous and reminded the Communist ministers of their previous undertakings and of the principle of ministerial solidarity. Thorez replied that an increase in wages would not result in an increase in prices, because the difference could come out of profits. After some fruitless argument, Auriol pointed out to the ministers that, in contrast with the Third Republic's Constitution, the new Constitution gave the President of the Council (i.e. Ramadier) the choice of his ministers and it was up to him, provided he still had the support of the Assembly, to say whether ministers who disagreed with the programme supported by the Assembly could remain in the government. In any case he, Auriol, was not going to accept the government's resignation if the Communists stepped down. It was for Ramadier to bring the whole affair to the Assembly, which could then say whether or not it continued to support him. At the end of the meeting, as the ministers left the room, Auriol kept back Thorez for a moment, and made a last-minute appeal to him. Red in the face, and very moved, Thorez replied, with tears in his eyes, that he could do nothing more: 'I know that what we are doing is very serious, but I am at the end of my tether.'[11] There is no reason to think that he was putting on an act. Born to a poor, coal-mining family, he was, or anyway conceived himself to be, a patriotic Frenchman, whatever his Muscovite allegiance. He also loved the trappings of power.

The rest of the drama was quickly played out, though not without some heart-stopping moments. Ramadier made the dispute a matter of confidence and the National Assembly voted him that confidence, with all the Communists, including the Communist ministers, voting against. By their own act, the Communists themselves appeared to have signed their death warrant. But then Guy Mollet put his spanner into the works. Though not a crypto-Communist, he could not imagine, as many other Socialists could not, a system where the Socialist party remained in government and the Communists moved into opposition. *'Pas d'ennemi à gauche'* had for long been one of the golden rules of French left-wing politics. Mollet persuaded the Directing Committee of the Socialist party to think and vote likewise, namely that the government should resign and allow the Assembly to pronounce upon a new prime minister. The Directing Committee's decision was however overturned by the Socialist deputies representing the parliamentary party. The way was at last clear for the Communists to be excluded from the government.

Despite their negative vote in the Assembly against Ramadier, the Communist ministers declined to resign, and on 5 May a curiously worded decree appeared in the *Journal Officiel*, stating that 'the functions [of the four Communist ministers] are considered to be at an end, following the way they voted in the National Assembly.' The four subsequently went to the Elysée to take their leave of Auriol. It was all very civilised. Auriol said how distressed he was by the crisis and thanked his visitors for their past collaboration and good will. Thorez thanked him for his words and confirmed that the Communists would do nothing 'which could create a rift between Republican parties'. Tripartism, which had come to lack any real substance, was finally at an end and the Communists, 'the first party of France', passed into opposition where, did they but know it, they were to remain for no less than thirty-four years. In the whole period of the Fourth Republic, no single event was more significant than this, the relegation of a party representing one-quarter of the electorate to the political wilderness, thus making the orderly functioning of the parliamentary system difficult, and often impossible.

Was it all a carefully laid plot to get rid of the Communists? The latter were later to claim that it was done under American pressure. But why did they go so quietly? The government, or at least some members of it, feared major Communist demonstrations on 1 May (Labour Day), and took extensive security precautions, which proved unnecessary. The best explanation is the simplest: the Communists, misreading the situation, manoeuvred themselves into a position whence their eviction followed naturally. They did not seek it and were not expecting it. In the early summer of 1947, after the announcement of the Truman Doctrine and the breakdown of the Moscow conference but before the introduction of the Marshall Plan and the onset of the Cold War proper, they seemed uncertain of their own and of Moscow's line.

At the height of the exclusion crisis, Auriol found on his desk a note, originating from secret but unnamed sources, purporting to describe the discussions within the political bureau and the local federations of the Communist party. According to this, party members were increasingly dissatisfied with the inability of their ministers in the government to influence policy. The best hope, the argument went, was to create a government crisis and get a new prime minister who would give them one of the big ministries. Thorez apparently argued against their thesis and Duclos also had reservations, which bears out the theory that Communist thinking was not united. Auriol added the comment that it was the tendency faithful to the Communist International which had carried the day, against Thorez, 'and that was why I insisted, more than ever, that Ramadier should not resign, unless brought down by the Chamber.'

But even Auriol, suspicious of Communist tactics and motives as he was, was not quite happy about what he was doing. 'It is not to be doubted', he wrote in his diary, 'that if I could have done it, it would have been better to dissolve the Assembly' – a course of action which the Constitution ruled out during the first eighteen months of a parliament's life, and even after that, two ministerial crises would have had to occur. The Assembly, Auriol noted, had been elected with a majority based on tripartism. 'The departure of the Communists changes the basis of that majority which will tilt towards the centre–left. Logically, the splitting of the majority would indicate going to the country [i.e. a general election] to choose another.' Wise old Auriol, with years of experience as a professional politician, realised that the dropping of the Communists involved a major redrawing of the political map.

Years later, Ramadier told a French author who was writing about the period that the events of May 1947 were a matter of French internal politics and had no international repercussions.[12] This is untenable. Certainly the Renault strike was, as already explained, the occasion for the break, but it was not the cause. Indeed, even before the final showdown with the Communists, Ramadier had found a formula for settling the claims of the Renault strikers. If the will had been there to keep the Communists in the government, it could have been done. Auriol went as far as he could to urge a compromise on the wages issue, but the will was emphatically not there, and with good reason. Faced with the negative attitude of the Communists on every aspect of foreign, colonial and internal policy, the other components of enlarged tripartism – MRP, Socialists, Radicals and Independents – were agreed that the moment of truth had come. None was more determined to get rid of the Communists than Bidault, who had returned from his Moscow humiliation breathing anti-Communist fire.

The departure of the Communists left public opinion largely unmoved, just as General de Gaulle's resignation had done fifteen months earlier. This was partly because they themselves reacted so peaceably. Immediately after the rupture, Duclos, never a man to mince words, said that people who were talking about a general strike were mad.[13] Another Communist spokesman declared that Communist absence from the government was only temporary. At the Party Congress held in Strasbourg at the end of June, the fiction of still being a partner of the government was somehow upheld. Most people at the time, whatever their political convictions, were convinced that the government of France could not for long be carried on without the Communists. Dumaine put it succinctly in his diary: 'A government without them faces a constant threat of social unrest, a government which includes them soon finds itself unable to function at all. The man in the street who tries to understand it all does not know whether to laugh or cry.'[14]

If the expulsion of the Communists was a crucial event (though scarcely noted as such at the time), the subsequent reaction to it of the Socialists was hardly less important for the future. The day after Thorez and his colleagues had taken their stately farewells of President Auriol, the National Council of the Socialist party decided to remain in the coalition. The discussion was impassioned, with Mollet, among others, arguing that their place was now in opposition. Only a slender majority – 2,529 to 2,125 – carried the day. But the deed was done. Unbelievable though it would have seemed at the Liberation, the Socialists had agreed to form part of a coalition which did not include the Communists. This was a milestone in the history not only of the French Socialist party but of post-war France itself. With tripartism one of the early casualties of the Cold War, the path was now open that led to the formation of the Third Force, that combination of MRP, Socialists, Radicals, plus a sprinkling of the conventional Right, which over the next few years was to supply the Fourth Republic with a succession of governments. Though stability was not, to put it mildly, to be one of their characteristics, they were successfully to defend the régime against the double challenge of Communists and Gaullists.

Already, the General's new tactics had introduced a fresh element into the political situation and most probably influenced Auriol and Ramadier in their handling of the Communist crisis. Rumours had been circulating in the early part of 1947 that the General was contemplating founding a new political movement. Auriol noted in his diary (11 February): 'He is regretting not being in power – he is going to do everything to get the top job back.' A month later, he was writing pessimistically that 'The Republic is not yet established and it would not take much to sweep it away. On one side the Communists, on the other the Right, with public opinion unsure of itself and discontented. All this is not good.' At the end of March 1947 at Bruneval, scene of an Allied raid in 1942, de Gaulle spoke to an enormous crowd of 'the day which is coming when, rejecting sterile games and refashioning the badly constructed framework into which the nation has strayed, thereby disqualifying the State from being a State, the great mass of French people will rally round France.'

It was just after this that Ramadier paid a nocturnal visit to

Colombey. ('Who is it who wants to see me?' asked the General, who was about to go to bed, and the servant's reply was: 'He says he is the head of the government.')[15] The purpose of the visit was to inform de Gaulle that in future he would only be accorded military and official honours in his role as the first Resistant; they would be withheld if he appeared as the political opponent of the government. In reply, the General, having expressed his aversion to political parties, said he was no Boulanger;* he remained a Republican but also a protagonist for strong powers being given to the head of the State. After two hours Ramadier left again for Paris, without, so he confided to a friend afterwards, having been offered so much as a glass of fruit juice. With extraordinary forbearance, he added: 'It is true, the cook had gone to bed.'[16]

A week later, at Strasbourg, de Gaulle formally launched the Rassemblement du Peuple Français (RPF), the Rally of the French People. 'It is time', he told the crowds, 'that French men and French women who think and who feel [that the Republic must not be allowed to disappear under a Communist dictatorship or collapse into anarchy] should rally round to prove it. It is time to create and organise the Rassemblement du Peuple Français, which, within a legal framework and over and above all differences of opinion, is going to promote and ensure the success of a great effort of common salvation and of a fundamental reform of the State.' The 50,000 spectators applauded long and loud, and three times the General had to return to the balcony of the town hall from which he had spoken.

Reaction was mixed. At the Elysée, where the two old Socialist friends Blum and Auriol lunched together the next day, the view was hostile. Blum said, and Auriol agreed, that de Gaulle had equated the State with himself. He would be the prisoner of his own illusion. The new movement would be dangerous, both for the régime and for de Gaulle himself, for it would be overtaken by totalitarian elements, and de Gaulle would become 'an absolute monocrat'. The editorialist of *Le Monde* (Rémy Roure, an old friend of de Gaulle's) was equally suspicious: either the RPF was a party like the others, in which case it was perfectly natural to

---

* General Boulanger (1837–91) led a movement in the early years of the Third Republic against existing parliamentary government and for military rehabilitation.

create it, or it was something else, an image of a so-called '*pays réel*', as opposed to the '*pays légal*',* in which case the dangers would become apparent. A week later came a written statement from the General, asserting that the RPF was not to be another party like the others, and declaring: 'The present system according to which rigid and opposing parties share power must be replaced by another, where executive power proceeds from the country and not from the parties.'

The thought, the wording itself, should have come as no surprise. Had the General not told the Assembly, on his last appearance there fifteen months earlier, that 'the point that separates us is a general conception of government and its relationship with the parliamentary régime'? Nonetheless de Gaulle's launch of the RPF was widely and with reason misunderstood. Criticising the party system while at the same time creating another party, even if it was called by a fancy name, seemed to many French people to be either inexplicable or somewhat sinister. As for the President of the Republic and the government, it was now to be war on two fronts: on the left, the ousted Communists, who were soon to abandon their low profile and move over to militant opposition; on the right (a label of convenience only, because Gaullism was not, at least at its inception, or in the mind of its founder, an orthodox, recognisable right-wing movement) the General's shock troops, with their constant sniping at the régime and the party system. No wonder that Auriol, after the Communist exclusion was successfully complete, took satisfaction from the tone in some American and British papers, which pointed out that France had some capable leaders, and that the President of the Republic had shown General de Gaulle that the Constitution could work very well, with the President enjoying far more power than the Gaullists would admit. These were fair comments. The Communist affair had been well handled. But it, and the founding of the RPF, had opened up

---

* The distinction between the *pays légal* and the *pays réel* was a formula first enunciated by the right-wing anti-Republican polemicist Charles Maurras. One among numerous examples of it can be found in his paper *Action française* for 11 January 1937: 'After Hitler, and who knows, before him . . . there is another enemy. It is the democratic Republic, the elective and parliamentary régime [i.e. the *pays légal*] legally superimposed like a grotesque and repugnant mask on the true essence of France [i.e. the *pays réel*].' The thought that de Gaulle might be re-echoing this Maurrasian hostility to democracy inevitably made his ideas suspect to many people.

a completely new landscape across which the young Republic and its leaders had now to make an arduous journey.

They were not helped, at this stage of their travails, by the internal economic situation, above all the food shortages, particularly of bread. Throughout most of 1947, French townspeople were having to make do with a miserly ration of 250 grammes daily of a peculiarly nasty yellow-coloured bread, made from maize imported with American credits. The farmers and peasants preferred to keep much of their wheat unthreshed or in their granaries or to feed it to their livestock. A millers' strike in the Paris region in May made the situation even worse. Public discontent was becoming ominous. At Nevers a rumour spread that two wagonloads of wheat were on their way for export abroad. It was untrue, but that did not stop a crowd of 6,000 people from sacking the Prefecture. At Lyon, the Prefect was reported to have cancelled bread rationing cards for May, whereupon he was besieged by 2,000 workers bearing placards with the words 'No bread, no work'. By the end of the month, Auriol noted that the wheat stocks were down to ten days' supply, and that by July there would be no stock at all. In early June, with the bread ration cut from 8½ ounces daily to five ounces, crowds gathered outside the Prime Minister's office in Paris, chanting 'Bread! Bread! Bread!'

Then came a wave of strikes, in both the public and private sectors, affecting metallurgy, the banks, the big stores, the railways and the mines. The strikers had genuine grievances. Ramadier himself was partly to blame, for postponing a wage review promised for July. Real wages had failed to keep up with prices. But however good their case, the strikers' demands, if satisfied in full, would have meant putting 10 per cent on the wage bill. As an MRP minister in the government put it. 'This cannot go on . . . the French people must choose. If the strikes continue it means suicide, and if that is the French people's choice, we cannot send the police to stop them.' He was to be proved wrong within a few months. Meanwhile with no trains and greatly reduced coal production, the life of the country slowed to a walking pace. Eventually the rail and other strikes were settled, with concessions on both sides, but inevitably with a further twist to the inflationary spiral and to the detriment of the government's policies on wages and prices. Another victim was government unity, in so far as that existed: the war between orthodox budgetary policy, as represented by Robert Schuman, the Finance Minister, and *dirigisme* – a controlled economy – as represented by most of the Socialists, broke out, as it was destined to do frequently in the years to come.

Auriol, sitting in the Elysée and reading prefects' reports on the state of the country for the period 10 August to 10 September, gave way to despair:

> Everyone is discontented, workers and civil servants . . . The madness is not far from panic, a sort of psychosis about rising prices is playing a major role, as well as fear . . . It emerges from all these reports that a gulf exists between the public authorities and the urban and rural masses . . . This regrettable state of affairs is beginning to look much more like a real crisis of the régime than a passing crisis of governmental unpopularity.[17]

Auriol's anxieties were well founded, but in fact even if the bread ration was inadequate and the economic situation appeared to be getting out of control, ordinary everyday life went on with a surprising degree of normality. There were queues at the Paris bakeries, but they were not as long, in that exceptionally hot summer of 1947, as those outside the city's swimming pools and the bathing places along the Seine. Whatever they may have thought privately about political and economic circumstances, no signs of panic afflicted these crowds in search of cool waters.

Coolness was a quality much in demand as the year wore on. The Marshall Plan, announced in early June, led directly to the hardening of the Eastern and Western blocs, as one by one the countries beyond the Iron Curtain refused to participate in the process of accepting and distributing American aid. In September, the leaders of the nine European Communist parties met in Poland, where Stalin's Cold War strategy was unveiled and the launching of the Cominform prepared.* Both the French and Italian parties came under severe attack for having played the parliamentary and governmental game. From now on, there was no question of the Communists acting as though they were ready to share in

---

* Literally an international office of Communist 'information', the Cominform was in practice a Soviet-controlled instrument whose purpose was to increase Communist militancy in Western Europe and strengthen the Soviet hold on the satellite countries of Eastern Europe. Its first headquarters was in Belgrade.

government. At the meeting in Poland, Duclos had to perform an act of humiliating self-criticism, confessing, on behalf of the party, to all manner of bourgeois crimes of opportunism and illusion, of becoming the 'witless lackey of imperialism',[18] and promising in the future to mobilise the movement against 'American imperialism'.

It was indeed a massive volte-face, all the more embarrassing (except that Communists do not seem to be embarrassed by such public contortions) in that Thorez had been in favour of the Marshall Plan. Even after the Soviet Union and its satellites had turned their backs on it, he was talking (end of July) about accepting 'the aid of our American friends'. Three months later he too was obliged publicly to confess his faults. They had not realised, he lamely explained, that the Communists had been 'expelled' from the government on American orders, and consequently they had failed to 'unmask the behaviour of the Socialist leaders'.[19] Those touching, and apparently sincere leave-takings at the Elysée, the eyes filled with tears, had presumably been (according to the new line) an aberration, a failure to see and denounce a trap, even after falling into it. There were to be no more mistakes of that kind. From then on, the Communists were in total and unremitting opposition. As Thorez put it, at a public meeting early in October, the task now was to 'rally all the forces in France against the American imperialists and their agents, running from the RPF to the Socialist party'.[20]

There had already been inklings of this change in Communist strategy. At the end of August, the Ministry of the Interior had furnished Auriol with an unsourced report, purporting to reveal Moscow's plans for action against the Marshall Plan and the role assigned to the Soviet Embassy in Paris in coordinating such action. Just how much credence should be placed in these intelligence reports, which fill the pages of Auriol's diaries, is difficult to say. The editor of the second volume of the diaries, Jean-Pierre Azéma, is inclined to be sceptical, especially about the alleged connection between the Soviet Embassy in Paris and the Communist party. He quotes François Billoux, one of the Communist ministers before their expulsion from the government, as saying, years later, that the so-called accounts of meetings of the Communist Politburo refer either to meetings which never took place or, if they did take place, to discussions which never happened. But then Billoux was scarcely an objective witness.

The reports emanated from several different sources, sometimes from those dependent upon the Ministry of the Interior (the Sûreté, divided into three sections and employing thousands of officials), sometimes from the Service of Foreign Documentation and Counter-Espionage (SDECE), with a staff of about 1,000 and answering to the Prime Minister, and sometimes from the Americans. Paul-Marie de la Gorce suggests that the latter made it their business, in these first rounds of the Cold War, to stoke up the fires of anti-Communism in France by exaggerating the dangers of a Communist coup. If this is true, and it seems plausible, Auriol unhesitatingly swallowed the line.

Towards the end of October 1947, with the autumn strike movement spreading fast, Auriol mentions in his diary having received 'extremely serious' information, confirmed by the intelligence section at the Ministry of the Interior, about the clandestine creation of Communist-inspired international brigades in France and elsewhere in Western Europe, linked with parachute drops of Soviet arms supplies. The task of these brigades, according to American sources, was to help the Communists seize power. Information along these lines continued to reach Auriol. Early in November, he describes at length another intelligence report about the activities and organisation of the international brigades led by foreign commissars, and the arms that were reaching them.

Ramadier, who had been making some enquiries into the matter, could not confirm this information. He may of course have been misinformed, or inadequately informed; or, more likely, the details about the international brigades owed more to fantasy than to fact. It is extremely doubtful that Moscow's strategy at this time, whatever its ferocity against the Marshall Plan and the so-called Americanisation of Europe, included urging the Communist parties in Western Europe to resort to force in order to gain power. Even Jules Moch, who as an energetic Minister of the Interior did more than anyone to crush the great wave of politically motivated strikes in the autumn, did not, at least at the time, go all the way with Auriol. In a memorandum sent to all prefects, he said that it did not seem that orders had been issued to push the strike movement to the point of insurrection.

Nevertheless, the French Communist party's change of tune, following the establishment in the autumn of 1947 of the Cominform, was a fact to be reckoned with, and no one was more eloquent and doom-ridden in reckoning with it than General de Gaulle. Already, at the end of 1946, months before the founding of the RPF, he had spoken to his closest supporters of the inevitability of another war. By the summer of 1947, he was issuing lurid public warnings about the Communist menace. At the end of June, in his native city of Lille, he spoke with passion of the Russian grip on Eastern Europe and of Communist designs in France, following this up a month later, at Rennes, in Brittany, with a formidable attack on those to whom he had first given a taste of power (in the post-Liberation government) but 'who have taken an oath of obedience to the orders of a foreign organisation aiming at domination, led by the masters of a great Slav power . . . Their goal is to establish a dictatorship in this country, as their companions have done elsewhere with the support of that power.'

This was the time when de Gaulle ceased to refer to the Communists by name (because that could have conjured up memories of their distinguished Resistance record) and started calling them 'separatists'. It was also the moment when the RPF, which had begun as a movement dedicated to institutional reform, turned into a truncheon with which to belabour the USSR and its clients in France and elsewhere. This at least is how it appeared at the time. Today, there is not much reason to question de Gaulle's genuine belief, in the autumn of 1947, that a war was impending between East and West, in which the role of the French Communist party would be a decisive and baneful one. In promoting the idea of the RPF, he was trying to awaken his compatriots to the dangers facing them and to the need to provide the State with the strong government required to defend itself. In furtherance of these efforts, he would have been untrue to himself had he not directed his fire at a wider target than that provided by the 'separatists'. The ruling government, the party system and the Constitution were equally the objects of his unchanging scorn.

The RPF, despite the fact that it was not supposed to be a party like the rest, decided to put up candidates for the municipal elections in October 1947. As part of the electoral campaign, the General spoke on 5 October to a huge crowd at the race course of Vincennes, on the eastern outskirts of Paris, mixing his diatribe against the Communists with references to the 'abyss' into which the political parties had plunged the country. His oratory and figures of speech were, as usual, extremely effective. As he described the political parties 'boiling up their little soup, over their little fire, in their little corner', the crowds roared with laughter. At a time when anti-Communism was just as strong an influence in some sections of French opinion as Communism was in others, it followed logically that de Gaulle should seek to use the international situation as a means of winning electoral support. But there was nothing artificial or disingenuous about his fears, however unjustified they later proved to be, that the Russians were contemplating aggression, that the Communists were plotting a coup, and that the moment might be at hand when once again he would be cast in the role of national saviour.

In any event, the elections were a dramatic success for the RPF. Forty per cent of the electorate voted Gaullist, the RPF capturing the municipalities of thirteen out of twenty-five big cities, including Paris, Bordeaux, Marseille, Lille, Strasbourg and Algiers. The Gaullist gains had been largely at the expense of the MRP, whose previous right-wing supporters switched their allegiance. The Left, both Communists and Socialists, held their vote, which meant that France was now divided, not into two but three roughly equal parts: the Gaullists, the Communists, and the centre parties – Socialists, MRP, Radicals and Moderates (i.e. conventional right-wing). As the Socialist and MRP parties were not numerous enough to command a parliamentary majority, much would depend in future upon these Radicals and Moderates. This was a far cry from the hopes and dreams of the men of the Resistance.

The victory for de Gaulle and the RPF was a sensational one. It showed that a large section of French people were fearful of Communism, discontented with the men and mechanisms governing them, and fed up with bread rationing and the muddles of food distribution generally. There was also, among some, genuine admiration for the person of the General. Although, with the founding of the RPF, he appeared to have become involved with the game of power politics and demagogy which he affected to despise, he had also managed to retain more or less unblemished his popular image of being above and beyond the normal frailties and temptations of political life. '*Il n'est pas comme les autres*' was a sentiment felt and expressed by a large number of people with no particular axe to grind. For at least a year after October 1947, it seemed that de Gaulle's return to power might be imminent.

But these had been municipal, not legislative elections. The Assembly elected in 1946 was still there and showed no signs of wishing to commit suicide, despite the General's orders to it to do so. 'The present National Assembly should be dissolved straight away,' ran his official statement after the municipal elections, 'but not without first establishing an electoral system based on majority voting with which to provide a future parliament with a coherent majority.' Predictably, the parties in the Assembly failed to oblige, which was the first setback for de Gaulle. How to achieve power by legal means (despite accusations to the contrary, he never showed any disposition to achieve it any other way) remained a lasting problem. It was not until 1958, when under the pressures of the Algerian crisis and the threat of civil war the Assembly voted him back into power, that the difficulty would be overcome.

The second setback for de Gaulle was the way in which the RPF, by the nature of the support it received at the polls, had been pulled sharply to the right. Among those who voted Gaullist on 20 October, and equally those who were elected municipal counsellors, were many Moderates (i.e. right-wing) and Radicals, both of whom, in many cases, made common cause with the RPF and climbed aboard the Gaullist, anti-Communist, bandwagon. This grouping of a disorientated Right was very different from what had been conceived as a reforming and innovative movement when it was launched by de Gaulle in the spring.

The municipal elections were followed by nation-wide strikes which threatened at times to turn France into a civil war battlefield. Already, in October, Parisians had experienced the discomforts of a Métro and bus strike, which dragged on for most of the month and very probably contributed to the Gaullist successes at the polls, as disgruntled citizens cast their votes for the party (even if it did not call itself one) that promised change. What was notable about the Métro strike was that it was started not by the Communist-dominated CGT but by the Christian and 'breakaway' unions, in favour of higher wages. There was no question that these claims, and those which accompanied the subsequent strike movement, were well founded. Food, on which three-quarters of the French working man's income was spent, was rising steadily in price, as were most other commodities; between January and November the price index had risen officially from 856 to 1336, and the existence of the black market made the real increase even greater. But something more than wage claims was involved in the outbreaks of violence which characterised the month of November.

Thorez's words about rallying French people against American imperialism and its agents evoked a quick response, once the elections were over, in Marseille, traditionally a city of violence and hot blood. By a narrow victory, the RPF had wrested control of the town council from the Communists. Just before the election the latter had granted large wage increases to the tram crews who provided the city with its public transport. The new, incoming majority compensated for this by increasing tram fares, the Communists decided to exploit this situation, and by 11 November most of the factories in the city and its surroundings were on strike. The next day, large crowds closed in on the lawcourts, where three of the previous day's demonstrators had been sentenced to prison. The mob forced the judges to revise their finding to one of suspended sentence, then moved on to the town hall, invaded the council chamber where the new council was sitting and beat up the new Gaullist mayor. From the balcony, the outgoing Communist mayor announced that the new mayor had resigned. 'Citizens,' he shouted, 'we have reconquered *la Maison du Peuple*.' The police and security troops did nothing, either then or later in the evening, when Communist-directed crowds attacked and pillaged the bars and nightclubs frequented by black marketeers and racketeers. The next day, 40,000 men in Marseille were on strike.

A few days later, the miners in the northern coalfields came out, partly in support of wage claims, partly in protest at the dismissal by the government of the Communist administrator of the Coal Board. The latter immediately set about whipping up the strikes, to which the government responded by ordering the security forces to use their arms in order to evacuate the mines. In one clash, fifty men were injured. It was the first time since the war that strikers had been fired upon. Elsewhere, the troops refused to fire and fraternised with the miners. The atmosphere was one of civil war, with the central government unsure of its authority.

In the midst of all this, there was a government crisis in Paris, when Ramadier, exhausted, ill and undermined by his coalition partners, resigned. Auriol turned to Léon Blum, by then aged seventy-five, who failed to win the Assembly's approval largely because, in his speech inviting its confidence, he chose to equate, as equal dangers, Communism and Gaullism. It was neither a tactful nor an accurate observation. The Communists were trying, often by violent methods, to paralyse the country. De Gaulle's threat was represented by his verbal admonition to the National Assembly to dissolve itself. There could be no realistic equating of the one challenge with the other.

Nevertheless Blum's unfortunate comparison, though it lost him support on the Right, was not entirely without substance. As the strike movement gathered strength, as the dustmen, sewage men, undertakers and other public services in Paris stopped working and the streets took on the appearance of insanitary disorder, as first the Renault and then the Citroën factories stopped work, de Gaulle, flushed with the triumphs of the municipal elections, called a press conference where he mounted an all-out verbal attack against the régime. Arguing that the authorities – i.e. the government – had no legitimate basis and were incapable of getting the situation under control, he compared the political parties to Kipling's chattering Bandar-log (the monkey people), who claimed to be kings of the jungle. And, in a phrase calculated to arouse the worst suspicions about his future moves, he made a parallel between the birth of the RPF and the beginnings of the Resistance after the collapse of 1940; the RPF, he declared, was 'an elemental force which corresponds exactly to French people's promptings and instinct'. It was a breathtakingly sweeping claim.

These were dark days indeed – literally so, because electricity cuts meant that for much of the time there was no current. As the strikes spread, as the political parties, before and after Ramadier's resignation, manoeuvred and intrigued in a way to justify de Gaulle's disparagement of them, so the entries in Auriol's diary became more and more sombre and dramatic:

> There is a danger that the lassitude and anxiety in the country will change into anger . . . The winter is going to be a hard one . . . Communists and Gaullists can easily exploit the situation and clash . . . We are on the edge of the abyss . . . The letters that I am receiving from old people, from people living in poverty, heartrending letters in which some say they would prefer the gas-chamber, remind me of the situation in Germany in 1923–24, with numerous suicides of middle-class folk, small stock-holders, retired people etc.[21]

In the streets of Paris, there was a daily deployment of large forces of police and *gardes-mobiles*. Clashes occurred frequently between Communist and Gaullist squads. The spread of the strikes to most of the railway system meant that food supplies began to be affected. Newspapers were down to two pages. Low gas pressure made it difficult to get a hot meal.

Ramadier's successor was Robert Schuman of the MRP, the former Finance Minister, a Lorrainer by origin. He had grown up in a province annexed by Germany after 1871, and had served briefly in a (non-combatant) unit of the German Army in the First World War. Slow-speaking (with a noticeable German accent), imperturbable, lion-hearted, shrewd, with a manner more resembling a monk than an active politician, he was certainly no demagogue or populist. His government was composed of the same elements as its predecessor and its immediate task was to face up to the rapidly deteriorating social situation. By now, 3 million workers were on strike all over the country. The Socialist Jules Moch was given the Ministry of the Interior. Eighty thousand troops were called up. Moch seriously considered a plan for ensuring control of the main lines of communication, temporarily abandoning the rest of the country to the Communists, who would have to be ousted later by troops transferred from the French zone in Germany.

Along with these desperate measures, the government decided to fight a parliamentary battle for the right to work. In the northern coalfields, with their tradition of violence (vividly depicted many years earlier in Zola's novel *Germinal*), physical reprisals were visited upon the blacklegs – *jaunes* in French trade union jargon – who were against the strike, and elsewhere non-Communist *jaunes* called for a secret ballot, to the rage of the CGT men. The government bill instituting prison sentences and fines for anyone interfering with the right to work took five nights and days to get through the Assembly, so violent and persistent were the delaying tactics of the Communist deputies. It took no less than 250 pages of the *Journal Officiel* to record it. '*Voilà le Boche!*' screamed Duclos as the Prime Minister, Schuman, took his place on the ministerial bench. (He had been the first non-Communist deputy to be arrested by the Germans in 1940.) Jules Moch, a Jew who had fought in both world wars and lost a son in the Resistance, was greeted with Communist shouts of 'Hitler' and 'Nazi'. Another Communist, ruled out of order, refused to leave the rostrum and remained there all night, encouraged by his Communist colleagues, until finally escorted away by the colonel commanding the Assembly's guard. This officer's task was complicated by the Communists who, each time that he approached the offending deputy, burst into the 'Marseillaise', requiring him to spring to the salute. This was the only humorous episode in the whole grim saga.

By early December, there were signs that the strikes were on the wane. They were certainly becoming unpopular with the public at large, and the excess of violence, even in a nation brought up on the memories of the Commune and its barricades, revolted many people. On 4 December, the Paris–Lille night express was derailed by sabotage on the line and twenty people killed. The identity of those responsible was never established. The Communists blamed Gaullist provocateurs. Moch accused the Communists, though no arrests and no charges were made. As well as putting through its emergency legislation, the government offered to meet union claims with a cost-of-living bonus, which was at first rejected by the CGT but accepted by the other, non-Communist unions. But by 10 December even the CGT sensed that, in face of energetic government measures and working-class weariness, it was losing control and ordered a return to work. 'The battle is won, I am master of the situation,' boasted Jules Moch.

The whole Schuman government was entitled to some self-congratulation. Its resolve and tenacity had helped to win the day, incidentally challenging Gaullist claims that the 'system' was incapable of handling a dangerous state of affairs with firmness and authority. The fact that Moch was a lifelong Socialist who did not hesitate to authorise the use of force against the working class made his feat the more remarkable. The Communists never forgave him for it, and among his own party he had enemies and critics, for his was a strong and difficult personality. But, even so, the ending of the strikes probably owed less to Moch's energies than to the non-Communist members of the work-force. One of the casualties of the strike movement was the unity of the trade unions and of the working class itself. The non-Communist, Socialist-inspired section, calling itself Force Ouvrière, abandoned the CGT and later set up on its own, encouraged and helped financially by the American Federation of Labour.*

This important development could not have occurred had the

* George Meany, leader of the AFL, said in a speech in Washington in the winter of 1953 that 'it was thanks to the money of American workers . . . that we were able to create a split in the French CGT . . .'

government not agreed to concessions which amounted in effect to an across-the-board increase in wages of 25 per cent and sometimes more. For despite the general tendency, shared in by Auriol and Moch, to regard the strikes as a Moscow-inspired Communist attempt to paralyse the country, they and everyone else could not overlook the fact that wages had fallen far behind prices, thus providing the work-force with genuine reasons for discontent. If the Ramadier government had shown more unity and determination in grappling with the wage/price problem, the Communists would not so easily have been able to exploit the situation. As it was, only by alleviating the discontent could the political motive behind the strikes be revealed for what it was.

But if these tactics – firmness in the face of disorder, allied with recognition that wages were too low – won for the government a famous political victory against the Communists, they also added up to an economic defeat. The new wage bill in the public sector could not be offset against greater productivity in the mines or elsewhere, because there was no increase in productivity and the strikes themselves had lost the economy close on two months' production. A new turn in the inflationary spiral was inevitable, accompanied this time by the need to devalue the franc. The men of the Fourth Republic can certainly be credited with having fought off the Communist and Gaullist challenge in this 'hot' autumn of 1947. 'We have had a brush with civil war and, given the possibility of Soviet intervention, with war itself,' wrote Auriol in the last pages of his diary for the year, 'and despite that France has begun her recovery.' But the price of victory had been a heavy one, whose economic effects were to be long-lasting.

There remains the question of just how far the Communists were prepared to go in their declared strategy of opposing the effects of the Marshall Plan and the 'Americanisation' of Western Europe. The wave of anti-Communism which the Cold War, the propaganda of the RPF and the conduct of the Communists themselves had unleashed, swamped nearly every channel of thought and analysis. 'Insurrectional' became the stock, preferred description of the nature of the strikes. But however genuinely men such as de Gaulle or Auriol thought that war was impending, it is today clear that Moscow, while firmly resolved to confront the American challenge, was not thinking of a violent seizure of power by Western Communist parties. Corroboration of this view seems to come from one of the intelligence reports reaching the Elysée at this time. It is an account of a speech made by Thorez to the Politburo of the French Communist party on 1 December 1947. Auriol's diary contains many such reports on the Politburo's proceedings. They need to be treated with some suspicion, although Auriol himself set a good deal of store by them.

According to this particular report, Thorez, who had just returned from a visit to the Soviet Union, strongly criticised what the party had been up to during his absence. The spreading of the strikes nationwide had, he said, put the Communists in a difficult position. They must now engage reverse gear and lie low while waiting for the enemy and preparing a plan of attack. It was important that the return to work should not be generalised, otherwise the secessionists of Force Ouvrière would be the winners (which is exactly what happened). 'Stalin told me, without beating about the bush, that if we go on as we are, he will deliberately abandon us.' Assuming this account is accurate, it gives a remarkable picture of Communist discomfiture and sense of failure. Thorez's earlier hopes of a French workers' party which would lead to a '*nouvelle et populaire*' democracy must have seemed very distant to all those who listened on that December day to their leader's harsh strictures.

Only a month later, however, according to another flow of information reaching Auriol from 'well-placed informers', Thorez was in much more combative mood. Again addressing the Politburo, he is quoted as saying (re-echoing de Gaulle's remark in 1940): 'We have lost a battle, we have not lost the war.' The strategy he prescribed was to destabilise the régime by periodic economic and political crises, 'so as to bring France to a state where no resistance is possible'. America would then get tired of coming to France's help and a serious crisis would occur. 'That will be the moment chosen by Stalin to unleash a tremendous drive on which victory will depend.'

Auriol was so alarmed by this that he telephoned to Moch, who confirmed it. So apparently did a telegram from the Vatican, reporting Polish information reaching the Pope according to which the Soviet Union, afflicted by internal difficulties, was forced to follow 'a policy of prestige which would bring about a world war'. Whatever importance or degree of authenticity is to be attached to this and other bits of intelligence reaching the Elysée, three things were clear as 1947 gave way to 1948: first, that the Communists, though they had suffered a reverse, still had the support of a great mass of the working class and thus an immense potential for making trouble; second, that de Gaulle and the RPF, by reason of the popular support it enjoyed, presented a potent, though non-violent, threat to the régime whose defence lay in the hands of the centre, and often discordant, parties; and third, that the best way of warding off 'adventure', whether it came from right or left, was and always had been to remove the main reason for popular discontent by bringing the economy, particularly the cost of living, under control.

CHAPTER 4

Fighting on Three Fronts

Though France has known, in the course of her long history, moments of great prosperity – the eighteenth century was one example, and another was the late nineteenth century, when the reparations bill after the Franco-Prussian war was quickly met – economic decline characterised the years leading up to the Second World War. It was accompanied by an economic philosophy generally described as 'Malthusian': a preference for high profit and small turnover, for social stability rather than economic advance, for the 'small man' – farmer or industrialist – in preference to larger and more efficient units, for tariff and other barriers with which to keep foreign competition at bay. Along with the belief in the small man went another, much cherished in left-wing circles, that real industrial and economic power lay in the control of *'les trusts'*, *'les deux cents familles'*, *'le mur d'argent'* – in other words, capitalists of boundless greed and selfishness.

To these already unpromising shibboleths and prospects was now added, in 1944–5, the devastation of war. The country suffered materially far more heavily in the Second World War than in the First. A quarter of all buildings were destroyed, compared with 9 per cent in 1914–18. The transport system, road and rail, which had been the target of Allied bombing and Resistance sabotage, was virtually in ruins. Coal supplies, the main source of energy, were totally inadequate to needs. Not only was domestic production, affected by the shortage of manpower, massively down on the none-too-brilliant 1938 output, but France, the world's largest importer of coal, could in this immediately post-war period manage to obtain only 10 million tons of imports, compared with the 23 million tons of imports in 1938.

Three tasks thus faced post-Liberation governments: to get the economy moving again by repairing roads, railways and ports so that the mines and the factories could raise their production levels; to plan a fair and efficient distribution of scarce raw materials, consumer goods and food; and to work towards long-term objectives designed to modernise French productive and economic activities.

In the first of these tasks a remarkable degree of success was achieved. By the time the Fourth Republic was born – that is, after the new Constitution had been approved by a second referendum in the autumn of 1946 – the repaired railways were carrying as many passengers as they had in 1938 and production had reached 80 per cent of its pre-war levels, even if productivity lagged behind 1938 figures.

The second of the three tasks – to control prices, wages and distribution during the period when production was catching up with demand – proved much more intractable. Perhaps if General de Gaulle, in the winter of 1944–5, had espoused Mendès-France's plans for drastic austerity action, the story might have been different. As it was, successive governments, consisting of coalitions of electoral rivals with deeply divided views on economic policy, proved quite unable to control the wage–price spiral. The radicals and the Right were by temperament and principle against planning and controls. So were the farmers, many of whom had done well out of the war and had no intention of surrendering their easy gains or subjecting themselves to directives from Paris about what they could grow and at what price they could sell it.

The only time during this period when a government took, and could be seen to take, effective action was when at the end of 1946 Léon Blum's minority, all-Socialist government imposed a 5 per cent cut on all retail prices. Shopkeepers were required to mark the reduction on their sale ticket and the operation was supervised by special committees of representatives of consumers and local authorities. The move was at first well received by the public, and in January 1947, for the first time since the war, prices, which had risen by 50 per cent in the second half of 1946, actually fell a point or two. But a second 5 per cent cut, announced by Ramadier, Blum's successor, was not greeted so warmly. Ramadier's multi-party, discordant coalition was not of a kind to inspire public confidence and prices began to rise again. The Blum–Ramadier experiment came to an end; the infernal spiral once more spun out of control.

The third task – planning and executing the plan for the long term – was undertaken with a much greater degree of success. On 5 December 1945, General de Gaulle found on his desk a five-page memorandum which advised him that the only way to break the wage–price circle was to modernise the French economy: 'The whole nation must be associated with this effort,' the memorandum said; 'the country will only accept the measures to be taken if it knows and understands clearly the real situation.' The author of the document was Jean Monnet, helped by a small staff of brilliant men, all resolved, in Monnet's own words, 'to make France into a modern country'. They worked on the memorandum in the requisitioned Bristol Hotel in Paris, their papers spread out over the beds and even the bathrooms.[1] Eventually they planted the acorn from which the Monnet Plan would grow.

Monnet's contributions to the achievements of the Fourth Republic need a book to themselves. The astonishing thing about him is that he had no technical qualifications, not even a university degree. The son of a well-to-do brandy producer from Cognac, while he was still under thirty Monnet spent much of the First World War in London, actively engaged in helping to coordinate Allied food supplies and shipping. After that war, he became for a time assistant Secretary-General of the infant League of Nations, after which he was involved as a merchant banker in financial affairs in different parts of the world. Soon after the outbreak of war in 1939 he became chairman of the London-based Anglo-French Council charged with coordinating Allied resources. It was he who generated the idea, as France was preparing to surrender in 1940, of an Anglo-French union. He spent three of the subsequent war years in Washington, where he was concerned with lend-lease arrangements. By this time, he had built up a formidable range of contacts, above all with American leaders, by whom he was held in the highest esteem.

Small, dapper, tireless, owing nothing to any political party, fertile in ideas, preferring fact to theory, action to words, Monnet was above all persuasive; though never losing his courtesy, he badgered people nearly to distraction, and was quite capable of getting his way by guile if more straightforward methods proved inadequate. He had no inhibitions when it came to dealing with de Gaulle. 'You talk about grandeur,' he told the General in August 1945, 'but today French people are pygmies. There will only be grandeur when French people are of the size which justifies grandeur. For that, they must modernise . . .'² On 3 January 1946, the *Journal Officiel* published a decree which authorised Monnet and his men to begin their work on 'a first overall plan for the modernisation and economic equipment of metropolitan and overseas France'. Parliament and the political parties had had no say in the matter, nor was the new organisation, answerable only to the Prime Minister, to be accountable to parliament. This fact, combined with Monnet's own personality, was to be the Plan's greatest asset.

Mindful of the bureaucratic morass into which French administrators can so easily stray, Monnet was particularly insistent that his new, specially fashioned machine should not fall under the sway of any of the established ministries. By the same token, he wanted to keep it small: the Plan's staff, secretaries and guards included, never exceeded a hundred, and Monnet's own immediate team was limited to four or five exceptionally talented men. Even the Paris headquarters of the Plan – a former private house alongside the church of Ste Clotilde, in the 7th *arrondissement* – was chosen specially for its un-ministry-like features. These were the outward, physical aspects of the new structure. Within, the novelty lay in the creation of eighteen 'modernisation commissions', each with thirty to fifty co-opted members, which held regular meetings attended by employers, trade unionists, officials and appropriate experts. These commissions discussed goals and how to attain them, all within the framework of the six priority sectors mapped out by Monnet and his staff: coal, steel, cement, transport, agricultural machinery and chemical fertilisers.

The guiding principle was to face the future by modernisation, which meant breaking with the bad habits and Malthusian thinking of the past and planning for increased production and productivity. The Plan deliberately turned its back on everyday needs, such as housing and consumer goods, in favour of investment, output, productivity and competition in the six chosen sectors. The target was to reach the 1929 level of production (the best pre-war performance) by 1949, and exceed it by 25 per cent in 1950. This aim, despite huge amounts of Marshall Aid investment, was only partially realised. The 25 per cent increase in production was still not achieved in 1952. But in the years that followed the inception of the Plan, an immense amount was done – the construction of the great Rhône dams, the electrification of the railway system, the re-equipment of the iron and steel industry, the development of the natural gas deposits at Lacq – to make possible future economic expansion.

One of the remarkable aspects of these procedures, which sound like a higher form of the corporate State but in practice were no such thing, was the readiness of employers and unionists to work together towards a common goal. At the end of 1946, for example, Léon Blum, then Prime Minister, announced that while the forty-hour week remained the legal limit – it was one of the sacred achievements of the pre-war Popular Front – a forty-eight-hour week was necessary if recovery was to be hastened. At the manpower commission of the Plan, chaired by a Communist trade unionist, this was accepted, and the union leaders, including the Communists, did not demur. This was the period when the Communist leaders, as components of the government coalition, threw themselves whole-heartedly into the task of reconstruction and recovery, apparently putting national interest above ideology and party considerations. After they left the government in 1947, and above all after the great strikes and the schism in the CGT, their attitude changed and their representatives no longer took part in the work of the Plan. But by then the Plan and its objectives were firmly and irrevocably established.

But where was the money to come from for the investment required by the Plan? It was a gigantic sum, equivalent to about a quarter of French national income. Monnet, always the optimist, refused to let this daunting obstacle hold him up. Six months after the launch of the Plan in January 1947, General Marshall, the US Secretary of State, made his Harvard speech. Monnet's optimism had been justified; help was at hand. As he put it in a long memorandum[3] addressed to Georges Bidault, the Foreign Minister, in July, after the Russians had turned their backs on the Marshall Plan, the aim of French policy was to obtain American credits with which to re-establish the economy on a sound footing. In a highly relevant piece of analysis, he pointed out that the immediate objective of European cooperation and the winning of credits would have longer-term effects:

> For an unlimited period, we are going to cooperate with the Anglo-Saxons [i.e. Britain and the US] and that cooperation will inevitably assume a political form . . . the existence of a strong Communist party will keep permanently open the wound that the rupture with the Russians has created in the conduct of French foreign policy . . . We have to realise that the coming years during which we will depend on American credits will be

a particularly difficult period . . . If the policy, now inevitable, of cooperation with the Anglo-Saxons is to be a fruitful one, it must be accepted by the immense majority of French public opinion.

There were certainly material advantages in such a policy, but that, Monnet went on, was not enough. Public opinion must also see 'the promise of future economic independence towards which the modernisation Plan, whose rapid application is made possible by American credits, is leading'.

In other words, Monnet was saying that France had no choice but to throw in her lot with Western Europe. The attractive idea of being a bridge, a halfway house between East and West, was no longer tenable. France needed American money if she was to recover her economic health and well-being, and there would be a price to pay for this ineluctable choice. That price, Monnet warned, included firstly a German settlement of a kind to make German resources, particularly Ruhr coal, available for the European recovery programme; and secondly an overhaul of French finances, necessary not only for the country's own good but also to encourage the Americans to lend the money and to ensure, if they did so, that it was not misspent.

Monnet's lucid reasoning could not be faulted. But he could only advise. It was up to the government and the political parties of which it was composed to take the necessary action, particularly in the battle against inflation. The huge wage increases which had helped to bring the strikes of autumn 1947 to an end called for special measures to limit their consequences. René Mayer, Finance Minister in Schuman's government, a right-wing Radical and a firm believer in economic liberalism, put forward a plan with three objectives: to establish a new level for prices, to reduce the budget deficit, and to devalue the franc. The plan involved the deregulation of industrial prices, the opening of a free market in gold (designed to coax out the hoarders) and the imposition of a special levy. It was another reminder that the *dirigiste* post-Liberation mentality was on the wane.

With Mayer – prosperous, well groomed, confident to the point of arrogance – the key post had passed into the hands of what today would be called a market forces man. But inevitably the adoption by the coalition government and the Assembly of the Mayer plan was characterised by the usual difficulties which arose whenever economic policy was in question. The Socialists did not at all like the way the current was flowing, especially Mayer's intentions for the gold market and a semi-amnesty for the hoarders. They insisted that 5,000-franc notes – which accounted for more than one-third of the money in circulation and were supposed to be the preferred currency of the black marketeers and hoarders – should be called in. As usual with such measures, the real culprits took steps to avoid them, while the general public was inconvenienced by having to queue to exchange their notes.

For all that, Mayer's plan, unpopular though it was, had a certain effect for a time. In January and February, prices rose steeply, under the influence of wage increases and higher transport fares. But they stabilised in March and, more important still, production began to pick up, reaching a coefficient of 113 in April, compared with 97 in 1947 (1938=100). Mayer was entitled to a certain satisfaction, and he cannot have enjoyed a session at the Elysée when Auriol suggested that he, Mayer, should see the employers' federation and get them to agree to a voluntary cut in prices, so as to encourage others to do the same. 'Give an example, like Stafford Cripps', exhorted the Socialist Auriol,[4] disregarding in his admiration of British efforts the world of difference which separated the austere vegetarian from the rotund and free-enterprise-minded Mayer.

In fact, something of the Cripps spirit seems to have crossed the Channel. Janet Flanner noted that the new taxes, the special levy and the calling-in of 5,000-franc notes had produced 'an odd, un-Gallic stoicism that is a substitute for morality'.[5] A stoic patience was indeed called for in this spring of 1948. Almost three years after the end of the war in Europe, many things were still rationed. An ordinary French family without priority got no petrol allowance at all (though a vigorous black market in petrol coupons flourished, fed in part by Breton fishermen who made more money by selling their coupons than by exchanging them for fuel for their fishing boats). There had been no butter ration since Christmas 1947. The shops in the cities were better stocked with consumer goods than a year previously, but many people lacked the cash with which to buy them. Auriol found it necessary to remind Schuman that the future of the government and even of social peace itself was linked to the housewife's shopping basket; the entire economy, he pointed out, depended on one thing alone: food and prices.

The economic outlook in this spring of 1948 may have brightened, but the political atmosphere remained clouded. The Third Force coalition, besieged on one side by the Communists and on the other by the RPF, stood in constant fear of a parliamentary dissolution and new general elections. To their credit, these centre parties had held together, despite their doctrinal differences, and presented a united front to the Communist threat of the previous autumn. But faced with the Mayer plan, whose effects were bound to penalise and offend in some way almost every French family, they could not help looking over their shoulders at the electorate and wondering what lay in store for them. RPF propaganda, strengthened by the support for Gaullism in the country at large, kept up a constant demand for fresh elections. In the parliamentary debates on the Mayer plan, the Gaullist sympathisers (although at that time they accounted in parliamentary terms for only a relatively small and informal group in the Chamber) entered into an unholy alliance with the Communists to embarrass and harass the government. It was a pattern often to be repeated in the future. Mendès-France, in conversation with Auriol, went so far as to predict that nothing could be done with the present parliament; it would be better to have new elections, provided the electoral system could be changed from a proportional to a majority one. Auriol did not agree. The important thing, he argued, was to remove the fear of new elections and thus enable the government and its majority to continue in office.

There was no doubting the intentions of the RPF and its leader. In a speech at Compiègne in early March, the General once more excoriated the régime and declared that 'Everything is ready to ensure that the country is steered towards its salvation and its greatness, as soon as circumstances allow the assumption of the necessary responsibilities.' This curious and obscure phraseology seemed to mean that the General was making a bid for power, but, as usual, without specifying how he was to get there. It was shortly after this (4 April 1948) that Schuman became the second Prime Minister to go to Colombey-les-Deux-Eglises to see the General. Just what his purpose was is not clear. He said afterwards that he had gone to discuss questions of national defence, in which he was not well versed. But presumably he also wanted to find out for himself whether any understanding was possible between the Third Force and its harshest critic. If so, he could have saved himself a journey. De Gaulle was no readier then than at any other time to have any truck with 'the system'. Although the meeting lasted for three hours and was friendly, it achieved nothing. Robert Schuman, de Gaulle told one of his followers, was a 'very good and honest man'. But, he added, Schuman 'has no illusions – he knows that his government isn't one and that he doesn't control it.'[6]

In this spring of 1948, as the chestnut trees bordering the Champs Elysées donned their new uniform of white and pink candles and the number of prams in the Tuileries Gardens bore witness to the post-war baby boom, two other clouds loomed up on the political horizon which were to prove just as dangerous to the government as the price of food. The first was that hoary old dispute, State aid to private (Church) schools – in other words, clericalism and its arch-enemy, *laïcité*.

Why this issue was for so long capable of exerting a bitterly divisive influence on French politics is bound up with French history since, and even before, the Revolution. To Anglo-Saxon minds, *laïcité* is a concept difficult to grasp. It is worlds apart from the English practice of an official religion coexisting with other denominations. Its origins belong to the revolutionary ideas of 1789, but distinct signs of it can be traced even earlier in the eighteenth century when the Encyclopedists and Voltaire (when he wrote '*Ecrasez l'infâme*' he was referring to the Church) proclaimed not only that the Church should be disestablished – in the English sense – but that religion should have only a minor place, if any at all, in public life. The Revolution, to which large numbers of French people today like to think of themselves as the heirs, went much further. A deliberate attempt was made, under the Terror, to uproot Christianity altogether from French soil. The First Empire, the restored monarchy and the Second Empire set the pendulum swinging the other way, but the builders of the Third Republic hastened once more to reverse this movement.

They assumed that the Church and those who served her were, and were likely to remain, ideologically unsuitable as well as unwilling to make the Republican system intelligible to and respected by the general public. This sentiment was summed up in Gambetta's passionate cry '*Le cléricalisme – voilà l'ennemi!*' Throughout much of the Third Republic, the Left and Centre-Left feared and mistrusted the priests and their right-wing lay supporters, who seemed to embody, at a moment when Republican roots were only shallowly planted, all the evils and wish for revenge of the *ancien régime*. This affirmation of *laïcité* called therefore for the exclusion of religious issues from all forms of public life, and especially for the withholding of taxpayers' money from ecclesiastical activities of any kind.

A second definition of *laïcité* concerned the Church as teacher. Here the Republicans considered that Church schools and those who taught in them were unfitted by their very nature to teach science or instil the spirit of the modern age. In late nineteenth-century terms, they were right. Certainly Jules Ferry, in the early years of the Third Republic, was convinced he was serving the national interest when he drew up strict regulations for religious teaching congregations and evicted the Jesuits from their schools. Ferry's creation of a system of universal, free, compulsory primary education became identified with the sanctity of the Republic itself.

The Dreyfus affair, which split France into pro- and anti-Dreyfus camps of extreme pugnacity, helped to bank up the fires of anti-clericalism. The Church and the Orders, especially that of the Assumptionists, were seen in their anti-Dreyfus allegiance to be a threat to the Republic itself. It was particularly galling to good Republicans that, more than a century after the Revolution, more than half the pupils in secondary schools should still be taught by priests and monks. In 1906, the left-wing government of Emile Combes – himself originally destined for the priesthood – decided to deal once and for all with the 'clerical menace'. A law was passed to expel all those Orders not authorised. Large numbers of Church schools were shut down, and exile imposed upon thousands of monks and nuns, revered and respected though they were by millions. There were riots in Brittany, tempestuous debates in the Chamber. The flavour of the period is caught in a speech of 1906 by René Viviani, a brilliant Socialist orator who was to become Prime Minister in 1914. Passages from it were placarded on walls all over the country: 'We have devoted ourselves to the work of irreligion. We have torn away human consciences from belief. . . . We have extinguished the stars in the heavens and they will not be lit again.'* There was nothing neutral or tolerant about this. It was a declaration of perpetual war.

The passions of those years had somewhat abated by the time the First World War was won. The fact that priests and members of the banished congregations flocked back to join the colours made direct

---

* I am indebted to M. Vincent Labouret for this quotation, and in general for valuable guidance on the *laïcité* issue.

persecution henceforward unthinkable. The Jesuits reopened their schools. Alsace and Lorraine, ultra-Catholic provinces returning to French possession, were a new counterweight to the violence of anti-clericalism. But old enmities die hard. Schoolteachers and university lecturers, representing one of the mainstays of the Socialist party, remained as vigilant as ever against any creeping attack on the principles of *laïcité*, such as subsidies to Church schools. In the Second World War, some of the hierarchy and many brave priests had opposed Vichy and been active in the Resistance. But at the Liberation, the Left and the *laïques* had reason to recall that a great many had not. On the other hand, while the newly formed MRP could not realistically be suspected of anti-Republican intentions or tactics, it was by definition a Catholic party, as keen to protect legitimate Catholic rights as the lay parties were to withstand any encroachment. Clashes were inevitable, and likely to be all the more bitter because of the crushing weight of historical memories and tradition.

These long-standing, quasi-ritual quarrels were not confined to the parliament in Paris or the headquarters of the political parties. Mutual intolerance between lay and clerical interests continued to prevail all over the country, in rural communes as much as in the large cities. Because of the centralised nature of much of French society and the preponderance of Paris as the begetter of ideas and breeding ground for political fevers, it is easy to forget that the fires of controversy could burn just as fiercely at the local level. A prosperous butcher in a small town, for example, who chose to send his children to the *école libre* (Church school) could expect to be denied the custom (and accorded the hostility) of the local schoolteacher and his or her family. *La vie de province* remained just as marked a feature of French life under the Fourth Republic as under the Third.

The reason why these old wounds burst open again in 1948 lay in the increasing uneasiness of the Socialist party at being part of the government coalition. As the decision taken after the dropping of the Communists had shown, most Socialists knew in their heart of hearts that they were doomed to this fate, forced on them, at least at that time, by the need to withstand, together with the other Third Force parties, the pressures of the Gaullists and Communists. But that knowledge did little to comfort their consciences when the Communists taunted them, as they frequently did, with being allied with reactionary forces – i.e. the Catholic MRP and the non-*dirigiste* Radicals. The party, anxious to demonstrate that it had not forgotten its principles, began to press for the nationalisation of private (Catholic) schools in southern mining districts. Most of the colliery schools in the north had passed uneventfully into the State system at the Liberation, but those in the south and centre of the country were some sort of left-over and were still private. These lay noises from the Socialists naturally evoked corresponding clerical responses from the MRP. The Socialists however held the winning card: a statute passed in 1945 made nationalisation of these twenty-eight schools a legal obligation, and there was, as well, a 'lay' majority in the Chamber to complete the victory.

The MRP struck back with a decree inspired by Schuman but signed, rather against her will, by Madame Poinso-Chapuis, the MRP Minister of Public Health. Hers is a name unremembered today, but one which occupies a tiny but significant site in the land-scape of the Fourth Republic. Irreverent foreign correspondents, grappling as best they could with the problems of *laïcité* and the Minister's difficult name, took to referring to her among themselves as Madame Poisoned-Chalice.

Her decree entitled family associations (Catholic bodies) to receive State subsidies and distribute these to families who found it difficult to meet the costs of private – i.e. Catholic – education. This seemed to call into question the principle of *laïcité*, and predictably the Socialists and Communists reacted sharply. The Socialist Minister for Education had not even been consulted, it transpired. In the end, the dispute was settled – but not before the coalition had come near to disintegrating – by a face-saving compromise which maintained the Poinso-Chapuis subsidies but made their application subject to State control. If it was all a storm in a teacup, the tea that was spilt was enough to leave some indelible stains on the fabric of the coalition.

The other cloud was of a different dimension altogether. The future of Germany was an issue that had dominated French thoughts about foreign policy since the end of the war. 1870, 1914, 1939 . . . it would have been an exceptionally detached French man or woman who did not associate German industrial and military power with French sacrifice and suffering. The connection between the terms of the Versailles treaty and the rise of Nazism, very little appreciated in France – between the wars there was no French Keynes to sound the warning note – was disregarded altogether in 1945. Even before the German surrender, de Gaulle was talking about the Rhine as the natural frontier of France. He foresaw the division of Germany into a federation of autonomous States, with the Saar economically linked with France.

A few days before the surrender in May 1945, Bidault, as Foreign Minister, officially put forward the French claim for the internationalisation of the Ruhr and French control of the Rhineland. But 1945 was manifestly not 1918. France, if finally not a defeated nation, was certainly not a victorious one. Her reduced condition, notwithstanding de Gaulle's visions of grandeur, was humiliatingly emphasised when she was left off the invitation list for the Potsdam conference in August 1945, at which the US, the USSR and the UK spent much time discussing Germany. For the next three years, at international conferences in London, Paris and Moscow, the unfortunate Bidault – able, patriotic, alternately idle and overworked, highly strung, excitable, often appearing to be and sometimes being the worse for wear through drink – unsuccessfully fought his corner. There were frequent differences between France and Britain over coal deliveries from the Ruhr. From the Soviet Union, for whose support against 'Anglo-Saxons' de Gaulle had bid in 1945, there was little cheer. Moscow would not even support France over the Saar, where the British and Americans were at least sympathetic.

As time went on, the shadows cast by the Cold War and France's need for American dollars made Bidault's task even less enviable. Monnet had been his usual perceptive self in warning that the going was due to become difficult. What was a foreign minister to do when faced with the irreconcilable needs to voice French fears of German reinstatement and to support the US in its resolve to withstand the Soviet threat?

American minds were quickly made up that European recovery could not be achieved without a productive and stable Germany. London was not far behind. At the beginning of 1948, Ernest Bevin proposed that the Franco-British treaty of Dunkirk, signed a year earlier and designed to provide against another German aggression, should be extended to embrace Holland, Belgium and Luxembourg, and be redefined as a defence against aggression from wherever it might come. A few weeks later came the Communist coup in Prague. Alarm bells were ringing all over Europe. The Soviet representative on the four-power Allied Control Council in Berlin, faced with the Anglo-American decision to effect monetary reform in their zones, walked out. Whatever the dangers and disappointments for France, the division of Germany, and building up of the western part of it into an economic and ultimately political force, was becoming inevitable.

In June 1948, agreement was reached in London between the UK, the US and France that the three western zones of occupation should be integrated into the Western European economy. The London Agreements also recognised the need to give 'the German people the possibility of arriving, within the framework of a free and democratic form of government, at the ultimate establishment of its unity, at the moment destroyed'. Thus ended, in effect, France's always unrealistic post-Liberation attempt to impose, as she was able to do after 1918, her own policy for Germany. When in 1958 General de Gaulle returned to power, he summoned senior officials from the Quai d'Orsay to brief him. 'What remains of my German policy?' he asked. '*Rien, mon Général*' was the uncompromisingly frank reply.[7]

Poor Bidault was exposed to a barrage of criticism for having put his name to the London Agreements. De Gaulle's scorn, and insistence that they should be rejected, was boundless and was to be expected. But from within the government also came protests and objections. The Socialist ministers, and Vincent Auriol himself, were fearful of taking a step which would formalise the splitting of Europe into two and, according to them, run the risk of provoking the Russians into a violent reaction. But the prospect of a re-established and possibly rearmed Germany was the most emotive issue. Jules Moch thought it would lead to war. Auriol, in the Council of Ministers, sent a note to Moch and another Socialist minister saying that if the government did agree to German rearmament, he, Auriol, would resign. He was naïve enough to think that international tensions would abate only if the heads of government of the four powers – USA, USSR, UK and France – would sit around a table 'without experts or notes, looking each other in the eye'.

There was a lot of bold talk, from Schuman, among others, about being firm with the British and Americans, telling them that they were embarked on a dangerous policy without providing France with proper guarantees. But Bidault put his finger on the vital point when he warned that there was not the ghost of a chance of reaping the benefit of Marshall Aid while at the same time saying No to the arrangements for Germany. 'If we want to go it alone, we shall lose everything. In the unfortunate situation where we are, we should only follow the logic of national interest . . . to get US help, we have to approve the London Agreements.'[8] Eventually the National Assembly gave its consent, but only by a narrow margin and only after Bidault had been reproached from left and right for having sacrificed the interests and security of France in London. One right-wing figure, Louis Marin, summed up all the French fears of Germany and the sense of humiliation at France's allies' treatment of her when he cried: 'We French are asked to sign [the London Agreement] with our eyes closed, like the caged nightingales that are blinded so that they will sing better.'

The shock imposed by the Poinso-Chapuis affair and the need to assent to the creation of a divided Germany robbed the Schuman government of much of its cohesion. A month later, at the end of July, the Socialists and the MRP again fell out, this time over military credits, which the Socialists, looking for a pretext to assert themselves, sought to reduce. Schuman resigned, and was succeeded by André Marie, an experienced Radical politician who embodied the ideas and practices of the Third rather than the Fourth Republic. He succeeded in persuading Léon Blum and Paul Reynaud, the archpriests respectively of democratic socialism and financial orthodoxy, to join his government. But he had the greatest difficulty in distributing jobs, as Socialists and MRP fought, like dogs over a bone, for the inclusion of this person and the exclusion of that. Bidault, the signatory of the London Agreements, and Mme Poinso-Chapuis, who had put her name to the notorious decree, both lost their jobs. It was a deplorable spectacle.

De Gaulle, who at Angers on 25 July made another of his blistering attacks on the 'manoeuvrings' of the system, was provided with some unusually powerful ammunition. But his indignation was equalled, perhaps surpassed, by that of the man whose post he was suspected of seeking. 'This has become the most painful, the most discouraging, the most degrading crisis,' wrote Auriol in his diary. '[There is] nothing noble, nothing doctrinal [nothing to do with] grand political ideas [about it].' His impatience was understandable, his analysis faulty. In fact, beneath the undignified struggles over jobs lay the unbridgeable ideological chasms which separated the parties of the Third Force – *laïcité* versus clericalism, *dirigisme* versus market forces, above all the Socialist fear, with the Communists in opposition, that by allowing themselves to be pulled too far to the right, they would risk losing their claim to be a working-class party. In the five years of the Fourth Republic's first legislature (1946–51) they upset six Third Force governments, although with a lack of consistency which emphasised the distance between their heads and their hearts, they continued to serve in all of them. As André Siegfried sagely pointed out, there was 'no possible majority with them or without them'.

These same chasms quickly swallowed up any hopes that the Marie government, which was supposed to signify 'stability and action', could survive. After only five weeks it collapsed under the weight of the arguments between Paul Reynaud and the Socialists. The former, quite properly asserting that France must not only put her financial house in order right away, by living within her means, but also prepare for the ending of Marshall Aid in 1952, put forward a recovery programme whose application called for the voting of special powers (Mendès-France had made similar proposals two and a half years earlier). The Socialists claimed that the plan could not succeed unless prices were lowered, otherwise social agitation would undo all the progress foreseen by Reynaud's proposed measures, as well as driving non-Communist unionists into the arms of the Communists. Reynaud reported that it was impossible to think and to say that the cost of living was going to diminish when it was going to rise. The argument raged on, culminating in a marathon, fourteen-hour meeting of the Council of Ministers on 27 August, at which all the same points were made over and over again. Reynaud said that the French people must accept a lower standard of living. Blum, in a moving speech, declared that it was essential to re-establish the purchasing power of the working class: '[This is] a trial of strength for the Fourth Republic, a fearful, perhaps a blood-stained, trial, for history is there to show that you cannot defend the Republican régime without the support of the people . . . We are fighting on two fronts [i.e. Communists and Gaullists], are we to fight on three?'

Reynaud, and those who thought like him, were just as well-intentioned and honest in advancing their beliefs that only orthodox economics could cure the patient as Blum and his friends were in arguing that this was the way to kill the poor ailing creature. In view of these entrenched positions, it was hardly surprising that once the Marie government had fallen, great difficulty was experienced in putting together another. Ramadier refused Auriol's invitation to head another administration, Schuman tried and failed (twice). In near desperation, Auriol tried to persuade Edouard Herriot, the Grand Old Man of the Radical Party, to step down from the presidency of the National Assembly (the speakership) and form a government, but he refused. Finally, early in September 1948, after France had been without a government for nearly a fortnight, Auriol turned to another, but less well-known, Radical politician who, even more than André Marie, incarnated the image of the Third Republic. Henri Queuille, originally a country doctor from the Corrèze, one of the underdeveloped departments in lower-central France, had held ministerial office between 1920 and 1940 in no less than nineteen governments, serving as Minister of Agriculture thirteen times. He joined de Gaulle in London in 1943 and was re-elected a deputy in the November 1946 elections. He made no pretence of being an intellectual or economist (his only published work was a book called *Le Drame Agricole*) or a great leader of men. But his gifts of modesty and common sense, combined with his intimate knowledge of the workings of the party system, made him an inspired choice, even if it appeared as an invitation to '*immobilisme*' – standing quite still so as to avoid being pushed over.

Queuille easily won the approval of the National Assembly and proceeded to form a government which (like most of the governments of the Fourth Republic) differed in its composition very little from its predecessor. He is credited with several homely sayings, illustrative of his simple if cynical approach to politics. One was that in politics, 'It is not a question of resolving problems but of silencing those who raise them.' Another – though this was of a later date, when he was again Prime Minister – was that 'I will do my best, the least harm possible . . . you can pass judgement afterwards . . . France must have a government.' One contemporary account, while recognising Queuille's modesty and integrity, speaks of him drifting along 'in a fog'.[9] No one could have foreseen that his government would last longer (nearly thirteen months) than any other in this first phase of the Fourth Republic. He reserved for himself the unenviable post of finance and economic affairs, and the Quai d'Orsay remained, as it had done since the war and was destined to go on doing, in the hands of the MRP (Robert Schuman).

Foreign and French commentators – including of course de Gaulle – might and did deplore the instability of the system, but in fact it maintained, at least as regards the men serving it, a remarkable degree of consistency.

It was not a moment too soon to provide France with a government. Another 'hot autumn' lay ahead. It was much the same story as a year earlier. Though the Communists certainly exploited the situation for political ends, specifically the obstruction of the Marshall Plan, they could not possibly have induced so many men to strike if there had not been a genuine and well-founded sense of grievance. As part of the financial recovery plan, direct and indirect taxes were raised and Paris Métro fares doubled. Although from mid-September onwards a growing wave of strikes among Paris metal workers, public transport and the aeronautical industry compelled the government to back-track on some of its measures, in the hope of restoring some of the purchasing power in pay packets, any improvement was immediately absorbed by a vicious increase in food prices. A reminder of the persisting chaos in the marketing and distribution system for meat was the government's introduction, early in October, of yet another 'meat plan' (the twenty-eighth since the Liberation).

On 4 October, the miners, upon whom the grip of the Communist-dominated CGT was particularly strong, came out. Though in fact their living standards were not so depressed as those of other French workers, 60 per cent of the 300,000-strong work-force voted for the strike in a referendum which followed the Queuille government's announcement of its recovery programme for the mining industry: 10 per cent of the work-force to be laid off, new measures against absenteeism, a new code of discipline. There followed a test of strength of unparalleled intensity. The strike order was generally followed, despite the non-Communist unions' opposition to it, and before long the CGT ordered that maintenance teams be withdrawn from the pits. This had never happened before.

Queuille, in his non-confrontational way, at first favoured letting the strike run its course, but stiffened by the energetic Jules Moch, then as in the previous year at the Ministry of the Interior, he decided to meet force with force. Forty thousand men from the French occupation forces in Germany were despatched to the northern coalfields to dislodge the pickets and reoccupy the mines. There were armed clashes, in which many were wounded and two killed.

Although by November the strikes were on the wane, with the order to resume working given by the unions on the 29th, it had been an anxious time – not perhaps as menacing as the previous autumn, but still calling for steady nerves and resolve.

Nor was the threat only from the extreme Left. De Gaulle, giving his first press conference for ten months, once more lambasted the 'so-called' parliament and 'so-called' government, and once more offered himself as the nation's saviour. But he was no nearer achieving this legally than before. The wily Queuille persuaded the majority in the Assembly to vote (by a narrow margin) in favour of postponing for six months the cantonal elections due in October. This thoroughly undemocratic procedure had at least the advantage – from the viewpoint of the Third Force coalition – of robbing de Gaulle and his movement of an electoral success which would almost certainly have equalled that which they enjoyed in the municipal elections twelve months earlier. They would have received a new puff of wind in their sails. As it was they had to content themselves with a fair measure of success in the elections held in early November (by indirect methods, not by universal suffrage) for the Council of the Republic, the upper house of parliament – a result achieved largely at the expense of the MRP. But given the limited powers of the Council of the Republic – far less than that of its predecessor, the Third Republic's Senate – and the fact that many elected on the Gaullist ticket then decided not to take the Gaullist whip, this outcome, though providing useful propaganda, was as useless as the cantonal elections would have been in helping de Gaulle to regain power legally.

The steadfastness and determination of the government in overcoming the strikes redounded to its credit, as it had done in the previous autumn's experience. Whatever de Gaulle might say, the men and the system which he scorned had shown themselves capable of mastering an ugly situation. But it was not necessary to look very far below the surface in the closing months of 1948 (when Paris, incidentally, was playing host to the UN General Assembly) to realise that France was '*l'homme malade de l'Europe*'. One foreign observer seeking to explain the strength of de Gaulle's and the Communists' appeal to their constituents wrote: 'It is necessary to realise how deep is the exasperation of the average Frenchman with the succession of "experiments" that have been successive Ministries' substitutes for an economic programme and his disgust at the prevarications and the bargains which have taken the punch out of any policy and sapped the authority and stability of government.'[10] At the Elysée, a similarly harsh analysis was being served up. Paul Auriol, the President's son and assistant Secretary-General at the Presidency, presented a memorandum to his father which argued that the root of French troubles was not so much the recent increase in taxes, the wage and price problem, or questions of foreign policy, as 'the lack of the State's authority'. The Communists, young Auriol wrote, based their appeal simultaneously upon wage claims and 'the desire for a better distribution of riches . . . as a sign of protest against the State's bad management'.

The RPF appeal, on the other hand, was founded, in Paul Auriol's words, on 'more and more vigorous protests against the State's financial chaos and against the fact that its lack of authority domestically leads to a lack of prestige abroad'. Appearances to the contrary, the differences between the Elysée and Colombey were not as great as might seem. In their different ways, both President and General shared the same broad diagnosis of what was wrong with France.

These thoughtful observations must be set against the picture given by others of both Communist and Gaullist tactics. Jules Moch, as usual, chose to see Communist encouragement for the strikes as part of an international conspiracy. Certainly he had some arguments on his side, including a letter from Thorez to Communist newspapers, describing the aim of the strikes as the overthrow of the government. It was also at this time that Thorez declared publicly that France 'will never make war against the Soviet Union'. But when Moch came to develop his thesis to the National Assembly in November, he was unable to support it with any convincing proof and the debate ended inconclusively. 'If you have any evidence, produce it,' said a non-Communist deputy who was also a well-known lawyer. 'If you haven't, shut up.'[11] A more realistic and cautious note was likewise sounded by Queuille himself, that repository of Third Republican Radical wisdom, with its slogan of '*Ni réaction ni révolution*'. In the Council of Ministers held as the strikes were drawing to a close, he warned against precipitate criminal proceedings for conspiracy against the State unless foolproof evidence was available. He would rather, he said, have a smaller majority than a larger, anti-Communist one which favoured active and massive repression ending in the release of nearly all the suspects; 'Courage is not giving way to imprudence and passion.'

The Communists themselves could have been under no illusions about their prospects if they had been successful in bringing down the government. No other party would have accepted their invitation to share power. Twelve months of violent hostility towards the ruling coalition, plus the increasing pressures of the Cold War, had placed them ever more firmly in permanent opposition and isolation. What was more realistic, though even here their hopes remained unrealised, was the possibility of bringing the country to a standstill, thus making impossible the application of the Marshall Plan. Auriol's diary, usually so full of information about what the Communists were (supposed to be) up to, is strangely silent during the period of the strikes. Only when they were over is there a report of the Politburo meeting, at which Duclos is quoted as laying down the not very exciting tactical line of working towards national instability so as to prevent a centre coalition from enjoying the people's confidence.

As for de Gaulle and Gaullism, he and his followers had given many examples of their passion, and now proceeded to indulge in some excesses. Already the RPF had been getting itself a bad name for the strong-arm tactics of some of its stewards and guards who were supposed to provide security at public meetings. These gatherings were beginning to assume the nature of para-military rallies, with armed guards surrounding the General and jeeploads of other pugnacious-looking men much in evidence. An episode in September 1948 at Grenoble, where a Communist was killed by a bullet apparently fired by one of these Gaullist security men, was especially damaging to the RPF's reputation.

Now Caffery, the US Ambassador in Paris, reported to Auriol a conversation that he had with Jacques Soustelle, one of the General's principal lieutenants, who was later to play a leading role in the movement that brought de Gaulle back to power in 1958.[12] Soustelle had said that the Americans ought not to hand over counterpart Marshall funds – i.e. the franc equivalent of Marshall dollars entering France, which provided valuable underpinning for the Monnet Plan – to the present, incompetent, government. Instead, Washington should withhold it until de Gaulle was back in power and would ensure it was not wasted. Caffery said he found this very disturbing. 'No more than I do,' replied Auriol. This was an example, neither the first nor the last, of the Gaullists playing the game known in French political jargon as *'la politique du pire'* – seeking to bring about the collapse of the existing system, whatever the cost, so as to be able to take over the ruins and build them up again in a way to suit and favour the new builders.

After a year (autumn 1947–8) which must be seen historically as a continuous whole, with the embattled coalition fighting (despite Blum's earlier warning) on the three fronts of Communism, Gaullism and the wage–price spiral, French fortunes began to look up, according to that inexplicable cycle which sometimes enables a government beset by difficulties somehow to survive them and find itself sailing in calmer seas. Queuille introduced a 'good housekeeping' budget, cutting civil and military expenditure (and incidentally depriving the Monnet Plan of some of its hoped-for credits). He managed, in his adroit way, to avoid the sterile confrontations between *dirigistes* and free-market men which had created so much trouble for previous governments; and this despite the fact that his measures included a plan for fiscal reform, usually the thinnest ice on which to choose to go skating. Auriol was full of admiration, as he had reason to be: Queuille had risen from his bed of influenza and, hardly able to stand, had effectively defended his budget against attacks on it by the Council of the Republic.

Indeed, Queuille's reputation as a politician whose fear of movement was so great that he preferred inaction at all times does not sit easily with the facts. It grew up partly because of his own somewhat cynical aphorisms about the art of government, partly because of his modest personality, which made him appear as the reverse of a statesman, an anti-hero who compared badly with such trenchant characters as René Mayer or Paul Reynaud or even Robert Schuman, monk-like though he was. It is significant that Queuille brought into his ministerial team, even if it was only to a junior post in the Ministry of Finance, another anti-hero, Antoine Pinay, who four years later, as Prime Minister, was to rival and surpass Queuille's performance as the 'little man' who knew how to inspire confidence.

A State loan was floated, and fully taken up, in January 1949, the first such successful loan since that issued just after the Liberation. Prices began to stabilise. The quality of life itself improved. Bread rationing finally ended in January, more than three and a half years after the end of the war in Europe, to be followed in the spring by the freeing of milk, chocolate, fats and textiles. The black market disappeared slowly. The return to normality received further emphasis when Josephine Baker resumed her role as the Folies-Bergères' leading lady. American journalists, by the spring of 1949, found themselves filing only 60 per cent of the amount they had been sending from Paris to their agencies and newspapers a few months earlier.[13] That in itself was a sort of negative achievement, a recognition that the invalid France was not only not going to expire (which was never at all likely – when do ancient civilisations like France expire?) but might even be out of danger.

There was a price to be paid for all this, and the near miracle was that for more than a year the conscience-ridden Socialists were ready to pay it. This price was the return of economic liberalism. René Mayer had begun it, with his recovery plan. Paul Reynaud tried a bit too brusquely to continue it, and now here was Queuille, together with the man he eventually appointed Minister of Finance, Maurice Petsche, who came from the authentic right wing and was used to the ways of big business. Without the country properly realising what was happening, without creating a lot of ideological heat and noise, Petsche reintroduced the manners and methods of the capitalist State, while leaving in place the post-war nationalisations and of course the Monnet Plan. A writer in *Le Monde*, Jean-Jacques Servan-Schreiber (later to become first editor of the pro-Mendès *L'Express*), noted perceptively on 23 June 1949 that the Europe which emerged from the war, 'a Europe of *les lendemains qui chantent*' (see p. 61) was changing: 'What is coming is a liberal, a "Radical–Socialist" Europe.'

Exchange control was swept away, funds for investment (apart from the Marshall Plan) were now to come from the banks, protection for unproductive sectors was to be dismantled so as to let in the wind of competition, a return to free collective bargaining was introduced. If this did not happen all at once – the collective bargaining law was not passed until February 1950 – there was not only a consistency in all these measures but, more important still, they worked. There was consistency, also, in personalities. Petsche was Minister of Finance solidly, despite three changes of government, from early 1949 until the 1951 general elections; Robert Schuman remained at the Quai d'Orsay throughout the same period; Pierre Pflimlin (MRP), who was to be the last prime minister of the Fourth Republic, was Minister for Agriculture for all this time.

The thirteen months of Queuille's government provided the country with some welcome respite. But it was as true as it was inevitable that the essential differences between the coalition parties had not ceased to exist. When in early October 1949 the patience of the Socialists finally ran out and they brought down the government with a demand for higher wages for underpaid workers and civil servants, it took nearly the whole month to stick the pieces together again, this time with Bidault heading a 'new' government – i.e. a team made up of much the same people, supporting much the same programme as before.

Eight months later, the same thing happened again: twenty-four hours before the outbreak of the Korean war in June 1950, the Socialists (who had left the government in February) torpedoed the Bidault government, wages and the status of civil servants again serving as a cause. It was nearly three weeks before René Pleven, Finance Minister under de Gaulle's provisional government, succeeded in reassembling the components of the sorely battered Third Force. De Gaulle still had plenty of ground from which to attack the shortcomings of 'the system'.

In fact the attractions of the General, whose stock, like the price of gold, tended to rise in times of trouble and fall when the going became smoother, began at this time temporarily to wane. There were several good reasons for this. Where Queuille represented both the wish for a return to normality and the means of fulfilling it, de Gaulle's ceaseless and strident criticisms of the régime seemed to promise, were he ever to regain power, anything but a quiet life. It was not that the Communist threat, external or internal, had gone away. But the coalition had shown itself, throughout a terrible year, capable of withstanding it without bringing about civil war. Moreover that same coalition, whoever might be leading it at any particular moment, had steered France firmly into the Western bloc (the treaty establishing the North Atlantic Treaty Organisation – NATO – had been signed in April 1949), which is where, despite some plague-on-both-your-houses feeling, the great majority of French people wanted her to be. What had de Gaulle, despite his pounding rhetoric, to offer instead? When finally the delayed cantonal elections took place, in the spring of 1949, the RPF failed by a considerable margin to repeat its previous successes.

The feeling of discouragement, of having missed the bus, is caught in a letter written at this time (April 1949) by Michel Debré, one of the closest to de Gaulle and the first Prime Minister of the Fifth Republic, to Georges Pompidou, *chef de cabinet* to de Gaulle from the spring of 1948 onwards and his successor as the second President of the Fifth Republic:

> I am pretty despairing about events and about men. Where are we going? . . . The General has up to a point tried to bring about the revolt of the *pays réel* [i.e. the masses] against the *pays légal* [i.e. the Establishment]. But the *pays légal* is good at self-defence . . . Will we emerge from the circle? Yes, with a catastrophe, no if there isn't one. It is better to think, hypothetically, that there won't be one. In that case, I don't see the future. Or rather, I see a slow decadence.[14]

Two months previously, André Malraux, in his typically melodramatic way, told a friend that 'de Gaulle's historical destiny is finished . . . now, to end it finally, there should be a grand assassination, we need a Ravaillac.'*

But although this relatively peaceful interval, after the great strikes of 1947–8 and before the onset of the Korean war, brought a much needed breathing space to the Fourth Republic, its institutions and those who served them continued to be held in low esteem by the general public. The month's interregnum that followed the fall of the Queuille government in the autumn of 1949 provided a spectacle which left many people angry and ashamed. Bidault, the next Prime Minister, in his opening declaration to the National Assembly, spoke of 'the indifferent eye turned by a tired nation' upon these parliamentary antics. Prices had stabilised, the shops were fuller than before of consumer goods, the monied bourgeoisie was making its way back into political and financial power, but none of this meant that politics and politicians in general were popular or respected. Bidault, in his cynical and witty way, knew very well that the ground upon which he stood could (and after eight months it did) open up from one moment to the next. 'What shall I find in my Christmas stocking?' he was heard to say as 1949 drew to a close. 'Some fruit, I expect, an orange, a banana – or its skin.'

Understandably, nothing contributed so much to the bad reputation of the Fourth Republic, in the eyes of French people as

---

* The murderer of Henry of Navarre (Henri IV).

well as foreigners, as these intermittent crises and the subsequent absence of any government, often for quite long periods. The exasperation was all the greater when the episodes finally ended with the establishment of another government of almost precisely the same composition and programme as the previous one. How much material harm these crises did to the country is partly unquantifiable. The members of the resigning government remained, until a successor had been established, in charge of day-to-day business (*affaires courantes*), and the senior civil servants, usually men of high calibre, knew what to do. But neither they nor their headless masters could make binding commitments on behalf of France. It was inconvenient, as well as humiliating, for the country to have no government in the weeks following the outbreak of the Korean war, just when Western policies urgently required to be coordinated and decided. France was one of the permanent members of the UN Security Council, and her properly authorised voice needed to be heard.

Probably the greatest harm caused by this government instability was of a psychological nature. Régimes, like people, tend to be taken at their own valuation, so that the public and foreign perception of French instability added greatly to the impression, already reported to Auriol by his son, that the main default of the Fourth Republic was the State's lack of authority. Auriol himself was certainly aware of this and spent part of a country weekend (January 1949) drawing up a comparative table of instability as between the Third and Fourth Republics. This emboldened him to say to Alben Barkley, Vice-President of the US under Truman, that while France might change the horses, the carriage continued to move forward. Barkley asked: 'What happens when you run out of horses?', to which Auriol's answer was: 'We go back to the original ones.'[15] Auriol was of course making the valid point (see p. 105 above) that while governments might fall, the men serving them reappeared, often in the same part.

Given this valuable element of continuity, the collapse of governments in 1949 and 1950 might not have had much effect upon the improved fortunes of France had it not been for the impact of the Korean war. Petsche's skilful application of a 'liberal' economy – in fact, the repudiation of most of the collectivist aims and hopes of the new men and parties emerging from the Liberation – might have enabled France to go on enjoying the benefits of price stability and a new-found confidence. As it was, that confidence began to ebb in the second half of 1950, a flight of capital began, and the bad old habit resumed of the State resorting to the printing press as a source of money. Wholesale prices began to edge upwards, the purchasing power of wage-packets downwards. Had the régime so derided by de Gaulle been better designed, it might have withstood these shocks better. But the setback – which affected all Western economies in some degree – was initially due to events outside French control.

As for the men who served this faulty system, they were not the poltroons and incompetents that much of popular opinion imagined them to be. Most of the politicians took their jobs seriously, and some of them were exceptionally able men. Auriol was unflagging in his efforts. At meetings of the Council of Ministers, he listened a great deal, taking copious notes, full of suggestions for compromise between the warring parties. 'It is my duty', he said, 'to watch over the continuity of the Republic.' A junior member of the government of those days (1949–51) has left some vivid glimpses of what a Cabinet meeting was like.[16] It sounds very different from the austere protocol of de Gaulle's time. At one end of the table Mitterrand, a Secretary of State (a much more junior post than the name suggests in English), would be reading an historical feature serial, *Les Grandes Amoureuses*, in the pages of the previous evening's *Paris-Soir*. Next to him, the Secretary of State in charge of electoral reform drew urns – funerary, not voting – on his blotter. Queuille said very little, preferring to leave things to Auriol. His main concern was to take problems one by one, and buy time: 'until Easter, until Whitsun, until the elections, until just after the elections, until the Tour de France . . .' According to Lapie, he had 'a fundamental knowledge of the psychology of ordinary people and of the provinces . . . and was not without malice, even in his silences'.

While most ministers talked only about their own departmental affairs, the confident, larger-than-life René Mayer was free with his advice on everything. Robert Schuman spoke slowly on foreign affairs, saying as little as possible. The fiercest arguments were always about agriculture and finance, with Petsche, the Minister of Finance, often fighting his corner alone. Once, at a Cabinet held at Rambouillet (the presidential château south-west of Paris), when the question of a minimum wage was under discussion, there had to be constant suspensions and walks round the garden, in order to lower the tension. In general, security was poor. Ministers tended to return to their departments after Cabinet meetings and tell their staffs – and later in the evening their men and women friends as well – what had passed. More than once the newspaper *Samedi-Soir* published accurate accounts of Cabinet meetings, which could only have come from someone present. Auriol was angered by this sloppiness. 'Ministers are incorrigible,' he wrote in his diary. 'In earlier days there was absolute discretion [a questionable statement] but now people gossip here, there and everywhere.'

To this picture of mild disorder in high places were added, in the early autumn of 1949, some much more lurid overtones. What became known as 'the Generals' affair' was another of those scandals to which French politics have for long been so prone. But this one, involving politicians, Army generals, the habitual internecine war between two branches of the intelligence services, and an unpopular war in Indochina, contained the seeds of all sorts of future troubles and disaffection. The story is of great complexity and leaves many questions unanswered. That is the nature of French scandals.

To understand it even dimly, it is necessary to go back to the outbreak of war in Indochina (December 1946). This was followed by a period of uncertainty in Paris, where those in favour of resuming negotiations with Ho Chi Minh – the Communists and some Socialists – were outnumbered by those – most of the MRP, the Right and the Gaullists – who opposed such a policy. The Ramadier government finally steeled itself to recall d'Argenlieu, who was replaced as High Commissioner by Emile Bollaert, a man of much more open mind, under whom the prospects for negotiations seemed to brighten. Ho Chi Minh suggested armistice negotiations, but the French terms for these were pitched so high by the military as to rule out any possibility of Ho's accepting them. By this time, the Communists were out of the government in Paris and the political balance had shifted towards the centre and the MRP, where the will to make concessions was minimal. One of its men, Paul Coste-Floret, was Minister for War. After a visit to Indochina in May 1947, he rashly announced that 'there is no longer a military problem'.[17]

Despite these unpromising auguries, Bollaert persisted, and prepared to make a speech on 15 August 1947 (the day when India was due to achieve independence) proclaiming an immediate cease-fire and conditional independence for Vietnam, just as Leclerc had recommended some months earlier. Whether Bollaert, had he been able to make the speech, would have saved six years of futile war must remain speculative, because the differences within the coalition in Paris meant that no approval for the initiative was forthcoming. All he was authorised to do, when he finally spoke on 10 September, was to suggest a status for Vietnam which would have denied her an independent army and her own diplomacy. Although Ho Chi Minh had refused similar terms a year before at Fontainebleau, he did now respond to Bollaert with counter-proposals of his own, but these went unanswered from Paris.

By now, the advent of the Marshall Plan, the onset of the Cold War and the declared resolve of the French Communist party to combat American 'imperialism' had all played into the hands of those who considered that Ho Chi Minh, rebel and Communist, was not someone with whom to be discussing matters which could affect the future of the French Union. Bidault's words in the National Assembly on 27 August, in a debate on Algeria, could equally apply to Indochina: 'There can be no concessions when it is a question of France, of its flag, of its presence and of its destiny.' Even the Communists, at this stage before they had gone over to the offensive, would not have demurred at the general sense of this. Pierre Cot, a fellow-travelling spokesman for Communist policy, emphasised in the Assembly's debate on Indochina in March, while arguing for negotiations with Ho Chi Minh, that 'none of us is thinking of a policy of abandonment. . . . France has a task and mission in Indochina.' This was in tune with the Thorez keep-the-Tricolour-flying line.

With Ho Chi Minh ruled out as a 'valid interlocutor', the initiative was back in the hands of the military. But, *pace* Coste-Floret, the war was far from over. The French autumn offensive against Vietminh forces, from which much had been hoped, was a failure and once more the search began for some sort of a political way out of the impasse. By now, Coste-Floret had moved to the Ministry for Overseas France. This remained an MRP 'fief' until the end of France's war in Indochina, and thus was to associate the MRP more and more closely with the prosecution of an unpopular and unsuccessful war. Coste-Floret was the main architect of the 'Bao Dai solution' which, in a lukewarm effort to meet Vietnam nationalist aspirations, recognised the ex-Emperor of Annam as the head of an 'independent' and unified Vietnam.

Bao Dai, despite his reputation as a playboy and lightweight, was no fool and knew that if he were to have any real standing he must not be seen as a French puppet. Lengthy negotiations followed before, in June 1948, he was ready to sign an agreement with Bollaert under which France recognised the independence and unity of Vietnam as an Associated State of the French Union – the very points that Ho Chi Minh had tried to win two years earlier. Nearly twelve more months were to elapse before this agreement was transformed into a formal Franco-Vietnamese treaty. Even then, Bao Dai's wish for separate diplomatic representation abroad – one of the outward and visible signs of a genuinely sovereign state – was largely denied him by Paris.

Coste-Floret's Bao Dai strategy, had it been speedily and ungrudgingly implemented, might have held out some hope of success. But it was not, and in any case the policy was by no means to everyone's liking. Many rank-and-file Socialists considered that France had conceded too little for the plan to work. For them, Bao Dai was a shadowy figure, incapable of rallying the Vietnamese people. In any event, the war, with its heavy call on French financial resources and military manpower, showed no signs of abating. On the other wing, conservatives and the Gaullist-influenced section of the MRP feared a sell-out. None was more inflexible than Bidault, who was insistent that when it came to patriotism – meaning, in this context, defence of French overseas interests – he had no lesson to learn from anyone. The influence of the gung-ho RPF upon the right-wing faction of the MRP, and hence upon Indochinese policy, was a vital factor in the failure of the Bao Dai experiment.

It was against this background of rumbling disagreement between MRP and Socialists that the Generals' affair unfolded. In April 1949 Ramadier, by this time Minister of Defence, despatched General Revers, Chief of the General Staff, to report on the situation in Indochina. He was a politically-minded, very able officer, given to intrigue, with Socialist and Radical contacts. He reported under two headings. Militarily, he recommended that, in light of the impending Communist victory in China, French garrisons in northern Vietnam should be withdrawn from the Chinese frontier areas to the Tonkin delta. Politically, he criticised the government's handling – which meant, in effect, Coste-Floret's handling – of the Bao Dai strategy, complained that France had no proper war aims, urged that full and genuine independence should be conferred on Vietnam and the other Associated States, favoured the creation of a national Vietnamese army, and proposed that a new French High Commissioner, of exalted rank and prestige, be appointed.

In August, parts of this report were alleged to have been broadcast by Vietminh radio. Even that presumably ascertainable fact was never proved beyond doubt, but the allegation inevitably gave rise to suspicions that somewhere there had been a leak. A few weeks later there was a curious episode in Paris at the Gare de Lyon, when a fight between a French soldier and two Communist Vietnamese students led to the discovery, in the briefcase of one of the latter, of copies of extracts from the Revers report. This man also had a list of Vietnamese living in Paris, one of whom confessed that he had been passed the report by a certain Roger Peyré, a shadowy adventurer who had worked for the Vichy *milice* (a French imitation of the Gestapo) and for the Gestapo itself during the war, and who subsequently became friendly not only with Revers but with General Mast, the officer whom Revers favoured as the new High Commissioner. Peyré had various financial interests in Indochina, as well as links with the SDECE, French counter-intelligence.* He told a friend that Mast's appointment 'would suit me very well'.[18] Moreover, Peyré claimed, Indochinese sources in Paris, to whom he had passed the report, had given him 2½ million francs, of which he had distributed a million each to the two Generals.

The Ministers of the Interior and of Defence (Moch and Ramadier, both Socialists) told Queuille, the Prime Minister, what had occurred, and it was decided that with delicate military negotiations pending in Washington, the cost of a scandal would be too great. The Judge Advocate General's department (Tribunal Militaire de la Seine) was called in and, accepting Ramadier's argument that only the political and not the military parts of the Revers report had been leaked, ruled that there was no case. Peyré and those arrested with him were released and the two Generals, who denied receiving money but admitted their friendship with Peyré, agreed to retire. The affair seemed to have been disposed of.

This was not at all the view of Coste-Floret, whose policies had

---

* SDECE (Service de Documentation Extérieure et de Contre-Espionnage) was the French equivalent of the British SIS, or MI6. It was constantly at odds with the DST (Direction de la Surveillance du Territoire), which corresponds to MI5.

come under attack in the Revers report. Impelled by personal as well as political feelings, he represented to Queuille that the whole business was an intrigue designed to secure Mast's nomination to Indochina, to the political benefit of Peyré and of Socialist party funds. At the end of September, a publicly circulated newsletter alleged that Revers had staged the leak and been paid for it. At that point, the Queuille government fell, to be succeeded, after the customary delays, by one led by Bidault.

The subsequent developments in this murky affair included: successful pressure on Peyré from SDECE to withdraw his first statement; his abrupt (and probably aided) departure, with his family, for South America; the replacement of Revers as Chief of Staff; the publication by *Time* magazine, at the end of December, of an attack on Revers as an alleged leaker of military secrets; a statement in January by Bidault to the National Assembly, which had hitherto fed only on rumours, albeit a rich crop of them; the onset of internecine war between the DST and SDECE; and the establishment of a parliamentary committee of inquiry. The latter's task was constantly hampered by inability to obtain requisite information and documentation, to keep its investigation confidential (its Communist member transmitted selected items of the proceedings to *L'Humanité*), and to trace the sources of Peyré's influence – the rapporteur complained of a 'wall of silence'.

The preliminary report of the committee was debated in the National Assembly in May 1950, when a majority of deputies agreed that Ramadier had acted in good faith; a Communist-inspired move to impeach him was thwarted. In November, the final report of the committee came before the Assembly, when the Communists mounted another, nearly successful attempt (possibly with the connivance of some of the MRP) at impeachment, this time against Jules Moch. He was alleged to have failed to prevent the burning of many documents relevant to the inquiry.

The committee found that Peyré had given a copy of the Revers report to his Vietnamese contact, through whom it found its way to the Vietminh. It also criticised Revers for his lack of discretion over the company he kept, but exonerated him, Mast and Ramadier from charges of accepting bribes. Nevertheless, it found both Generals wanting in their conduct, and they were dismissed the Army. (Twelve years later, in 1962, the *Conseil d'Etat*, the highest administrative tribunal, found that Revers' dismissal had been illegal.)

As usual with such scandals, the inquiry left many questions unanswered. What exactly had been the relationship, and who benefited from it, between Revers, Mast and Peyré? What about Revers' counter-allegations that it was Coste-Floret and his friends who staged the leak, because of the latter's objections to the criticisms in the Revers report? Coste-Floret's response to this last claim was that he, who had been to Indochina to see things for himself shortly after Revers had submitted his report, had made equally critical comments on the military and political situation there. This was true, but there was no doubt about the hostility of the Minister towards Revers and his associates. Coste-Floret openly accused Revers, Mast and the Socialists of plotting the replacement of Bao Dai by their own candidate, General Xuan.[19]

The unanswered questions and the unsatisfactory workings of the committee of inquiry increased rather than allayed public misgivings about the affair, which succeeded in discrediting the Socialists, deepening the already considerable suspicions between them and the MRP, and greatly adding to public cynicism about politics, politicians and the workings of the State. The spectacle of two branches of the intelligence services at one another's throats, though nothing new, was particularly unedifying. Probably the principal beneficiaries were the Communists, who were able to mock everyone – the coalition parties, the security services and the Indochinese war. The greatest losers were the Army, whose growing sense of disenchantment with their role in the war and the lack of support it received from Paris was increased by the demonstration of generals playing politics.

Though the Generals' affair may have added to it, this distaste of the Army for Republican politicians and the system within which they worked was nothing new. A private conversation with a very senior retired general of impeccable reputation and with a fine Resistance record helps to explain in historic terms the feelings of the military towards the civil power. 'You have your Queen and country,' he said, 'but we have no monarchy, and as for our country, it has been disgracefully treated by the Republican political system. I was never brought up to believe in the Republic as an ideal or something to look up to. Before the [Second World] War, we regarded Lebrun [the last President of the Third Republic] as a joke. What we did have respect for was the flag and our military traditions.'[20]

This admirable old officer had been a friend of Revers, and his colleague in the Resistance, and confirmed that he was an intriguer: 'He was by nature a plotter, but I never took the so-called Generals' affair seriously, it did not have much effect upon the Army.' Whatever doubts it may throw upon the real consequences of the Generals' affair, such evidence from such a source is impressive in the way it confirms the low esteem in which the military held the politicians. This familiar theme, becoming more and more insistent as time went on, was a decisive element in the background music of the Fourth Republic.

CHAPTER 5

Light over Europe,
Storm-clouds Elsewhere

On the evening of 9 May 1950, a press conference was called at the Quai d'Orsay. There, in the ornate setting of the Salon de l'Horloge, Robert Schuman, the Foreign Minister, unveiled a document whose contents were to provide a new and original starting-point for post-war French foreign policy. 'Almost exactly five years after the unconditional surrender of Germany,' said Schuman, reading in his quiet German-accented voice from a preamble which he himself had drawn up earlier in the day, 'France performs the first decisive act in the construction of Europe and associates Germany with that act. European ideas must be entirely changed. This change will make possible other actions in common, which up to now have been impossible.'

What Schuman was doing was to introduce the plan for a European coal and steel community, designed not only to control through internationalisation the output of European coal and steel – specifically that of German factories and mines in the Ruhr, thus helping to allay French fears of a renascent Germany – but also to pave the way towards new and untried forms of European cooperation. The key passage in the document which Schuman presented to the journalists and the world that afternoon read: 'Through the pooling of basic industries and the establishment of a new High Authority, whose decisions will bind France, Germany and the countries belonging to it, this proposal will establish the first tangible institutions of a European federation indispensable to the preservation of peace.' The story behind this remarkable announcement is a good deal more important (and uplifting) than the sordid and conspiratorial details of the Generals' affair. Not that the preparation of the Schuman Plan, as it came to be known, was lacking in conspiracy of a sort.

Its point of origin was, as so often in post-war French affairs, Germany and the need, now that the Cold War was in danger of becoming hotter, to integrate her into the Western society of nations. The French had already had to accept, however reluctantly, the division of Germany and the establishment of a West German Federal Government. There followed the Berlin blockade and the restitution, over French protests, of the control of the Ruhr to West Germany.

In November 1948, at the Armistice ceremonies at Compiègne (scene of the German and French surrenders in 1918 and 1940 respectively), Vincent Auriol, deeply suspicious like most men of his age of German intentions, had said it was 'unpardonable to allow the arsenal of the Ruhr to be restored to the hands of Hitler's accomplices'.[1] Strong words, emanating from the President of the French Republic, but worse was to come. Not only was the control of the Saar (economically attached to France since the end of the war) a subject of intermittent argument between Paris and Bonn, but the need to rearm Germany was ceasing to be unthinkable and becoming, in the light of the newly established NATO strategy of defending Europe as far to the east as possible, a distinct possibility. If ever there was a moment for a French initiative, this was it. The Americans had specifically stated that at the three-power conference – US, UK, France – to be held at Foreign Minister level in London on 10 May 1950, they looked to France for a new approach to the German problem.

But what was this to be, given the state of French feelings about Germany? From Bonn had already come suggestions of a startlingly far-reaching kind. In an interview with an American journalist in March 1950, the new Federal Chancellor, Konrad Adenauer, had proposed a complete union of France and Western Germany, a fusion of economies, parliaments and nationalities.[2] It was an offer comparable to that put forward in May 1940 for a Franco-British union. But just as that fell on deaf ears, so now this German olive-branch withered away almost as soon as it was picked. French sensibilities were far too tender. 'Adenauer wants to create Europe around and for Germany,' wrote *L'Aube*, the MRP party paper. If this is what the MRP, with its broadly internationalist outlook, thought, then how much more averse was conventional, orthodox French opinion to the prospect of a Franco-German marriage in which inevitably a rebuilt Germany would become the dominant partner.

Not that all French opinion was as hidebound as this. In the summer and autumn of 1949, at the newly established Council of Europe in Strasbourg (a purely consultative, non-executive body), various stirring motions were passed in favour of a united Europe equipped with real powers. One of them spoke of creating a European political authority. But as all such ideas had to be approved (or more usually disapproved) by the governments of the countries represented in the Council, nothing more was heard of them. Paul Reynaud suggested to the Strasbourg Assembly a public authority to control and administer European steel production. But he too soon realised that his idea was not going to bear fruit; governments would kill it in the bud.

Enter Jean Monnet, the magician who could be counted on to produce something new and unusual and to pursue his objective with the cunning and tenacity of a leopard stalking its prey. He describes in his memoirs[3] how some of his best ideas came to him while walking in the countryside and how, disturbed in mind about the impasse in Franco-German affairs and the construction of Europe, he walked for two weeks in the Swiss Alps in the spring of 1950. When he returned to Paris, the outlines of what would eventually be the European Coal and Steel Community (ECSC) were already in his head:

> If we on our part could eliminate the fear of German industrial domination, the greatest obstacle to the union of Europe would be removed . . . A solution which would put French industry on the same starting-point as German industry, while freeing the latter of the discriminations born of defeat, would re-establish the economic and political conditions of an understanding indispensable to Europe . . . Still more, it could be the very yeast of European unity.

Conscious of the approaching three-power conference in London, Monnet set to work with his intimate advisers at the Commissariat au Plan, to draw up a scheme for the pooling of the coal and steel production of France, Germany and as many other European countries as wished to join under an international Authority (this wording was changed in drafting to 'High Authority'). An essential element of the plan was that the decisions of the High Authority would be binding upon France and Germany and other participating countries. In other words, where coal and steel were concerned, international decisions arrived at in common would override the authority of national governments. It was a daring concept. No wonder Monnet told almost no one what he was doing. When the plan was announced by Schuman on 9 May, neither parliament nor the ministries most concerned had been consulted, and nor had French steel masters or the heads of the nationalised coal industry, to their subsequent concern and anger.

Monnet and his men had not only laid the most extraordinary egg. They had also to find someone to hatch it. Monnet thought immediately of Schuman, who because of his own history would seem to have been created to preside over Franco-German rapprochement. But things nearly went wrong when Schuman's *directeur de cabinet*, Bernard Clappier, having shown some initial enthusiasm for Monnet's explanation of his plan, then failed to be in touch. The latter, sensing a lack of interest, sent a summary of the plan to the Prime Minister, Georges Bidault. What would have happened if Clappier had not, rather belatedly, expressed an interest on Schuman's behalf, and the matter had rested with the Prime Minister, could be one of the questions in the guessing game of modern history. Bidault, for all his qualities, was emphatically not the person to be godfather to a Franco-German entente. Moody, quick to take offence, a stalwart defender of French sovereignty, more 'Atlantic' than European, according to Monnet it seems doubtful whether he even read the document, though Bidault in his memoirs denies this.[4] Though it was lying on his desk when Monnet went to see him a few days later, Bidault claimed angrily that he, not Schuman, should have been the first to be informed.

As it was, Schuman, who studied Monnet's scheme during a weekend at his home in Lorraine, saw in it the new French initiative which hitherto had been lacking. Two confirmed 'European' ministers, René Mayer and René Pleven, were let in on the secret, as was the senior official at the Quai d'Orsay, Alexandre Parodi. They were all sworn to silence. As Monnet put it, 'We were determined to mount the operation outside the ordinary diplomatic channels and do without ambassadors.' But one diplomatic contact was indispensable. A member of Schuman's personal staff was despatched to Bonn, bearing letters for Adenauer, who approved whole-heartedly of the idea for a coal and steel community. This news was telephoned to the Elysée, where the Cabinet was in session, and Schuman was at last free to tell his colleagues, though only in the broadest terms, what was in the wind.

René Mayer, with his customary eloquence, supported Schuman, as did Pleven, and the other ministers (including Bidault) agreed.* Only Petsche, the Finance Minister, a confirmed foe of Monnet and his subtle ways, demurred. At last, after eighty years of mutual fear and distrust, Franco-German reconciliation had become a realistic hope instead of a distant dream. Except to the architects of the plan, and perhaps not even to them, it did not seem exactly like that at the time. After the press conference on 9 May, a journalist who found some difficulty absorbing the portent of what he had heard said to Schuman: 'So, it's a step in the dark?' 'That's right,' was the calm reply, 'a step in the dark.'[5]

The French government, and Monnet himself, an Anglophile of more than thirty years' standing, would have liked Great Britain to be among the countries attending a conference whose purpose would be to establish the High Authority. That anyway is the version propounded by Monnet when he came to write his memoirs years later. But among those who, in accordance with Monnet's secret tactics, had been kept in the dark was the British government. René Massigli, the French Ambassador in London, a public servant of great distinction and experience, was instructed to inform the British Foreign Secretary, Ernest Bevin, only a few hours before Schuman made the plan public at his press conference on 9 May.[6] While doing as he was told, Massigli was extremely suspicious of the methods employed, the more so when it emerged that Dean Acheson, the US Secretary of State, who was in Paris on 7 May, had been made party to the plan two days before the French government itself was informed. Was this a piece of Franco-American collusion at the expense of the British? Massigli's fears were soon confirmed. Bevin was predictably very annoyed at being confronted with what seemed to be a *fait accompli*. He accused Acheson, by now in London, of cooking up the whole plan with Schuman.

Massigli also discovered during the course of a visit to London by Monnet at this time that in Monnet's view any government

---

* Mayer could lay claim to an impressively long-standing commitment to the European idea. In 1943 in Algiers, he had prepared, at the request of de Gaulle, a study of a possible future federation of Western Europe.

agreeing to participate in negotiations on the French plan would have to commit itself in advance to the principles of the plan.* By this time hot under the collar, Massigli protested that there was not a politician in London – i.e. of any party – who could accept, blindfold, such a commitment. He was of course entirely right, for the Labour government could not bring itself to make, as the French insisted, a prior commitment to something which did not exist, whose consequences were unknown and whose practical impact had yet to be defined. Notes and telegrams shuttled to and fro across the Channel, but to no avail. British reluctance (fully shared by the Conservative opposition) to become involved in the construction of a Europe where some decisions would escape the veto of national governments was unshakeable, and was to remain so for at least another ten years.† At a less lofty level, British objections were also based on practical considerations. As Herbert Morrison, who for some of this time was standing in for the ailing Bevin, put it, 'The Durham miners wouldn't like it.'[7]

Formulae were floated which would help to draw Britain into the negotiation, but in a special, reserved position. Monnet would have none of this: 'To consent to British participation on those terms of a special position', he advised the French government, 'would be to resign ourselves in advance to the substitution of the French proposal by a concept which would be no more than a caricature of it . . . Soon, there would no longer be rules in common, nor the independence of the High Authority.' In other words, Monnet suspected that London's only interest in the negotiations to establish a coal and steel community would be to water down French designs for a degree of supranational control. He may well have been right.

---

* Massigli seems by this time to have abandoned any effort to keep his temper over Monnet's tactics. He is said to have accused him and his team, on their arrival in London, of behaving like an elephant in a china shop: 'You've broken up everything and now you ask me to repair the damage.' (Massigli, *Une comédie des erreurs* (1978), p. 203.
† The records (*Documents on British Policy Overseas*, Series 2, vol. I, pp. 75–6) reveal a sharp difference in interpretation of the Schuman Plan as between the Foreign Office and the British Embassy in Paris. The former thought it hastily conceived and inadequately thought-out. The Ambassador in Paris, Sir Oliver (later Lord) Harvey, found it a bold step forward, a turning-point in European and world affairs, a startling and revolutionary proposal 'which must not be allowed to fail'. The verdict of history leaves no doubt as to who was right.

In any event, he saw that this would ruin any possibility of realising the Schuman Plan as originally conceived.

The gap was unbridgeable. Indeed, Massigli was not the only person to suspect, rightly or wrongly, that Monnet's conduct of the affair had been carefully calculated to ensure British abstention from the negotiations, thus making it far easier to attain his aims. 'The feeling is growing', wrote the *Economist* in mid-June, 'that France has been less than loyal towards her British partner.' Many prominent Frenchmen regretted this development, for another of the constant strands in French thinking about Germany consisted of a wish to offset German power with British support. But as that could not be won on acceptable terms, those countries – West Germany, Italy and the Benelux trio – which had accepted the French plan as first proposed, went ahead with France and negotiated the treaty. It was finally signed on 18 April 1951 and ratified by the French National Assembly eight months later, by the comfortable majority of 377 for, 235 against.

The process of ratification did not go altogether smoothly. Apart from the predictable disapproval of the Communists, many Socialists were doubtful: Jules Moch kept the flag of *laïcité* flying by pointing to the dangers of a Europe dominated by the Vatican – i.e. the Christian Democrat axis being forged between Schuman and Adenauer and the Gasperi government in Italy. Monnet, the man usually reported to be capable of persuading almost everybody of almost anything, showed up curiously badly in a parliamentary setting. Summoned to appear before a parliamentary committee to explain and defend the ECSC treaty, he seemed to forget its details.[8] For him, the father of the treaty, now signed by its six participants, there was nothing left to explain. His natural field of action was behind the scenes, not in the public arena.

In the end, the treaty somewhat trimmed the supranational status of the High Authority, but enough of it remained to provide – this was Monnet's purpose all along – a stepping-stone to more elaborate and far-reaching European institutions. Even more than its importance as an experiment in international organisation, the story of the European Coal and Steel Community is a reminder of what, amid the shifting sands of the Fourth Republic, a few determined men could achieve. The Massiglis and Petsches of the world might suspect and dislike Monnet's methods and ambitions, but only a fool could deny his effectiveness in getting results, or question the value of the Schuman Plan as the means of burying the hatchet between France and Germany. In the twenty months between the plan's inception and the ratification by Paris of the consequent treaty, the government fell and was replaced by another no less than five times (if the episode in 1950 is included, when Queuille formed a government that lasted only two days before being strangled at birth by an adverse vote in the National Assembly). Yet throughout this time, the work of putting flesh upon the bones of this French-conceived and entirely novel animal went on more or less uninterruptedly. The irony was that while Schuman, Monnet and others who thought like them believed that they, and the German government in Bonn, had laid the unshakeable foundations for Franco-German reconciliation, a far sterner and less easily resolved test was shortly to dominate and ultimately to poison the whole of French political life: it was called German rearmament.

But before that, and in a way that guaranteed trouble in the future, the Fourth Republic was in difficulties over its colonial affairs, in particular in North Africa. There, Tunisia and Morocco were French protectorates, their internal sovereignty recognised by France, while Algeria, divided into three departments, was legally and constitutionally considered an extension of metropolitan France. In all three territories, the influence of the *colons* – white settlers or government or municipal employees of French nationality though often not of French origin – was strikingly disproportionate to their numbers. In Tunisia, for example, though theoretically foreigners in a foreign country, they had become in fact privileged Tunisians, the more prominent of whom filled official positions at different levels of the Tunisian administration, and thus effectively helped to run the country. Dominating everything was the all-powerful figure of the French Resident-General, while ranged against him stood the Tunisian nationalist movement, the Neo-Destour, led by Habib Bourguiba, the future President of an independent Tunisia. As early as 1945, it had rejected a French programme of minimum reform and had taken its case to the Arab League and the United Nations. Agitation continued to grow. The liberal-minded Resident-General, Jean Mons, a Socialist and former *directeur de cabinet* of Léon Blum, sought in 1947 to introduce more Tunisians into the civil service and give more powers to the Prime Minister. But these measures met with fierce opposition from French officials, determined to maintain the system of direct administration.

Two years later, in 1949, Mons authorised the return from exile of Bourguiba. Though a supporter of close cooperation with France, the latter was scornful of the spirit of domination implicit in the concept of the French Union. 'It looks today', he had written from his Cairo exile in 1946, 'like a colossal manoeuvre of a colonialism at bay.' This was the unpromising legacy that the 1946 Constitution-makers in France had bequeathed, and Bourguiba, once back home, was quick to proclaim the Neo-Destour's aim of universal suffrage and a democratic Constitution. In April 1950, he presented a seven-point plan to Paris for a change in the Protectorate status of Tunisia. For a moment, it seemed as if statesmanship was going to prevail. In June, Robert Schuman, the Foreign Minister, spoke in a speech at Thionville of 'independence which is the final objective for all the territories within the framework of the French Union'. The speech had been drafted for the Minister within the Quai d'Orsay. Whether or not he really meant what he was saying – people could never tell with Schuman, so interior and cryptic was his thought process – his words evoked such a sharp reaction from the Right, the military and the jingo press that the Bidault government was forced to abandon (assuming it ever seriously considered adopting) this conciliatory approach.

Some administrative reforms were introduced, but predictably failed to satisfy either the nationalists or the Europeans. The indigenous Tunisian authorities, increasingly set upon achieving complete sovereignty, complained of 'French timidity and the systematic obstruction of certain senior French officials'. In a mirror reaction, the French in Tunisia, by now encouraged and supported by the RPF, did all they could to resist anything which could pave the way to internal autonomy, seen as the slippery slope to independence. Given the differences within the government majority in Paris, there was in fact no French policy, in the sense of a consistent government line calculated to ensure the best outcome for France. *Colon* interests, represented for the most part not by rich industrialists or businessmen but by '*petits blancs*', fought hard, with the help of the Paris colonialist lobbies, to safeguard their privileges and impede the course of 'Tunisisation' of the administration. Against them, the Socialist party in France supported the idea of independence for Tunisia within a French framework, whatever that formula might mean in practice.

In the other Protectorate, Morocco, General Juin (he had not yet been created a Marshal) had been Resident-General since 1947, in succession to a liberal-minded predecessor who had fallen foul of the local French administrators and *colons*. Juin's instructions from Paris were to bring about a form of Franco-Moroccan co-sovereignty which would effectively confirm the French living in Morocco in their political rights. Such a policy was guaranteed to meet with opposition from the Sultan who, while not anti-French (there was a parallel with Bourguiba here), had been encouraged by his meeting with President Roosevelt in 1943 to espouse the cause of reform and nationalism. Juin was told to stand no nonsense; if the Sultan were to prove recalcitrant, then either his voluntary abdication must be effected or his forcible dethronement engineered. The situation thus created was bound to ensure trouble. Caught between the pressures of the nationalists and those of the Resident-General, the Sultan leant more and more towards the Istiqlal nationalist movement, so abhorrent to French administrators in Rabat and their friends and supporters in Paris.

Himself a product of French–Algerian stock, Juin soon fell out with the Sultan. In November 1950 the latter appealed directly, and unsuccessfully, to Auriol to modify Morocco's status as a Protectorate, and shortly afterwards Juin, mindful of his instructions, delivered an ultimatum: renounce the Istiqlal or abdicate. To back up the pressure, the cooperation of the powerful Pasha of Marrakesh, El Glaoui, was called in aid. A march on Rabat of 'loyal' Berber horsemen was the result, demanding the Sultan's submission and threatening deposition. In the end, he had to yield to Juin's ultimatum, but the nationalists knew this had been done under constraint. The effect was to strengthen rather than demolish the force of Moroccan nationalism.

French left-wing opinion saw clearly enough what had happened. A cartoon in *Franc-Tireur* depicted the 'Berber horsemen' ludicrously got up in the uniform of the French CID – the Sûreté: bowler-hat, large moustache, large boots and untidy umbrella. But the divided Pleven Cabinet had shown itself unwilling (or unable) to impose any other policy, and in many right-wing circles the humiliation of the Sultan was seen as a salutary move. After that, there could be no reconciliation between the sovereign and the authoritarian Resident-General. His recall, in August 1951, made no difference, because he was largely instrumental in choosing his own successor, General Augustin Guillaume, who was

just as imperious and dismissive of Moroccan nationalist sentiment.

These colonial difficulties were in part created, and certainly
increased, by the habits of High Commissioners, Residents-General
and senior French officials in Indochina, Tunisia, Morocco or almost
any other imperial outpost, who tended to obstruct, to apply their
own ideas, and to disregard or on occasion disobey their instructions
(where they had any) from Paris. Shortly after he ceased to be
Foreign Minister in 1953, Robert Schuman complained of these
tendencies in an article in *La Nef*, a high-brow publication edited by
Lucie Faure, wife of the Radical politician Edgar Faure. Describing
the position of the Residents-General in Tunis and Rabat, he noted:
'They have a vast and varied scope for initiative, which they are
always tempted to extend, particularly when their views and those
of the French population coincide. They interpret instructions from
Paris and decide how they are to be carried out.' He concluded with
the thought that 'No important reform affecting relations between
France and Morocco is possible without a return to precise ideas
of responsibility and hierarchic subordination.'[9] Schuman was in a
position to know what he was talking about. In singling out this
preference in overseas trouble spots to take matters into their own
hands, he was identifying the weakness in the State's authority which
characterised the Fourth Republic, and of which Vincent Auriol and
other perceptive observers were so painfully aware.

An earlier example of this, and of the problems for French
colonial policy posed by the presence in colonial territories of
the *colon* element, was Madagascar. There, the French authorities
after the war had initiated political reforms as a result of which a
moderate nationalist party, pledged to bring about independence
within the French Union, had come into being. This process was
overtaken by events when, in March 1947, a popular uprising
of appalling ferocity led to the murder of many Europeans and
pro-French Madagascans and the burning of their houses. There
were only 37,000 *colons* among a total population of 4,200,000, but
so embattled did they understandably feel that they went on the
rampage. The original rebellion was undeniably cruel in its effects;
the repression, carried out by the *colons* on their own account and
by French troops – an expeditionary force of 18,000 men arrived in
April – was horrific. Nearly 90,000 Madagascans were slaughtered
and native populations uprooted. The French commander stamped

out the rebellion with savage thoroughness, effectively nipping in the bud for many years to come all prospects for the peaceful advance of the island towards independence.

In Paris, only the Communists, then still in the government, protested against the repression. The blame for the rebellion was placed by the colonial authorities upon the moderate nationalist party (who denied responsibility), and the Communists and the overseas representatives in the National Assembly were the only deputies to vote against the lifting of parliamentary immunity from the three Madagascan deputies, which was effected without their case being heard. Their trial as alleged instigators of the rebellion opened in July 1948, when two of them were condemned to death (the sentences were remitted) and one to life imprisonment.

Another Madagascan, not a deputy, who had confessed to his part in the rebellion and then retracted, on the grounds that he had been tortured, was sentenced to death after a separate trial. Although the French High Commissioner in Madagascar – Pierre de Chevigné, a prominent member of the MRP – was advised that this man's presence at the trial of the deputies could be desirable, he ordered the sentence to be carried out forthwith. In Paris, Auriol remonstrated strongly but too late. Though de Chevigné did his best to restrain the excesses of the local hard-liners, he provided, in the case of the hurried execution, another example of the man on the spot acting on his own initiative at the expense of his own government's wishes. In French public opinion, the Madagascan affair aroused little interest, apart from indignation at the murder of Europeans. This was fully understandable, but it meant that *colon* interests had it all their own way.

In Algeria, the story was similar. There, in May 1945, faced with the rising tide of Arab national nationalism, the French authorities took what proved to be the unwise step of deporting one of its leaders, Messali Hadj. Protest riots followed, and at Sétif, in the Constantine region, Muslim nationalist demonstrators murdered more than 100 Europeans with great brutality. The ensuing repression, if not so appalling as in Madagascar, was still horrific enough: French-controlled forces devastated the region, killing between 6,000 and 8,000 Muslims. In metropolitan France, concerned with its own problems and with the end of the war in Europe, the event was inadequately reported. But its impact on the future of Muslim–French relations in Algeria was pernicious and long-lasting, and provided the worst possible background for the new statute for Algeria. Passed by the National Assembly only after considerable delay due to lack of agreement, this sought to establish an Algerian Assembly of 120 delegates, half of whom were chosen by an elected European college consisting of 460,000 citizens of French status, plus 58,000 assimilated Muslims, and half by an elected Muslim college made up of 1,400,000 unassimilated Muslims.*

A Socialist deputy and former Governor-General of Algeria, Maurice Viollette, who before the war had tried unsuccessfully under the Blum Popular Front government to give the Muslims a squarer deal, now taunted *colon* interests who wanted to bar the first, European, college to Muslims. These interests had not been so concerned, he pointed out, on the battlefields of the Second World War, when Muslim components of the French Army shared with Europeans the same experience of fighting and dying under fire. His oratory failed to prevail against the weight of opinion in the Assembly. So did that of an Algerian Muslim member, representing a moderate nationalist movement, who warned that 'We are in the majority, we have our own personality and we have paid the blood tax' – another reference to the sacrifices of war. The statute, as voted, did introduce some much-needed reforms. It foresaw votes for women, new programmes for education and an end to the prevailing, undemocratic, system of local representation (*communes mixtes*). It also was intended to begin the move away from assimilation. But itself the result of compromise in the National Assembly, the new legislation failed to appeal either to the Muslims, who were hostile or indifferent, or to the Europeans, already alarmed by the successes of the nationalists in the municipal elections of October 1947.

In fact, they need not have worried. The statute, which did go some modest way towards installing democracy, was never properly implemented. Seven months later (February 1948) the liberal Governor-General, Yves Chataigneau, an object of hatred by the *colons*, was replaced by the Socialist but authoritarian Marcel-Edmond Naegelen, who proceeded to master-mind a massive electoral fraud.[10] As a result, the elections produced results which

---

* 'Assimilated', in this context, meant 'meritorious' Muslims – civil servants, recipients of higher education, holders of the Legion of Honour, leading ex-servicemen, etc.

exceeded even the hopes of the *colons*: in the first, European college, the Right, the Centre and the RPF won fifty-four of the sixty seats; in the second, the genuine nationalists and the Socialists managed to win only nineteen seats, the remaining forty-one going to 'administration candidates' – i.e. French stooges or '*béni-oui-ouis*' in French political slang. Most of the statute, with its provisions for agrarian, educational and other serious reforms, was pigeon-holed, and Algeria continued in effect to be ruled from the offices of the Governor-General in Algiers and from the Ministry of the Interior in Paris. From now on, the nationalists knew that if their aims were to be achieved, it could not be done within the law.

Apart from a very few, mostly Socialist, deputies with specialist knowledge and deep convictions, or small reviews concerned with colonial questions, notably the left-wing Catholic *Témoignage Chrétien*, French politicians and public opinion generally had no difficulty in closing their eyes and refusing to recognise that traditional colonial empires – French as well as British and Dutch – could never be what they were before the war. (Only the Portuguese managed, at least for the time being, to keep the lid screwed down on their overseas possessions.) Where French sight could discern it, the rising tide of nationalism was seen as something to be withstood and beaten back, with force where necessary or with political trickery, as in Algeria. The great exception to these generalisations was the Communist party and its constituents. Support for liberation movements in colonial and subordinate territories was an essential part of Soviet and Communist ideology and tactics. That very fact, now that the Cold War was an established element of international life, contributed to French resistance to colonial change or any diminution in French sovereignty.

The war years of French humiliation and defeat already provided a strong motive – largely lacking in British thinking about decolonisation – for pretending that the French empire, even if it was now called the French Union, was an unchanged and unchangeable feature from the pre-war landscape. To that pretence was added the pressures of *colon* interests. The *colons* may have been short-sighted, illiberal, obstinate. But they had, as they saw it, their rights, which in many cases they had enjoyed for generations, and they were not going to see these threatened with erosion if they could help it. And apart from the justice or otherwise of their case, the numbers created a political problem which could not be wished away. The British withdrawal from India would have been a very different affair had 10 per cent of the population there had British status, which was the proportion of French *colons* in Algeria.

These factors helped to build up a large and powerful resistance to change, transcending French political differences and factions. The arguments could even be elevated into a special form of *realpolitik*. Nobody could deny the role that the outlying parts of the French empire had played during the war, either by adding to the strength of the Free French cause, or giving Vichy a certain amount of leverage vis-à-vis the Germans. From those memories, it was but a small step to the assumption that France's claim to be a great power rested upon *la France d'outre-mer*. A former French diplomat recalls Paul Auriol, the President's son and a member of the Elysée staff, saying to him: '*La France n'est rien sans ses colonies.*'[11]

Such sentiments were shared across a very broad spectrum of opinion. During the war, Pétain lauded 'the Empire' and the way in which the native populations, 'part of our responsibilities as well as of our trials, have shown themselves to be true sons of a common country'. Only a few weeks after the war ended, a black delegate from French Guyana, Gaston Monnerville (later to become President, or Speaker, of the Council of the Republic, the upper house of the French parliament), told the Consultative Assembly that 'without the Empire, France today would be no more than a liberated country . . . Thanks to her Empire, France is a victorious country.'[12] It is not surprising, in this atmosphere, if decolonisation, in post-war France, was a word little used or thought about.

One of those Socialist deputies who did see further than the end of his self-interested or deluded nose was Pierre-Olivier Lapie, whom we have already met, as a Minister, quizzically observing the goings-on at a typical Cabinet meeting. In the autumn of 1949, as an official French delegate to the Fourth UN General Assembly in New York, he had to defend the French Union against its international critics, particularly those from what is today called the Third World. This he did as best he could, but was well aware of the mounting anti-colonial pressures, especially from the US. He wrote to Robert Schuman in Paris, warning him of the urgent need to make political progress in French African possessions and in Madagascar, to breathe life into the organisms of the French Union, and to achieve self-government in Tunisia and Morocco. He never received any answer, although Schuman himself was known to be sympathetic to such arguments. As for Lapie's generally enlightened views on what should be the future of the French Union, he had to admit that in 1949, there was no one to agree with him, even in his own party.[13]

Unpromising though all this was, and boding ill for the future, at least the inherent dangers for France were not immediate. This could not be said of Vietnam, where the situation was fast deteriorating. The Bao Dai régime, starved of all real power by French administrators on the spot as well as by successive governments in Paris, began to look more and more like a French puppet administration, and an ineffective one at that, unable to stamp out the prevailing corruption or to win or retain the respect of the French Army upon which the régime depended. Very few people, either in Saigon or Paris, had any further faith in a military solution.

To that extent, the Revers report, whatever misuse was made of it, had hit the nail on the head. The military cost of the continuing and undeclared war – technically it was still an operation against 'rebels' – was becoming ever more burdensome, in terms of men and money. Every year, the equivalent of three-fifths of an average annual graduation of cadets from the military academy of St Cyr – more than 320 officers – were being killed, and the other two-fifths wounded.[14] At the end of 1949 and the beginning of 1950, Mao Tse-tung's establishment of power in China and his recognition of Ho Chi Minh's government brought important material support for the Vietminh, as also did recognition by the USSR, determined not to be left out of a classic colonial struggle. With the coming of the Korean war, however, French efforts in Vietnam suddenly became part of the worldwide and (according to Western values) God-blessed struggle against Communism.

From now on, there were hopes and prospects that the financial burden could be partially offset by the arrival of American arms and money. The aim of a French military solution, never a realistic one, could now be replaced by a strategy of holding on until American help arrived. But this change could not immediately ease the situation on the ground, which took a sharp turn for the worse in the autumn of 1950. The Revers recommendation that the posts on the Chinese frontier should be evacuated was approved by the Committee of National Defence in Paris, but hesitations, muddle, orders and counter-orders meant that the command to withdraw from the most distant of the posts, Cao Bang, was not given until

September 1950. By then, it was too late. The retreat turned into
a rout. More than 2,500 of the 3,500 garrison of the fortress were
killed or taken prisoner. By the end of October, the French had lost
the other posts, suffered more heavy casualties and been driven out
of northern Tonkin.

For the first time since the start of the war, French domestic
opinion, in the face of these disasters, began to show an interest. In the ensuing debate in the National Assembly, the Pleven
government was blamed on all sides, though its critics were divided
between those who wanted a stronger prosecution of the war and
those, including Mendès-France, who argued for negotiations. The
debate ended with a typically vague motion giving the government
a mandate to 'reinforce the Army as required' but also stressing
the international and anti-Communist nature of the struggle – an
indirect bid for American aid.

In addition to these divisive factors, there was the incessant
propaganda mounted by the Communists against what they called
'*la sale guerre*'. This was motivated by a wish both to support
Ho Chi Minh in what had become a hot part of the Cold War
and to stir up French opinion against the policy of its leaders to
commit France to the Western bloc. The campaign fitted neatly
into the larger, international, Communist-inspired campaign of the
Peace Movement, of which Picasso's famous dove was the universal
symbol. Picasso also helped to create a Communist 'martyr' with
his drawing of Henri Martin, a young naval petty officer who, after
serving in Indochina, returned home and set about persuading his
service comrades that the war was unjust. He was condemned in
1950 by a military court to five years' detention, and '*Libérez Henri
Martin*' became from then on a familiar rallying cry at Communist
and Communist-sympathising gatherings. Sartre contributed a long
preface to a book about the young man.

It is perhaps surprising, looking back, that the '*sale guerre*' campaign did not have more effect outside its natural constituency
of the Communists and their friends (unlike the Peace Movement, which commanded wide support in non-Communist and
Communist circles alike). The answer was that the Indochinese
war, where it was not simply ignored by public opinion, was seen
as a contribution to world freedom or as a continuation of the
French *mission civilisatrice*, a time-honoured formula for justifying
the French presence overseas.

Meanwhile Juin, who before the reverses in the north had been sent from his Residency in Morocco to make a special report on the Vietnam situation, produced his own conclusions. For him, to negotiate with Ho Chi Minh would be a sign of impotence whose effect would be enormous in 'overseas' France. He recommended, re-echoing the disgraced Revers, withdrawing from the mountainous zone in the north, a concentration of efforts and deployment, changes in the high command and speeding up the creation of a native Vietnamese army. Faced with this grave situation, the government in Paris embarked on a marathon series of meetings which in many respects typify the difficulty experienced by Third Force administrations in arriving at any important decision. One MRP minister argued that it was impossible to abandon Indochina, with all that that would mean for other parts of the French Union. (This, with special reference to French North Africa, was a constantly recurring theme.) Pleven, the Prime Minister, said that help – he meant men as well as material – must be provided by France's allies or else national servicemen must be sent to reinforce the expeditionary corps. Schuman, still at the Quai d'Orsay, was exceptionally outspoken for a man usually of such calmness of temperament:

> These contradictions and confusions among the military, not only over there [in Indochina] but here in Paris, have got to stop. We expected, from our arrangements with Bao Dai, to turn Vietnamese opinion, as well as that of our neighbours and allies, in our favour. We have not done so. Let us have the courage to realise this. Before getting involved in peace negotiations, we have got to define clearly our political and military objectives.

In the ensuing discussion, at least three different courses of action were envisaged, and finally it was decided to appoint General de Lattre de Tassigny as supreme commander and High Commissioner in Indochina. He was a fine officer with a magnificent military record, and a flamboyant, even theatrical, personality, a form of French Field Marshal Montgomery. (Because of his tendency to play to the gallery, he was known to the wags as General de Théâtre de Marigny, a prominent Paris theatre.) These febrile discussions ended with Vincent Auriol, in his no-nonsense way, pointing out that the agreements with Bao Dai (meant to signify independence for Vietnam) had not been loyally carried out on the French side, and that there were now more French officials in Indochina than formerly. It was the old story: when the incoherence in Paris did lift long enough for a clear and positive policy to be defined, that policy was frustrated by interested parties on the spot.

De Lattre's energy and charisma did much to re-establish the position and restore morale to French forces. By June 1951, General Giap had to abandon his thrust against the Red River delta and revert to guerrilla tactics. But to achieve this result, de Lattre required urgent reinforcements. They could be supplied only by despatching national servicemen – the preferred choice of the General Staff – or by robbing North Africa of some of its garrisons. By this time (early 1951), a general election in France was in the offing and Queuille, who in March had succeeded Pleven as Prime Minister after the latter resigned because of difficulties over electoral reform, was unwilling to run the political risk of requiring conscripts to serve in Indochina. Instead, North Africa was milked: eleven regular infantry battalions, three armoured regiments, four artillery units and two engineer battalions were 'lent' to de Lattre, on the understanding that they would be returned by July 1952. In the event, only two battalions came back.[15] Help was also forthcoming from the US: de Lattre effectively 'sold' the Indochinese war to the Americans, who from the end of 1951 onwards began to pour in equipment for the French expeditionary corps as well as for the new Vietnamese army.

De Lattre had certainly performed near-miracles, and his untimely death from cancer in January 1952 was a heavy blow. But even his successes had not brought the war any nearer to an ending, and by the time he left for Paris and his death-bed he had shot his bolt and his officers were openly critical of him and his authoritarian ways. The metropolitan French contingent in the expeditionary corps – 54,000 officers and volunteer other ranks, serving alongside 120,000 colonial troops and members of the Foreign Legion and 260,000 Vietnamese forces – had nothing but contempt for the political ditherings of the ministers and parliamentarians in Paris. Their vacillations were well described by Michel Debré, a Gaullist member of the right-wing opposition, in a speech in the Council of the Republic at the end of 1953: 'The French people', he said, 'feel that this war is out of their control and in the hands of destiny. . . . They have the impression . . . that France does not know what she wants and that we are fighting aimlessly, without a clear objective. What is painful is not so much the fact of fighting and accepting sacrifices; it is that we are apparently fighting without any goal.'

In 1957, three years after the war had ended with a humiliating defeat for France, General Henri Navarre, the last Commander-in-Chief, voiced the same complaint. The first reason for the defeat, he wrote, from which all others flowed, was 'the absence of a policy: from start to finish, our leaders never knew what they wanted or, if they knew, were incapable of stating it. They never dared to tell the country that there was a war in Indochina. They could neither commit the nation to war nor to make peace. . . . They were capable only of taking day-to-day bastard solutions which were always overtaken by events.'[16] Mendès-France could not have put it more strongly.*

But these strictures against the politicians, however well-justified, should in fairness have been applied to the nation as a whole, of whom its political leaders were but the faithful reflection. If there was a conspiracy of silence about the Indochinese war, it was one readily accepted by those conspired against. At times, it seemed indeed as though Paris was determined to encourage ignorance of or indifference to this distant war. No record of honours awarded in the campaign appeared in the *Journal Officiel* after 1948, and although the status of war veterans was granted in 1952 to men who had served in Indochina, the ruling was not applied until after France had withdrawn from the war.[17]

Such short-sightedness simply fed the malaise in the Army, a malaise which had so profound an influence in the events of 1958 that killed the Fourth Republic. It went back to the defeat of 1940, to the occupation years and the role of the Resistance, and to the post-Liberation period. In 1946, the demobilisation of officers and NCOs made necessary by budgetary economies meant that 45 per cent of the former and 40 per cent of the latter had to leave the Army. A year later, the Ramadier government increased Army resentment by linking service salaries with those of the civil service, in a way that was both financially disadvantageous and humiliating. A second lieutenant with several years' service stood

* Laniel, Prime Minister at the time of Dien Bien Phu, also wrote a book, *Le Drame indochinois* (Paris, Plon, 1957), attacking both Navarre's strategy and his conduct.

at 250 on the wage index, compared with 282 for a third-category postal employee and 310 for an assistant magistrate. 500 was the index figure for a lieutenant-colonel with twenty-four years' service, while a second-category departmental customs director stood at 600.[18] After the establishment of NATO forces, the discrepancies between French Army pay scales and those prevailing among the allied forces became painfully evident. Worse still from the point of view of military morale in Indochina itself was the fact that the Vietminh had got hold of the leaked Revers report and had managed to reproduce 2,000 copies of its military portions, thus proving that French national security bore closer resemblace to a sieve than a safe.

Poor pay and reduced status may not have been the principal cause of service resentment, but they certainly added to the feeling that the nation as a whole had little respect for or interest in its Army. 'Condemned to fighting and losing unpopular wars, the French officer watched with mounting resentment as his prestige dropped from an already depressed level in 1945 to a position of social neglect and scorn unknown to his rank since the Bourbon restoration.'[19]

This sense of isolation from French society found a parallel in the feeling of physical remoteness created by service in Indochina. Officers returning on leave often felt themselves to be strangers among their own people and longed to be back with their units in the Indochina countryside, living the life of straightforward military values. Jean Lartéguy, a former paratroop officer who later wrote some highly readable military novels, gives vivid expression to these feelings as he describes a party of officers returning home after their release from Vietminh prison camps:

> The paradise of which they had dreamed so much in the camps was slowly approaching and already they no longer wanted it. They dreamed of another paradise that all of them were thinking of. They were not suffering sons who were returning home to have their wounds cleaned, but strangers. Bitterness mounted within them.[20]

The French Army in Indochina, above all some of its incompetent and disobedient generals, and the irresolute politicians in Paris, must bear some of the blame for the débâcle. The Revers report had said as much. But Lartéguy's is the psychological background which must constantly be borne in mind when putting into perspective the events of 1958, or the scene at the Arc de Triomphe described in the opening pages of this book.

Nevertheless, despite the worsening situation in Indochina and continuing instability at home, the Fourth Republic, having shown in 1947 and 1948 that it knew how to fight off the Communist challenge, continued successfully to demonstrate that it could withstand the pressures from both extremes, Gaullist as well as Communist, while at the same time enabling France to press on, notwithstanding the setbacks caused by the effects of the Korean war, with her economic recovery.* From the fall of the first Queuille government in early October 1949 until the general election in June 1951, the Third Force went on holding the centre ground, which was the only possible ground to occupy, seeing that there was no clear-cut right-wing or 'liberal' majority ('liberal' in the Continental sense, meaning laissez-faire, non-*dirigiste* economic policies) and no clear left-wing one either, given the permanent political exile of the Communists.

Most of the instability – i.e. the successive collapse of governments and their replacement, sometimes after weeks of political vacuum, by a team of the same people – was due to the Socialists. Increasingly at odds with some or all of their partners over *laïcité*, economic policy, military credits for Indochina and the defence of civil service wage levels, ever more conscious that they were consistently outflanked on the left by the Communists, they helped to bring down Queuille in 1949, Bidault, his successor, in 1950 and Queuille again in his short-lived and unsuccessful attempt to form a government to succeed Bidault. At one point they left the government (Bidault's), after serving for three months in it, because of wages policy, thus apparently breaking the solidarity of the Third Force. But they were back again as usual in the succeeding government which René Pleven managed to form, still opposed to 'liberal' economic policies, still the upholders of *laïcité*, still reluctant to be associated so closely with the Right, but possessed once again of the key post of Minister of

---

* As a result of the Korean war, the US and to a lesser extent Britain embarked on a massive rearmament programme. Because of stockpiling, a big rise in the price of raw materials threatened the recovery of all Western economies.

Labour, which had become as much a part of the Socialist heritage as the Ministry of Foreign Affairs had come to belong to the MRP.

It was at this time – July 1950, within a year of the general election – that Vincent Auriol, walking one day with his quick, light infantry, step in the park at Rambouillet with Jacques Dumaine, gave the latter a potted but invaluable analysis of the political and parliamentary situation:

> The present Assembly, with its extreme left opposition some one hundred and eighty strong, has become a distorted reflection of the country. The working classes are not adequately represented in the government, especially as the Communists do them a disservice by remaining constantly in opposition. On the right, the irreducible band of Gaullists [in fact, only twenty-four deputies in the Assembly elected in 1946 accepted the Gaullist whip although there were about eighty in general agreement with Gaullist ideas] force the machinery of parliament even further out of gear; if we subtract the strength of this permanent deliberate opposition from the total membership of the Assembly, there remains only 380 deputies available to carry out the duties of legislation. Among them must be found the future rulers of the country. The margin is too narrow.[21]

Auriol's arithmetic also helps to explain why the same names and faces kept popping up whenever 'new' governments were formed, like the members of a stage army who, having exited from one side of the stage, reappear presently from the opposite side. In view of the daily pressure and harassments to which the prime minister of this ill-assorted coalition was subject, those who accepted the charge, often more than once, must have been imbued either with a masochistic craving for total exhaustion or with a laudable sense of public duty. Four years later, speaking of his experiences as Prime Minister, Mendès-France told the National Assembly on 3 December 1954 of the way in which a government was 'nibbled at, undermined by arguments on matters of minor importance, lobby campaigns, frightful polemics . . . It is what is called "wearing out" [*usure*], in the ominous jargon of the technicians.'

He certainly had good reason to talk thus. A graphic account of the circumstances he was describing is given by one of his ministerial colleagues about the scene when Mendès was presiding

over a ministerial meeting in August 1954, called to discuss the
much-disputed treaty for the European Defence Community:

> The meeting lasted from 5.45 to 12.15, with an hour-and-a-half
> recess just before 10. It was extraordinarily passionate. Pathetic
> appeals from some followed protestations from others of their
> willingness to make personal sacrifices. The Prime Minister him-
> self, ill at ease in this atmosphere, was the victim of a veritable
> breakdown which required a brief interruption of work. 'I am not
> upset,' he repeated, 'I am exhausted . . . I cannot go on – it's
> inhuman.' I looked at him at the end of the session, slumped in
> his chair, his head forward, his features ravaged by fatigue, with
> large dark pouches under his eyes. . . . I was filled simultaneously
> with sympathy, pity and anxiety.[22]

Another head of government, Edgar Faure, complained of the
unfairness of the permanent state of warfare between the Prime
Minister and six hundred deputies: 'The deputy organises his life
as he pleases, he can get a substitute to vote for him, he can
dine, he can sleep. This relief is forbidden to the Prime Minister.' The surprising thing, Faure went on to say, was that it was
still possible to govern. 'Among all the tendencies of an unstable
government [the Prime Minister] is the catalyst. Only the policy
which he carries out is rarely his own. It is a continual compromise
between the wish to achieve everything and the fear of smashing
everything.'

The first legislature of the Fourth Republic (1946–51) drew to
a close in a flurry of pre-electoral activity. The coalition parties were
deeply divided upon the best way to amend the electoral system, but
as the elections came ever nearer, on one principle at least they were
agreed: the need to weaken the Communists without building up
the RPF. The 1946 electoral arrangements, if unchanged, would
achieve precisely the opposite. Six months of discussion led to no
less than eight different projects being rejected by the Assembly.
Faced with this impasse, the Prime Minister, Pleven, resigned in
March 1951 (with one honourable exception, Georges Bidault in
June 1950, all the prime ministers of this first legislature chose to
surrender – i.e. resign – rather than succumb in battle, in the sense of
being overturned by an absolute majority of the National Assembly,
as laid down by the Constitution). He was quickly succeeded by
the resilient Queuille, who managed with his legendary finesse to

steer through parliament a new electoral law designed to stymie the Gaullists and above all the Communists. It was a combination of proportional representation and first-past-the-post. Everywhere outside Paris, party lists of candidates could form alliances or *apparentements*. Party programmes remained distinct, but for the counting of votes and distribution of seats any such alliance winning an absolute majority of votes would carry all the parliamentary places in the constituency concerned. Within such an alliance seats were distributed according to PR. The system meant that the Third Force parties could combine and thus enjoy the advantage of size, which otherwise would have passed to the Communists and Gaullists.

These two parties naturally were indignant about the new law, which the Communists, when they were not calling it fascist, called a 'thieves' ballot'. (The ruling Christian Democrat party in Italy introduced the same electoral practice, for the same reasons.) It did indeed look like a device designed – rigged was a more usual criticism – to ensure the re-election of members of the centre parties. But the thinking that lay behind it could be justified by the circumstances. Had ordinary PR obtained, it is probable that the election result would have yielded up three more or less equal groups, Communists, Gaullists and Third Force parties. None of these would have had a majority, and though the result might accurately have reflected the divisions within national opinion, parliamentary government would have been impossible. Why not, the argument ran, enable the coalition majority to present itself at the polls as a more or less unified electoral choice? Which party and which politicians within it made use of this argument is not clear. No one seemed anxious to claim paternity for it. It appears to have come from within the MRP. The important thing is that it was finally approved by a parliamentary majority.

Against the advice of some of his most influential supporters, de Gaulle, faithful to his resolve to have nothing to do with the 'system' and also convinced of the dishonesty of the new law, ruled that Gaullist lists should not be allied to any others. If he had swallowed his pride and his scruples, and allowed Gaullist candidates to ally themselves with other, probably right-wing, lists, he might have stolen a march on the coalition by adopting its own tactics. But that, of course, would have meant compromising with the enemy. As for the Communists, no one was going to form an alliance with them in their pariah position.*

It is doubtful how much these political subtleties meant to the ordinary French man or woman in 1951. Ever since the Liberation, he or she had been far more preoccupied with the difficult business of living than with the manoeuvrings of political parties or the rise and fall of governments. In this, the French were no different from their European neighbours. The Cold War and its pressures, above all the possibility that it might turn into a hot war in which French territory would be fought over or, worse still, atomised, had indeed entered national consciousness. But on the home front, the same old problems – housing, food, the cost of living – were the predominant concern of most people.

The 15th of March 1951 was the last day for paying one's income tax, an experience far more real and painful than anything that might be going on at the Palais Bourbon. Prices were moving up again, which had everyone worried and talking of nothing else: since 1950, knitting wool had risen in price by 65 per cent, coffee by 55 per cent, pork chops by 50 per cent, workmen's overalls by 55 per cent. At the end of March, two weeks of strikes for more pay brought the transport system in Paris and then in most of France to a standstill. Unlike those of earlier years, these strikes were non-political and peaceful. People walked to work more or less uncomplainingly. Their minds, as they did so, were less on politics than on the prospect of having to walk home again in the evening.

---

* In a conversation with the author in Paris (December 1989), Jacques Chaban-Delmas, one of the leading Gaullists in the Fifties, made the claim that had the General allowed RPF candidates to form *apparentements* with other parties, the party would have swept the board and brought de Gaulle back to power, instead of his having to wait another seven years. Exceptionally, he allowed Chaban-Delmas, the mayor of Bordeaux, to use the *apparentement* system there, with the result that Gaullist lists enjoyed spectacular local victories. But unless the RPF had been so successful nationally as to win an outright majority of parliamentary seats, and thus be in a position to govern alone, this argument skims over the fact that the General would have had to cooperate in forming a government with some of the other parties. At no time (until 1958) did he give the least sign of permitting himself this indulgence. Chaban-Delmas was not incidentally quite correct in supposing that Bordeaux was the only place where RPF lists were allied with those of other parties. There were other examples of *apparentements* between the RPF and other lists, principally in the Catholic areas of western France.

The contrast between the supposed attraction of political ideologies and the real worries of the people was admirably summed up by a third year student at the National Institute for Political Studies, who said he had made a big mistake talking about Marxism, existentialism, Christianity. 'These are only words, only bla-bla-bla. They fade away when faced with a requirement infinitely more profound, more essential, more general, more demanding: the beefsteak.'[23]

Voting in the general election took place on 17 June 1951 – eleven years to the day since Pétain announced on the radio that France had fallen. The result showed, unsurprisingly, that the electorate was deeply divided. The Communists lost eighty seats, leaving them with 103, but this was because of the electoral system; their popular support of 5 million votes or 25 per cent was almost untouched. At the other end of the spectrum, the Gaullists (RPF) secured 4 million votes (21 per cent), many of them at the expense of the MRP, and won 118 seats, thus becoming the largest party in the new Assembly. The two parties which had been most prominent at the Liberation and had played the leading part in establishing the Fourth Republic fared worst: the MRP lost half their votes (mostly to the RPF) and the Socialists saw their previous 4½ million votes reduced to 3 million. But the *apparentement* system had paid off: the components of the Third Force – Socialists, MRP, Radicals and conventional right wing – had a narrow majority in the country (51.5 per cent) and a (notionally) comfortable majority of seats in the Chamber.

This was more than could be said of the Communists and Gaullists, in the highly unlikely event that they agreed on any lasting basis to make common cause. Had the electoral law remained unchanged, the picture would have been different, with Gaullists and Communists winning more than half of the seats. But however comforting theoretically these results were for the Third Force, the fact was that no majority existed among its parties for or against *dirigisme* or *laïcité* or European defence. The seeds of instability, far from being uprooted by the election results, had been embedded even more deeply in the soil of the Fourth Republic.

The most interesting outcome of the election was what appeared to be the Gaullist success. Electoral success it certainly was: though it had its greatest impact largely north of the Loire, and owed much to right-wing voters who had previously supported the MRP, it also was due to support from the working class, the 'little people' in country villages or the suburbs of large towns, for whom the person of the General, his attacks upon the status quo and the RPF's programme represented a force of protest and dissatisfaction and the promise of better things. To this extent, Gaullism was comparable to Bonapartism, a malady to which some sections of French opinion have been intermittently prone ever since the first Emperor spread his spell. But the glow of satisfaction at Gaullist headquarters in Paris did not last long. Indeed, it hardly dawned. According to a senior member of his staff, 'On the morning of 18 June 1951, the General knew that [the RPF] had not succeeded.'[24] One hundred and twenty seats were not enough.

Putting on the best face he could, de Gaulle, in a press conference he gave on 22 June, claimed the RPF's right to form a government as 'the French grouping which has won the greatest number of votes and . . . the greatest number of seats' (in Gaullist reckoning the Communists, whose share of the popular vote was larger, could not be considered a 'French party'). But once again he made it clear that the RPF would not participate in governments 'formed by others'. This was entirely consistent, but left the Gaullists, despite their 120 seats and their wide measure of support in the country, as effectively high and dry as they were before. Control of one-sixth of the National Assembly could provide no stepping-stone to power. Thus the 1951 triumph of the RPF was hollow and marked the beginning of its decline as a new and popular political current. In his memoirs, written years later,[25] Jacques Soustelle noted that 'the RPF, having failed to win all, could lose all. . . . A terribly difficult game was beginning: that of parliamentary Gaullism.' This observation, because of when it was made, is obviously not prophetic, but it is an accurate summary of what subsequently happened to organised Gaullism.

The transition from the first to the second legislature of the Fourth Republic provides a chance to explore the intellectual climate which prevailed from the Liberation onwards. The student with his witty and cynical references to the primordial status of the beefsteak undoubtedly spoke for a great mass of people. But France as the nation of ideas and concepts, where the noun 'intellectual' is almost a trade description (instead of, as in Britain, a term of mild abuse or at least a cause for suspicion), had not ceased to exist because of four years of war and occupation. Even before the country had been rid of the enemy, the intellectual tide began to flow strongly in the direction of Sartre and Marxism.

Here there is an important distinction to be made between Sartrian philosophy and the social *mores* deriving from it. Sartre's thoughts, first formulated in his key philosophical work *L'Être et le Néant* in 1943, harked back to Kierkegaard and Heidegger. Sartre postulated first of all a kind of void, or *néant*, into which man is born, then the possibility that man can emerge from this void – i.e. can exist – by exerting his own personal choice and responsibility, however 'absurd' such a choice will be. This in turn means becoming *engagé*, or committed to a role or tendency in social and political affairs, and this in its turn implied, in post-Liberation conditions, a commitment to a form of left-wing near-Communism. This analysis of problems of personal responsibility, especially in relation to political action, embraced and expressed all the Sartrian hatred of the bourgeois ethic that had permeated pre-war France and led to her decline.

Sartre's humanist, if austere, philosophy found a ready audience among the disenchanted post-war generations. Simone de Beauvoir, his inseparable companion, called the first autumn of peace (1945) '*l'offensive existentialiste*'. The impact was sustained by his review *Les Temps modernes*, founded in 1946 to publish the work of existentialist writers such as de Beauvoir and Maurice Merleau-Ponty. As well as being a serious, though frequently obscure, philosopher, Sartre through his novels, his journalism and his work as a playwright was in these post-war years very much the *maître-à-penser*, that typically French model of the intellectual as mentor and messenger. His message accorded well enough with the hopes for change which characterised the post-Liberation period.

But existentialism also assumed another, distorted, dimension. In the Paris bars and cafés around St Germain des Prés sprang up a movement (though that is too formal a word) of young people given to jazz, talk, the wearing of jeans, check shirts and sandals and a general air of licence and rebellion against the established order. These adolescents had little in common with Sartre's severe precepts. The singer Juliette Greco or still more the jazz trumpeter/singer/novelist/playwright Boris Vian (who did collaborate for a time with Sartre on *Les Temps modernes*) were their idols and symbols. But fanned by the winds of publicity and made notorious by the increasing number of tourists and other visitors who came to see their antics, these people declared themselves to be existentialists. It was not the first time in the history of French culture that philosophical ideas had given rise to a revolution in the style of living: at the end of the eighteenth century, the influence of the Encyclopedists brought about changes in habits, ways of thought and even moral values in a considerable cross-section of French society. But this was no comfort to Sartre. 'These young people have nothing to do with me,' he complained, 'and I have nothing to do with them. Very few among those who are called existentialists have ever heard of *L'Être et le Néant*. But the word sounds good, they have decided that it is a theory which exalts the taste for existence, for living one's life without constraint. All my enemies have exploited this mistake by accusing me of perverting the present generation of youth. This is now so widely believed that I am powerless to establish the truth.'[26]

This indignation was no doubt well founded, but it was also true that Sartre himself was a great frequenter of the Left Bank cafés, where in the company of Simone de Beauvoir and Albert Camus he would drink heavily and listen to Camus' fund of dirty stories. The brilliant editorialist of *Combat*, which was the post-Liberation intellectuals' required reading, Camus, once a faithful member of the Algerian Communist party, gradually fell out with Sartre, who he felt attached too much attention to politics – just as Sartre felt that Camus put excessive emphasis on universal moral values. As a novelist, Camus enjoyed far greater success and exerted far more popular influence than Sartre. *La Peste*, in which the onset of plague in wartime Algeria is presented as the image of the Occupation, sold 100,000 copies immediately and was translated into many languages. But politically the two men, Sartre and Camus, grew apart; the former was much more pro-Communist than the latter, who became indeed, as time went on, increasingly uncertain about where he stood; he told a colleague on *Combat* that if there existed a party of people who did not know what they thought, he would join it. One cannot get much further from *engagement* than that.

In fact, for all his fame, Camus' somewhat muddled philosophy, culminating in *L'Homme révolté* (1951), in which he spent a large amount of space attacking Marxism without providing many alternative forms of protest, left him intellectually isolated, even if he remained, for many of the younger generation, something between a lay saint and the keeper of moral conscience. Years later, when the Algerian war came to challenge French scruples, he could not, or would not, as an Algerian-born citizen, face up to the moral issues involved in what had become a cruel war of independence.

Despite the trivialisation of serious ideas by St Germain café society, existentialism, whatever the interpretation put upon it, did come to represent and express a mood that captured the irrationalism, the disillusionment, amounting in some cases to despair, which prevailed in much of Europe during the immediate post-war years. Despair did not however mean inaction. There was also the need for *engagement*, which meant, initially, rejecting bourgeois values in favour of Marxism – though Sartre, notwithstanding his violently anti-bourgeois stance and his avowed Marxism, never went all the way with the tenets of the Soviet-style Communist system, whatever his right-wing enemies might say. In some of his writings, he seemed to be seeking (like so many of his countrymen) a middle way between the Communist and 'Atlantic' systems. In *Qu'est-ce que la littérature?*[27] he wrote:

> All is lost if we want to choose between the powers who are preparing for war. To choose the USSR is to renounce formal freedoms without having the hope of acquiring the material ones . . . But after the victory of America, when the Communist party will be obliterated, with the discouraged, disoriented and, to risk a neologism, atomised working class, and with capitalism all the more merciless because it will be master of the world, do we believe that a revolutionary movement starting from nothing would have many chances?

He goes on to argue that literature's best chances are linked to the birth of a Socialist Europe, defined as 'a group of States organised democratically and collectively of which each one, while awaiting better things, would give up a part of its sovereignty for the benefit of the whole'.

This interesting premonition of 'Third Force' Europe could not and did not displace the Communist party as the principal object of *engagement*. With its Resistance record and its revolutionary aims, the party had established a strong claim for the sympathy and support of intellectuals. Though it drew massively for its backing on the working-class vote, it never ceased to be during these years a rallying point for the revolutionary temperament and tradition which is part of the French psyche. 'The Communist party produces almost invariably a number of traditional reflexes of great emotional power. . . . A large number of Frenchmen tend to identify the Communist party with freedom, peace, the nation [*la patrie*] and social justice.'[28]

Existentialism and the cult of Sartre may have been the visible preoccupation of the Paris cafés and university lecture halls, but the real sub-soil of almost all intellectual activity in the post-war years was made up of left and extreme-left trends of thought. It was virtually impossible to be considered as an intellectual unless you were known to share Communist, or at least near-Communist sympathies. Those within the charmed circle regarded those outside it as either idiots or *salauds* (bastards), who could not or would not accept what Sartre called '*l'horizon indépassable du Marxisme*'. 'The Communist world was so complete, with its daily and weekly newspapers, its cultural and political magazines, social affairs and rallies, national and international congresses (not to speak of its cell meetings), that one could believe it was the whole world.'[29] This belief was not of course shared by the larger part of the population – workers, employees, small farmers, agricultural labourers – who went their different ways far more preoccupied with the difficulties of daily life than with the ideological conceits of the intellectuals.

Among the latter, attitudes varied from the slavish loyalty of poets such as Aragon, one of the founders of surrealism, and Eluard, another surrealist who was one of the group around *Les Lettres Françaises*, to Picasso and the fellow-travelling Vercors (pseudonym of Jean Bruller). At the other end of the scale, signifying the complete rejection of Communism, stood François Mauriac and Raymond Aron, a friend in youth of Sartre, later to become a writer with *Le Figaro* and a professor at the Collège de France (roughly equivalent to a fellowship of All Souls), and a brilliant exponent of 'liberal' thought. Sartre himself temporarily broke with the Communist party with the success of his play *Les Mains sales* in 1948, but the coming of the Cold War caused him to adopt the stance of a loyal fellow-traveller and a supporter of the campaign against the Indochinese war. In an article ('*Les Communistes et la Paix*') written in the early Fifties, which contrasts strangely with his earlier thoughts about the unacceptability of either the Eastern or Western bloc, he argued that Communism was the only true mouth-piece for the French working class and that Marxism was the foundation of all culture.

Not that Sartre and his fellow-travelling followers had it all their

own way. As writer, thinker and politician, Léon Blum remained
a figure widely respected by the non-Communist Left. Moreover,
as the Forties drew to a close, Communist cultural domination was
challenged from another quarter. The onset of the Cold War and
the political isolation of the Communist party nurtured the growth
of anti-Communism as a counterweight to the appeal of Marxism.
The resulting division into two camps took on new emphasis as the
Kravchenko affair burst upon the public. In November 1947, *Les
Lettres françaises* published an article by its editor, Claude Morgan,
on the French translation of a book called *I Chose Freedom*. Victor
Kravchenko, the author, had been a member of a Soviet purchasing
commission in the US. There he defected and wrote (or, as his
opponents maintained, had written for him) a scorching description
of the Soviet system and especially its concentration camps where
enemies of the régime and countless innocent people were put
away. Morgan was among the fiercest of the critics, maintaining
that the book was the work of American intelligence and no more
than a piece of anti-Soviet propaganda. Kravchenko (and/or those
advising him) decided to take *Les Lettres françaises* to law.

The ensuing court case, which came on in Paris in January 1949
and lasted for three months, was widely reported and made a sensation. Morgan's witnesses included many well-known intellectuals
and Resistance figures – Communists and those in sympathy with
them, who refused to believe (or at least admit) the comparison
between Soviet and Nazi concentration camps. Kravchenko was
awarded damages, though they were only a fraction of what he
claimed. But the case served to illustrate the unbridgable chasm
that had opened up between the two camps.

Not that the anti-Communist bloc was composed solely of
solid, passionately convinced ranks of believers in Western –
i.e. American-inspired – values. At the very highest level, in the
Elysée itself, Vincent Auriol, though a confirmed anti-Communist
and a supporter of the Atlantic Treaty, was deeply opposed to a
general anti-Soviet campaign which could force the Russians into
a dangerous corner. Many thinking French men and women, while
accepting that France's destiny lay naturally and inevitably with the
West, regretted the division. Albert Camus was another who talked
about the necessity to find a third way between the two power blocs,
denouncing both capitalist and Marxist utopias. Though de Gaulle
later yielded to no one in his anti-Communism and his conception

of France as part of the Western world, he too, at least before the winds of the Cold War began to blow at gale force, did not like the prospect of being squeezed between two giants.* He talked in terms of Europe as a balancing element (he was subsequently to abandon entirely this earlier treatment of the US and USSR as equivalent entities, constantly naming the Soviet Union as the potential and likely aggressor).

None of this amounted to neutralism or international Third Force-ism. That school of thought was represented by *Le Monde* and its contributors, prominent among whom was Etienne Gilson. An authority on Thomas Aquinas and a member of the Académie Française, he was no Marxist or even Socialist, in fact not a political figure at all. Nonetheless he supported with eloquence and conviction – particularly in two articles which the paper published in the spring of 1949, at the time of the signature of the Atlantic Treaty – the thesis of national independence and the avoidance of association with either bloc. It was as much a pacifist as a neutralist argument; remaining aloof from the rivalries of the great powers was, so the reasoning went, the best chance of not getting drawn into a war started by one of them. Under its brilliant though gloom-filled editor, Hubert Beuve-Méry, this became for many years the editorial policy of *Le Monde*. It could not accurately be dubbed right-wing or left-wing, or indeed ideological in any strict sense of the term. And although *Le Monde*'s readership lay almost entirely among the educated classes, the appeal of neutralism, in the sense of not wishing to get drawn into a third world war, evoked a wide emotional response.

A pointer to the distress caused by the advent of the Cold War, and the consequent need for France to move into one of its camps, was a special number, published in 1951, of *La Nef*. It was devoted to the *mal du siècle*, meaning the apocalyptic mood of much of nineteenth-century literature as the Romantic tradition withered away. The response of readers showed that the *mal* was not

* In a conversation in April 1948 with his private secretary de Gaulle said: 'It's frightening, the way American pressure is developing. If ever that young country, by force of circumstances, becomes master of the world, one daren't imagine to what lengths her imperialism will go. We must certainly keep a close eye on them.' (Claude Mauriac, *The Other de Gaulle*, translated by Moura Budberg and Gordon Latta (London, Angus and Robertson, 1973, p. 287.)

confined to the previous century. 'Our age is one of total anguish,' wrote one reader, and a student of political science re-echoed the words: 'It is impossible for a young person not to be anguished ... We do not know whether tomorrow we will be Russian, American, or whether we can remain French.' The playwright Henri Bernstein went further: 'Pessimism and anguish existed in the nineteenth century, but *not* this nearly universal sense of insecurity and deadly peril which is the principal element of our moral climate. The idea of community no longer exists: no one, today, believes in tomorrow.'

The neutralist urge had no political consequence. At election time, no one ever stood on a neutralist programme, for the good reason that there were no votes in neutralism. Furthermore, Bernstein's gloomy analysis was the literary effusion of one man. It did not and could not represent the feelings of tens of millions of French people, most of whom had some hopes, though not perhaps very high ones, of tomorrow. Nonetheless, polls carried out by the Institut Français d'Opinion Publique (IFOP) showed that in 1947, while 36 per cent of those questioned thought that the Soviet Union wanted to dominate the world, 29 per cent thought the same thing of the US. By the early Fifties – i.e. after the coming of the Cold War – these opinions had come down much more heavily against the Soviet Union as the likely aggressor. But, significantly, in a poll taken in October 1954, asking the question what France should do in the event of a war between the two superpowers, 22 per cent said it should side with the Soviet Union, while 53 per cent wanted it to take no part at all. This was the French equivalent to the German *ohne mich* tendency.

The geographical, political and financial logic of an alliance with the US and the West, and France's need for US dollars and a shared defence effort in face of the Soviet threats, were factors recognised by the great majority of French people when they consulted their heads. But their hearts often pulled them in other directions. Sometimes heart and head came together, in a surprising way, to deplore the division of Europe, and France in particular, into two opposing blocs. Even such a suave and sophisticated observer as Jacques Dumaine, a man at the other end of the social and political spectrum from the St Germain clubs or the fellow-travelling coteries, could with suitable reserves and qualifications argue the case against treating the Communists as outcasts. In his diary for November 1948, he deplored General de Gaulle's calling them separatists: in so far as they were inspired by Muscovite fanaticism, they must, he argued, be resisted, 'but to declare that they no longer belong to the French community is a dangerous rhetorical untruth . . . the great majority of them are firmly rooted in French soil and will remain so.'[30] He was right, though not many people of his class and upbringing would have permitted themselves such thoughts.

The other notable trend in post-Liberation thinking and way of life was represented by what, for simplicity's sake, could be called the Catholic revival. Given the previous record of the Church and its relationship to everyday life, this was something of an intellectual and religious upheaval. For generations, the Roman Catholic hierarchy and clergy identified themselves, or were perceived as doing so, with the bourgeoisie and the faithful peasantry, from whom much of the priesthood was recruited. Some representatives of the Church sided openly with such extreme right-wing movements as Maurras' Action Française.* During the war, many (though by no means all) bishops sympathised with Vichy, whose paternalist doctrines suited them very well. With the collapse of Vichy, this old-style clericalism stood at a discount. The emergence of a new, liberal-minded Catholic political party, the MRP, coincided with the appointment of more modern-minded cardinals and bishops, and with increased activity by such movements as the Jeunesse Ouvrière Chrétienne (JOC) and its rural counterpart, the Jeunesse Agricole Chrétienne, which by 1950 numbered 70,000 young people. The Catholic trade union movement (CFTC) grew to be a vigorous if unequal rival to the Communist-dominated CGT. In the world of ideas, the review *Esprit* (1930–50), edited by Emmanuel Mounier, struck an echoing chord. An anti-Marxist, pro-Socialist Catholic, Mounier, through his philosophical creed called 'personalism', tried to reconcile the teachings of the Church with Socialism.

Especially, the experiment of the worker-priests captured popular imagination. In 1944, the Mission de Paris was established, with

* Maurras and L'Action Française dominated right-wing thought throughout the earlier years of the twentieth century, Maurras himself being passionately anti-Dreyfus. Later, he became an outspoken apologist for the Vichy régime, and described his life sentence, imposed by the *épuration* courts, as 'the revenge of Dreyfus'.

the task of exploring the world of the largely de-Christianised proletariat. Priests, most of them young, shed their clerical garb and went to work in the factories in Paris and the major provincial cities, sharing the lives and cares of those who lived and toiled there. Almost inevitably, some of the hundred or so priests involved became infected by their environment, espoused Marxism and were militant in the CGT. Others joined the Peace Movement. The Vatican, as well as right-wing opinion in France, was critical and in 1953 came a stinging condemnation from Rome of the whole experiment. A year later the French hierarchy, with some reluctance, virtually closed down the mission, ordering all worker-priests to cease political and trade union activities and forbidding them to spend more than three hours a day in the factory. About sixty disobeyed, some of them renouncing their priestly status and joining the Communist party. Their numbers may have been small, their influence limited, but a best-selling novel, Gilbert Cesbron's *Les Saints vont en enfer*, gave wide publicity to, and attracted much sympathy for, their plight.

The extent and effects of this Catholic revival must not be exaggerated. Large sections of the French population remained de-Christianised. A poll held in 1950 on whether a reference to God should be added to the preamble to the Constitution gave the following results: in favour, 37 per cent, against 33 per cent, indifferent or don't know 30 per cent. These figures were not very different from those recording the final referendum on the Constitution itself – approximately one-third for, one-third against, one-third don't know.

The conclusion – not a particularly surprising one, in view of the upheavals suffered by France and the rest of Europe – is that post-war opinion was in general troubled, divided, rudderless, looking for something different without knowing what, or where to find it. Samuel Beckett's contribution in the Fifties to the Theatre of the Absurd, the plays in which nothing happens, nobody comes, nobody goes, was itself an eloquent expression of an era. An English reviewer of the first London performance of *Waiting for Godot* described it as a 'metaphor which makes a particular appeal to the mood of liberal uncertainty which is the prevailing mood of modern western Europe'. If that was one anguished theme of the times, another, embodying feelings of disgust and desperation at the established order of things, was voiced by the heroine of a

Françoise Sagan novel. Not for her the ferment of the genuine or self-styled Paris intellectuals, or the impact of the new, socially-minded Catholicism. 'At least when one is young,' she says, 'in the trickery which life consists of, nothing seems to me more desperately desirable than imprudence.'[31]

CHAPTER 6

The Shadow of German Rearmament

The 1951 general election results were such as to increase, rather than reduce, the prospect of governmental instability. In the ensuing eighteen months, three governments came and went. It took one month, after the elections, to form a new government under René Pleven. He only lasted until January 1952, when another three weeks elapsed before Edgar Faure, a youngish Radical, succeeded in bringing the power vacuum to an end, but for barely more than a month until he too collapsed, to be succeeded by Antoine Pinay, whose premiership lasted exactly ten months.

The underlying reason for this display of French party politics at their most unruly was the same in each case: with 118 Gaullists (RPF) in intermittent opposition on one wing and 103 Communists in the same position on the other, there should in theory have been enough votes in the centre to provide a stable majority of a Third Force variety. In fact, there was, as usual, insufficient agreement between the centre parties to provide any such majority, or rather, there were as many majorities as there were problems.

This new situation became clear early in the Pleven period, when the Gaullists decided to show their strength by breathing new life into the never-dormant issue of *laïcité*. Two bills, both providing modest financial help for parents sending their children to private (i.e. Church) as well as to State schools (and thus infringing the strict principle of *laïcité*), were passed by the Assembly. One of them was government-inspired, the other bore the name of its MRP author, Charles Barangé. A 'clerical' coalition of 313 MRP, classic Right, RPF and some Radicals voted for; voting against were the 255 Communists, Socialists and the rest of the Radicals – in other words, the supporters of what they liked to call the '*défense Républicaine*'. For the Socialists, gravely wounded in their hearts and minds by this offence to one of their most sacred principles, the Barangé bill was the breaking point with Christian Democracy (the MRP). Not until the death agonies of the Fourth Republic, in May 1958, were they ready again to be in the same government as the MRP. But this did not mean that they had lost their power or that their votes in the Assembly ceased to count. Nor did it mean that they would never again vote with the MRP.

The new pattern of shifting majorities was illustrated once more when the Socialists, along with the Communists, MRP and RPF, approved Pleven's incomes policy (rejected by the Radicals and the Right) and still again when they were in the 'European' majority (including the MRP) which in December 1951 ratified the Coal and Steel Community (against Communist and RPF opposition). And it was the Socialist withholding of their votes on financial policy that finally laid Pleven low in January 1952. His successor, Edgar Faure, was even less successful at holding together this fissiparous majority. After a month, having failed to win Assembly support for tax increases, he stepped down and thus opened the way to one of the more remarkable men and episodes of the Fourth Republic.

If Dr Henri Queuille, acceding to the premiership in 1948, had signified a return to Third Republican methods and rhythms, Antoine Pinay, who was voted in as Prime Minister on 6 March 1952, seemed an even more realistic incarnation of the pre-war years and earlier, when much of French society was composed of 'little men', little businesses, limited fields of vision. His little round pork-pie hat, his little moustache, his modest way of public speaking, his own descent from farming and bourgeois stock, his total non-exposure to foreign civilisations or languages, his position as Mayor and Deputy of St Chamond, a medium-sized town south-west of Lyon, his profession as head of a tanning enterprise there – all these elements combined to give the impression of a simple, undistinguished and unmemorable man. (Though there was nothing undistinguished about his First World War record, when like Ramadier, another Prime Minister, he was awarded the Médaille Militaire for bravery on active service.)

As a parliamentary deputy at the time of the fall of France, in July 1940, Pinay had identified himself with the majority of his countrymen by voting for full powers for Pétain, an act which cost him a few days of imprisonment at the Liberation. This stigma was soon erased and he was back in parliament, sitting on the right of the Assembly, by 1945. His entry into the Hôtel Matignon, the No. 10

Downing Street of France, marked even more than Queuille's had done the end of the era which had begun with the Liberation.

But like his friend Queuille, there was more to Pinay than at first appeared. There must have been, because of all the prime ministers of the Fourth Republic, only three – de Gaulle, Mendès-France and Pinay – left behind them a clear and lasting impression on the public's memory. Though his methods and often his thought processes may have been simple, he was not without native wit and cunning, and he ruled as the leader of the most right-wing coalition which the country had known since the Twenties era of Poincaré. At the same time, he had the common touch. His populism extended from fireside chats on the radio to well publicised visits to cheese or charcuterie shops to see for himself how their products were being priced. 'I am Mr Consumer,' he told the public, 'and I am going to make the Hôtel Matignon the headquarters of a league of consumers consisting of 43 million French people.'[1] He was indeed extraordinarily successful as his own public relations man, rarely letting an opportunity go by to emphasise his *petit bourgeois* economical habits and common sense. This was the impression – of calmness, down-to-earth-ness, a firm hand on the tiller – that he wanted to give, and this is what he succeeded in doing.

Reserving to himself the key post of Minister of Finance, he saw his principal task as the reduction of the rate of inflation and a halt in the vicious spiral of wages and prices. He was well served by a team of expert advisers, among whom was Jacques Rueff, who had been on Poincaré's staff. Financial orthodoxy was the order of the day, with the emphasis on saving and a reduction in credit and investment. This certainly helped to bring down inflation, even if it also put a brake upon the economy. But Pinay's methods were also more direct ones. Within a week of assuming office, he sent for the representatives of the big retail shops, with branches all over the country, and appealed to them to act on prices. Soon price tags were appearing on goods, announcing reductions under the words *'Défense du Franc'*. Then it was the turn of the federation of small and medium businesses to be summoned to the Prime Minister's office, then the chemists, the butchers, the hairdressers . . .

Nothing like this had ever been seen. Effects soon followed. Between February and July 1952, the index of wholesale prices fell from 152 to 142.8, retail prices from 148.5 to 142.8. Pinay's critics said that this was luck, and up to a point they were right. He had had the great good fortune to take over the economy just when, with the Korean war over, raw material prices were coming down internationally and industrial investment was expanding. Maurice Petsche had also brought the economy under control, only to see, two years previously, his fruitful work largely destroyed by the effects of the outbreak of the Korean war. But the psychological shock of the Pinay experiment was very much due, whatever the exterior influences, to his own efforts. No wonder that the crowds shouted, when he paid a visit to the Lyon fair in April 1952, 'Hold on, hold on, Monsieur Pinay, we're with you.'[2] In the atmosphere of political disaffection and the growth of the 'them and us' syndrome which so characterised the post-war years, this was a new sound indeed. It showed, not for the first time, that what the average French person really cared about was not Indochina or the renaissance of Germany or even, putting things in order of priority, the Soviet threat, but the cost of living and improvements in the quality of life.

Undoubtedly the brightest jewel in Pinay's crown was the loan issue floated in his name in May 1952. It was loaded with glistening inducements, including exemption from taxation and death duties, and with the return on capital invested linked to the price of gold. It proved to be one of the most successful State loans launched in the twentieth century. Large and small investors alike hastened to buy the stock. The death duty exemption alone made it a highly interesting proposition – hence the slogan, much bruited about at the time – *'Mettre en Pinay avant de mettre en bière'*.*

Not all of the Pinay period in power was marked with the same degree of prudent management and achievement. At the same time as the loan was making its triumphant impact, there was a ludicrous episode involving a government drive against the Communists. On 27 May 1952, the American General Matthew Ridgway arrived in Paris to succeed Eisenhower as Supreme Allied Commander Europe. He had been the commander of United Nations forces in Korea, and for some time past, Communist propaganda had been busy linking his name with the alleged use by the Americans of bacteriological warfare there. The day following his arrival, the 28th, the Communist party organised a huge protest demonstration, which was countered by large forces of police and *gardes républicains*. In

* 'Get into Pinay before getting into your coffin'.

the course of the ensuing clashes, one man was killed, 27 police and 200 demonstrators injured and 718 people arrested. In the late evening, Jacques Duclos, who was acting Secretary-General of the party while Thorez was receiving medical treatment for partial paralysis in the Soviet Union, was arrested – *in flagrante delicto* said the police, that being the only way in which a deputy could be arrested without his parliamentary immunity having first been withdrawn by a vote of the National Assembly. It was to say the least a questionable claim, seeing that the arrest took place after the demonstrations were over.

In the boot of Duclos' car was found a basket containing two (dead) pigeons. Pinay's fire-eating Ministers of the Interior and of Justice were determined to show that nothing less than a plot against the State was involved, and the birds were therefore designated carrier pigeons. Searches and perquisitions against Communist branches all over the country were ordered and many arrests made, Communist newspapers seized, and an alleged conspiracy 'discovered' at Toulon. While right-wing papers splashed lurid stories about the pigeons and the 'plot', to many people the affair looked suspiciously like a police frame-up.[3] Could the government really be preparing to outlaw the Communist party? It was as though McCarthyism, then at its height in America, had crossed the Atlantic and settled in Paris (though those intellectuals and others who drew this comparison conveniently overlooked the fact that, unlike the situation in the US, there existed in France a strong and potentially subversive Communist party, supported by a quarter of the electorate). Despite his parliamentary immunity, Duclos was detained until, on 1 July, a court dismissed the charge of conspiracy and ordered his release. He always maintained that the pigeons had been given him to put in the pot.

Not all of the government agreed with the methods employed by the two hard-line ministers. Pleven, the Minister of Defence, took the unusual step of issuing a communiqué saying that the documents seized at Toulon contained nothing secret, and Pinay himself, with his habitual good sense, feared that the affair would make the government look ridiculous. So it did, but the ineffectiveness of subsequent Communist agitation against Duclos' arrest and the disarray within the party in face of the campaign mounted against it showed just how far it had isolated itself or been isolated from the body politic.

One important shift in the political balance marked Pinay's term in office. This was the beginning of the disintegration of the RPF. Looking back on the event, it was inevitable. Deputies, even Gaullist deputies imbued with the aloof and unswerving spirit of non-cooperation of their leader, could not be expected to remain for ever untouched and undefiled by the parliamentary waters swirling around them. Besides, not all of the 118 RPF deputies were of such unshakeable loyalty. Some of them were former right-wing figures who had marched under the Gaullist flag for the purpose of getting elected. Twenty-seven of them decided to vote for the investiture of M. Pinay, who without their support could not have become Prime Minister. Thus a new majority was born, from which both the Socialists and the true-blue Gaullists were absent. It was the height of irony that the success of Pinay, the supporter in 1940 of Pétain and of the armistice, should have been due in part to those who had entered parliament under the auspices of the founder of Free France.

But it was not only these twenty-seven backsliders who were responsible for digging the grave of the RPF. At the end of May 1952, forty-one RPF deputies wrote to the General, saying that while they remained faithful to the aims of the RPF as defined in 1947, the methods of achieving power needed to be reconsidered. 'All methods which lead to systematic, sterile and unpopular opposition seem to us to get nowhere. . . . It seems to us impossible to modify the system while remaining outside it.'[4] De Gaulle, although only a few months previously he had told an RPF congress that 'we are ready to study with others the measures to take in common in order to get the country back on the rails', replied to the forty-one that the RPF would not compromise with the régime 'as it is'.

By the end of the year, forty-five RPF deputies had left the party. Some of them formed a new group which itself before long merged with the conventional right wing, now more or less unified under the general title of Centre Nationale des Indépendants et Paysans. Thus the subtle strategy of Vincent Auriol, who was resolved to fight off de Gaulle's challenge, paid off. Faced with the reluctance of the Socialists on the one hand, and the refusal of the hard-core Gaullists on the other, to support any conceivable government, he came to the conclusion that the only solution, if the Republic was to survive, was to divide the Gaullists. Antoine Pinay was his secret weapon in this task.

The General was naturally displeased at this turn of events. He had already had cause for annoyance when, after the fall of the Pleven government in January 1952, Auriol had sent for Jacques Soustelle, the leader of the RPF parliamentary group, and asked him to form the new government. The President was perfectly correct in doing this; Soustelle was the head of the largest party in the Assembly. But he also had in mind the seeds of division and discomfort that this approach would sow in the Gaullist camp. He was not wrong.

Oral accounts exist, and have been pieced together by various writers and historians, of the stupendous scene between de Gaulle and Soustelle which followed. They differ as to when it took place. Some think it was later, after the fall of the Pinay government. Soustelle, in his memoirs, is imprecise, although he does record a telephone conversation with the General in January, when the latter was so carried away that he, Soustelle, had to hang up. Lacouture[5] goes for the January date and sets the scene in the Paris headquarters of the RPF, where the General, surrounded by his advisers and senior people, is presiding over the regular weekly meeting of the RPF steering committee. Soustelle is absent, not having returned from the Elysée. 'We can't take any decision without the Prime Minister,' says the General sardonically. '. . . I would like to know his programme, what's going to happen to me in this business, what post will the Prime Minister offer me, Under-Secretary for the Arts? Sports? Education perhaps?'

At this point Soustelle arrives and seems unaware of the storm that is brewing. He explains that he has asked Auriol for a breathing space in order to take soundings. De Gaulle can no longer contain himself. 'You are all the same,' he says. 'It's enough to roll out a red carpet under your feet for you to walk on it, no matter where it is leading.' Soustelle, who has turned pale with shock, adds that he has told Auriol that he, Soustelle, does not think he can succeed in the formation of a government, and has said as much in a communiqué. 'Read it,' commands the General. Soustelle does so. It is a singularly obscure and jargon-laden statement. 'But that's idiotic,' says the General. 'What does it mean?' And stalks from the room without shaking hands with anybody.

De Gaulle was hot-tempered, given to mordant sarcasm and wounding words. No doubt he was upset by the conduct of Soustelle, who not long before, as Secretary-General of the RPF, had been one of his principal lieutenants. Weeks later, when he had calmed down, he spoke to Soustelle in far more philosophic tones. But the episode serves to show, despite its massive support by the electorate, what a hybrid and insecure affair the RPF was, at least in its parliamentary form. Eighteen months later in May 1953, following heavy losses in the municipal elections the previous month, de Gaulle, without formally dissolving the RPF, withdrew from its parliamentary deputies the right to speak or act in its name. 'The shattering of illusions is upon us,' his statement concluded. 'Now we must prepare the way of recourse' (i.e. the moment when the country would turn again to him).

It was the death of the experiment that had begun so spectacularly. The Gaullist deputies, while continuing to share and express many of the General's views, were left free to enjoy the delights of the parliamentary game. Deprived of the title RPF, they became Social Republicans (RS). It cannot have been through error or forgetfulness that de Gaulle, when he came to write his memoirs, devoted only a few lines to the RPF. Despite the fervour and conviction with which he had launched it, it was not something he chose to look back upon with any pleasure or satisfaction.

All this while, as Auriol was outwitting the General and Pinay was performing his economic miracle – for it was a miracle, even if it had only a brief lifespan – a time bomb was ticking away. It was labelled 'German rearmament'. Pinay had made no reference to it in his investiture speech, which was one reason why he had succeeded in winning a majority. Those dissident Gaullists would never have favoured him with their votes if he had pledged himself to action on this issue. Even as it was, they tried, unsuccessfully, to make the price of their support the ejection of the pro-European Robert Schuman from the Quai d'Orsay. The bomb's official title was Communauté Européenne de Défense, European Defence Community (EDC), or in everyday parlance the European army, and it had been assembled by French hands seventeen months earlier, during the first legislature.

In the summer of 1950, only six weeks after Robert Schuman had launched his (or rather Monnet's) plan for a European Coal and Steel Community, came the outbreak of the Korean war. Overnight, the international climate underwent a crucial change. Among those Frenchmen who at once saw what this would mean was Monnet himself. He knew that the Americans would not accept this Far Eastern Communist thrust lying down. They would resist in Korea and expect their allies to resist with them, and in Europe they would call for a strengthening of Western defences in face of the increased Soviet threat, including the rearmament of Germany.

This would create a crisis all over Europe. Only five years after the end of the war, the idea of a reborn German army would be greeted with dismay and opposition by everyone, including the Germans themselves. As for France, had not Robert Schuman, less than a year previously, on the occasion in 1949 of the ratification of the Atlantic Treaty, solemnly assured the National Assembly that 'Germany is not armed and will not be . . . It is unthinkable that she could accede to the treaty as a nation susceptible of defending or contributing to the defence of other nations.' Other, more perspicacious or perhaps more cynical Frenchmen thought differently. Beuve-Méry, the editor of *Le Monde*, gave considerable offence when he wrote that the Atlantic Treaty contained the seeds of German rearmament 'as the baby chicken is in the egg'. In the Assembly the next day, Schuman dismissed this as 'the most monstrous error that has been made in this field'. Now Monnet saw the Schuman Plan, with its promise of Franco-German reconciliation and of a new concept of European unity, gravely prejudiced before it had been possible to give it even the semblance of reality. On holiday in August 1950 on the Ile de Ré, off the Atlantic coast, he overheard two young soldiers on leave talking in a café. 'With the Schuman Plan,' he somewhat improbably reports one of them as saying, 'one thing is sure, which is that the soldier will never again have to go to war.'[6] For Monnet, it was paramount that this confidence should not be betrayed.

He was quite right about the pressure for German rearmament. Even before the outbreak of the Korean war, voices had been raised – notably those of Field Marshal Montgomery, the deputy Commander-in-Chief of NATO forces, and General Bradley, Chief of the US Chiefs of Staff – urging that Germany should contribute to the defence of Europe. In Bonn, advisers to the US High Commissioner, John Jay McCloy, were working on plans for rearming the Germans, which included the idea of an integrated and supranational European army. Nothing of this was surprising. Whatever doubts might be entertained about American obsession over the Soviet threat, it remained a military fact that in face of 60,000 East German military police and twenty-seven Soviet divisions in East

Germany, with many more behind them, NATO disposed of only twelve ill-equipped divisions with inadequate air support.

At the Consultative Assembly of the Council of Europe in Strasbourg in August (which was not supposed to concern itself with defence matters), a resolution was adopted in favour of the immediate creation of a European army under a European minister of defence, which would include a German contingent. Winston Churchill, then Leader of the Opposition, made a ringing speech about the Russian threat and the need for German rearmament. (He had floated this idea some months earlier, in a House of Commons speech.) In the proposed European army, he now said, 'we shall all have an important and honourable role to play' – a form of wording which, in view of the Conservative government's subsequent refusal to have anything to do with the EDC except wish it well, created the conditions for future misunderstanding.[7]

As regards practical results, the Strasbourg resolution counted for nothing. The real action was in the US. There in New York on 12 September 1950, Dean Acheson, the Secretary of State, told a meeting of the three powers (US, UK and France) that the Germans, rearmed at divisional level, must be brought into NATO. Although he was not specific on details, and there was no reference as such to a German army, the American military had already let it be known that they were thinking in terms of twelve German divisions. Acheson's main point was that the US would only reinforce its own forces in Europe and set up a unified command if the European allies were ready to do likewise and to agree to the creation of German units. He himself was dubious of these tactics, which were inspired by the Pentagon rather than the State Department. He nonetheless set aside his doubts and delivered what amounted to an American ultimatum. Schuman was in an unenviable position, faced with the threat of American disengagement from Europe or German rearmament. He began by trying to buy time. The French government, he said, would be ready to discuss German rearmament only when there existed properly integrated NATO forces with which German units could be merged.

The British sided with the Americans, and in the full NATO meeting that followed, so did Canada, Italy, the Netherlands and Norway. The other members of the alliance, in Acheson's words, 'hung back, watching the French'.[8] The latter, for all their resistance (strengthened by the arrival from Paris of the fiercely anti-German Jules Moch, the Minister of Defence) and attempts to defer any immediate moves, knew that the cards were stacked against them. 'Don't press so hard,' said a senior member of Schuman's team. 'We will find a solution.'⁹ Schuman himself, by the end of the NATO meeting, was putting water in his wine. German rearmament had been proposed, he said (in fact, he used the coded phrase 'German participation in the defence of the West'), and this would need to be examined. 'What I cannot do, and what my government cannot do, at the present moment and in actual circumstances, is to make a premature decision on this problem.' Joseph Bech, the genial Luxembourg Foreign Minister, was more reassuring still: bidding Acheson to 'relax', he said that in Paris plans were being drawn up for a European military arrangement based upon the Schuman Plan. When Acheson asked why, in that case, Schuman did not say so, Bech replied: 'He doesn't know it yet.'¹⁰

The Luxembourgeois had evidently been in touch with Monnet or with one of his staff. For sure enough in Paris that indefatigable fighter, while still the head of the French modernisation plan that bore his name and chairman of the six-power negotiations for the Coal and Steel pool, was secretly at work on a project designed to provide for a German contribution to European defence without creating a German army. (This at least is Monnet's own version of events. Others could also claim paternity for the European army idea, but there is no doubt that Monnet's part in it, and his influence with Pleven, who succeeded Queuille as Prime Minister in July 1950, was all-important.) The key to the problem was a European army for which, in Monnet's words, 'no precedent or model existed and which we had a few days to invent.'¹¹ He advised Pleven that the way to proceed was down the lines of the Coal and Steel plan, namely to create a unified European army, under the direction of a supranational authority, into which German units could be progressively integrated. He further advised that this plan should not be put into practice until the Coal and Steel agreement had been signed. He was afraid that the difficulties and fears attaching to German rearmament might slow down or impede the agreement, which lay at the very heart of the new Europe that was his goal.

On 24 October 1950 Pleven, having got the approval of the Cabinet, made a statement to the National Assembly. Once the Coal and Steel treaty had been signed, he said, the government proposed the creation of a European army linked to the political institutions of a united Europe. This would be achieved through the maximum possible fusion of human and material elements, under a single political and military authority. A defence minister would be appointed by the participating governments, with his own budget and procurement programme, and national military contingents would be incorporated 'at the level of the smallest possible unit'. Pleven omitted, to Monnet's annoyance, the words in the original draft which referred to these units wearing the same uniform. As for countries with existing armies (i.e. France among others), they would retain control over those forces not to be integrated. The government intended to invite Great Britain and the free countries of Continental Europe to complete this plan once the Coal and Steel treaty had been signed.   The statement was approved by the Assembly by 349 votes to 235, which seemed on the face of things satisfactory enough. But even at this early stage, the ground had been laid for future confusion and differing interpretations. The government had contrived to give the simultaneous impression that the programme for strengthening NATO would not be delayed, and that German rearmament was still a long way off. Furthermore, the French plan was instantly recognisable as discriminatory against Germany, all of whose forces would be integrated in the European army, while other countries such as France and Italy would retain control over some of their military machine. In particular, the reference to British participation was ambiguous. Only a few months previously, London had declined to commit itself to a negotiation (for the Coal and Steel community) which contained a supranational element and whose final outcome remained to be worked out. Why did Pleven and Monnet think the British attitude would be any different over the European army scheme with its supranational machinery? Had they perhaps been deceived by the oratory of Churchill who, like other Conservative leaders in opposition in the late Forties and early Fifties, tended to regard the European issue not so much as an article of faith (which they soon turned their backs on after regaining power) but rather as a useful stick with which to beat the Labour government?

In the debate, Pleven was indeed asked what would happen if Britain did not participate. He replied as best he could, maintaining that he was unable to answer hypothetical questions. But already a fog was beginning to obscure the outlines of the European army plan. In London, Massigli considered that British non-participation was inevitable, and he could not imagine how an effective defence of Europe could be envisaged without the British. In his memoirs he wrote: 'It was to take four years for our Europeans [i.e. those of the Monnet school of thought, of which Massigli was emphatically not a member] to understand this.'[12]

The formal American reaction to the Pleven plan was diplomatically couched: it was 'welcome', it called for 'sympathetic examination'. In fact, Acheson was appalled. To him, the plan was 'hopeless',[13] a view concurred in by the Pentagon. Initial British reactions were scarcely warmer. In a conversation in November with Guy Mollet, the Socialist leader, Ernest Bevin, said he could not understand the plan.[14] In the months of confused and confusing inter-Allied negotiation that followed, and which included strenuous spoiling efforts by the Russians to prevent any measure of German rearmament, the French appeared to retreat from their original position. By the end of 1950, they were ready to accept the idea of German military units at something not far short of divisional strength – combat teams of some 10,000 men. But Adenauer and the German government also had something to say. For them, the discriminatory arrangements of the original Pleven plan were unacceptable, as was the continued status of Germany as an occupied country. They were in a strong position: either German rearmament would take place on their terms – and neither government nor opposition wanted a newly created German army as such – or not at all.

This stance was in complete contradiction with the French position, which continued to consist, in essence, of an attempt to delay German rearmament and the granting of German sovereignty for as long as possible and to preserve the discriminatory parts of the Pleven plan. The 'French position', as a description of a consistent and authoritative line of policy, is indeed a misnomer for the situation as it stood in mid-1951. As Acheson wrote, in an excess of English-style understatement, 'France was not of one mind on policy towards Germany.'[15] While the combat team idea was taking shape, Vincent Auriol was telling visitors that the Germans were vengeful, nationalistic, and could not be trusted. While Schuman and Monnet were agreeing with Adenauer that within the embryo Coal and Steel Community, France and Germany would be on a footing of equality, the French negotiators for the European army were defending exactly the opposite thesis.

Two developments occurred in the summer of 1951 which helped to point the way out of the impasse. The first was the influential contribution made by David Bruce, the US Ambassador to France, to the cause of EDC. The American government, prompted by McCloy in Bonn, had proposed, in the interest of speeding things up, to press on with German rearmament forthwith, integrating German units into the NATO structure as an interim and time-saving measure and leaving EDC, with its supranational element, to take its chances later on. Bruce, a skilled and experienced diplomatist and a true friend of France, saw at once that the French, whatever their uncertainties over EDC, would be bound to reject out of hand this crude rush towards a rearmed Germany. A major crisis within the Atlantic alliance would ensue. In a long and closely argued telegram to Washington, he sought to persuade his government that the EDC was the best, the most rapid and least painful method of securing US defence and other interests in Europe. Making explicit 'its strong support for setting up of the European Army and its political framework promptly', the American government would, said Bruce, be in a better position to insist on French execution of the plan.*

The second event was the exercise of his persuasive powers by Jean Monnet. In June 1951, he sold the Pleven plan to Eisenhower, by now the Supreme Allied Commander in Europe. Deliberately avoiding too much emphasis on the military aspects, Monnet argued that the key to German rearmament lay in the unification of Europe, failing which each nation would continue the power-play for itself. The West's strength, he conceded. did not depend upon the number of its divisions but on its unity and the common purpose within

* Events proved the falseness of this prophecy. Bruce's telegram sent from Paris as no. 25 on 3 July 1951, in answer to State Dept. telegram no. 7155 of 28 June (*Foreign Relations of the United States* for 1951, Department of State series, US Government Printing Office, Washington, DC), later became a case study at the Institute for the Study of Diplomacy at Georgetown University. It was a lucid and effective piece of reasoning, and helps to explain Bruce's later unswerving, some would say undiscriminating, loyalty to EDC, together with that of his assistant William M. Tomlinson, seconded to Paris from the US Treasury. In a conversation in Florida with the author in March 1989, Mr Douglas Dillon, one of Bruce's successors as Ambassador in Paris, described Tomlinson as a Euro-fanatic, under Monnet's thumb. Monnet pays a glowing tribute to Tomlinson in his memoirs. Whatever may be thought of his judgement, none could question Tomlinson's zeal and industry.

it. Eisenhower, always more a political than a military general, was receptive and delighted. Almost surpassing Monnet in the expression of lofty ideas simply defined, he said: 'You mean, it is more a human than a military problem?' Eisenhower's Chief of Staff, Alfred Gruenther, who was among those present at the meeting, began to fret at this high-falutin' tone, but his superior rebuked him: 'Military divisions are one aspect of things, but the real affair is human. What Monnet is proposing is to organise the relationship between men and I am for it.'[16]

A few days later, in an important speech in London, Eisenhower made Monnet's arguments his own and thus gave his very considerable backing to the European army idea. Meanwhile in Washington, Acheson, influenced no doubt by Bruce, was himself having a re-think, the result of which was to line up official US government support behind the scheme, as being the only one in sight likely to result in a military solution acceptable to France and Germany. It now remained for the European army negotiators in Paris, hitherto bogged down on the issue of equality of rights for Germany, to reflect these new developments.

General elections had meanwhile intervened in France (June 1951), and in the month that it took to put a new government together, the old one, including Robert Schuman at the Quai d'Orsay, carried on dealing with 'current affairs'. It was in these circumstances that the French negotiators changed their tune. The discriminatory parts of the Pleven plan disappeared, while the supranational element remained, without being clearly defined. 'Everything has been done to keep England out . . . Is that what they want?' was the first reaction of Massigli in London.

Many more months of negotiations were needed before the treaty establishing an European Defence Community was ready for signature. The Americans continued to give it their support, but Britain, by now under a Conservative government led by Winston Churchill, while paying it lip-service, steadfastly declined to take any part in it. Churchill himself described it rudely as a 'sludgy amalgam'[17] but nonetheless undertook, always provided that British participation was not involved, to do everything possible to bring it about. In another confused and confusing statement, he told the House of Commons in December 1951: 'We do not propose to merge in the European Army but are already joined to it.'

Monnet, always the optimist, held the view that the EDC project

would be adopted and that within three years there would be a
European Federation. David Bruce, by now appointed US observer
to the interim committee of EDC with the special task of urging
on the creation of the European army, shared these illusions.
Both he and Monnet would have done well to pay more attention
to developments on the French political stage. The 1951 general
election had thrown up a National Assembly of a very different
composition to that which greeted the Pleven plan when it was first
announced. The Socialists were no longer in government and 118
Gaullists (RPF) had the greatest number of seats in the Chamber.
The latter's congress in Nancy, in November, after listening to
a barrage of criticism of the EDC from the General, formally
condemned it. The Socialists were scarcely less critical – not of
the EDC as a concept but of the shape it was taking; according
to the ever-vigilant Jules Moch, the modifications to the original
plan were such as to create no more than a camouflage for a
reconstituted *Wehrmacht*. The Communists, with 100-plus seats,
were from the start totally and unshakeably hostile to EDC and
all forms of German rearmament.

Even more indicative of trouble to come was the debate in
the National Assembly in February 1952, during the brief prime
ministership of Edgar Faure. Schuman boldly asserted that none
of the alterations to the Pleven plan affected the original concept.
Much remained to be negotiated, he said, but the political objective
of a united Europe was at the heart of the matter. To some observers,
he gave the impression of someone on the defensive, and although he
was, predictably, applauded by his own MRP benches, the rest of the
Chamber was less enthusiastic. Bidault and Pleven spoke, but were
less well received than a left-wing member of the MRP, for whom
a British counterweight in Europe was essential. Jules Moch made
the same point, while Communists and RPF raked the whole EDC
idea with their fire.

The government motion in favour of the EDC on which the
debate ended, and on which a confidence vote was asked for,
expressed the usual and in some cases contradictory reservations,
particularly on the issue of British participation. It was approved
by 327 votes to 287, the minority including, as well as Communists
and Gaullists, twenty Socialists, ten Radicals and six MRP. In their
doubts and hesitations, and even in the minds of some of those who
voted for the motion, were mingled all the cross-currents of French

thinking at that time: straightforward fear of German rearmament, a desire for détente with the USSR, now that the Korean war was over, dislike of seeing control over part of the French Army being handed over to a supranational authority, strong feelings about the necessity for British participation. In parliamentary and political terms, the debate was not a good augury for the future of the EDC. The majority of ninety-four which had greeted the Pleven plan when first announced in October 1950 had dropped to forty sixteen months later.

It was mid-May 1952 before the EDC treaty was ready for signing. In the preceding laborious negotiations, some of the original ideas about the European army had disappeared. There was no longer to be a common European minister for defence, the size of the units was now fixed at 13,000 men – far removed from Jules Moch's hopes for German battalions – and with twelve of these near-divisional strength German formations, it was difficult to pretend that the outcome was not going to be the establishment of a German army. On the other hand, enough remained of the supranational element to attract the fire of Gaullists and others who objected most strongly to precisely this aspect of the plan: article 1 of the treaty spoke of common institutions, common defence forces and a common budget.

The French did secure guarantees from London and Washington against a possible later withdrawal of Federal Germany from the EDC, including the stationing of British and American forces in Continental Europe. But there was no pledge on how long this commitment was to last. In brief, the treaty was a hybrid, unsatisfactory in some respects to all its signatories, and likely to be specially displeasing to the French.* At the signing ceremony at the Quai d'Orsay on 27 May 1952, the usually cautious Acheson indulged himself so far as to say that what they had witnessed that day was 'one of the most important events of our lifetime . . . the unity of the free peoples of Western Europe'.[18] He must have pondered on the wisdom of these words two days later, when

---

* In February 1989, in Paris, the author asked a former senior French Ambassador what he had thought of EDC when he first became aware of its detail. At the time, he was serving at an overseas post, so played no part in the fevered Paris arguments. Nevertheless, 'I was against it.' 'Why?' 'Because I thought it was *une connerie*' – of which the polite translation would be 'a nonsense'.

at the Elysée Vincent Auriol gave him an hour's long lecture on the folly of encouraging Schuman in the rearmament of Germany.[19]

If the Pinay government can be accorded the credit for bringing the EDC treaty to the signature table, it certainly wins no prizes for bold action thereafter. Fearful of what might happen were the treaty to be submitted to parliament, it held back from doing so during the rest of its term of office (Pinay fell at the end of 1952, a victim of largely MRP-nourished suspicions of his sluggish intentions towards the EDC, and of the completely opposite fears of the Gaullists that he might bring on the ratification process). Ostensibly, the reason given for the delay was that France needed to secure further guarantees and clarifications from her partners and allies. In fact, no efforts were made to engage in the negotiations which might achieve such additions to the treaty. Eight months were allowed to go by, during which opposition to the treaty mounted. De Gaulle's attitude, of course, was utterly hostile – he outdid Churchill's 'sludgy amalgam' by describing the European army as a 'ghastly mess', 'an artificial monster', 'a robot', 'a Frankenstein'[20] – but some of the senior Radicals, notably Herriot and Daladier, came out against it, and Edgar Faure, the former (and future) Prime Minister, maintained that France could not ratify the treaty while so much of her military effort was being expended in Indochina.

It has been argued[21] that the treaty could have been ratified had it been presented to the Assembly in 1952 or even 1953, instead of being kept on the shelf, gathering dust and opprobrium. This is anyone's guess. It is true that some of the big guns, among them that of Marshal Juin, had not yet been fired against the treaty, true also that the Monnet conception of a new Europe was still popular among people who thought about such matters. On the other hand, parliamentary arithmetic, even at that early stage, was not encouraging. If Edgar Faure, in February 1952, had managed to secure a favourable majority for EDC of only forty, and that before the details of the treaty were complete and known, who could say whether that majority might not have vanished altogether when presented with the actual text? As for the new Europe, it was one thing to construct a supranational framework around the coal and steel industries, quite another to try to do the same for national armies, the historic expression of national pride and independence. This was particularly true of the French Army. As de Gaulle put it, and his message carried farther than the ears of convinced Gaullists,

'France is, of all the great nations which have their own army today, the only nation which is to lose hers.' In their enthusiasm to intensify the construction of a united Europe, the 'Europeans' of the Monnet school, strongly supported by the Americans, with their simplistic tendency to think that if there could be a United States of America so there could be a United States of Europe, had overreached themselves.*

The proof of that was yet to come. What is certain is that the EDC treaty was finally laid before parliament on 29 January 1953 by the René Mayer government which had succeeded that of Antoine Pinay. Mayer only won his prime ministership from the Assembly by promising new negotiations for additional protocols to the EDC treaty and for arrangements for the closer association of Great Britain. In addition, he undertook not to ask for a vote of confidence when the Assembly came to approve or disapprove the treaty. It was not much of an endorsement for one of the main elements of a policy statement. Yet Mayer had to attract not merely the same Gaullist votes that had proved indispensable to Pinay, but the main body of Gaullist deputies, as he could count neither on the Socialists nor on all the 'classic Right', who had never forgiven him for his calling-in of 5,000-franc notes back in 1947. He also had to agree to drop Schuman and replace him at the Quai d'Orsay with Georges Bidault, generally thought to be, if not anti-EDC, at least not so ideologically committed to the idea of Europe and Franco-German reconciliation as Schuman.

In parliamentary terms, the fact that Mayer (and his successor Joseph Laniel) held office by courtesy of the Gaullist bloc, anti-EDC to a man, meant that the prospects for the treaty were dimmed still further. This was not Mayer's fault: like Laniel after him, he was a genuine 'European' and wanted to see the treaty ratified. But he was the reverse of Bunyan's pilgrim: more beset with dismal stories, the less his strength. By the end of May, the Gaullists who had helped to put him into power helped to turn him out again, precisely because he seemed to be clearing away the obstacles to submission of the treaty for parliamentary ratification. Thus EDC,

* Paul Hoffman, the tall and burly American administrator of the Marshall Plan, is said on one occasion, exasperated beyond self-control by the tergiversations of the Europeans, to have seized the short and slight Bidault by the lapels and, almost lifting him off the ground, shouted: 'Integrate, damn you, integrate.'

even before it became a topic of public debate and discussion, was beginning to be a political minefield which could only be crossed by aspiring candidates for high office with the use of dissemblance, subterfuge and the giving of fresh hostages to fortune.

At least René Mayer, unlike his predecessor, was not guilty of inertia. His government prepared additional protocols to the treaty, designed to maintain 'the unity and integrity of our Army and of the French Union' and also to provide for a settlement (favourable, naturally, to France) of the Saar problem. In effect, this was turning the clock back to the earlier French position, previously abandoned, of securing special and discriminatory advantages for France. As a senior official at the Quai d'Orsay put it, 'First we tie up Germany, then, in the cause of the equality of rights, we tie ourselves up with her, then we rack our brains to get untied'.[22]

In the circumstances, it was something of a triumph for French diplomacy that the new protocols were agreed and signed by the six participant nations by the end of March 1953. But the Saar issue remained outstanding, and a source of friction with Germany, and more discouraging still for EDC and its supporters was the appointment by the foreign affairs and defence committees in the National Assembly of Jules Moch and General Pierre Koenig, both implacable foes of EDC, as their respective rapporteurs.

Raymond Aron, normally as clear-sighted a commentator as can be imagined, considered (together with his American co-author) that from January 1953 to August 1954 there was 'the greatest ideological and political debate France has known since the Dreyfus affair'.[23] This is an exaggeration. The 'affair' in its time divided French society from top to bottom. Families split apart, sons refused to speak to fathers, brothers to sisters, blows were struck, household ornaments smashed – in some respects, these rifts have still not healed. By contrast, the EDC argument, despite the torrent of passionate words, spoken and written, which poured forth for and against it, did not enter to anything like the same degree into public consciousness. The treaty itself, with its 132 articles and accompanying protocols, was not exactly popular or easy reading; there must have been many, perhaps a majority, of French people who, like Ernest Bevin, understood nothing about it.

In so far as opinion polls carried a message they showed that feelings about the EDC, as about so many other matters of public interest, were profoundly divided. In September 1951, 42 per cent of those questioned were in favour of the European army, 26 per cent against and 32 per cent had no view. A year later, these figures read: 48, 30 and 22 per cent. Nine months after that (June 1953), they were 43, 23 and 34 per cent. By July 1954, with the treaty still unratified by parliament, but after much ink and oratory had flowed, 36 per cent of those questioned were in favour of EDC, 31 per cent against and 33 per cent expressed no opinion. As usual with opinion polls, much depended upon how the question was put: 'German rearmament' carried a different connotation from 'European Defence Community'. Furthermore, it was rarely made clear to the public, either by the pollsters or the politicians, that the option about whether or not to rearm Germany had already been foreclosed – by the effect upon Western European strategy of the Cold War, by American pressures, by France's dependence upon US military and financial support. What had to be decided was not whether but how Germany was to be rearmed.

But if comparisons with the Dreyfus affair are inappropriate, it is true that the EDC issue caused governments to fall, affected the composition of parliamentary majorities and divided and embittered large sections of the 'Establishment' – the senior civil service (especially the Quai d'Orsay), the political parties, the press and the Army. It hung, like a great, grey, indissoluble cloud of pollution, over everything. Hervé Alphand, the French official who was head of the negotiating team that helped to draw up the EDC treaty, complained that the Quai d'Orsay showed signs of undisguised hostility, which the government did nothing to stop.[24] This was certainly true of some of its members. Alphand became as passionately attached to the cause of EDC as some of his colleagues, notably Massigli in London, were bitterly against it. Such was his strength of feeling that when the National Assembly finally killed the treaty, in August 1954, this brilliant servant of the State, hard-boiled and worldly to the point of cynicism, is said to have given way to tears.

In the Army, anti-German feeling, though it may have been present in the minds of some of the older officers, was never a predominant influence. Indeed, senior generals such as Paul Ely, the French representative on the NATO standing group, were early supporters of the idea of German rearmament. But on the whole, senior serving officers said little or nothing in public, whatever their private feelings. This was far from being the case with their retired colleagues. General Weygand came out against the EDC in a magazine article, and his views were shared by a Gaullist deputy, a retired General, and Koenig, a former General, appointed rapporteur of the Assembly's defence committee for its consideration of the treaty.

As discussion of the EDC became more widespread, groups of younger officers, colonels and majors, began to be influenced by, and to make their views known through, a widely circulated publication, *Message des Forces Armées*. This expressed the discontent and indignation of all those who disliked intensely the prospect of part of the French Army being absorbed into a European hybrid, without their seniors making any effort to protest. The only Marshal of France, Juin, who had in the early stages apparently given his blessing to the concept of a European defence community, began to listen to these voices coming from the middle ranks. He ended by joining the chorus with such vigour and disrespect for the government that he was dismissed as its military adviser (see p. 2). It is certainly not too fanciful to see in the activities of these younger officers, as critical of their own superiors as they were of their political masters, the origins of that revolt against authority, expressed in the name of patriotism and military honour, which a few years later was to challenge and defeat the Fourth Republic.*

Unlike the Army, among the anti-EDC parties and politicians anti-German sentiments were a constant factor. The Communists, along with the Gaullists the only party to be undivided in its hostility to EDC, made unending play with the horrors of a rearmed Germany. In a European army, one Communist deputy warned, Frenchmen 'would be obliged to serve under the orders of Nazi generals who yesterday were ordering the execution of their relatives'. Some of the classical Right were of the same mind, arguing that a Franco-German reconciliation was a chimera, which could only lead to German hegemony. But among the Right there were divisions, just as there were among the Radicals and the Socialists. Herriot, the grandfather of the Radical party and a former deportee, threw all his considerable weight behind anti-German fears, as did Daladier, Prime Minister at the time of Munich. Among the Socialists, Jules Moch, with his visceral feelings about Germany,

* Among these officers was the future General Jacques Faure, later renowned for his conspiratorial efforts on behalf of Algérie française.

considered that the original Pleven plan had been disfigured entirely. The left wing of the party thought that any form of German rearmament was unacceptable. The Gaullists, who found themselves allies of the Communists in this respect, kept emphasising the effect EDC would have upon the French Army. For them, as for their leader, what mattered was not German rearmament but the independence of France, a far more fundamental issue involving not just opposition to the supranational aspects of the European army but the bigger questions of NATO command structures in Europe and the American exercise of supreme command.

At one of his press conferences (November 1953),* General de Gaulle gave voice to these sentiments in words of exceptional bitterness. This 'monstrous treaty' was the work, he pointed out, of the *'inspirateur'* (Jean Monnet) who in 1940 'tried to integrate King George VI with President Lebrun, the House of Lords with our Senate, the Home Guard with the Garde Républicaine' (the proposal for a Franco-British union). Now, said the General, he was trying to do the same for France and Germany. 'Since victorious France has an army and defeated Germany has none, let us suppress the French Army. After that we will make a stateless army of Frenchmen and Germans, and since there must be a government above this army, we will make a stateless government, a technocracy. As this may not please everybody, we'll paint a new shop sign and call it "community"; it won't matter anyway, because the "European army" will be placed at the entire disposal of the American Commander-in-Chief.'

The General's scorn for the US and Britain knew no bounds. 'It is curious . . . how the Americans are using open and secret pressure to compel France to accept the EDC which can only condemn her to decay. . . . Britain too, though for different reasons, is demanding that we ratify the so-called European army, though nothing in the world would induce her to join it herself.' But, he went on, 'there are French people who stand, today as in the past, for the independence of France. Not long ago, the Resistance smashed a system which accepted for the State the law of the enemy. The RPF

* These were usually held in the ballroom of a Paris hotel. It was at once obvious that many present were not journalists, but selected members of a Gaullist claque, ready with pre-arranged questions which would enable the General, who habitually spoke without notes, to unleash another of his copious supply of derisive or ironic shafts.

blocked the path to those who intended to make us the slaves of the Soviets. Every means should be employed to fight against a régime which would commit the abuse of stripping France of her own decision-making process.'

In a way, this hostility to EDC, emanating from so many disparate sources, served to rekindle, as de Gaulle had hinted, the memories and traditions of the Resistance, when men and women of different origins, loyalties and convictions stood together in a common struggle against a common enemy, a crusade for the honour and independence of the French nation. Added to this heady mixture of prejudice and emotion was the complicating fact that even the supporters of the treaty saw it in different lights. For some, such as Bidault, it was the least unsatisfactory way of getting Germany rearmed. For others, such as Jean Monnet and his friends, it was a further, and desirable, step on the road to European integration. No wonder that Aron and others succumbed to the temptation to compare EDC with the Dreyfus affair. It was an unreal comparison, in any popular or lasting sense. But there is no doubt that for some years, EDC influenced and distorted the French political process in a way that at the time seemed to combine warnings of a typhoon with the rumblings of an earthquake.

The overthrow of René Mayer's government in May 1953 was followed by the longest crisis of the Fourth Republic. Paul Reynaud, Mendès-France, Bidault and André Marie all tried unsuccessfully to form a government. When at last after thirty-six days a little-known right-wing figure called Joseph Laniel succeeded, largely because of the weariness then prevailing, in getting himself voted in as Prime Minister, he too had to give undertakings that no ratification of the EDC treaty would be attempted until the Saar question was settled and new arrangements were made with Great Britain. For the first time, three Gaullist ministers and two under-secretaries entered the government, thus bringing the opponents of the EDC into the front line. Gaullists and Communists remained solidly anti-EDC, the MRP preponderantly in favour – though the attitude of Bidault, as Foreign Minister, was always liable to personal mood and petty jealousy. Earlier, in March 1953, he had talked to Dillon, the American Ambassador, about what he called the 'Schuman myth', suggesting (spitefully and wrongly) that he, Bidault, had originated these imposing European ideas for which Schuman got the credit.[25]

Laniel himself, a rich and burly Norman, had a good Resistance record (he had been a member of the CNR) and was not as dim, stupid and uncultivated as the Paris intelligentsia held him to be. A collector of fine porcelain, his typically Norman disposition of not liking to say Yes or No, or indeed anything much, added to his reputation as a numskull. But that this was a partial view is suggested by the fact that he was also seen as a possible candidate for the presidency of the Republic when Vincent Auriol's seven years' term of office was up at the end of 1953. Bidault was another contender, as was that great survivor Dr Queuille. Over all these and other hopefuls loomed the baleful presence of the EDC.

When, just before Christmas 1953, René Coty, a mild, pleasant, undistinguished Senator, also from Normandy, was elected President after no less than twelve rounds of voting, he commented: 'I have no illusions: if I am President of the Republic, it is because I have been having a prostate operation. This exempted me from having to come out for or against the EDC.'[26] This was pleasingly witty, but it could not efface the effect that the Versailles election had upon the public opinion in France and abroad. The episode presented the Fourth Republic at its worst: reeking with intrigue and personal rivalries, and lacking any sort of dignity. The American Embassy's report to Washington could not have put it better: 'The spectacle of confusion and impotence . . . is widely considered as one of national humiliation and as involving a serious weakening of the democratic fibre of the country.'[27]

Earlier that autumn, in Washington, there had been a three-power meeting (France, US, Britain) when Bidault, under pressure, reminded his Anglo-Saxon colleagues that while it was quite normal for them to emphasise the importance of European integration – i.e. the need to get a move on with EDC – its direct effects would be felt only in France, for France was the only one of the three countries to give up any sovereignty. Reading the records of these meetings – there was another three-power gathering, this time at the summit level (Eisenhower, Churchill, Laniel/Bidault), in Bermuda in December – it is impossible not to feel a certain sympathy for the hapless French ministers who had to endure this constant prodding and pushing by their allies, neither of whom was being required to take such a momentous step.

The French record of procrastination over their own plan, of failure to seize the nettle, was indeed a sorry one and a great impediment to the strengthening of the West's defences. But it must have been hard at Bermuda for Bidault (Laniel fell ill there, so that Bidault effectively became head of the French delegation) to be subjected to a massive onslaught from Churchill ('three years completely wasted . . . The British were partners, with EDC but not in it . . . not prepared to advise his fellow countrymen to undertake more . . . The British, thank God, still had the Channel . . . Sorry to have to speak in this way'), some of it delivered in a choking voice and with tears in the eyes.[28] 'What a remarkable actor,' commented one French eye-witness.*

Hard also for the French, a few days later, to listen to John Foster Dulles, the US Secretary of State, at the NATO meeting in Paris, warning them, in effect, that rejection of the EDC would be the end of the world. His fleshy jowls shaking in indignation, his eyes behind their steel-rimmed spectacles full of self-righteousness, he told a press conference that unless ratification of EDC were soon forthcoming, the US would be compelled to make an 'agonising reappraisal' of its policies. Far from having a settling effect upon French parliamentary opinion, one senior official in the Quai d'Orsay, himself pro-EDC, considered that Dulles' homily 'finished' EDC and that it must have been deliberate.[29] As 1954 dawned, the Laniel government was no further forward on the road to ratification. Its only mandate was a vaguely worded motion resulting from ten days of confused debate in the National Assembly, in which no one and no party shifted from their previously known position. The motion simply opted for the 'continuity of the policy of building a united Europe'.

It was not only over European policy that difficulties abounded. For some time the situation in the North African protectorates of Tunisia and Morocco had been steadily deteriorating. Early in 1952, Paris turned down flat a Tunisian request for an all-Tunisian government and administration. One of the main representatives of the North African lobby, Senator Colonna, had earlier addressed

---

* According to stories in the French press, additional offence was given when Churchill, greeting his colleagues at Bermuda airport, appeared to spend more time stroking the mascot – a goat – of the Welch Fusiliers, the regiment which was doing the honours, than in talking to the French Prime Minister. The French press agency reported that while the creature was '*un animal sympathique*', its recurrent presence at the entertainments held as part of the conference was 'a little too prominent'.

a memorandum to the government in which he argued that 'the Tunisians cannot be much trusted and they are incapable of either administering or governing their own country – we must continue to hold all the command posts.'[30] Soon after that, the newly appointed, hard-line French Resident-General ordered the arrest of Bourguiba and other Neo-Destour leaders. A few weeks later, he had the Prime Minister and three other ministers in the Tunisian government arrested and banished to the south of the country. Nationalist riots and French repression followed, and thousands were arrested by the French authorities.

Opposition in France to these strong-arm methods was not confined to the usual 'liberal' organs of opinion, such as *Le Monde*, or the Communists or fellow-travelling papers. The Socialists, no longer in the government, were indignant, and so were some sections of academic and trade union opinion. But a parliamentary debate held in May on Tunisian affairs was a fiasco. Successive motions were defeated by a series of changing majorities and the debate ended with no concluding vote of any kind. Where parliament was concerned, France had no Tunisian policy. No more depressing example could be imagined of the confusion and helplessness of Fourth Republican legislators when confronted with questions of empire.

Later in the year, the sky darkened still further when the Bey, by now completely disillusioned by French policies or the lack of them, refused to cooperate with the French-installed puppet government and appointed what amounted to an alternative government of nationalists. Tension increased with the European extremists turning up the heat. Pamphlets began to circulate in Tunis, imprinted with the mark of a red hand, and some members of the Bey's government received threatening letters. Then in December one of the leading nationalists, Ferhat Hached, was murdered. He was head of the Tunisian trade union movement and had contacts with the American Congress of Industrial Organisations (CIO) and the American Federation of Labour (AFL). His death caused an international sensation. The killers were never found, but the 'red hand' organisation was suspected and rumours circulated that the Resident-General's office could have been in the know. In Paris, the National Council of the Socialist party passed a motion deploring the policy of force; the text was censored by the Resident-General's office.

Self-government for Tunisia was something that the *petits blancs* were determined to resist. From their viewpoint, their attitude was easily explicable. What was at stake was their privileged position and their secure jobs in the public sector. Among their supporters in Paris was a powerful and opinionated figure, equally ferocious against Communism and North African nationalism, who held a variety of ministerial appointments between January 1952 and June 1954. Léon Martinaud-Déplat was a Radical of the old school and administrative Secretary-General of the Radical party (it was he who as Minister of Justice was involved in the affair of Duclos' pigeons).

It would be neat and easy, given the strength of his insistence on the maintenance of French domination over Tunisia and Morocco, to describe him as a reactionary colonialist, intent solely upon preserving French status and privileges. There was a good deal of this in his attitude, just as there was no doubt about his role as a political operator. But as a leading Radical-Socialist, he was in some measure the heir to and exponent of the old left-wing tradition of nineteenth-century French colonialism, which saw in overseas conquests and the spreading of French influence the chance to introduce the civilising benefits of Republican values, extending to the races thus colonised the inestimable privilege of sharing in those values. Tunisia and Morocco being Protectorates and not colonies, the application to them of this policy of assimilation was a legal nonsense. That did not bother Martinaud-Déplat. For him and those who thought like him, direct French rule was the only conceivable system in the North African territories. He and his friends were also exponents of the domino theory: any concession in Tunisia would have immediate repercussions in Morocco and eventually the trouble would spread to Algeria, part of the sacred soil of France itself. (The same argument applied to any prospect of negotiating with Ho Chi Minh.)

Martinaud-Déplat's power to influence events in North Africa was closely bound up with the political situation in Paris. The absence of the Socialists from Pinay's coalition meant that the Radical role became crucial. Successive prime ministers came to depend upon as many of the ninety-plus Radical voters as could be mustered for the application of chosen policies. This was especially true of EDC, where Radical opinion was divided. Martinaud-Déplat himself was pro-EDC, and his personal influence with his colleagues became therefore of great importance. Nor did matters stop there. Radical help was also needed in support of the Laniel government's attempts to re-stabilise the economy by cutting back public expenditure, attempts which in the summer of 1953 brought on a wave of strikes in the public sector. It was the greatest strike movement that France had experienced since the days of the Popular Front though, unlike the events of 1947 and 1948, it was everywhere peaceful.

By mid-August almost 4 million workers were on strike, and the country semi-paralysed (although the French tendency for everyone to go on holiday in August limited the effect). The Laniel government had a major trial of strength on its hands. Here again it needed all the support it could get, including that of the Radical ministers. It emerged from the encounter intact, but at the double cost of another demonstration of the impotence of the State and of creating a deep wedge between that State as an employee and the millions of people who worked for it.

Thus the interlocking nature of different problems left Martinaud-Déplat and his hardline friends in a decisive position vis-à-vis North African policy. The Socialists could and did protest against repressive actions there. The President of the Republic – though Auriol was in many respects the prototype of those who wished to keep the Tricolour flying wherever it had flown before – complained, after Ferhat Hached's murder, of the effect upon world opinion of crimes committed against Tunisians. But Martinaud-Déplat and the strong-arm men had a firm grip on the North African situation and were not letting go of it. Although the Laniel government, faced with growing violence between European and Arab extremists, did adopt more conciliatory policies in Tunisia, they were not enough to satisfy nationalist demands. By the spring and summer of 1954, when Tunisia was fast sinking into chaos, the choice had become one of all-out war against the nationalists or negotiations with them.

The Tunisian imbroglio had its counterpart, in a still more intense form, in Morocco, a country with far greater economic potential, far greater inducement for private investment, and therefore far higher stakes. There Juin, who had found, or rather had placed, himself at loggerheads with the Sultan, was succeeded in 1952 as Resident-General by General Guillaume, a man of Juin's persuasion and indeed choosing. He proceeded, after the disorders in Casablanca which followed upon the murder of Ferhat Hached in Tunisia and which led to killings on both Moroccan and French sides, to dismiss

from any position of responsibility any prominent Moroccan holding or suspected of holding nationalist sympathies. In Guillaume's
view, nationalism equalled Communism, every nationalist was a
Communist agent. This simple and convenient equation was fully
shared by Martinaud-Déplat and the colonial lobby in Paris.

The final target of these men could not fail to be the Sultan
himself, with his proclaimed nationalist sympathies. With the active
encouragement of Juin and Martinaud-Déplat and the colonialist
press in Paris, a plot began to take shape in the summer of 1953
for the deposition of the Sultan. Had not such a necessity been foreshadowed in the original instruction to Juin as Resident-General?
The time had come to put it into effect. It involved enlisting once
again the willing services of El Glaoui, the octogenarian Pasha
of Marrakesh, a bitter enemy of the Sultan (and also a friend
of Winston Churchill). In March, at his palace in Marrakesh, a
'petition' was organised, supposedly signed by hundreds of pashas
and *caïds* – though some of them later said they signed under
constraint – asking that the Sultan be deposed.

Three months later in Paris, at the Académie Française, Juin,
a newly elected member, made an unprecedented verbal assault
on François Mauriac, a fellow 'Immortal' and a vigorous critic,
speaking and writing with the voice of Christian conscience, of
repressive French policies in Morocco. Among the audience was
El Glaoui himself. Singled out for Juin's special commendation –
'ardent defender of the cause of Franco-Moroccan friendship, in
Morocco today he personifies loyalty to France' – the old man
rose from his seat in the spectators' gallery and received a public
ovation. It was an extraordinary scene. A few days later, Mauriac
wrote in *Le Figaro* that this sitting of the Academy 'was scarcely
worthy of a great country'.

What passed in Paris between El Glaoui, Juin and the rest of
the North African lobby can only be guesswork. What is certain is that on his return to Morocco, El Glaoui summoned his
followers, had his puppet candidate, the aged Sidi Mohammed
Ouled Moulay Arafa, named Iman Imam, or religious leader,
and sent his Berber cavalry, who had played such a dubious role
in the 1951 crisis, to encircle the capital, Rabat. On 20 August,
Guillaume returned from Paris, armed with fresh instructions. In
theory, the choice was between challenging El Ghaoui's horsemen,
a course of action which would have opposed France and perhaps

French troops to the man described by Juin as France's best friend, or leaning on the Sultan to abdicate. In fact, there was no room for doubt. Guillaume told the Sultan that for the sake of law and order and his own safety, he and his sons must leave the country.

Moulay Arafa, El Glaoui's man, was then proclaimed temporal sovereign and the deposed monarch was flown to Corsica in a French military aircraft, on his way to exile in Madagascar. On arrival, he saw troops waiting. 'They're not going to shoot me?' he asked. 'Sire,' replied the official deputed to meet him, 'formal instructions have been given that Your Majesty should have the benefit of French hospitality.'[31] The plot had apparently worked perfectly; the cause of *la présence française* had been triumphantly reasserted and the stuffing knocked out of Moroccan nationalism. That at least was the theory. In fact, within a few weeks, Morocco was again the scene of violent incidents and prolonged unrest. It passes comprehension that Laniel, a few months later, could claim that he had settled the Moroccan problem.

The degree of direct complicity of the French government in these murky proceedings is not easy to establish. For one thing, the government was deeply divided. Laniel, the Prime Minister, was doubtful about the Sultan's deposition, but was ready to trust Guillaume. Martinaud-Déplat, Minister of the Interior, made no pretence of his views. For him, French North Africa must be seen as a whole. If Moroccan nationalism was allowed its head, the effects would be bound to be felt in Tunisia (just as, for him, the reverse was true). His fellow Radical, Edgar Faure, by now Minister of Finance, strenuously opposed this strong-arm policy and specifically the dethronement of the Sultan. So did several other ministers, in varying degrees, though only one, to his honour, resigned: François Mitterrand, future President of the Fifth Republic, who held a junior post. The trouble was that, with the need to maintain the government majority in favour of the Faure programme of economic and financial recovery, the views of Faure and those who thought like him were paralysed; resignations of senior ministers would have caused the collapse of the government, a luxury not to be afforded in that summer of strikes and unrest. Pleven, Minister of Defence in the Laniel government, was a similar case: as the author of the Pleven plan for a European army, now formalised in the EDC treaty, he felt bound to restrain his doubts over Moroccan policy because the

MRP was the strongest supporter of the EDC and Bidault was its man at the Quai d'Orsay.

Bidault's own role in the Moroccan business was particularly serpentine. A strongly worded paper by the Director of African and Near-Eastern Affairs at the Quai d'Orsay, written after the event, complains of the intrigues and manoeuvres of senior French officials in Morocco and concludes that the government was faced with a *fait accompli*.[32] But Auriol himself began to wonder whether Bidault was not privy to the plot, so shifty were his answers to awkward questions. There is plenty of evidence that he saw no objection, indeed quite the contrary, to the forced departure of the Sultan. Twelve years later, in his memoirs, he said as much: 'In 1953 the Laniel government was led, at my suggestion, to remove the Sultan from the Moroccan throne, where he had ruled for 25 years.'[33] Once El Glaoui's machinations had had their intended result, this is indeed what Bidault recommended to the Council of Ministers.

Whether or not Bidault was part of the plot, the government of which he was a leading member certainly underwrote what Guillaume had done. Fear of civil war if the *fait accompli* was not officially sanctioned seems to have been the guiding thought. But some ministers complied with a heavy heart. 'You are going to appear impotent rogues,' Edgar Faure told his colleagues, in a burst of plain speaking. Paul Reynaud, one of Laniel's deputy prime ministers, cynically suggested that the Sultan's deposition could be justified to American opinion by saying that he was supported by the Communists.

What was ominous in all this for the future of the Fourth Republic was firstly the widely shared impression that the Moroccan affair had been the outcome of a plot hatched, in Rabat and Paris, not just by political die-hards but by senior French officials including Guillaume himself; secondly that the government was too weak or too divided, or both, to do anything about it or to initiate any alternative policy; and thirdly that French opinion, faced with the rival claims of colonial conservatism and liberalising instincts over North Africa, was deeply divided, as it was destined to be in later years over Algeria. The ferocity of the hard-liners is illustrated by a threatening letter which a *colon* in Casablanca sent to Mauriac, after the latter had accused the government of being one of the conspirators in the Moroccan plot: 'You might as well know,' this enraged colonial farmer wrote, 'that if you continue to write such tripe [in support of Moroccan nationalism] you are going to have an accident one of these days. You're a dirty dog and a traitor to Marshal Pétain . . . *à bientôt, salaud.*'[34] Here was the genuine touch of thuggish right-wing intolerance which was later to characterise the feelings of many North African *colons* about their opponents in France. Something of the same spirit could be found in the Army. A senior former French official recalls[35] a slightly later period in Morocco, when regular French officers were seconded to help to train and advise units of the Moroccan army. When they returned to their own messes, their brother officers turned their backs on them.

The person who emerged from the Moroccan affair with renewed arrogance and disdain was Juin. There were rumours firstly that a military putsch in France in his favour was being planned; secondly that he would be a candidate in the forthcoming elections for the presidency of the Republic. There was nothing in either story, and a fortnight after the Sultan had been sent on his way, Juin defined his own position in a public speech: 'Those who have floated this idea [of his candidature for the Elysée] do not know me. You would not want me to abandon my title of Marshal of France in order to assume functions which consist more of boring drudgeries than of the exercise of power . . .' The tone, and the choice of language, seemed to be deliberately insulting about the office of President. No wonder that Mauriac wrote, shortly afterwards, of the dangers facing the Republic which he defined as '*l'appel au soldat*'.

Auriol himself had already marked down Juin as a haughty and uncontrollable, or anyway uncontrolled, officer. Two years earlier he wrote in his diary, when Juin was Resident-General in Rabat and showing every sign of being his own master, 'I do not forgive him for the agitation he has created and for the personal policies that he is carrying out, and with the deep respect I have for the idea of the State, I am against generals and high commissioners behaving like satraps.'

It would be inaccurate to describe the mass of Army officers in 1953 as disaffected or disloyal. Indeed, many of them, whatever their contempt for the politicians, never strayed, then or later, from the path of duty and obedience. But the malaise in the Army, to which EDC, the unwinnable war in Indochina and the spectacle of political disarray in Paris all contributed, was by now a growing threat to the régime. It is not too capricious, even using hindsight, to see in the example set by Juin – his obvious contempt for Republican institutions, and the fact that he, Algerian-born and the only living Maréchal de France, could be thought to represent and speak for the Army in North Africa – one of the first ripples of the great wave that in 1958 was to wash over and drown the Fourth Republic.

Auriol was being prophetic to a degree he could not have dreamed of at the time, when he wrote in his diary, after the plot had run its course:

> It was a *coup d'Etat*, against Morocco, against the Sultan, and against the Republic . . . Everything worked as though it had been deliberately planned – and it had been deliberately planned . . . There is no more government, no more State in France, there are gentlemen over there who take the decisions according to their own interests and passions.[36]

Although the Fourth Republic had five years of life ahead of it, these thoughts of its first citizen read today like a funerary oration over its corpse.

CHAPTER 7

The annus mirabilis *of Mendès-France*

If by late 1953 the situation in North Africa was unpromising, that of Indochina was nearing the stage of disaster. De Lattre's death in January 1952 marked an end to the apparent upswing in French fortunes, as well as the loss of an inspired and inspiring leader. But though de Lattre certainly re-established morale and helped to rally the Vietnamese to fight for their own cause, this upswing was more apparent than real. It is arguable that ever since the autumn of 1950, when the French had withdrawn from their positions close to the Chinese border and left Communist China free to supply the Vietminh, the outcome of the war had in effect been decided.

By March 1953, Giap had shown that Tonkin, considered by de Lattre to be 'the bolt to the door to South-East Asia', could be bypassed by his highly mobile forces. In contrast, the French Expeditionary Corps was deplorably inflexible. Of the half-million men it finally comprised, 350,000 were tied down by static tasks. General Raoul Salan, de Lattre's successor, planned to restore mobility to these static elements by handing over pacification tasks to the armies of the Associated States, for whom American equipment was beginning to arrive. This plan was developed by General Navarre, Salan's successor, chosen by Prime Minister René Mayer for the somewhat bizarre reason that he knew nothing whatever about Indochina, never having served there. Navarre quickly understood that his task was not to win the unwinnable war but to 'create the military conditions for an honourable political solution which would be adopted when the time was ripe'.[1] He had been told as much by Mayer: 'Seek an honourable way of getting out' had been the instruction. Navarre therefore planned, in 1953–4, to adopt a largely defensive strategy in the north, where the weight of Giap's divisions was concentrated, and then in 1955 to launch a general offensive which would enable France to negotiate from strength. The government in Paris, unable, or at least unwilling, to supply Navarre with all the men and material he had asked for, in effect gave him a free hand to do the best he could in the circumstances.

Over the years, successive governments were repeatedly warned by their military advisers that with the means at hand the war could not be ended militarily. The logical conclusion should have been either to reinforce the military effort by sending national servicemen (politically unacceptable) or to end the war, even if that meant giving to Ho Chi Minh what earlier governments had refused to give. Various attempts were made, it is true, to initiate secret approaches to the Vietminh, notably by Antoine Pinay, during his prime ministership, and by René Mayer during his. But they came to nothing, and the war continued, with its heavy toll of human and material losses but with no clear war aims.

There is no disputing that the burden was a heavy one. From 1945 to 1954, 20,685 French soldiers of all ranks lost their lives (including de Lattre's only son), along with 11,620 members of the Foreign Legion, 15,229 Africans and North Africans, 27,666 Vietnamese embodied in the French Expeditionary Corps, and 17,597 soldiers of the Associated States (Vietnam, Laos and Cambodia), a total of nearly 93,000. Between 1952 and 1955, French military expenditure, much of which went on Indochina, accounted for about one-third of the budget. But there were compensations, some of them of a highly disreputable kind. The traffic in piastres, the Indochinese currency, was one of these.

The official value of the piastre had been fixed by Paris, in a decree dating from December 1945, at 17 francs. Its real value was about seven francs. Encouragement was thus given to illicit operations, from which a number of people, chiefly Vietnamese and French administrators (including Bao Dai personally), and the Vietminh, were thought to have benefited largely. Just how much these frauds cost the French Treasury and rewarded the Vietminh is hard to say; the parliamentary commission set up to establish the facts found it difficult to answer such questions. But public opinion, once the piastre 'scandal' had burst upon it, quickly became convinced that there was murky business afoot and that some hard-faced men were doing well out of the war. The Communists were able to press home with renewed vigour their charges of '*une sale guerre*'.

Even the Army, while professing distaste for these fiddles, was opposed to a devaluation of the piastre, which would have removed the temptation to speculate. René Mayer explained to the parliamentary commission of inquiry into the piastre affair: 'There was also the question of the morale of the Expeditionary Corps. . . . [De Lattre's staff] very often was among the main opponents of any kind of devaluation which would have affected the arrangements of those fighting in Indochina for sending money to their families, for their savings, and for the capital which they could build up in France for their families or themselves.'2 (Devaluation was unilaterally carried out by Paris in May 1953, after de Lattre's death.)

Another important element in the Indochinese equation was the contribution made to the French economy by American aid for the war. Between June 1950 and May 1954, according to US statistics, Washington handed over aid totalling $3.6 billion, equivalent to 80 per cent of the cost of the war.* Thanks to this supply of dollars, which began to flow just as Marshall Aid came to an end, France was able to finance her foreign imports, at the same time as she was relieved of much of the expense of the war. It was not long before the Communists were making use of the disagreeable but not entirely groundless comparison: American dollars in return for the sacrifice of French and native lives.

A further product of the war was that it enabled French governments and even more their opponents to justify continued prevarication over or actual hostility to EDC. The argument was that the military demands of the Indochinese commitment made it difficult if not impossible for France to contemplate a scale of German rearmament which would leave the level of German forces in Europe superior to that of the French. There was something in these arguments, but they would have held more water if those same

---

* These figures differ according to sources and are open to varying interpretations. In *The Two Vietnams* (London, Pall Mall Press, 1963) Bernard Fall distinguishes (p. 458) between US funds allotted to France under NATO and the mutual Security Program ($4 billion), funds voted by Congress for Indochina ($1.4 billion) and such funds actually expended up to the time of the cease-fire ($954 million). Fall puts total French expenditure on the war at $11 billion. Contrast this with Mendès-France (investiture speech May 1953), who said that 'half the cost of the war' was being met by the US. What is certain is that the access to fresh sources of foreign exchange was an important prop for the French economy.

governments had raised the length of conscript military service to two years, which is what it was at the time in Britain.

At the end of October 1953, with no sign or prospect of a military solution in Indochina – realistically, there never had been one, as Leclerc had realised years before – the National Assembly held a typically inconclusive debate on the subject. The final motion invited the government to do everything possible to 'achieve, through negotiation, the general pacification of Asia'. Even at this late hour, it was impossible for a government depending for survival upon Gaullist, MRP and right-wing support to sponsor a motion which explicitly foreshadowed direct negotiations with Ho Chi Minh and the likely abandonment of the French presence – though Laniel did undertake to 'study every constructive proposal' coming from the Vietminh.

Just previous to this, a Vietnamese congress in Saigon, a body of nationalist delegates who were simultaneously anti-Vietminh and anti-French, had given considerable annoyance in France by making it clear not only that Vietnam wanted its independence – already promised to all three Associated States by Paris – but that it did not choose to remain within the French Union. As one left-wing newspaper (*Libération*) put it, 'In those circumstances, what the devil are our soldiers doing out there? Why not bring them home immediately?' This certainly echoed a growing sentiment in public opinion, even though some ministers in Laniel's government, notably Georges Bidault and some others of the MRP contingent, as well as the confirmed colonialist Martinaud-Déplat, were staunch opponents of French withdrawal from Indochina. But how could the French presence, and the continuation of the war, together with the means to continue it, be justified once the principle of independence for the three Associated States had been conceded, at least in theory? 'In theory' is a highly necessary qualification. In fact, despite seemingly bold decisions taken in Paris to dismantle the old colonial system in France's Far Eastern empire, nothing really changed. 'In the last years of French rule, there were more French officials in Indochina than there had been British serving in all India at any period of our rule.'[3]

Late in October, Vincent Auriol received at the Elysée a Vietnamese Catholic bishop, who said that his country wanted independence. 'But you've got it,' replied Auriol, at which the bishop complained that despite promises of independence, 'We have seen no change, we've still got your High Commissioner, your officials . . . Nothing has changed in the state of mind of French officials and we are still under direct [French] rule.' Auriol wrote in his diary: 'I felt that what he was saying was right.'[4] Given this background, it was scarcely surprising if the increasing inconsistency of French objectives began to become apparent even to those for whom the Indochina war had always been a closed, or at least an unreadable and unread, book.

The denouement was not long in coming. In January 1954, a four-power meeting (US, UK, USSR, France) took place in Berlin, the first of its kind to be held for nearly three years. Its purpose was to see, following the death of Stalin, whether agreement could be reached on the future of Germany. It could not, but what emerged, almost as a by-product of the meeting, was an agreement to convene a conference at Geneva in April, for a discussion of Far Eastern matters, including Korea and Indochina, by the interested powers, one of which was China. The Americans at first opposed this, because of the recognition of China it implied, and Bidault was also reluctant. While not ruling out a negotiated solution, he wished such a negotiation to be conducted from strength, and in no case directly with the Vietminh. Only a few weeks later he was to tell a pro-negotiation Socialist who had been authorised by the government to make contact with the Vietminh that Ho Chi Minh was on the point of surrender, and it would only be lending him strength to seek contacts with him. But that is precisely the prospect that the Geneva conference offered, and was intended to offer.

The truth was that the groundswell in France for an end to the Indochinese war was now so strong that no government could withstand it and survive (just as the Laniel government felt unable openly to originate direct negotiations with Ho Chi Minh). Not long after, Laniel, the Prime Minister, told the National Assembly that while previously there had been conflicting views on whether negotiation or force of arms was the best way out of the Indochinese imbroglio, the time for such arguments was now past: 'We are in fact unanimous in wanting to settle the conflict by means of negotiation.' But with whom? At the end of the previous November, Ho Chi Minh gave an interview to the Swedish newspaper *Expressen* in which he said he was ready to negotiate without making the withdrawal of the French Expeditionary Corps a precondition.[5] As usual, the government in Paris was divided, as between those, a majority, who wanted international negotiations and those who favoured direct contacts with the Vietminh. Bidault condemned the *Expressen* offer as 'a propaganda manoeuvre'. In the event, Ho's initiative went unanswered.

Laniel's references to negotiation may have been politically realistic, indeed long overdue, but militarily, in terms of the fight with the Vietminh, they were a dubious contribution. The agreement at Berlin to hold a Far Eastern conference at Geneva meant, in effect, that negotiations for a political settlement were already on the international agenda before any substantial military advantage could be established on the ground. Navarre, the Commander-in-Chief in Indochina, always considered that the announcement of the Geneva conference was a major factor in the battle for Dien Bien Phu. The camp's fate, he was to write later, 'was sealed on the day that the Geneva conference was decided on'.[6]

According to General Navarre, the final humiliation of France was the result not of the fall of Dien Bien Phu, but of Geneva; the politicians, not the military, were ultimately responsible. Apart from the effects, real or imagined, of the Berlin conference upon the course of the war in Indochina, Navarre had some good reasons for grievance. At a meeting of the National Defence Committee in Paris in July 1953 he had made it plain, while unveiling his two-year plan for the future conduct of the war, that if he was going to be required to defend Laos against a Vietminh attack, he would have to resort to a tactic he did not like – the establishment of 'hedgehogs', or combined air and land bases, of which Dien Bien Phu was a prime example. Juin, at the same meeting, agreed that if Navarre did not receive the reinforcements he was asking for (and he did not get all of them), then he had no choice but to go for the bad strategy of 'hedgehogs'.[7] The meeting left Navarre with no firm instructions about Laos; he was to use his own judgement, according to the military and political circumstances at the time.

The committee of inquiry set up after the Dien Bien Phu débâcle was largely inconclusive in its findings, but did consider that Navarre had been left without proper guidelines. This was a grievous example of pusillanimity in Paris. The government knew that if French good faith towards the component parts of Vietnam – i.e. the Associated States – was to be sustained, it would be desirable to be seen defending Laos. But they stopped short of saying so and, more importantly, of providing the means to mount a realistic defence.

Despite the shortage of reinforcements, Navarre got off to a good start with his plan, launching some daring raids on Vietminh positions which showed that the long-term build-up did not mean an end to offensive operations. By November 1953, these successes caused the Laniel government to wonder whether the conditions of negotiating from strength had not arrived. Navarre advised not; better to wait, he said, until the following spring and summer, when the military situation would have improved still further.

It was at this point that Giap began to deploy his forces in a pattern designed to suggest that the expected attack on Laos was under way. Lacking any proper political guidance, Navarre decided to defend Laos. In effect, he walked into Giap's trap. On 20 November, six French paratroop battalions were dropped onto the bowl-shaped site of the village of Dien Bien Phu, 170 miles west of Hanoi, near the border with Laos. Navarre was criticised at the time, and still more after the war was over, for his error of judgement in choosing Dien Bien Phu as a 'hedgehog' base, totally dependent as it was upon the air for supplies and reinforcements. (General Cogny, responsible for operations in North Vietnam, bore just as much, if not more, of the blame.)

It was indeed a rash decision, even though Navarre had warned the politicians about the undesirability of 'hedgehogs'. The garrison's fate was effectively sealed as early as mid-March 1954, when a massed Vietminh attack put part of the airstrip out of action. Apart from the problem of supply, a fatal French error had been seriously to underestimate the Vietminh's capacity to achieve artillery superiority. With their gun emplacements dug into the hillsides overlooking the camp, the Vietnamese gunners were largely invulnerable to French counter-battery fire or strafing from the air. The unhappy colonel commanding the French artillery was so overcome by the enormity of the miscalculation that he committed suicide soon after this first Vietminh assault.

Navarre was not to know, when he abandoned his earlier plan for a slow build-up and committed himself to taking on the enemy in pitched battle, that Giap too had decided to make Dien Bien Phu the decisive battlefield, to which he was to commit almost all his fighting force. Navarre's later claim that the prospect of the Geneva conference contributed to the disaster at Dien Bien Phu cannot be proved, but it is certainly true that the impending conference raised the price of victory (and thereby the price of

defeat) at Dien Bien Phu to mountainous heights, for the victor
on the battlefield would have a superior chance of being the victor
at the negotiating table. After the Vietminh attack in March on
the base, it could have been no coincidence but a calculated piece
of timing that Giap mounted his final and successful assault at the
end of April, with an eye to its maximum effect on the first formal
meeting of the Geneva negotiators on Indochina.

The period between mid-March and the fall of the Laniel government in mid-June was one of high drama, heavy with consequence
for the future of the Fourth Republic. Nor was the drama confined
to France. In Washington, the attack on Dien Bien Phu was viewed
with alarm, representing as it seemed to do the promise of a threat
to the whole of South-East Asia. Even before that, the Americans,
while continuing to express admiration for the fighting forces in
Indochina, were disturbed by the increasingly clear evidence that
French aims were no longer to win the war, but to get into the best
possible negotiating position. President Eisenhower began to talk
about dominoes (if Vietnam 'fell', neighbouring countries would also
be in danger of 'falling'), and when General Ely, the French Chief of
Staff, mentioned to his US counterpart, Admiral Radford, the need
for increased air support at Dien Bien Phu, he got a sympathetic
hearing, though in fact views were divided in Washington about
the desirability, and the consequences, of American intervention.
The great majority of Congress and of the Chiefs of Staff opposed
it. But three powerful figures – Vice-President Nixon, Foster Dulles
and Admiral Radford, Chairman of the Joint Chiefs – were all
in varying degrees attracted towards some method of 'stopping
Communism'.

It was not until 4 April, after Navarre had reported that an
American air strike, specifically on the Vietminh artillery positions,
could have a decisive effect, that a formal French request for such a
strike was conveyed to Washington. The predictable answer came
back that Congressional approval would be necessary. This was not
the only US objection. Instead of a single strike on Dien Bien Phu,
Dulles wanted the whole of Indochina saved from Communism.
His plan was to internationalise the war. The Americans were
determined not to move alone; the support of the other allies,
especially Britain, was needed. It was not forthcoming, either then
or at any other moment during the crisis, either as regards Dien
Bien Phu or over the Dulles plan for internationalisation. Anthony

Eden, the British Foreign Secretary, did not share the interventionist views of Foster Dulles, who claimed to see a parallel between the Indochinese situation and the Japanese invasion of Manchuria in 1931, as well as Hitler's reoccupation of the Rhineland. For Eden, French appeals for help 'were all too reminiscent of the French demand for our last RAF squadrons in 1940'.[8] Winston Churchill, the Prime Minister, agreed entirely with Eden. What the British government was being asked to do, he robustly declared, was to 'assist in misleading Congress into approving a military operation which would in itself be ineffective and might well lead to the verge of a major war'.[9]

This first rejection did not deter Paris, as the situation of the beleaguered garrison at Dien Bien Phu worsened, from trying again. On 23 April, Bidault told Dulles, who was in Paris for a NATO ministerial meeting, that unless the US could provide massive and urgent support for Dien Bien Phu, it would be necessary to seek a cease-fire. Once again, the response was negative. Nearly everyone on the American side, with the exception of Radford, now seemed convinced that nothing could save Dien Bien Phu, though Dulles was still thinking in wider terms of 'stopping Communism' in South-East Asia by means of concerted action involving the US, the UK, France, Australia, New Zealand, Thailand and the Philippines.

Neither the British nor the French thought anything of this idea. The government in Paris was concerned not to endanger the chances of a compromise settlement at Geneva, and above all was totally preoccupied with Dien Bien Phu. They had reason to be. No one who lived through those weeks in Paris could ever forget the atmosphere of despair and disarray. Early in April, there had been the scene at the Arc de Triomphe (see Prelude, pp. 2–3). Three days after this, General de Gaulle, emerging from his self-imposed silence at Colombey-les-Deux-Eglises, came to Paris and held a press conference at which he attacked the EDC, approved Marshal Juin's defiance, and insisted that the régime should be of a kind to ensure that 'France exists in her own right, that she has a policy, that she has a system of independent and balanced defence, that she is an atomic power and that she has nuclear arms'. He also announced that on 9 May, the anniversary of the victory in Europe, he would go alone to the Arc de Triomphe to pay respects to the Unknown Soldier (which he duly did, but without the crowds he had expected turning up, even though it was only two days after the garrison at

Dien Bien Phu surrendered). If this attempt to exploit the distress of the public somewhat misfired, it did nothing to bring comfort to those in power. De Gaulle's strictures about incompetence and lack of policy rang only too true.

As the shadows closed in on Dien Bien Phu, French ministers became almost obsessional in their efforts to persuade the Americans to intervene. One of them suggested that if US aircraft were to bombard the terrain round Dien Bien Phu, they could be marked with French insignia and be considered part of the Foreign Legion.[10] Bidault was more than usually devious, telling the British that France would fight on even after the fall of Dien Bien Phu, and suggesting the opposite to the Americans. Laniel was personally distraught at the thought of the fate awaiting the Dien Bien Phu garrison; one of the messengers at the Hôtel Matignon kept asking him whether anything could be done to save it.

Ely sought another meeting with Radford, also in Paris for the NATO meeting, and pleaded with him for US intervention. He recognised that it could make no difference to the situation at Dien Bien Phu, but said that it would be psychologically important for France and Vietnamese opinion. He referred to Operation Vulture (*Vautour* in French), the code name for a possible air strike; Radford professed not to know the word, which is inexplicable. Not only was he the leading American interventionist, but senior US officers had already visited Saigon and Tonkin to make plans for the air strike. They envisaged sixty Flying Fortresses, based in Manila, escorted by 150 fighters from the US Seventh Fleet, flying successive sorties, each of which would drop 450 tons of bombs.

Dillon, the US Ambassador in Paris, thought that lacking any US intervention, the Laniel government would fall and be replaced with a successor pledged to negotiate with Ho Chi Minh and to the withdrawal of French forces from Indochina. What difference the air strike would have made is impossible to know. But as a prophecy of what actually did happen, the Ambassador's judgement cannot be faulted. Dulles, in Paris, reported to Eisenhower that 'France is almost visibly collapsing under our eyes . . . Dien Bien Phu has become the symbol out of all proportion to its military importance.' The second part of this statement was undeniably true, but the first was another example of the tendency to describe situations in lurid terms and colours which was often the hallmark of the Dulles style.

That same tendency seems to have shown itself in a remarkable conversation which took place between Bidault and Dulles in Paris at the time of the second French appeal for American help. Dulles suddenly said to the French Foreign Minister: 'And what if I (or we) give you two of them?' 'Two what?' 'Two atomic bombs.' Bidault was flabbergasted, and with reason. Whatever Dulles said or meant, Bidault was not disposed then or at any other time to take seriously the offer of two atomic bombs 'to save Dien Bien Phu'.[11] The matter is fully discussed by McGeorge Bundy in his book,[12] which concludes that at the very least, Dulles said enough to Bidault 'to create a misunderstanding'. But Bundy also shows that a Pentagon study group did examine the question of using nuclear weapons at Dien Bien Phu, and concluded that 'three tactical A-weapons, properly employed, would be sufficient to smash the Vietminh effort there.' Dulles knew about the findings of this study group, and it is plausible that this is what he had in mind in his conversation with Bidault.

Six months later, Dulles himself said he had no recollection of making any such offer to the French. Nonetheless at the time – end of April 1954 – he was telling the NATO meeting that such atomic weapons 'must now be treated as in fact having become conventional'. But none of this means that the US, in the fevered days leading up to the fall of Dien Bien Phu, came anywhere near making a formal proposition to use nuclear weapons in Indochina, nor that the French ministers, whatever the straws they were frantically clutching at, came anywhere near wanting or considering such use. (At a later stage, when the government came to discuss the French negotiating position at Geneva, some of its members, notably Paul Reynaud, were ready, in their desire to bring pressure to bear on China, to contemplate the use of US nuclear weapons against China.)

The fall of Dien Bien Phu to the Vietminh occurred on 7 May, twelve days after the opening of the Geneva conference. Although its inevitability had been fully recognised for some time, the effect of the defeat on French opinion was immense. For a month, the courageous efforts of the 16,000-strong garrison of seventeen nationalities to withstand the attacks of the Vietminh, who numbered 40,000, had been described in gruesome and admiring detail in the French press. When the end came, the French Expeditionary Force lost seventeen of its best battalions, thousands of French Union soldiers were taken prisoner, and there were 4,000 within the camp left seriously wounded, many of whom never recovered. During the siege, 1,530 volunteers, replacements for specialists who had been killed or wounded, parachuted into the camp, 94 of them only one day before it succumbed; 800 of these heroes were Vietnamese. It was understandable that the Americans should deplore the fact that 'the fall of a small outpost' appeared to be the prelude to a general French capitulation. But this was to misunderstand the tragic significance which French opinion and the French press, for so long ignorant of and indifferent to the war, attached to the fall of the fortress. A cartoon in *Le Figaro* in April, called '*Dernier Réduit*', showed prominent government ministers, including Bidault and Pleven, the Defence Minister, in a dug-out, using their last cartridges on themselves. For years afterwards, the very words Dien Bien Phu resounded, like the tolling of a passing bell, in French ears.

For many the defeat symbolised at once the end of French claims to be a great power, the beginning of the end of French colonialism (though that road still had some way to run), and the inadequacy of the political system and the men who manned it to measure up to requirements. This at least is how the débâcle was seen by what might be called the Establishment. In his memoirs, Gladwyn Jebb (later Lord Gladwyn), British Ambassador in Paris 1954–60, noted that the fall of Dien Bien Phu was felt 'by a good many Frenchmen, more particularly among *bien pensants* and the *gratin* [orthodox conservatives and the upper crust of Paris society], to be national humiliation.'[13] Public opinion as a whole, so far as it could be measured by the polls of the Institute of Public Opinion, told a somewhat different story. In July 1947, less than eight months after the undeclared war had begun, 52 per cent of those questioned favoured fighting on until victory, 48 per cent wanted negotiation or withdrawal. By October 1950, the war party's figures had dropped to 38 per cent, the negotiators' had risen to 52 per cent. In May 1953 the figures were 15 and 50 per cent, and by February 1954 they had changed again to 7 and 60 per cent. These results point clearly not only to a major shift in thinking but also to a steady decrease in the rate of response, suggesting growing indifference. But these indications in no way softened the impact or diminished the distress caused by the surrender at Dien Bien Phu.

There was no indifference about public attitudes, after the fall of the camp, towards the Laniel government. No one had a good word to say for it, and the fact that it was enabled to hang on to power for another month was due solely to the reluctance of its critics in the National Assembly to bring about a government crisis while the Geneva conference was in progress. In the middle of May, it survived a vote of confidence by only two votes, and from then on was no more than a ghost, a fact which did nothing to strengthen Bidault's already weak hand in Geneva. Finally, on 12 June, the government, at the end of a debate on Indochina, succumbed to a vote of no confidence.

The debate was characterised by some fierce exchanges between Bidault and Mendès-France, with the latter accusing the government of which Bidault was a member of being the embodiment, for years, of 'imprudence and, more recently, . . . of impulsiveness, irrationality, continual contradiction'. The charges were true, but Bidault, whatever his contribution to the collapse of the government's credibility (he had, for example, refused at Geneva to have any contact with the head of the Vietminh delegation), was in an impossible position. As he reminded the deputies, every word spoken by them, every article published in the press, evoked an immediate and sometimes fearsome echo at Geneva. He was soon relieved of his agony. On 17 June 1954, Mendès-France was voted in as Prime Minister by a huge majority which included the ninety-nine Communists, the first time since 1947 that they had voted for any Prime Minister-designate. Mendès at once made it plain that in order not to create any undesirable obligations and compromise his position at the Geneva conference, he was subtracting these votes from his total. This still left him with more than the required constitutional majority.

It was a remarkable achievement, the more so because President Coty had not gone through the usual crisis rigmarole of consulting parliamentary groupings, asking Monsieur X to form a government, and when he proved incapable of doing so encouraging Monsieur Y to try his hand. In the past, this process had tended to lead, through sheer weariness, to the third or fourth or fifth candidate winning the Assembly's vote. Instead, Coty appealed directly and straight away to Mendès-France, the chief and most potent non-Communist critic of the government's Indochinese policy, or lack of it, and indeed of most other policies. The President (unfortunately for the historian he did not, like Auriol, keep diaries) must have been well satisfied with his choice. Yet despite the triumph of the investiture debate, and the sense of a new and invigorating wind blowing over the foetid swamps and marshes of French party politics, the arithmetic of the Assembly had not changed. There were still as many majorities as there were problems. For those with eyes to see and fingers to count on, the path of the future, for all the promise that a new man with new ideas brought to it, was strewn with obstacles and mantraps.

The ex-Gaullists, under their new label of Social Republicans, had voted for Mendès-France: that ensured trouble when he came to address himself to the EDC, still an unexploded bomb in the undergrowth. On the other hand, more than 80 per cent of the MRP, champions of the European idea and quasi-hereditary guardians, ever since the Liberation, of the Quai d'Orsay and, more recently, of the ministry for relations with the Associated States, had abstained. Their growing personal hostility to Mendès and all his works (which he reciprocated) was to be an important element in the coming months. It was not the least of the ironies of this time that the public Mendès tried to appeal to, the hopes he held out, were the same as those which the MRP, the new, left-of-centre, reforming Christian Democrat party, had attempted to represent just after the Liberation. On the right, the classical conservatives were against him from the start. Even his own Radical party was divided in its views of him; between his cold logic and liberal views and the reactionary guile and stance of a Martinaud-Déplat there was a wide and unbridgeable gulf.

It is not, of course, accurate to describe Mendès as a new man, nor his ideas as new. Ever since his unsuccessful bid in 1945 to persuade de Gaulle to make the difficult choice for France's economic future (see pp. 20–2), he had been someone marked by the originality and unswerving nature of his thinking. Nowhere was this more true than over Indochina. As early as October 1950, when French policy seemed fixed on the Bao Dai experiment – continuing to fight the Vietminh while building up a supposedly independent Vietnamese State – Mendès had spoken in the Assembly about the 'incoherence' of French policy, about the ineluctability of choice: either allocate many more men and much more money to the prosecution of the war, or seek a political settlement involving big concessions. From then on, he continuously delivered similar warnings, even though their message evoked far less response than the more strident '*sale guerre*' slogan of the Communists.

In his unsuccessful bid for the premiership in the long summer crisis of 1953, he used one of his favourite phrases, 'to govern is to choose', meaning that France could not attack all her problems piecemeal and at once; in particular, he said, the burden of the Indochinese war had become too heavy and a peaceful solution was desirable. It was an impressive speech, sounding a rarely heard note of realism and candour. But it excited, in the minds of some, dark suspicions of Mendès' real intentions on foreign policy and Indochina. Was he seeking to detach France from the Western alliance? In the lobbies, his enemies busied themselves fanning these suspicions, mixing in with them more than a dash of anti-Semitism.* On that occasion Mendès failed by thirteen votes to secure the necessary constitutional majority, but as he himself remarked prophetically, the debate which he had initiated would not go away.

In the first number (10 May 1953) of the new weekly magazine *L'Express*, which was to become one of his main mouthpieces, Mendès again promoted the idea of negotiations over Indochina: 'Our negotiating position was better last year than now, it is probably less bad now than it will be next year.' And it was again in *L'Express*, exactly one year later, just after the fall of Dien Bien Phu, that he published his 'Appeal to Youth', in which the ideas that went into his successful investiture speech the following month are set out. The thought and wording in the appeal were significant. He wrote of 'this new battle of the Liberation which is beginning . . . for the great crusade of renewal for which we are hoping for France.' General de Gaulle could have penned these words.

There was indeed something identifiably Gaullist in Mendès' criticisms of the ideological and party squabbles of the post-war years, the inadequacy of the ad hoc approach to problems which demanded, if a dynamic France with a bright future was to be created, consistent and long-term policies. In his investiture speeches of 1953, when he failed, and 1954, when he succeeded, he had acknowledged his debt to de Gaulle, 'symbol of French continuity and guiding spirit of the Resistance', as well as to Poincaré, the apostle of

---

* The anti-Semitic prejudice which ran, and still runs, through much of French society was frequently turned against Mendès. Nor did it come only from the conventional, anti-Dreyfus, Right. After Mendès at his investiture in 1954 had made it clear that he was not going to count the Communist vote, Jacques Duclos was heard to say, in the lobbies, 'Cold-footed little Jew' (Alexander Werth, *The Strange History of Pierre Mendès-France* (London, Barrie, 1957), p. 88).

Above: Robert Capa catches the spirit of the Resistance in this picture of the Champs-Elysées on Liberation Day, 26 August 1944. The unity symbolised by the composition of the group in the jeep was to prove short-lived.
Below: Later the same day, General de Gaulle leaves Notre-Dame after a thanksgiving *Te Deum*. The service had to be shortened because of rifle fire within the cathedral.

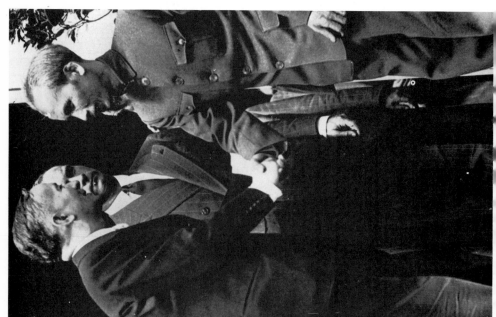

Left: Georges Bidault (l.), Prime Minister in July 1946, greets the Vietminh leader Ho Chi Minh. The latter had come to Paris to negotiate (unsuccessfully) the arrangements for the independence of the Republic of Vietnam. *Right:* Recording the results of the national referendum held on 13 October 1946. It narrowly approved a new draft constitution and thus brought the Fourth Republic into existence.

Above: The strike at the Renault factory on the outskirts of Paris which precipitated the dropping of the Communists from the coalition government in May 1947. *Below:* Parisians at the Gare St Lazare queue patiently for a bus in strike-bound Paris, December 1947.

Violence in the coalfields in October 1948.
Strikers at the St Etienne pits attack police guarding a mine.

The faces of the Fourth Republic. On the steps of the Elysée at 3 a.m. on 25 November 1947 Robert Schuman presents his government to Vincent Auriol, President of the Republic. Left to right: René Mayer (Radical), André Marie (Radical), Paul Coste-Floret (MRP), André Maroselli (Radical), Jules Moch (Socialist), Daniel Mayer (Socialist), René Coty (Independent; later to succeed Auriol as President), Pierre Schneiter (MRP), Robert Schuman (MRP), Marcel Naegelen (Socialist), François Mitterrand (Resistance Union), Christian Pineau (Socialist), Vincent Auriol, Joannes Dupraz (MRP), Georges Bidault (MRP), Pierre Pflimlin (MRP), Pierre Abelin (MRP), Pierre-Henri Teitgen (MRP).

Above: Jean Monnet, one of the principal architects of the French economic recovery: 'small, dapper, tireless, persuasive'. *Below:* Antoine Pinay, the little man with the little hat, sees for himself the results of his efforts, as Prime Minister in 1952, to bring down prices.

Above: A helicopter hovers over the doomed fortress of Dien Bien Phu, March 1954. *Below:* Reading the bad news: the Cartier-Bresson photograph of a Paris news-stand which sums up the mood of public anguish as military disaster looms.

Above: Mendès-France
the milk-drinker:
'rather too well-
publicised' a
campaign.
Below: Pierre Poujade
the demagogue: he
called Mendès' milk-
drinking an insult to
France, 'world
producer of wine and
champagne'.

General Massu (r.) with his parachute troops in Algeria.

Above: The mob in Algiers breaks into the government offices. This was the beginning of the movement that was to lead, three weeks later, to the collapse of the Fourth Republic. *Below:* After the storming of the government offices, members of the 'Committee of Public Safety' show themselves on the balcony to the crowds below.

Above: 'Why should I, at the age of 67, begin a career as a dictator?' General de Gaulle at his press conference in Paris on 19 May 1958 responds indignantly to a question about his ideas on freedom. *Below:* The great 'Republican' demonstration on 28 May 1958 against de Gaulle's return to power: 'as unexciting as a Sunday school picnic'.

Above: President Coty greets General de Gaulle at the Elysée, a few days before the formal transfer of power by the last President of the Fourth Republic to the first President of the Fifth. Madame de Gaulle is in the background. *Below:* At the Arc de Triomphe, 8 January 1959, the new President, watched by the old, rekindles the flame of the tomb of the *Soldat Inconnu*. It was shortly after this that de Gaulle so abruptly took his leave of René Coty.

financial discipline, and Léon Blum, the social reformer. By any calculation, it was an impressive triple heritage to claim. The General's political thinking was reflected again in what Mendès had to say to the Assembly about the proper relationship between executive and legislature:

> Parliament legislates and controls the executive, but the executive must be in a state to govern . . . It must not be stopped in its work by the constant fear of being voted out . . . Parliament has the right to withdraw its confidence [from the government] at any moment; the government must be able, at any moment, to act as though it had twenty years of tenure.

No wonder the new Prime Minister, himself a former bomber navigator in the Free French air force, won the support of the Gaullists.

Even if Mendès was not a 'new' man, there was something about his style and approach that made a refreshing contrast with the other familiar figures of the Fourth Republic and their ritual performances over the obstacles of the political steeplechase. His dynamism, for example, his almost frenetic energy, struck anyone who had dealings with him. Edgar Faure tells the story of how, after two days of unremitting labours on the formation of a government, Mendès felt the need for fresh air and went for a stroll with Faure, whom he had appointed his Minister of Finance, in the Bois de Boulogne. They stopped at a kiosk where Mendès bought ham sandwiches. 'This is the first solid food I've had for forty-eight hours,' he explained.[14]

Although Mendès was later to oppose strongly the way in which the General returned to power in 1958, there was no doubt about the genuineness of his admiration for his former leader. One of the first things he did on becoming Prime Minister was to send a message to the exile of Colombey-les-Deux-Eglises (the date was 18 June, the anniversary of the General's 1940 appeal from London to stricken France), paying tribute to the 'lessons of patriotism and devotion to the public good which your confidence allowed me to receive from you'. They had a lot in common, this seemingly ill-assorted pair: love of their country, dissatisfaction at what was happening to it, the will to lead, an unusual width of vision. But de Gaulle was unshakeable in his conviction that no good could come out of the existing political system. In a statement issued soon after Mendès became Prime Minister, he said that 'Whatever the intentions of some men may be' – an obviously benevolent glance towards Mendès – 'the present régime is incapable of yielding anything, save illusions and stray impulses.' The two men met face to face in October 1954, Mendès setting aside the protocol of his Prime Ministerial rank in order to call upon de Gaulle at the hotel where the latter always stayed for his visits to Paris. Despite the General's caustic style it was a friendly encounter. This was not surprising, seeing that de Gaulle agreed with what had been done over Indochina, Tunisia and above all EDC. But while praising the 'ardour, the strength, the worthiness' of the Prime Minister, he would go no further. 'From time to time,' he told his visitor, 'people may well wave their hats as you go by, because you are someone new and likeable, but when you have got rid of what is bothering this régime [i.e. German rearmament], it will get rid of you.'[15] It was an accurate if easy forecast. And when Mendès asked him how to change the régime, he received the typically embittered reply, 'I tried to change the régime, but you didn't give me much help, and I failed – as for you, you are not even determined to try.'

Did 'Mendèsism', in the sense of a range of ideas about what France needed and how she should be governed, amount to an individual political philosophy or was it predominantly a matter of style? The style was certainly novel, as was the evidence that Mendès had thought long and consistently about these matters. He also had the advantage, for one who was trying to give France a fresh start, of having belonged to none of the governments of the Fourth Republic (his membership of de Gaulle's post-Liberation team preceded the final adoption of the Constitution), and therefore bore no responsibility for the mistakes of the past. On the other hand, this benefit was offset by the fact, exemplified by his post-war years of isolation, that he was an outsider, without any real grass-roots support, in or out of parliament. Despite his membership of the Radical party, he had little or nothing in common with the comfortable, bourgeois, easygoing habits and personalities which had helped to give to the Third Republic the label of *République des camarades*. His personal manner, in which a degree of intellectual arrogance blended with a desire to score off old enemies, had its disadvantages. Above all there were always the parliamentary facts of life – the absence of any stable majority – which confronted Mendès as they did every other Prime Minister. Talking about renewal and a new battle for Liberation may have struck, indeed did strike, a popular chord among all those who were resentful at the many disappointments and frustrations of the post-war years, and longed for something better. But such hopes and promises could only briefly make people forget that Mendès was still the prisoner of the political system.

In mid-June 1954, however, his style reigned supreme and caught the imagination of France and of the world. In nothing was this more true than his bold gamble over Indochina and the Geneva negotiations. He gave himself, he told the Assembly – and the Russians, the Chinese and the Vietminh – four weeks to reach agreement and a cease-fire. If by 20 July there was no satisfactory solution he would resign, having previously sought parliamentary authority to send national servicemen to reinforce and continue the struggle in Indochina. This was fighting talk, just the stuff to disarm those critics who stood ready to accuse Mendès of preparing to do a sell-out. As André Siegfried pointed out, this was the only known example of the vanquished serving an ultimatum on the victors.

There were further surprises when it came to forming a government. Not for Mendès the time-honoured formulae of *dosage* – handing out offices according to the relative importance of the component parts of the coalition. Not for him either the reintroduction of tired old faces: in his government there was no Pleven, no Queuille, no Bidault, no Reynaud, no Schuman, no Martinaud-Déplat. The break with the past could hardly have been emphasised more strongly. Instead, the Ministry was small – sixteen instead of the usual twenty-two or so – and its average age was relatively low (Mendès himself was only forty-seven). Some of the appointments were made on a personal, not a party, basis, and the ex-Gaullists (Social Republicans) were given some of the plum jobs, including the Ministry of Defence.

Mendès also brought a highly individual touch to the choice of his personal staff or *cabinet* – always in France a more influential and openly political group of advisers than the Private Office of a British minister. Some of them, notably Georges Boris, who had worked with Léon Blum before the war, aroused suspicions about where Mendès' foreign policy might be leading. Famously anti-EDC, Boris favoured a rapprochement with the Russians, which explains the doubts expressed by Dillon, the US Ambassador, in a telegram to Washington in July. Dillon admired and got on with Mendès, but found some of his entourage 'questionable' because containing 'a number of individuals about whom we are not too happy'.[16] The same description could have been applied to the editor of *L'Express*, Jean-Jacques Servan-Schreiber, who at a certain moment was an unofficial member of Mendès' team at the Quai d'Orsay (Mendès was his own Foreign Minister). Brilliant but immoderate, his was not a personality usually associated with ministerial *cabinets*, and in addition to this, the admiring, almost fawning treatment given by *L'Express* to everything that the new Prime Minister said and did was of a kind to embarrass some of his friends and annoy all of his enemies.

Whether such misgivings were well founded or not, nothing could distract from Mendès' triumph when his Indochinese gamble came off. On 21 July, an armistice for Vietnam, Laos and Cambodia was signed at Geneva and their independence recognised. Vietnam was effectively partitioned at the 17th parallel, the French Army was to be withdrawn from the north within 300 days, and the Vietminh were required to evacuate Laos, Cambodia and South Vietnam. The political arrangements were less satisfactory. The French position was complicated by the existence of the régime in the south of their own quasi-puppet Bao Dai, which prevented them from entertaining the Vietminh's proposal of a united Vietnam freely associated with the French Union. Although such a State would almost certainly have fallen quite soon under total Communist domination, it might have suited French interests better than the agreement – which was never implemented – for free elections to be held two years after the cease-fire to determine the future of the divided country.

When he came to give an account of the negotiations to the National Assembly, Mendès carefully refrained from claiming that the results of Geneva were a success: 'I would not like anyone to have illusions,' he told the Chamber, 'about the substance of the Geneva agreements. The text is sometimes cruel because it embodies facts that are cruel. It could not have been otherwise.' He could and should have been more generous in acknowledging the work done in Geneva by Bidault and the French negotiating team before the fall of the Laniel government. During that period of the conference, the partition of Vietnam had already been agreed upon, to the point that one of the military experts on the French delegation, Colonel de Brébisson, estimated Mendès' chances of being able to complete the deal as 80 per cent certain. In the light of this, Mendès' achievement at Geneva was not perhaps such a diplomatic triumph as his supporters claimed it to be. Nevertheless, the Prime Minister got a good reception, as he deserved to do, from the Chamber. Some of the Indochina die-hards prophesied that Vietnam would end up being lost to Communism (in the fullness of time they were proved right), but even Bidault, embittered though he was by the spectacle of Mendès the successful peacemaker, tempered his criticism. Peace had been achieved, he said, 'not of course at any price but all the same at a very high price'.

Whatever ammunition the Prime Minister's enemies stored up for use against him at a later time, this was not the moment to belittle what he had done. Public opinion, which had earlier shown so clearly that it had enough of the war, was now unreservedly thankful that there was to be no more bloodshed. Mendès was the hero of the hour. Overwhelming majorities in the Assembly approved the Geneva agreements and Mendès' part in bringing them about. The disgruntled MRP failed to follow the herd, abstaining in the vote that approved the government's action as a whole. The *vox populi* took a different view. In the Latin Quarter in Paris on the night of the Assembly's votes, there were student demonstrations in favour of Mendès. *Le Figaro*, by no means pro-Mendès in general, wrote soberly: 'We are in mourning. Half our positions in the Far East are lost,' but 'M. Mendès-France has worked hard and well for his country in Geneva. . . . If the terms are cruel, at least they leave no stain upon our honour . . .' The editor of *L'Aurore*, a paper rivalling the Beaverbrook press in its championing of imperial causes, acknowledged the nation's gratitude to Mendès for having acted 'with the authority and dignity of the representative of a great country in the service of a just cause'.

Looking back today upon the affair, it is possible to wonder whether Mendès' dramatic gesture of the four-week time limit was really necessary or relevant. One French Indochina expert doubts it.* Both the Russians and the Chinese, he maintains, had shown that they were anxious to bring the war to an end, and would

---

* M. Jacques de Folin, a former French diplomat, who was a member of Mendès' Quai d'Orsay *cabinet*. In conversation in Paris with the author in February 1989, he also supplied the information about Colonel de Brébisson's estimate of Mendès' probability of success.

have brought pressure to bear on the Vietminh. According to this view, the gimmick of a time limit, though it may have captured the imagination of the National Assembly and of French opinion, had more to do with Mendès' desire to break with the past by being unorthodox than with the mechanics of the Geneva conference. The point may be valid but is unprovable. What does seem clear is that even if Mendès had not issued his 'ultimatum', he would not thereby have secured any more favourable a settlement. Though by 20 July the military situation, following the fall of Dien Bien Phu, was not as catastrophic as the rattled French General Staff in Vietnam was representing it to be, it was far from providing a promising basis for negotiation. The real measure of Mendès' accomplishment was to avoid – and here he was greatly helped by the mediating skills of Anthony Eden – complete French humiliation by arriving at the least bad arrangement in the circumstances.

A further memory of those times, which goes some way to offset the praises heaped upon Mendès, comes from another French diplomat, in 1954 a young man serving in the Quai d'Orsay.* He remembers – and this is interesting in view of other doubts about those close to the Prime Minister – how bizarre was the bearing and general air of self-satisfaction of some members of the entourage after the signing of the Geneva agreements. 'They seemed to glory in what had happened, at a time when relief over the end of the war was tempered with the consciousness of defeat, of blood spilt for nothing.' These strictures could not be applied to Mendès himself, this witness thought. His conduct and attitude had been 'irreproachable'.

The wave of admiration that followed Geneva carried him safely past another of the rocks on his perilous voyage: early in August, the Assembly accorded him the special powers he had asked for in order to grapple with the economic and financial situation. By this time, he was following in the footsteps of Pinay by giving regular radio broadcasts – 'fireside chats' on Saturday evenings – because he believed, as Pinay had, that the task of governing required not only a parliamentary majority but the support of the people at large. He appreciated, but discounted, the fact that

---

* M. Emmanuel de Margerie. He was French Ambassador in London and Washington during the Eighties. (Conversation with author, Washington, March 1989.)

this was going to alienate some of the professional politicians. 'In certain circles,' he told one of his biographers, 'I provoked a sort of scandal . . . as though politics were not the concern of everyone, as if they were reserved for a few specialists and professionals, who alone had the right to deal with them.'[17] It was a perceptive and accurate observation, but not one to endear him for long to the occupants of the '*maisons sans fenêtres*'* as the Palais Bourbon, the seat of the National Assembly, is familiarly known.

Hardly was the ink dry on the Geneva documents than Mendès put on another of his spectacular performances. It was as though he had determined that the word *immobilisme*, so often used to describe the passivity of previous governments, should be struck by him personally from the political vocabulary. He had undertaken, in his investiture speech, to redeem earlier, but unfulfilled, French pledges to bring about self-government for the protectorates of Tunisia and Morocco: 'We are ready to resume the dialogue unfortunately interrupted.' Now, on 31 July, the French public was astounded to read in its evening newspapers and hear on its radios that the Prime Minister, accompanied not only by the (Gaullist) Minister at the newly created Ministry for Tunisian and Moroccan Affairs, but by Marshal Juin, had flown to Tunis and there, in the royal palace at Carthage, told the Bey in formal terms that the French government 'recognised and proclaimed, without afterthought, the internal autonomy of the Tunisian State' and was ready 'to transfer to Tunisians and Tunisian institutions the internal exercise of sovereignty'.

It was indeed high time to take the Tunisian situation in hand. The Bey had withdrawn all forms of cooperation, no Tunisians could be found to form a government, and terrorism and counter-terrorism were on the increase. Mendès, the day before his flight, told the Council of Ministers of his intentions and got their agreement, though that of the Gaullists was reluctant. But how did Juin, the Algerian-born, authoritarian architect of the Sultan of Morocco's dethronement, get himself mixed up in this adventure? Had he

---

* The double meaning here is first that the building has indeed no windows to its façade facing the Place de la Concorde, and second that the deputies are reputed (fairly or unfairly) to be totally engrossed in their own political games, oblivious to the wishes and feelings of ordinary people.

changed his noticeably hidebound mind about how to deal with Arabs? There is no knowing exactly,* but what is sure is that Mendès had shown remarkable skill and powers of persuasion in courting Juin and getting him to give, by his presence, tacit approval to the Carthage declaration. He had also provided another, dazzling, example of his style, of which all his enemies could find to say was '*C'est du cinéma*,' in the sense that he managed to give the impression, often the reality, of perpetual motion. By the evening of the 31st, a Saturday, Mendès and his party were on their way back to Paris, but not before he had found time to record his usual Saturday evening broadcast.

Naturally, the *colon* lobbies did not take this lying down. It drove a coach and horses through their contention that they had an inalienable right to live and enjoy effective power in Tunisia as though it were their own country. Their fears that the giving of an inch would all too soon be followed by the taking of an ell were immediately confirmed. Bourguiba, the Neo-Destour nationalist leader, promptly greeted the Carthage declaration as an important step towards the complete independence of Tunisia, which was not at all what Mendès had said. In the ensuing debates in the National Assembly, despite violent attacks by Martinaud-Déplat on the government and on Bourguiba, Mendès won an easy victory. He probably owed this in part to his refusal to extend to Morocco the reforming zeal he had so energetically displayed towards Tunisia. Despite the worsening situation in Morocco, where the puppet Sultan's nomination had, predictably, done nothing to relieve the tension, Mendès evidently felt he could not take on the problems of two protectorates at once. Instead of initiating steps to restore the deposed Sultan to his throne, as some of his supporters hoped he would, he limited himself to hoping that an agreement could be reached with the existing Sultan.

With the armistice in Indochina achieved, the special economic powers voted, a new line towards Tunisia laid down, Mendès was left with the most difficult and delicate of all the unfinished business which he had inherited: the EDC. His own feelings, as far as he had formulated them, were hesitant. In the debate of

* One theory, advanced by Edgar Faure in his memoirs, is that Madame Juin was not with her husband when Mendès' invitation came. She would have persuaded the Marshal to refuse.

February 1952 he had voted for the principle of the EDC. But since then he had been highly critical of previous governments' foreign and defence policies. He had included in his team some leading Social Republicans (ex-Gaullist), all stridently anti-EDC, like their former leader whose views they shared. In joining the Mendès government, they had calculated that here was the best chance, and the best man, for disposing once and for all of the hated project.

The Communist vote had gone to Mendès (even though he discounted it) for something of the same reason. It was but a step from here for his critics and enemies to accuse him, despite his rejection of the Communist support, of seeking to stand French foreign policy on its head. In the investiture debate in June, an MRP deputy, Jean Lecanuet, had summed up these suspicions when he asked whether the Prime Minister-designate was trying 'to call into question our entire international policy, and above all our European policy, thanks to a new majority [*majorité de rechange*], which would lend special significance to new solutions'. This was coded language for hinting that with Gaullist and Communist support, Mendès was going to kill off the EDC, loosen the ties with the US and the West and enter into closer relations with the Soviet Union.

People were always making these and similar accusations about what they thought or feared Mendès was planning to do. In France, it is called a *procès d'intentions* (literally trial by intent), in which the presumption that the person concerned is thinking of doing – or not doing – something can neither be proved nor disproved. His critics of the time, and for years afterwards, always maintained, for example, that Mendès at Geneva had secured the Indochinese settlement by trading it with the Russians against a pledge to torpedo the EDC. There is not the smallest proof that this was true (although one of his senior ministers and fellow Radicals, Edgar Faure, a man for whom expediency was second, if not first, nature, is said to have encouraged Mendès to strike just such a bargain). But these were the kind of suspicions which Mendès' personality and methods aroused. A former member of the US Foreign service, serving in his Paris Embassy at the time, recalls going to the airport sometime in the summer of 1954 to meet Mrs Clare Boothe Luce, the US Ambassador in Rome, on her way through to New York. That formidable woman, who saw a Red under every bed, told him that she knew, on the best information, that Mendès was a Communist.[18]

Whatever his own, decidedly lukewarm, feelings about EDC, Mendès, on acceding to power, was sure of one thing: the EDC boil would have to be lanced, the sooner the better. He said as much in his investiture speech, deploring 'the great and painful quarrel' that had come to divide French people, and pleading for a rapprochement which could reconcile all to the fact of German rearmament. Reaffirming France's commitment to the Western alliance, he undertook to report to parliament, before it rose for the summer recess, new propositions 'enabling us to create the widest national consensus which is indispensable for any plan of European defence'. In the weeks to come, this was to be a constant element in Mendès' thinking: after the years of delay (not of his doing) he did not believe there was a parliamentary majority for EDC, or if there was, it was likely to be one so slender as to be inappropriate for a decision of such magnitude.* The day after the investiture debate, the *Times* correspondent in Paris reminded his readers that in speaking as he had about EDC, Mendès appeared to treat the matter as a purely French problem, whereas there were five other parties to the treaty; 'M. Mendès-France has killed the EDC treaty as it stands today.' If indeed he was such a murderer, he was not the only one. On 18 June the defence committee of the National Assembly voted by twenty-nine votes to thirteen for the rejection of EDC.

There are at least two possible ways of telling the story, an intensely dramatic one, of what happened in the next ten weeks. The first, to which a lot of responsible people in France were then and still are ready to subscribe, is that Mendès was determined from the outset to bury EDC and replace it with the straightforward admission, subject to safeguards, of Germany to NATO.[19] He was mistrustful of a Monnet-type Europe and wanted a British link. He therefore prepared amendments to the treaty as signed of such a

---

* On one occasion, Dulles reminded him that the Third Republic's Constitution had been passed by the narrowest of margins. This was true. The decision of the 600-strong National Assembly to approve a Republican Constitution was adopted on 30 January 1875 by a majority of one vote. In another context, Churchill is supposed to have said that for a government to govern, the size of its majority is irrelevant: 'One is enough.'

far-reaching nature as intentionally to alter the very basis of EDC and guarantee the opposition of the other five signatories, four of whom had already gone through the process of parliamentary ratification (only Italy had not). He then brought on the long-delayed debate in the National Assembly, which by a sizeable majority threw out EDC lock, stock and barrel. The debate was not even a proper discussion of the issues involved, because of the parliamentary procedural tricks which brought it to an end. At no point did the government stake its existence by making the vote a matter of confidence, as it might be thought appropriate to have done in respect of an international treaty formally signed by France more than two years earlier. Even the ministers in Mendès' coalition were allowed to vote as they wished.

The other, pro-Mendès, version is that, knowing he would never get the treaty as it stood through the Assembly, he tried honestly to secure the agreement of France's partners to enabling amendments. The latter – under what amounted, according to this reading, to strong American pressure – stood their ground, whereupon Mendès was compelled, in order to bring the whole sorry saga to an end one way or another, to refer the treaty to the Assembly for a decision the nature of which was inevitable. In this, he rendered a signal service to his country, dispelling the cloud that had been allowed for far too long to darken the political scene, and clearing the way towards the unavoidable objective of German rearmament.

So far as possible, the facts should be allowed to speak for themselves. The first thing Mendès did, in furtherance of his investiture promise to seek the widest possible consensus, was to ask two of his ministers – General Pierre Koenig, anti-EDC, and Maurice Bourgès-Maunoury, pro – to see what points of agreement could be established as between partisans and opponents of the treaty. This exercise predictably achieved nothing. The differences were and always had been too wide, not over the principle of German rearmament but about the supranational elements of the treaty, regarded by its supporters as an essential contribution to Franco-German reconciliation and the construction of the new Europe, by its antagonists as an unthinkable surrender of French sovereignty, profoundly affecting the French Army. So Mendès was left with no choice but to seek the aid of France's partners in repackaging the treaty so as to make it saleable to parliament.

He explained the situation clearly to Dulles in a conversation in Paris in mid-July.[20] The latter, while expressing confidence in Mendès, was in his doomsday mood (he always was over EDC): if France again procrastinated, the damage would be 'incalculable'. Mendès put it another way: the worst thing that could happen would be the rejection by parliament of EDC. Yet that, as things stood, must be the outcome, because there was no majority. The US had been misled, Mendès said, about the possibilities of ratification. The National Assembly was divided into three groups: a pro-EDC faction, another, agreeable to German rearmament but against the EDC, and a third, consisting principally of the Communists, opposed to German rearmament in any form.

The only thing to do, Mendès told Dulles, was to try to winkle sixty to eighty of the second group away from opposition and into the pro-EDC lobby. The only way to do that was to seek modifications in the existing treaty. Dulles warned him that this would lead to an 'unacceptable' situation for France's partners. Both men, it seems fair to say, were in good faith, although it is relevant to wonder whether at this stage Mendès had fully appreciated the odds against his quest: modifications in the treaty likely to win over the Gaullist and other 'anti-supranationalists' would have to be so fundamental as to transform EDC into a different animal altogether.*

As the month of July wore on, Mendès continued successfully to conceal his own sentiments. He could scarcely be blamed, so difficult, almost impossible, was his situation. The pro-European elements in his government were threatening to force his resignation if his 'compromise' solution went too far. The ex-Gaullists were muttering about overthrowing him on the EDC issue, thus creating a situation which could lead to a crisis of the régime. Various of his advisers were by this time at work on preparing suggestions for the modification of the treaty, some of them prominent members of the Quai d'Orsay who had been trying, in the words of David Bruce, the special US Ambassador to the embryo Defence Community, 'to kill or thwart European policy for the last three years'.[21]

---

* Perhaps he did realise this. M. de Folin (conversation with author, Paris 1989) recalls, just before setting out for the Brussels conference, hearing the Prime Minister say, while pointing to a copy of the treaty with its annexes and accompanying protocols, 'If so much as a comma of that is changed, it will be a dead document.' There was no tone of regret as he said it, yet he was going to Brussels with the precise purpose of trying to persuade France's partners to make substantial changes.

In the event, Mendès rejected the advice of those who would have changed EDC into a 'little NATO' (the Six – France, West Germany, Italy, Belgium, Holland and Luxembourg – plus the UK), and instead laid before the government a series of proposals or protocols designed to preserve the essence of the treaty while allowing for the criticisms of its opponents. That at least was supposed to be the effect, but it did not work out that way. The protocols would have extended the duration of the treaty to run concurrently with the life of NATO (fifty years); its supranational clauses would only become operative after eight years; military integration would only take place in the forward areas – i.e. Germany, meaning no German units would be stationed on French soil; EDC would lapse if NATO lapsed; and in the event of German reunification, member States could if they wished withdraw from the treaty. Before these draft protocols assumed final shape, the Quai d'Orsay anti-EDC group went to work on them again, so that they emerged, as a telegram from the US Paris Embassy to the State Department put it, in a form 'unacceptable beyond our worst expectations'. Whether or not the protocols really did drain the treaty of most of its substance, they certainly reintroduced the principle of discrimination against Germany. On the other hand, three of Mendès' principal Gaullist ministers resigned rather than approve the protocols which, they claimed, did nothing to alter the supranational element and confirmed the narrow, six-nation nature of the treaty. At this point Mendès must have known, if he did not know it already, that he was attempting to square a circle.*

So far in the story, it should not be difficult to feel sympathy for Mendès in his predicament. But then he did something which could be calculated to arouse – as it did – the worst suspicions of London and Washington about his long-term intentions and the future direction of French foreign policy. On 12 August he told the American and British envoys in Paris that in view of his difficulties over EDC, he thought that the Western reply to a recent Soviet note proposing yet another four-power conference on 'European security' should not close the door to such negotiations. He did not actually make the attempted ratification of EDC conditional upon such a conference, but argued in a (for him) convoluted

---

* See the account by Robert Buron quoted above, p. 145, for the strain imposed by the affair upon the Prime Minister.

way that French public opinion must be assured that it was the Soviet government under Khrushchev which was responsible for lack of progress – i.e. which was making German rearmament unavoidable.

Despite Mendès' ingenious explanations about how the ratification process could go forward simultaneously with what looked like another delaying exercise, it seemed to be one more example not just of French procrastination but of the ever-present French desire to seek, despite successive failures in this direction in the past, a rapprochement with Moscow. The fact that the Kremlin had been directing a particularly virulent campaign against the EDC made Mendès' attitude all the more open to misrepresentation. In London, the Foreign Office was 'disappointed, anxious and alarmed',[22] while Dulles declared himself to be 'deeply shocked and disheartened'.[23] Winston Churchill, who in Eden's holiday absence was doubling up the posts of Prime Minister and Foreign Secretary, recorded his weariness 'with this deeply injurious French procedure of delay'.[24] Of all the cards to play at this moment, when Mendès needed all the understanding he could get, none was more fatally likely to incur the impatience and hostility of France's allies than this last-minute reintroduction of the Russian joker.

It was in these unpromising circumstances that Mendès went to Brussels on 18 August 1954 to try to sell his protocols to France's five partners. Rarely has there been, above all among allies, a more spectacularly unsuccessful and bad-tempered conference. (It even began under a bad omen. On its opening day came the news of the death of Alcide de Gasperi, the former Italian Prime Minister and one of the 'fathers' of post-war European unity.) Paul-Henri Spaak, Prime Minister of Belgium and host and chairman of the conference, a confirmed European and a statesman in the true sense of the term, did his best. (That at least is one interpretation of his handling of the conference. Its validity is questionable, seeing that Spaak was unwise enough to advise Adenauer not to see Mendès alone, a piece of rudeness which gravely offended Mendès.) But with the other five all finding the French protocols unacceptable, if only because it would be necessary to refer them back to national parliaments, there was little that Spaak or anybody else could do.

French historians make much indignant play (as Mendès did at the time) with the role of David Bruce, who was in Brussels throughout the conference, bringing (according to this French version) improper pressure to bear upon the Five. Under instructions from Washington, he certainly did see that all six delegations were aware of the US government's adverse views about the protocols, including the opinion that they watered down, postponed or virtually eliminated the supranational elements in the treaty. Both Bruce and his enthusiastic assistant Tomlinson kept in close touch with Spaak about the way to run the conference. They were in and out of Spaak's outer office all day long.[25] All this was no more than their duty. But these and other pressures were of a kind to cause Parodi, the head of the Quai d'Orsay, who was fiercely anti-EDC, to write Mendès an angry note beginning: 'You have been subjected to the strongest, the most patently pre-organised and the most indiscreet pressure that I have ever seen used against a French government.'[26] Mendès found no difficulty in falling in with such a view.

As the point of breakdown approached, Dulles cabled Mendès, telling him, for the umpteenth time, of the fearful consequences if EDC were to fail and threatening (for that is what it amounted to) to confer, were the Brussels conference to collapse, with the Five and the UK, to the exclusion of France, about German rearmament.[27] Whether such heavy-handed tactics were the best or the only possible ones in the circumstances seems doubtful, to say the least. But that was Dulles' way, and his patience certainly had been tried very hard. As for his belief in the quasi-sacred nature of the supranational principle, the Americans had from the start viewed EDC through this particular rose-tinted magnifying glass; the influence of Jean Monnet had had a good deal to do with that.

Compared with the question of whether these American pressures were impermissible, Mendès' own conduct in Brussels, as witnessed and described by those present, is a good deal more interesting, both as a psychological study and as a contribution to the question of whether, as his enemies continue to this day to claim, he 'killed EDC'. The conference began by trying to discuss the French draft protocols point by point, but this soon proved futile and Spaak introduced what he intended as a compromise proposal. According to this, the Six would agree to meet after EDC had come into operation – i.e. after the French ratification – to discuss the French points with a view to possible amendment of the treaty. This would have avoided the difficulty of having to refer the protocols to national parliaments, which none of the Five was ready to do. But Spaak's paper began with a review of French foot-dragging over the past three years and Mendès (who could not be blamed for these delays) took violent exception, creating an extraordinary scene and demanding that page of Spaak's paper be withdrawn and destroyed. The Dutch Foreign Minister told Mendès that discussions would be easier if he were to show less temper and pathos. Mendès retorted that the situation justified some pathos.[28]

In his memoirs,[29] Spaak says he did not know whether Mendès' indignation was real or assumed: 'It consisted of one of those dramatic performances which he liked to put on from time to time.' Spaak also found that Mendès was the most emotional politician he had ever had to deal with:

> Any discussion with [him] soon takes a personal turn, where his feelings play a bigger role than his convictions. . . . [During the conference] he never stopped building up complexes about his partners. . . . He was convinced that no one liked him, that no one had confidence in him, that he was appearing like an accused man before prejudiced judges.

He also never stopped doodling on the paper in front of him, drawing, Spaak noted, not flowers or animals but 'huge opaque walls, the walls of a prison . . . he really had the sense of persecution'.

Spaak was not the only person to record this trait in Mendès' personality. David Bruce reported a conversation with him in Brussels in which Mendès described himself (correctly) as the hapless inheritor of his predecessors' errors and lack of good faith and complained of being abandoned by his European allies and suspected by the US, at a moment when 'he sorely needed sympathy and aid'. As for the political situation back in Paris, Mendès said that his enemies were 'licking their chops and organising against him'.[30] If this was pathos, it was surely not a piece of play-acting but the genuine article. Fifteen years later, Mendès was still smarting from the memory of his experiences in Brussels, which included the appearance in the French press, just as the conference was opening, of two pro-EDC articles, one by Robert Schuman, declaring that Mendès' proposals to the Five were unacceptable. 'I do not want any French negotiator ever to find himself in such a position,' Mendès wrote in an article in *Le Figaro* in April 1969.

Worse was to come. The professional experts in the six national delegations in Brussels had some promising talks which could possibly have opened the way to a compromise. Mendès promptly disavowed such efforts, rebuked his officials and told them to avoid any more such contacts.* He had made up his mind that no good was going to come out of Brussels, in the sense that the accommodation offered by his partners would not be enough for him to secure a convincing majority for EDC in the National Assembly. Spaak was astonished and angry when Mendès, in a tête-à-tête conversation, pulled from his pocket the text of a statement he proposed to read to the next session of the conference. It was a formal recognition of failure, just when (according to Spaak) 'enormous concessions' by the Five to France had opened up the prospect of success.

Just how 'enormous' those concessions were depended, of course, on who was measuring them. In Mendès' eyes, the conference was doomed to fail unless the other five powers agreed to go back to their parliaments for further amending action on the treaty. This is just what the Five were not ready to do. As against Mendès' assertion that his government would fall unless the conference accepted his proposals, Spaak reminded him that the Belgian government also would be brought down if the supranational elements of the treaty were weakened or returned to the Belgian parliament. The deadlock was utter and complete, and made all the more rigid by the clash of strong personalities. '[Mendès'] obstinacy and intransigence', wrote Spaak later, 'even seemed to him an additional trump card in terms of internal French politics. . . . For his success, he was ready to sacrifice the organisation of Europe.' In a characteristic display of generosity, Spaak also felt able to write that despite his hostility towards Mendès over the latter's conduct on EDC, 'I have to recognise his exceptional qualities of intelligence, character and courage.'[31]

EDC lay dead upon the Brussels conference table. Mendès had helped to kill it, in a way that seemed to his partners to be petulant

---

* One official, Jean Sauvagnargues, a future Foreign Minister under the Fifth Republic, who despite this ban wanted a further conversation with Robert Rothschild, Spaak's *directeur de cabinet*, had to pretend he had left his pipe behind in Rothschild's room. (M. Robert Rothschild in conversation with author, London, April 1989. The story is all the more piquant in that Sauvagnargues did not smoke a pipe.)

and uncompromising and evoked their indignation. The duty of the government which he led was, according to them, to exert every effort to defend the treaty before the French parliament. He seemed to be showing a singular reluctance to make this effort.

Their wrath was explicable. But for months past, EDC had been a poor sickly creature with very little chance of survival, and there is something both unreal and unattractive in the picture of non-Frenchmen, be they American, Dutch, Belgian, German or Italian, trying to tell the French Prime Minister that there was a majority in his own parliament for the treaty when he, who could claim at least equal and probably superior knowledge of such things, was convinced that the opposite was true. Something of the same process was repeated at Chartwell, Winston Churchill's country home in Kent, whither Mendès flew straight from Brussels.* Both Churchill and Eden urged Mendès to use his immense authority to get EDC through the French parliament, and spoke of the 'very grave dangers' of rejection. Mendès warned that with no concessions from Brussels to help him (the attitude of the Five, he complained, had been prearranged, not only among themselves but with the Americans), rejection by the Assembly was unavoidable. He explained that he could not make the matter one of confidence without bringing down his own government.[32] The Foreign Office minute on the meeting concludes, in a masterpiece of understatement, with the thought that the UK ministers, like the Five in Brussels, were 'left in some uncertainty about M. Mendès-France's real position and intentions'. Yet Mendès had made his attitude clear enough: he wanted quick international action, once EDC had been rejected, to restore German sovereignty and provide for German rearmament and he said, prophetically as things were to turn out, that a France which had rejected EDC would never dare to reject an alternative, even if it meant Germany in NATO. Before leaving Brussels, Mendès had managed at last to see Adenauer, whom he

---

* Despite the seriousness of the situation, personal relationships at Chartwell were pleasant. Churchill greeted Mendès as 'Mr France', and teased him about his milk-drinking campaign (see p. 233). When Mendès explained that all he was trying to do was to encourage his countrymen to lead a simple life, Churchill replied enthusiastically that his doctor had recommended the simple life to him also, a directive he explained as meaning nothing but champagne and brandy to drink and only cigars to smoke. (Author's conversation, March 1989, with Sir Frank Roberts, one of the Foreign Office officials present at the Chartwell talks.)

reassured as to the need for Franco-German accord. Even if EDC had expired in Brussels, Mendès certainly intended to show proof that there was life beyond death.

It only remained to bury the corpse. At long last, the National Assembly was to be called on to debate EDC. On 27 August, contrary to the advice of Coty, the President of the Republic, the Cabinet decided against making the matter one of confidence. It did so, in the words of Jacques Fauvet, because if it had not 'there would have been no debate for the reason there would no longer have been any government'[33] – i.e. its anti-EDC members would have resigned and brought on a crisis. For the same reason, ministers were left free to vote according to their individual opinion – an unusual procedure in respect of an international treaty formally entered into by a French government. Mendès undertook to give an objective account of the Brussels breakdown but most of the people listening to him, both when he appeared before the parliamentary committees and in the Chamber itself, did not interpret his attitude in this way. In particular, he laid much emphasis upon possible alternatives to EDC. Had he not discussed them at Chartwell? (There was something disingenuous about the way in which, after Brussels and Chartwell, 'leaks' to the press suggested that Mendès had received important encouragement from Churchill about these alternatives; as the French record of the Chartwell conference faithfully reveals, there was no such encouragement, and Eden specifically warned Mendès about the 'very serious difficulties' attaching to any alternative to EDC.)[34]

A flurry of parliamentary procedural manoeuvres preceded the Assembly's vote on 30 August. The pro-EDC forces, smelling defeat, tabled a 'prejudicial motion', recommending suspension of the debate to enable fresh negotiations to take place in Brussels. Their opponents promptly introduced a 'previous motion', which according to the rules took precedence over the prejudicial one; its approval would mean the abrupt termination of the debate and the total and irrevocable rejection of the treaty. Mendès, although resigned to (eager for?) such rejection, genuinely wanted a proper debate about the whole affair, and persuaded both factions to withdraw their motions. But the pro-EDC lobby, increasingly desperate and now seeking merely to win time by postponing the debate, resubmitted its motion, whereupon, just as surely as night follows day, the 'anti' lobby reintroduced theirs. This time, a co-signatory of this 'previous motion' was Edouard Herriot, the veteran Radical figure who for years after the war was President (Speaker) of the Assembly – an old man still commanding wide respect. It was he who spoke to the motion. Crippled with rheumatism and unable to mount the steps to the speaker's rostrum, he addressed the packed Assembly from his place.

It was a dramatic scene. Not only did the deputies fill the red benches right round the hemicycle but the public galleries were full and in the inadequate press box there was scarcely room to move. 'On the threshold of death,' boomed Herriot – though ailing and eighty-two, there was nothing wrong with his voice – 'let me tell you that EDC is the end of France, that it is a step forward for Germany and a step back for France, that when a people no longer runs its army – and France would not under EDC – it no longer runs its diplomacy.' How mistaken the Americans were, he said, in thinking that EDC was good for France. He recalled that as Prime Minister in 1924 he had brought about the first reconciliation between France and revolutionary Russia. Today, every possibility of agreement with Russia should be exhausted. The old man received a standing ovation. He may have muddled up his facts and figures and ignored shouted corrections, but for the anti faction, and for some of the wobblers as well, he had provided a diet to appeal to every taste: French patriotism, anti-Germanism, anti-Americanism, the desirability, in the cause of peace, of making another approach to the Russians.

The Chamber then proceeded to vote upon the decisive 'previous motion'. It was carried by 319 votes to 264. Fifty-three Socialists voted for – i.e. anti-EDC – and fifty against, a split which was crucial to the result. With the names of more than sixty deputies down to speak, the debate was cut short and EDC buried, without, as an emotional Paul Reynaud immediately pointed out to the Chamber, its author (Robert Schuman) or its signer (Antoine Pinay) being allowed to speak in its defence. In the course of one afternoon, the Assembly had drawn a sponge across the slate upon which French European policy had for the past four years been inscribed.

At the announcement of the vote the Communists rose and sang the 'Marseillaise', while the MRP and the rest of the defeated pro-EDC faction howled 'Back to Moscow'. In the lobbies afterwards, Mendès as good as said 'I told you so': his regret was that France's partners at Brussels and her Anglo-Saxon allies had been ignorant about the true feeling of the National Assembly.* Later, replying in a broadcast to those who claimed that EDC had been killed by a piece of procedural trickery, Mendès said that if there had been a vote upon the treaty itself, the majority against it would have been not 55 but 110.

Despite the speed and skill with which Mendès – much helped, as at Geneva, by Eden – reassembled the fractured pieces of French foreign policy, and got parliamentary approval for an alternative, non-supranational framework for German rearmament, the death of EDC was for him not so much a triumph as a weapon for use by his enemies. Many people, of course, were delighted at what he had done. Beuve-Méry, in *Le Monde*, rejoiced at the death of a treaty 'born in ambiguity, ripened in intrigue, lies and corruption'. But the MRP, who called the result of the debate 'the crime of 30 August', never forgave him, nor did most of the other supporters of EDC, including an assortment of ex-Vichyites. This collective hostility was now linked with that of the colonalist lobbies, who considered Mendès a scuttler from empire, in a way that proved fatal for what he had called 'the new battle for Liberation'. For the moment however, his style and obvious determination to mark a break with the past ensured his popularity with public opinion. 1954 was still his *annus mirabilis*, when the French parliament and people turned to him, the saviour figure, as they did to Pétain in 1940 and were to do again to de Gaulle in 1958, to relieve them of their troubles. As parliament rose for the summer recess, the sound of knives being sharpened, soon to become loud and menacing, was barely audible. In the cinemas, when Mendès appeared in the newsreels, he was generally greeted with a burst of applause. This was not the reception normally accorded to the political figures of the Fourth Republic.

* In a chapter in his and Raymond Aron's *La Querelle de la CED* (Paris, Armand Colin, 1957), apportioning blame for the collapse of EDC, Daniel Lerner says that 'the important American mistake was "guessing wrong" not at the end but at the beginning. . . . Rigid State Department support of EDC helped to sustain an acrimonious quarrel [in France] . . . and pushed French partisans into extreme positions.'

CHAPTER 8

A Donkey's Kick

It is just as possible for new governments to benefit from the wise foresight of their predecessors as it is for them to be handicapped by the outcome of earlier follies. Mendès' inheritance was no exception. In seeking, through the use of special powers, to set the French economy to rights, he saddled himself with a massive task, above all in terms of structural change. But unlike immediately post-war prime ministers, who had to contend with shortages, inflation and labour unrest, he was able to enjoy the advantages of what one historian has called 'the astonishing period of expansion in stability',[1] an evolution that had preceded Mendès' accession to power. It had been achieved partly through the previously adopted policies of his Finance Minister (and successor as Prime Minister) Edgar Faure, partly through the effects of the Monnet Plan and its successor the Second Plan, whose seeds, germinating without disturbance in the economic soil, were now putting forth promising growth. Between 1945 and 1954, industrial production rose from 50 (1938=100) to 159, and by the end of the Fourth Republic in 1958 it had reached the figure of 213. 'French industry had never experienced such rapid progress, not during the *belle époque*, nor during the nineteen twenties.'[2] In terms of gross national product per capita, France's performance had been, though much more modest than Germany's economic miracle, superior to the UK's, and the same was true for exports. French economic growth under the Fourth Republic was founded primarily upon strong internal demand, and this meant, in many sectors, increasing consumer satisfaction.

The motor industry was a good example. In post-war Europe, owning a car, or at least some form of motorised transport, became a key test of relative well-being, one whose appeal was universal. In France, the total number of private vehicles more than doubled between 1951 and 1958 (1.7 million to 4 million). By the end of the Fourth Republic, one in seven French people owned a car. The demand for and supply of two-wheeled conveyances – motor cycles and 'mobylettes' – increased similarly. The streets of Paris and the provincial towns, which in the immediate post-war years had been uncluttered and a positive pleasure to walk in, were by 1954 increasingly filled with the products of French factories, the little 4CV, four-door rear-engined Renault predominant among them. The nationalised Renault concern accounted for one-third of the market, Citroën (its remarkable 2CV, a mechanically propelled peasants' cart, was not yet off the drawing board but soon would be), Peugeot and Simca taking up the rest. A similar upsurge in the production of and demand for consumer durables marked the years of the Fifties. No self-respecting Frenchman will ever admit that on a personal scale things are going his way, still less that the improvements might be the fruits of government policies. But at least by the mid-Fifties some of the earlier and genuine grievances of the ordinary French consumer had been partially relieved. This should in theory have made it easier for governments to govern.

There were however reverse and sombre sides to this picture, and none more depressing than housing. The Monnet Plan had quite deliberately disregarded this sector, concentrating instead on heavy investment. This meant that post-Liberation France, with almost no new housing built between the wars, had the worst housing record in Europe. Eighty-five per cent of dwellings in Paris dated from before 1914, and the figure for the larger towns was 63 per cent. Rural housing was no better. Rents had been frozen since 1914, which made private or corporate investment in housing unattractive. Efforts by successive governments to remedy this situation had proved ineffective or inadequate or both. The result was that not nearly enough new houses were built. By 1953, new constructions were running at only 100,000 annually, whereas the need was for the building of at least 300,000 houses a year for twenty years.

In Paris in the winter of 1954, a socially aware priest, the Abbé Pierre, launched a dramatic and effective campaign to draw attention to the scandal of the shanty towns (*bidonvilles*) in the capital's suburbs of Saint-Denis and Nanterre. The response, in terms of shock and a determination to get something done, was on a national scale. But even before this, governments had begun to display greater energy. Between 1953 and 1955, the State more than doubled its funding for the construction of what in Britain would be called council housing, so that by 1958 the target of 300,000 homes annually was almost reached. At the same time, generous credit advances were provided for would-be home owners.

These measures, timely though they might be, were not however the whole answer. The familiar pattern of the weakest going to the wall showed itself once more in the allocation of new homes. Forty per cent of these, in the years 1955–60, went to white-collar workers (salaried staff, the liberal professions), 40 per cent to blue collars (employees, artisans, small retailers), leaving only 20 per cent for labourers, unskilled workers and the non-active. To be needy was by no means an automatic qualification for a new home. 'Housing remained a major source of frustration; the sovereignty of money was undisputed, and the weakest were left behind.'[3] Inequality as one of the ingredients of human existence remained a constant factor. The fledgling car owner, proudly taking his family for a country outing in his little Renault, might have been typical of a new generation of more or less contented French citizens. But even if this was so, against him and those like him must be set the 1954 statistics of 45 per cent of households claiming to have difficulties in making ends meet (for the households of labourers the figure was 71 per cent, for workers 49 per cent).[4]

If there was one subject above all others in which Mendès might be expected to demonstrate his proficiency, it was economics. In his investiture speech, he had laid down the two principles on which his government's economic policies would be based: the expansion of the economy for the benefit of the workers and the restructuring of businesses and commercial activities which owed their survival to artificial subsidy or some other form of protection. These were obviously long-term aims. The habits and customs of a long-established production and distribution cycle cannot be overturned in a month or a year, above all in a country as generally impervious to change as mid-Fifties France. In the shorter term, there was already an effective policy in operation, in the shape of the eighteen-month plan devised by Edgar Faure, Finance Minister under the Laniel government. By maintaining Faure at his post, Mendès to a large degree gave his blessing to the Faure plan, with its successful emphasis on private investment and cheaper credit and its judicious mix of private initiative and public intervention.

But Mendès himself had wider visions. How often, in the past, had he spoken, in and out of parliament, of the need to renovate the economic structure of the country, to modernise its industries and agriculture in such a way as to prepare its entry into the world of international competition and new technology. In terms of forward thinking (as well as properly thought out ideas) Mendès was ten years ahead of Harold Wilson and his 1964 slogan of a white-hot technological revolution . . . Thus under the special economic powers granted by parliament in August 1954, about 120 decrees were promulgated, embodying State encouragement and support for the conversion of agriculture and industry, loans for municipal housing, and a far-seeing programme for education and scientific research, including nuclear research. Nothing of all this was particularly controversial in political terms, although in predictable Pavlovian reaction the Right and the employers labelled it *dirigisme* and the Communists scorned it as neo-capitalism.

It was when the heat was turned upon vested interests that sparks began to fly. Shortly after assuming office, Mendès' picture began to appear in the newspapers with a glass of milk in front of him. He was not the first prime minister to try to attack the evils of alcoholism. René Mayer and Pinay before him had increased taxation on spirits. But Mendès, aided by the ever-adoring *L'Express*, threw all the weight of his personal authority and example behind the anti-alcohol campaign. His milk-drinking habits became known far beyond the frontiers of France. They could well be, after all these years, the single most memorable characteristic associated, at least in the average non-French mind, with the Mendès-France experience. But his efforts, which included the provision of free milk in schools, did not stop there. Among the many economic decrees to be issued were a number restricting the considerable privileges of the *bouilleurs de cru* (home distillers), cutting down on the numbers entitled to such privileges, forbidding altogether the possession of travelling stills, and encouraging the conversion of sugar-beet into sugar instead of the (largely unwanted) alcohol which ever since the First World War the State had been buying in from the *betteraviers* (sugar-beet growers) at the expense of the taxpayer. In 1952, the subsidy – for that is what it amounted to – cost the exchequer more than half the amount that Pinay, in his anti-inflationist efforts, had saved by cutting the crucially needed housing programme.

It was beyond question that such measures were justified. The sugar-beet/alcohol situation was not so much a contribution to alcoholism as a financial racket, which should have been ended long before. But this was a comparatively minor scandal by contrast with the home distillers. Originally, these were genuine farmers who were allowed, free of tax, to distil ten litres of pure alcohol annually for their own use. Before 1914, there were 800,000 of them. By 1954, this figure had swollen to 3½ million, many of them claiming the privilege on the basis of a few fruit trees in the garden. Moreover, the limit of ten litres was frequently exceeded, sometimes by huge margins, and most of this spirit found its way into the commercial products sold in shops and bars which accounted for such a high rate of alcoholism, especially in Brittany and Normandy. As member for a Norman constituency, Mendès knew the problem at first hand.

Whether or not this campaign, to which he so signally attached his own name, contributed in the long term anything important to the fight against alcoholism is an open question. In any case, the decrees of August 1953 (pre-Mendès) and September 1954, designed to reform the sugar-beet system, were practically annulled by further decrees, the result of pressure from the alcohol lobby, in May 1955 and September 1957. What is certain is that Mendès' effort brought down upon his head the potent wrath of the farming and drink lobbies, who wielded considerable political influence – not surprisingly, seeing that the distillers represented half the adult male population in twenty departments and a quarter in another forty. Every sort of accusation was made against Mendès, including the charge that he only wanted obligatory milk distribution in schools for electoral reasons. Pierre Poujade, the founder and leader of a new pressure group, the Union de Défense des Commerçants et Artisans (UDCA), a populist orator with a turn for vulgar invective, made heavy (and often anti-Semitic) play of Mendès and his rather too well publicised milk drinking, describing the scene where the Prime Minister was served a glass of milk at an international reception as an insult to France, 'world producer of wine and champagne'.

These were not the only forces to be rallying themselves against the government and its controversial chief. As already described in the previous chapter, Mendès' conduct over the EDC had guaranteed him the undying hostility of most of the MRP and the pro-EDC faction. When at the end of the year he succeeded – this time by making it a matter of confidence – in getting the National

Assembly to ratify by the narrow margin of 287 to 260 the London and Paris agreements which embodied German rearmament, most of the MRP abstained or voted against. Other opponents included all the Communists (the only party to be entirely consistent in its opposition to German rearmament) and many Socialists, Radicals, Gaullists and members of the conventional Right – among the latter Paul Reynaud and Pinay. Though it was a remarkable achievement on Mendès' part to have replaced EDC, in only three months, with something else that maintained the unity and added to the strength of the NATO alliance, it was not a performance, as the voting figures showed, to win him many new political friends or admirers (at least in France; Dulles, forgetting his dire prophecies about what would happen if EDC were rejected, called him 'Superman' – to many French ears a dubious compliment, coming from such a source). This time, as the ratification debate ended, there was no uproar or singing of the 'Marseillaise', only (in the words of one reporter) 'a deep, almost tragic silence', finally broken by the enraged screams and shouts of the Communists. Through the minds of many deputies must have run the thought of four years of time wasted and passion spent. They would have been inhuman, most of them, had they applauded the man who had not only prepared a new and bitter medicine but also forced them to swallow it.

But there was more to all this than just hurt feelings and disappointed hopes. Enmity towards Mendès was directed against a wider target than the perpetrator of 'the crime of 30 August' – the death of EDC. Ever since the Geneva conference and the declaration on Tunisia, his foes, who as well as the MRP included some of the most virulent, anti-Semitic, far right-wing sources of opinion, had been busy spreading rumours and smears to the effect that Mendès, his entourage and his 'progressive' left-wing supporters were preparing to lead France out of the Western alliance and towards the Communist camp. These circles professed to find confirmation of their suspicions in the dismissal, very soon after Mendès came to power, of Jean Baylot, the Paris Prefect of Police, a man who over the years have been almost fanatical in his anti-Communist zeal; it was on his orders that Duclos, with his famous pigeons, had been arrested in 1952. Did not this prove, asked Mendès' enemies, that the new government was changing ideological tack, that anti-Communism was from now on to be a reason for reproof? Within an hour of the news becoming known, forty deputies telephoned the Hôtel Matignon to protest.

This was the background to another 'affaire' in the long French tradition. The *'affaire des fuites'*, which centred upon a leakage of military secrets from the Committee of National Defence, took the form of an immensely complicated cat's-cradle of plots, informers, rival intelligence services and, above all, a stop-at-nothing effort by Mendès' critics to discredit and undermine him.

It began with revelations from an extreme right-wing police commissioner, Jean Dides. In July 1954, this man, later to be a Poujadist deputy, who had a chequered career which included working with the Germans under the occupation, was concerned with Communist surveillance, and produced what he claimed was evidence that there had been leakages of defence secrets to the French Communist party and thence to Moscow. It was true there had been leakages, though not demonstrably to the Communists. One of them dated back to the time of the previous, Laniel, government. This was the work, as the outcome of a criminal trial later revealed, of two left-wing civil servants from the secretariat of the Ministry of Defence. But Dides and his friends at the Prefecture were now claiming that the traitor was one of Mendès' ministers. The finger appeared to point first towards Edgar Faure, then to Mitterrand, Minister of the Interior and future President of the Fifth Republic.

Shortly after this Dides was relieved of his anti-Communist responsibilities and given a humble post at the port of Paris. This in no way cooled his missionary zeal in spreading rumours about Mitterrand. In this murky business, with police and security services manipulating the facts and doctoring the paper work for political ends, Mitterrand had to withstand a sustained series of attacks and innuendoes from the Right and far Right, in which hatred of Mendès 'the crypto-Communist' was mixed up with hatred for Mendès the 'scuttler' of empire (Indochina, Tunisia).

The 'affair' came up for debate in the National Assembly early in December, when a right-wing deputy (incidentally one of the leaders of the sugar-beet lobby) tried to smear Mendès and Mitterrand and claimed that Indochina had been lost because of treason at home. The Mendès-France government was a nest of neutralists which had destroyed Dides' highly effective counter-espionage unit, he said. Mitterrand was able to show that Dides' evidence had been 'doctored' and that he, Mitterrand, had resigned from the Laniel government not because of leakages but in opposition to its Moroccan policy. It was high time, he added, that 'an end was put to all these "parallel" police services grafted onto the regular Republican police.'

Though well justified as an observation, this was little more than a pious aspiration. One of the most deplorable aspects of the Fourth Republic, contributing to its decay and decline, was the permanent interplay, under the cover of anti-Communism, between politics, the octopus-like and frequently rival intelligence services, and the police. 'Credulous, unscrupulous and enmeshed in party intrigue, these services did much to discredit the régime they were supposed to serve before they finally betrayed it in May 1958.'[5] French history perhaps to a greater degree than in most other nations, has a way of repeating itself. Nearly twenty years before, right-wing slander campaigns against Roger Salengro, Minister of the Interior in Léon Blum's Popular Front programme, had driven him to suicide.

At the end of the '*fuites*' debate, Mendès' government won only a modest majority – 287 to 240 with 88 abstentions. His enemies had convincingly shown the depths to which they were capable of descending. They were not in the least ashamed of this, but what had also been demonstrated was the detestation – the word is not too strong – which the personality and policies of the Prime Minister were capable of arousing in right-wing and extreme right-wing circles. If this was the price of eschewing the *immobilisme* of previous governments it was proving a heavy one to pay. Here again, history was repeating itself. Mendès' capacity simultaneously to attract loyalty and enthusiasm, calumny and loathing, was directly comparable with the violent and contradictory reactions evoked by Léon Blum as leader of the Popular Front in the Thirties. The *fuites* affair, like most other affairs, was never completely cleared up. It is even possible that the Communists may have connived with the extreme Right in spreading forged information so as to embarrass Mendès. What is certain is that, as usual in such cases, some of the mud flung tended to stick.

In the autumn of 1954, mud of a different kind, destined in the end to inflict far more lethal demage than the *fuites* business, was thrown up in North Africa. On 1 November 1954 the Algerian war broke out. Few people saw it like that at the time. The disorders brought about by what appeared to be a rebel movement, principally in the Aurès mountains, cost no more than a few French lives. But the pre-concerted and coordinated nature of the uprising left no doubt that here was the beginning of a revolutionary struggle for independence. This was delicate ground for the government. Its right-wing critics could and did quickly claim, as they had been doing for months, that this showed how one thing led to another: the 'scuttle' from Indochina had been followed by liberal measures in Tunisia which sparked off troubles in Morocco which were followed by unrest in Algeria. It was the domino theory translated into French, and in this case the analysis had something to be said for it.

Mendès and Mitterrand, the responsible Minister (Algeria, technically a part of metropolitan France, came under the Interior Ministry), reacted sharply. Military reinforcements, including parachute battalions, were immediately despatched to the trouble spots. Both Mendès and Mitterrand, in strong contrast with what they were later to think and say, declared publicly that '*L'Algérie c'est la France*', the latter adding that 'all those who disturb the peace and support secession as well as their accomplices will be thwarted by every possible means. . . . The only negotiation is war.' As well as the military measures, the main nationalist party in Algeria, Messali Hadj's Mouvement pour le Triomphe des Libertés Démocratiques (MTLD), was outlawed, its documents confiscated and its followers arrested.

But this show of determination could not save the government from the venom of its enemies. This time they had something better to go on than the '*fuites*'. In an Assembly debate in early December, Georges Bidault, one of Mendès' most implacable opponents, complained of what he called the 'mysteriousness' of his, Mendès', colonial aims – 'What *do* you want, where *are* you going?' A right-wing deputy accused the government of having, within a few months, lost Hanoi, Haiphong, Pondicherry and the other French settlements in India (an amicable and overdue arrangement with Delhi had indeed provided for the transfer of these pocket handkerchiefs of French territory to India), and if it went on like this it would lose Tunis, Casablanca, Oran and Algiers. A more serious attack – though not lethal, that was yet to come – was mounted by René Mayer, the former Prime Minister, himself a Radical deputy from an Algerian constituency. He became head of and spokesman for all those interests, in France and Algeria, who were determined to maintain unbroken French domination in an Arab and Berber territory where only one-tenth of the population were European French citizens.

The most apt comment on this attitude came from a Communist deputy, who with perfect accuracy pointed out that although Algeria was supposed to consist of three French departments, it was in reality a colony and treated as such. This was because the reforms embodied in the statute of Algeria, voted by parliament in 1947, had never been properly applied (see p. 134). The administration of the country remained effectively in French hands and genuine Muslim opinion was ridiculously under-represented in the second, Muslim, electoral college. Mitterrand resolved to get the statute into operation, in the belief, shared by Mendès, that the Muslim masses could be weaned away from the appeal of the rebellion by greater social and political rights. To this end, he launched a plan which would have given the majority in Algeria a greater, but still a strictly limited and French-supervised, say in its own affairs. As is usual with such efforts, the plan satisfied neither *colon* nor nationalist factions. In particular, the aim of fusing local, native police forces with metropolitan police forces on the spot horrified *colon* interests, for it would have meant partially entrusting the control of law and order to outsiders, even if they were French.

These same interests were equally shaken when, at the end of January 1955, the Prime Minister appointed as Governor-General of Algeria Jacques Soustelle, a former Secretary-General of the RPF, an opponent of the EDC, with the reputation of a mildly left-wing intellectual. It is ironical, in view of Soustelle's subsequent role as a fanatical *Algérie française* supporter and one of the architects of the plot that brought the Fourth Republic to its inglorious end, to think back to the reception given to his appointment. 'Soustelle is a neutralist,' thundered *Le Figaro*. 'Crypto-progressive' was the epithet of *L'Aurore*, the standard-bearer for the *colon* lobby. *L'Humanité* saw the appointment as one more attempt by Mendès to shore up his wavering government. That was also how it appeared to many of the deputies of Mendès' own Radical party. Was not this just the sort of political chicanery – bidding for Gaullist votes by giving an important job to a leading Gaullist – which Mendès had earlier condemned when practised by others?

The European population in Algeria equally did not like the idea of Soustelle (when nearly two years later he was recalled by the then

Socialist government, *colon* crowds in Algiers, sensing him their best apologist, tried to prevent him from boarding his ship). The *colons* and their supporters were automatically suspicious of any nomination by Mendès. This was also increasingly true in Paris about any action by the government. The business of carrying out *procès d'intentions* against Mendès – judging him not on what he was doing or promised to do but on what he was suspected of planning to do – had reached unprecedented lengths. In mid-January 1955 he handed over foreign affairs (the Quai d'Orsay) to Edgar Faure, replacing him at the Ministry of Finance with a youngish MRP deputy, Robert Buron, a man out of sympathy with the main stream of his party. If by this Mendès thought he might win over some MRP support, he was badly mistaken. Buron noted, after seeing one of his party leaders, that for most of its senior members, 'Mendès was marked with original sin. . . . Not only is there no question of a rapprochement but it must be anticipated that at the first opportunity 60 or 70 MRP votes against the government will be joined with those of the Radicals, the Right and, according to circumstances, the Communists or the RPF.'[6]

On this reckoning, despite Mendès' continuing popularity among the younger generations and among the rank and file, as opposed to the deputies, of his own Radical party, his chances of survival were growing weaker daily. He had tried, the previous autumn, to bolster his government's strength by inviting the Socialists to join it. But the latter, under Guy Mollet's leadership, preferred to remain on the sidelines; for him and many of his pro-European colleagues, the memory of the fate of EDC was too recent to forget. Once more the bane of EDC, like an ancient curse, had exerted its evil influence. It had been, in pre-Mendès days, the cement of the coalition between Socialists, MRP and the non-Gaullist Right. Once that cement had been removed, it was inevitable that the building should begin to crumble.

Yet as the shadows closed around him, Mendès made little or no attempt – it was in any case probably too late to do so – to assuage his critics or try the use of the soft answer to turn away wrath. His champions were no more tactful. François Mauriac, in his weekly column in *L'Express* called '*Bloc-Notes*', coined the expression 'the party of Dien Bien Phu' to describe the MRP. Their men had, it is true, dominated French foreign and colonial policy for many years, and could fairly be held to blame for some of the mistakes, but rather more than most people, politicians strongly resent being reminded of their shortcomings. Mendès' own efforts in this direction were just as uncompromising. By taking every occasion to emphasise that before he entered the Matignon all had been chaos and darkness whereas now all was sweetness and light, by showing himself hypersensitive to criticism of any kind, he had within a few months brought about an effect exactly opposite to the spirit of national unity which it had been his declared aim to foster. Many of the smears and attacks against him were ignoble, some of them the work of ignoble men. But in the final count it was his own personality which contributed as much as any of several other factors to his downfall. The lines that Edmond Rostand puts into Cyrano de Bergerac's mouth could just as aptly be used for Mendès:

> . . . *Eh bien, c'est mon vice,*
> *Déplaire est mon plaisir.*
> *J'aime qu'on me haïsse.* *

The end came in the first week in February, and the occasion was yet another debate in the National Assembly – only a month had passed since the last one – on North African affairs. This time, René Mayer moved in for the kill. Although a member for an Algerian constituency and a disappointed supporter of EDC, he did not, as a Radical, share the bitterness of the MRP and, a Jew himself, was certainly not anti-Semitic as so many of Mendès' enemies were. But he pulled no punches and his speech was highly influential. He argued that the Tunisian negotiations – the sequel to Mendès' lightning visit to Tunis the previous July when the principle of internal autonomy was reaffirmed – were having 'a bad effect' on Algeria. He had no wish to see France 'adapt' herself in North Africa, as she had already 'adapted' herself in Indochina and India. He would be voting against the government, he said, not just because of its North African policies but because (speaking directly to Mendès) 'I do not know where you are going, and I refuse to believe that a policy of "movement" cannot find a happy medium between what is called *immobilisme* on the one hand and reckless adventure on the other.' It was the same accusation, couched in

* Well yes, it is my vice, Giving offence is my pleasure. I love people to hate me.

almost identical terms, mounted only three months previously by Georges Bidault.

This was the climacteric. Here were all the rumours, innuendoes, insinuations of the preceding months boiled down to one simple thought, expressed through the medium of a former prime minister, a man of high intelligence and wide experience: Mendès was not to be trusted. Mendès fought back angrily against what he called Mayer's 'donkey's kick' – *coup de pied de l'âne* (kicking a man when he is down). French policy in Tunisia, he reminded the Assembly, had already received its approval. The only other course in North Africa was one of force and oppression. (Already in the debate there had been a horrifying glimpse of this, when an Algerian Muslim deputy had spoken of tortures being perpetrated by the police in Algeria against Muslims. Those living in the *bled* (countryside), he said, 'know at last what electricity means . . . not from electric bulbs but from the electric gadgets that are inserted into various parts of their body'.) As for Algeria, what was M. Mayer grumbling about? Mendès reminded him that there were now increased numbers of troops there, which would not have been possible without the Indochina settlement. This North African debate, he said with increasing bitterness, was only an excuse for overthrowing the government (he was quite correct there), and what was tragic was that this would be done by an unholy coalition of colonialists, lip-service liberals (i.e. the MRP) and the Communists. He ended, in a Chamber still crowded at 4 o'clock in the morning, by putting the question of confidence.

At 4.50 a.m. the result of the vote was announced: 273 for the government (all the 105 Socialists, 52 Radicals out of 74 – this where René Mayer's influence in detaching 20 votes had been decisive – 5 MRP out of 82, 45 Social Republicans (ex-Gaullist) out of 70, 22 Right out of more than a hundred other fragments); 319 against (all the Communists, the mass of the MRP, the majority of the various right-wing groups, and 17 of the more right-wing Gaullists). Mendès had accurately prophesied the motley composition of the majority which would overturn him.

The usual pattern, after a vote of non-confidence, was for the defeated Prime Minister to leave the Chamber and go to the Elysée to present his government's resignation to the President of the Republic. But Mendès, at this grave moment, appeared to wish to prove that he was not as other men. He left his place on the ministerial bench and walked, not out of the building but up the steps of the rostrum, where he proceeded to harangue the deputies, who were first astonished, then outraged. It seemed to those witnessing the scene an extraordinary exhibition of hubris.* What he had to say was that what he and his government had done could not be undone. 'Men come and go, but national necessities remain . . . How can the nation forget the hopes that we have aroused, how can you doubt that the nation has acquired a taste for truth, now that it knows its bitter but salutary flavour?' Against a rising tide of verbal protest and banging of desk tops, he shouted his last words: 'I hope that tomorrow, in a better atmosphere, we shall give the country new reasons for hope and that we may overcome those hatreds of which we have often given such a sorry spectacle to the world. *Vive la France.*' Then he really did leave the Chamber, amid loud booing from the Right, the MRP and the Communists, and cheers from the Socialists and a few other Centre–Left benches.

The Mendès-France experiment had lasted for seven and a half months. However unorthodox and arrogant his final speech to the Assembly may have seemed, Mendès had spoken truly when he talked about hopes aroused and truths faced. After his defeat, he received 10,000 letters of support, and the opinion polls at the time showed that 53 per cent of those responding thought that the Mendès-France government had performed better than its predecessors. Seventy-nine per cent considered that its greatest achievement was the Indochinese settlement. If anything, Mendès' defeat was more regretted in Western capitals than in France, where governments were not expected to last for long. He had certainly, over EDC, aroused suspicions in London, Washington and elsewhere. But he was widely regarded abroad as a phenomenal and welcome newcomer to the familiar procession of political figures whom the world had got used to seeing trudge across the stage each time there was a crisis in Paris. The real question however consists

---

* Jacques Fauvet maintains in *La IVe République* (Paris, Fayard, 1959), p. 286, that the episode was due to Mendès' miscalculation of the final vote. He had prepared his farewell speech in the expectation that the adverse vote would not amount to an absolute majority of the Assembly and would not therefore make his resignation mandatory. Before resigning voluntarily, he wanted a last word. In fact, the 319 votes cast against his government were an absolute majority and killed it stone-dead. Mendès' defiance, whatever its motivation, thus appeared as intolerable bravado and a breach of political protocol.

not of these immediate reactions but of assessing the impact upon French political life of the Mendès-France style and his vision of government. Here the verdict, even with hindsight, must remain an open one. He undeniably faced up, in a way no previous government had done, to the most pressing problems – EDC and Tunisia principal among them – and established through his broadcasts and speeches a direct link – here Pinay had shown the way – with the general public. But this was not enough to overcome the limitations imposed by the party system or the animosities aroused by the vigorous approach and the oblivion to special interests which lay at the heart of the Mendès method.

As his performance in the Assembly on the night of his downfall suggested, Mendès did not consider himself beaten. The Mendès-France government was dead but not, if he could help it, Mendèsism, where that term could be considered to cover the continuation of certain policies, the adoption of certain methods and the propagation of a certain faith. This life after death took two forms. Firstly, Mendès' successor, Edgar Faure, who only won the premiership after a long-drawn-out crisis in which Pinay for the Right, Pineau for the Socialists and Pflimlin for the MRP all tried unavailingly to form a government, gave every sign of wishing to continue Mendès' policies. Within a few months, he had finally disposed of the last obstacle to German rearmament by inducing the Council of the Republic (the second Chamber, successor to the old Senate) to approve the London and Paris agreements. He had also completed the process, begun by Mendès, of establishing new relations with Tunisia. It was North Africa, and specifically Tunisia, which had served as the excuse for Mendès' enemies to overturn him. That it was only a pretext was demonstrated when the Assembly ratified by a large majority the Tunisian Conventions enshrining internal autonomy and Bourguiba was allowed to return to Tunis.

Why this about-turn, why had the critics of Mendès' colonial policies suddenly found it possible to approve an important part of them? It was certainly not the case that all at once a fervent wish to decolonise had swept, like a cleansing wave, over the *jusqu'au-boutistes* – the last-ditchers who later were to exert so strong an influence over Algerian affairs. The answer lay largely in the fact that although the new Prime Minister appeared to be practising a system of Mendèsism-without-Mendès, he was in fact playing the game by different rules. To state the obvious, Faure was not Mendès, and many people were very glad of that fact. Where the latter was intolerant of criticism, full of self-righteousness and scornful of blandishments, his successor was a political operator of great skill, intelligence and subtlety, a man with few political enemies (though Mendès was soon to become one of them), someone who would have found it easy and natural to re-echo one of the favourite sayings of his sixteenth-century compatriot, St François de Sales, that more flies are attracted by a spoonful of honey than by a whole barrel of vinegar.

Faure's methods were as different from those of Mendès as it was possible to be. In the name of political realism he reverted, before his investiture by the Assembly, to the practice of negotiating directly with the parties about ministerial posts. The result was a team formed according to the time-honoured principle, disregarded by Mendès, of *dosage* – jobs for the parties and for their boys. The MRP, rejoicing in the fall of their enemy, returned to the government with four portfolios, the Social Republicans (Gaullist) had an equal number, so did the Radicals, while the classic Right were awarded five, including the appointment of M. Pinay to the Quai d'Orsay. With such adroitly organised support, it was not surprising that Faure succeeded in winning approval for the finishing of business left unfinished by his abrasive predecessor.

But if this was only the appearance rather than the reality of Mendèsism, a second way of keeping the flame alight was pursued by Mendès himself, in the form of his attempts to reshape the Radical party in his own image. The previous autumn (October 1954) Mendès, then Prime Minister and the star of the party, had carried all before him at the Radical congress held in Marseille. There Herriot, the Grand Old Man of the party, had grandiloquently declared: 'This is the Congress of Mendès-France – *devant lui j'incline ma personne et mon passé – je lui confie le Parti*.'* Yet despite this triumph, only three months later one-third of the Radical deputies voted for his downfall.

The truth was that the Radical party, the most opportunist, facing-all-ways, fundamentally conservative (with a small 'c') grouping in the French political spectrum, was only partially, perhaps no more than slightly, *Mendèsiste*, in terms of Mendès' own standards and definitions. Martineau-Déplat was still there, a powerful

* 'To him I yield my person and my past. I entrust him with the party.'

anti-Mendès influence, and most of the Radical federations in the country stopped well short of Mendèsism. This was the tide that Mendès had to try to turn, and he sought to do so by pressing for an extraordinary congress, which was held in early May 1955 in Paris. It was a stormy affair, pitting Mendès against Martineau-Déplat – two violently differing philosophies and personalities. Mendès appeared to enjoy a great success, being loudly applauded by the delegates when he declared that the Radical party was a party of the Left and that it must address itself to the younger generation, 'among whom a will for renewal has been aroused' (i.e. by himself). What Mendès was trying to do was to prepare the way for a new, non-Communist and dynamic left-wing bloc, to be supported by the masses. That meant first of all an agreement with the Socialists. Such an aim was completely at odds with the other, Martineau-Déplat-inspired and traditional concept of the Radical party as a political hinge and the guarantor against sudden or possibly any change.

Anyone wishing to learn about the kind of France which Mendès was seeking to create (as against the kind which his enemies suspected and accused him of seeking to create) should study the speech he made in his own Norman constituency of Evreux on 23 July 1955.[7] More philosophical than most of his speeches, it consisted of a penetrating analysis of how the democratic system in France was not working properly, and a series of suggestions for reform. True democracy, he said, rested upon the fusion of the State and the citizen. But in France 'the citizen and the State have turned their backs on one another', with the State, in the form of successive governments, lying to the people – about Indochina, about EDC, about inflation. He referred to, and discussed remedies for, the instability of French governments, and argued in favour of fewer meetings of the National Assembly (to enable deputies to perform their other duties properly) and legislation by decree. This would not impinge upon the Assembly's right to overthrow a government whenever it wished, but would provide for the adoption and application of vigorous policies. The speech included a passage on citizenship, on the need to put the general interest first, and it ended with the familiar call for a 'national awakening'.

Had it been possible to translate these ideas into action, it is arguable that the Fourth Republic would not have ended as it did, in impotence and humiliation and by means of recourse to another saviour figure with far more radical ideas about how the nation should be awakened. Even so, Mendès' proposals, if applied, could not have dissipated the darkening clouds over North Africa. It is noteworthy that the Evreux speech contained little on that, although Mendès did reveal that he was receiving about ten letters a week from anxious parents whose sons had been called up to serve in Algeria. What mattered, he said, was not these individual anxieties, understandable though they were, but that there should be no war in Algeria at all. But he did not, at least on this occasion, throw much light upon how this desirable end was to be achieved.

The irony was that while Mendès was busy with the reform of the Radical party and the task of preparing a new future for France, Edgar Faure, eschewing the theatrical and intense style of his predecessor, was enjoying a period of seeming calm and stability. It was not over-optimistic, in that hot summer of 1955, to think that France was at last emerging from the dark troughs of the post-war years on to the sunlit plateau of peace and prosperity. This had not of course been brought about simply as a result of Faure's premiership. He happened to arrive in power at a propitious moment, with the economy expanding, a standstill on the wages front (with the exception of some violent strikes in the shipbuilding industry, which did not spread to other sectors), and the apparently insoluble problems of the past, such as Indochina and German rearmament, finally disposed of. It even seemed possible to believe that the much called-for national renaissance, exemplified in such economic achievements as the opening of the great dam at Donzère-Mondragon or the completion of the pipeline linking Paris to the lower Seine, was taking place without the drastic revisions and upheavals predicted by de Gaulle and to a lesser extent by Mendès.

Events in North Africa shattered these innocent dreams. In Morocco, where the earlier conspiracy to exile the legitimate Sultan and his substitution by a feeble puppet had afforded no relief in the cycle of violence and instability, a fearful massacre occurred on 20 August 1955, the second anniversary of the previous Sultan's overthrow. The trouble came principally not from the larger cities with their concentration of nationalist sympathisers, but among the Berber rural population, from whose tribes the French had traditionally recruited soldiers for their own army. At one centre, Oued Zem, forty-nine French people, including fifteen children, were slaughtered. In the inevitable French military repression that followed, roughly one thousand Moroccans were done to death. Despite this, and the customary display of insubordination by senior French officers and officials in Morocco over Faure's plans for getting rid of the puppet Sultan, those plans matured sufficiently, helped by a change of heart by the unpredictable old El Glaoui, to enable the deposed Sultan to be restored to his throne in mid-November, underwritten by a vague formula of 'independence within interdependence'. It was a considerable achievement for Faure, but it cost him the resignation of his Gaullist ministers and the support of the Gaullist and right-wing elements of his parliamentary majority. However enviable might be the Prime Minister's skill at shuffling the political cards, he was as much a prisoner as his predecessors of the equation according to which there was no stable and reliable parliamentary majority for any policy at any time.

But it was not only Morocco which blew up on 20 August. On that day in the Constantine area of Algeria there was an upsurge of rebel violence, followed by fierce French reprisals. One hundred and twenty-three Europeans, including women and children, were massacred. Reprisals accounted for more than 1,200 rebel lives (French sources) or 12,000 (FLN – Front de Libération Nationale – sources). By now it was clear that in Algeria, France had to contend not with a few patches of local dissidence but with a brutal, organised and resolutely led independence movement. Soustelle's well-meaning efforts to make contact, through members of his staff, with rebel leaders came to nothing and were abandoned. Soustelle himself, who earlier had promulgated a far-reaching programme of social and political reforms designed to bring about 'integration' (whatever that meant, for it meant different things to different people), was deeply shocked by the anti-European violence of 20 August and began his remarkable 180-degree turn away from liberalism toward his final, pro-*colon* stance. In any case, his hopes for reforms were irretrievably dashed when, at the end of September, the Muslim members of the Algerian Assembly – most of whom were thought to be reliable French stooges, '*béni-oui-ouis*' – rejected the whole idea of integration. This meant, effectively, that the reform programme was dead before it had had a chance to live. From now on, the emphasis was to be on the military build-up with which to contain and suppress the FLN.

In mid-October, the National Assembly debated Algerian affairs.

Faure stuck to the integration argument, though anyone who stopped to think knew that its literal application would have meant about 120 Algerian deputies sitting in the Palais Bourbon. Though the debate ended on a vote of confidence in the government (310 to 254, the minority comprising mostly Communists and Socialists) it failed in fact, as past debates on Tunisia had also failed to do, to produce any clear policy. If secession was unthinkable, assimilation too dangerous and integration impractical, what was left? In default of anything else, the only answer was to be found in the old Indochinese formula: 'pacification' first, then reforms and a new but yet-to-be-defined relationship. One of the most striking speeches in the debate, though its effect was nil, came from the eighty-five-year-old Maurice Viollette, who had been a pre-war liberal-minded Governor of Algeria and who, at the time of the discussion of the new Algerian Statute, had pleaded in vain (see p. 134) for a more enlightened approach. Now, in gruesomely prophetic terms, he spoke of 'the last chance to avoid disaster . . . As much as thirty years ago, I said that if the Muslims of Algeria were not given a square deal, they would take the law into their own hands.' He was haunted, he declared, 'by the thought of what is to happen to both France and Algeria'.

A few days later, in a speech in Normandy, Mendès sounded the same note. Unkept promises, he said, lay at the root of the Algerian troubles: 'Integration, to the [Muslim] Algerians, implies complete equality, but in Paris the word is often used merely as a meaningless slogan.' This was profoundly true. In all the public statements of the time, whether made under the Mendès or the Faure governments, there was a continuous ambiguity about the practical and desirable aims for an Algerian policy. Even the use of such a word as autonomy had its dangers, because, as the aspirations of Tunisia and Morocco showed all too clearly, it could be thought to mark the beginning of the slippery slope towards independence. The nearest it was possible to get towards recognising the realities of the Algerian situation was to employ such double-speak as Edgar Faure did when he referred in his investiture debate to 'an integration of Algeria which respects its original nature and its own personality'.

In the autumn of 1955, it was not necessary to be half as quick-witted or pragmatic as Edgar Faure to see, in face of the burgeoning crisis in Algeria, that no good counsel or proper evaluation of the national interest was likely to emerge from the Assembly elected in

1951. Although its full mandate would take it to June 1956, it was visibly running out of steam. Not that this was the Prime Minister's only motive for doing what he did. The rivalry between him and Mendès for the soul of the Radical party was by now a running battle. By going to the country early he could hope to catch Mendès and his supporters insufficiently prepared. Only a week after the Algerian debate, Faure tabled a bill calling for general elections to be brought forward. The ensuing confusion was a prime example of the Fourth Republic at its spectacular worst. Though the Assembly did finally approve of early elections, most of the month of November was spent in bewildering and Byzantine manoeuvrings both within the Assembly and between the Assembly and the Council of the Republic over the form of the electoral law.

Here the enmity between Mendès and Faure reached new heights, culminating in the Radical congress in Paris. For the Radical party, it was an epic occasion. The walls of the Salle Wagram, where it was held, were hung with suitable slogans – '*L'opinion publique est impatiente*' (Saint-Just), '*La République est toujours en péril*' (Alain), '*Le Parti Radical est le Parti qui tient parole*' (Herriot) – with Phrygian bonnets, the impeccable sign of Republicanism, painted above them. Unlike earlier Congresses, this time the majority of the delegates were pro-Mendès and anti-Faure, and a great burst of booing greeted Faure when he arrived in the hall. Mendès tore into the record of his, Faure's, government which, though ostensibly carrying out Mendèsist policies, had shown itself, so Mendès claimed, to be a Centre–Right coalition, whereas Mendès' plans for a rejuvenated Radical party were that it should be the mainspring of a Centre–Left grouping. The quarrel was not only ideological – French Radicals, like pre-Thatcher Conservatives, do not have much time for ideology – but was a personal clash between two able men of differing temperaments and ways of thought, both ambitious for power and ruthless in their quest of it. For the moment Mendès, in terms of control of the Radical party, held the upper hand. But a remarkable denouement was impending.

As the interminable and indeterminate discussions dragged on in the lower and upper chambers of parliament about the electoral system, so an increasing number of Radical, Socialist and Communist deputies who did not want a snap election, certainly not before the adoption of an electoral law to their liking, resolved to bring down the government. Along with this hodgepodge went the larger part of the Gaullists (Social Republicans) and many of the classic Right, who could not forgive Faure for having 'lost' Morocco, just as they had chosen the 'loss' of Tunisia as the pretext to overthrow Mendès. When Faure, at the end of November, declared a procedural matter concerning electoral reform to be one of confidence, the vote went against him. But the drama lay in the fact that his opponents, like Mendès on the night of his downfall, had not done their sums correctly. The voting figures were 318 against the government, 218 for it and 83 abstentions. 318 was an absolute majority of the Assembly, and as this was the second time within eighteen months that a government had been overthrown by such a majority, the way was open, under the Constitution, for a dissolution.

A fierce discussion among the members of the defeated government about what to do next ended by Faure's decision to dissolve. It was the first time such a procedure had been invoked in Republican France since Marshal McMahon, the second President of the Third Republic, had used it in 1876. By a coincidence, the decree announcing the dissolution appeared in the *Journal Officiel* on 2 December, the anniversary of Napoleon III's *coup d'état* of 1851. Such historical associations are dear to French hearts, and Faure's critics and enemies, Mendès and his supporters prominent among them, hastened to make the ominous but juicy comparison. A few days later, Mendès used his control of the Radical party's executive to expel Faure, along with some of the die-hards (a term inapplicable to Faure), such as Martineau-Déplat.

Public opinion, even more alienated than usual by these febrile machinations in Paris, seized on the dissolution as the one positively welcome development in weeks. 'Parliament is mostly a despised institution today,' noted Janet Flanner.[8] But along with the rejoicing, she also reported 'violent denunciations of Faure's dissolution order as a reactionary plot, an anti-democratic *coup de force*'. None was more vehement with this sort of criticism than Mendès. In his signed editorials in *L'Express* he lashed out against what he called 'rigged elections', 'guilty men' and 'a plot against *la Patrie*'.

Mendès was in a difficult position, and he knew it. Although he had 'purged' the Radical party, he had an impossibly short time – the elections were set for 2 January 1956, one calendar month after their announcement – to organise the 'new Left' of which he was the symbol and representative and to propagate its ideas. His first move was to put together an electoral coalition between his sort of

Radicals, the Socialists, an important section of the Gaullists, and part of the small group of near-Radicals led by François Mitterrand. This diverse alliance went under the name of 'Front Républicain', a title with more publicity value than political content. Its mouthpiece was *L'Express*, transformed for the period of the election into a daily paper and enthusiastically devoted to the task of preparing the way for the return to power of Mendès-France. That this was by no means a flight of fancy was shown by public opinion polls which, by the close of the election campaign, found that 37 per cent of the electorate wanted the Front Républicain to win, as against 24 per cent for the outgoing, Faure-led majority and 13 per cent for the Popular Front formula being pushed – unsuccessfully, in face of the Socialists' habitual refusal to cooperate – by the Communist party. The same polls revealed 27 per cent in favour of Mendès as Prime Minister, as against 8 per cent for Pinay, 6 per cent for Faure and 3 per cent for Thorez, the Communist leader.

Ranged against the Mendès coalition were, apart from the Communists and the Poujadists, the elements of the outgoing coalition – what Front Républicain propaganda called 'the guilty men of Dien Bien Phu . . . of the chaos of North Africa . . . of social *immobilisme* at home'. It was composed of the MRP, by now a shadow of its former, post-Liberation, left-of-centre vigour and scope; the non-Mendès Radicals, led by Edgar Faure and calling themselves the Rassemblement des Gauches Républicains (French party names are for the most part meaningless, the only rule, in a country owing its political ethos to the Revolution and having more recently experienced the Vichy years, being that no matter how right-wing or reactionary a party may be, it should never allow the word 'right', or anything suggesting it, to creep into its official designation); and the classic Right, financed principally by the Employers' Federation and by the farming and colonial lobbies. Faithful to the rule set forth above, they functioned under the bland device of the 'Union des Indépendants et des Paysans'.

There was not much enlightenment for the sorely tried electorate, as it approached the polls, in the party programmes. The Right put out a series of unremarkable brochures one of which dealt with 'the defence of Christian civilisation', another with 'the struggle against Communism'. Almost nothing was said about Algeria and North Africa, lack of a national policy for which was Faure's main reason for calling an early election. The MRP, intent on showing that whatever its enemies might insinuate, it was still imbued with liberal thinking, went strong on social reforms; on Algeria it side-stepped, saying merely that it stood for the re-establishment of law and order, for a greater say by Muslims in the administration, and for industrial and agricultural reforms. The (Mendès) Radicals went a little further than this, calling for a proper application of the 1947 Statute, free elections and the purging of French administrators. In the course of the campaign, Mendès himself made it clear that he regarded Algeria as a major issue.

Throughout December, *L'Express* kept up a bombardment of news and comment about Algeria, concentrating on French rather than Arab atrocities. In the context of popular feeling about the inalienability of the French position there, this probably did Mendès' prospects more harm than good. Even he stopped well short of the Communist position, which was in favour of an Algerian Republic with its own government and parliament. His 'plan' was for a general election in Algeria within six months (because of the security situation it had been agreed that, despite the fiction that Algeria was an integral part of metropolitan France, there would be no election there in January), making it possible to discuss the future Statute with 'the legitimate representatives of Algeria, so as to find a solution on Tunisian lines'. This was grist to the mill of Mendès' opponents, and especially to the Algerian *colons*, for whom internal autonomy *à la Tunisienne* was an unacceptable step towards independence. The Socialist party programme, though it too spoke of the need for a properly representative Algerian Assembly, left future relationships with France undefined, referring vaguely to 'association, federation or any other organisation desired by the populations' – the plural form denoted that Algerian French and Muslims alike were to do some joint desiring, not a promising prospect. Guy Mollet, the Socialist leader, described the Algerian war as *'imbécile et sans issue'*. Within a few weeks, as Prime Minister of the government which emerged from the elections, he was to find himself prosecuting the war with redoubled vigour.

It is a little too easy, with hindsight, to blame the parties for failure, in their electoral programme, to face up to the realities of the worsening Algerian situation. It is certainly true that despite the difficulties of negotiation with the FLN at that stage, when militarily and administratively the French held the upper hand in Algeria, an agreement – if it could have been made to stick –

would have saved years of bloody and fruitless struggle, just as an agreement with Ho Chi Minh in 1946 would have made the tragic Indochinese experience unnecessary. It is quite conceivable that such arrangements for Algeria could have provided for the protection of *colon* interests – though whether that would have been considered acceptable by the majority of *colons* is highly doubtful. When some years later General de Gaulle, restored to power, set about following more or less this line of action, he brought the murderous weight of *colon* and Army reaction down upon his head.

The fact was that in France in 1955, and for a long time after that, another sort of reality existed, which was the refusal, the sheer inability, of the majority of French people to contemplate the possibility of Algeria ceasing to be totally and unquestionably French. So many politicians and public figures had for so long – and they included Mendès himself – been asserting that Algeria was French and must ever remain so, that it was unthinkable, whatever private doubts and fears might be harboured, to suggest the least hint of the contrary. Mendès came as close to it as anyone – always excepting the Communists – with his references to the urgent need for a peaceful solution before the Algerian war swallowed up hundreds of billions of francs, leaving nothing over for investment and reform in France itself. But that line of argument brought a quick response from the Right, namely that to seek negotiations with 'terrorists' would simply encourage them. 'If you try to apply the Tunisia solution to Algeria,' Mendès was told by Jean de Broglie, a right-wing opponent in his Norman constituency, 'then it'll be the end of French rule in North Africa.'[9]

It was not only the classic Right which was the champion of *Algérie française*. Pierre Poujade and his movement had, to the scorn or merriment of the Paris know-alls, decided to put up candidates for election. If other party programmes lacked precision about Algeria, that charge could not be brought against the Poujadists. Madame Poujade, a pretty brunette, was a *française d'Algérie*, and after the Poujadist congress held in Algiers in November 1954, her loud-mouthed husband and his followers warmly espoused the cause, denouncing Mendès, Faure, Mitterrand and Pinay for planning to abandon Algeria (despite the fact that when in office, these had consistently stood for the maintenance of French sovereignty).

This was a new and, as it turned out, a well chosen turning in Poujadist tactics. The beginning, in 1953, had been in the picturesque little town of St Céré in the Lot department, where Poujade eked out a precarious existence as a stationer. It took the form of a protest movement against what it considered to be the unfairly applied and excessive tax burden laid by the State upon small shopkeepers and artisans. To that extent, it entered into the centuries-old French tradition of resistance to tax inspection and to the uncomprehending interference of administrations in Paris. Flaubert, in his *Dictionnaire des idées reçues*, couples together *octroi* (town dues, or rates) and *douane* (customs), and says of them that *on doit se révolter contre et la frauder*. Encouraging people to repel the tax-inspector was not only an historic posture but also one likely to be popular among a large number of people.

There was no coincidence in the fact that Poujadism drew most of its strength from the area south of a line running from St Malo to Geneva. This was the so-called *désert français* – all those economically stagnant departments made still more backward by rural emigration to the cities. Here was where the 'small man' was preponderant and, in the inflation-ridden, black-market-dominated post-war years, relatively prosperous. Continuing shortages and unceasing consumer demand had led to an unreal expansion in the service economy. St Céré itself was a typical specimen: for a population of 3,200, there were twenty-seven shopkeepers, a proportion of 120 consumers to every shop. But as goods began to flow more freely and inflation subsided these small retailers began to feel the pinch. The growth of the multiple store was a further threat to their livelihood. Understandably, their first cries of anguish were directed against the tax-inspector.

Poujade was exceptionally qualified to make these cries heard: literally so, for he had a stentorian voice and a natural gift for populist rabble-rousing oratory. He also had some of the demagogue's platform tricks, such as a display of virility, achieved by performing a sort of strip-tease, throwing off, as he warmed to his speech, his coat, his pullover and his shirt. His enemies accused him of being a fascist (*L'Express* dubbed him Poujadolf) and he did have youthful pre-war connections with the extreme right-wing Doriot movement. But he later served with the Free French air force, and UDCA propaganda was initially against officialdom and the rich rather than against the Left. The Communists indeed began by lending it their full support.

Then after the Algiers congress in the autumn of 1954, UDCA began to change its tune. By this time Mendès was in power, and an openly anti-Semitic flavour began to characterise Poujade's speeches, combined with a generalised curse on all politicians and on parliament as constituted. The movement also turned into one for the defence of 'empire', and thus appealed to a wider audience than the disgruntled mass of small tradespeople and tax-resisters. As it did so, its political aims became more, rather than less, obscure. By mid-1955, Poujade was talking as though the fight with the tax-man – where he had a not unrespectable case – had become a secondary matter. He began to think and speak in terms of corporatism, of summoning a new *Etats-Généraux* in which would be represented the different social and commercial interests of the country – tradesmen, farmers, workers – though what the relationship of this would be to parliament or indeed to the original Poujade movement was far from clear.[10]

Once the short electoral campaign began, the violent side of Poujadism began to show itself. Gangs of thugs roamed the constituencies and numerous candidates had to abandon their meetings, as the Poujadists roared out their pithy slogan of '*Sortez les sortants*' – throw out all those deputies who are standing again. This was by far the politest and most printable of their war cries.

No one following the election trail in the provinces in December 1955 could fail to be struck by the extraordinary contrast between the fevered activities of the parties and politicians in Paris and the calm, almost detached attitudes of the country people and townsfolk outside the capital. True, there was in many places a Mendès-versus-Faure polarisation, and almost everywhere the Poujadists were busy trying to challenge or interrupt other people's meetings, in preference to holding one of their own. In view of their almost total lack of anything which could be called a programme, they were probably well advised. In some of the country districts Mendès' attack on alcoholism and emphasis on milk-drinking had not been forgotten; in the Jura, in eastern France, the electoral fief of Edgar Faure, someone asked the latter where he stood on the matter of alcohol and he had the presence of mind to reply that he did not stick exclusively to milk. Algeria, as a subject of discussion, let alone contention, rarely cropped up (though Mendès, in his

Norman constituency, kept telling his meetings that Algeria was the gravest and most urgent question of all), and nor did German rearmament, by now a *fait accompli*.

But one familiar old war-horse could be heard snorting and pawing the ground, as it had done for most of the twentieth century: *laïcité* (represented by the principle of not giving State aid to Church schools) still exerted a powerful hold on Socialist emotions. This was especially true in Lille, for example, where in the 1951 elections the centre parties, including the Socialists, had made common cause with the other centre parties by 'relating' their lists (*apparentements*) and as a result won all ten seats even though the Communists topped the poll. This time the Socialists, still smarting from the way in which the non-lay parties had conspired together in 1951 (the Barangé law) to restore a small degree of State subvention to Catholic schools, refused to enter into any such arrangement. For a moment there was even a danger, averted by a 'gentlemen's agreement' among the non-Communist parties, that the Socialist Federation of the North – the most powerful in the country and a key to Socialist politics all over France – might seek to ally itself with the Communists in opposition to the 'clerical' front.

Voting in the election took place on 2 January, and the following day the Eiffel Tower caught fire. There was not the smallest connection between the two events, but the fire, in that it was completely unexpected, seemed to symbolise the surprise which greeted the election results. The flames were quickly brought under control; not so the results. If Edgar Faure and the dissolutionists thought that they were helping to ensure the creation of a new chamber that would be more manageable, more capable of agreeing on policies than the old one, they had seriously miscalculated.

On the left, the Communists and fellow-travellers increased their holding of parliamentary seats from 95 to nearly 150. On the extreme right the Poujadists, to everyone's stupor, including their own, polled nearly 2½ million votes and won fifty-three seats. Up to a point this was the result of the protest vote, which in 1951 had gone to the RPF, being transferred to Poujadism; the RPF polled nearly 3½ million fewer votes in 1956 than in 1951. But this was only a partial explanation. The new movement – like the RPF it could hardly be called a party in the ordinary sense – scored its biggest successes in the south, the traditional source of Communist, Socialist and Radical strength, where Gaullism was weakest. This was a generalised form of protest – against past government policies, against the fact that post-war modernisation had done little or nothing for these backward parts of France, against the reduced position of France in the world. Out of this jumble of motives and emotions, a new and unpredictable parliamentary grouping was born. Its name was Union et Fraternité Française (UFF). Its members were drawn mostly from the class whence Poujadism derived its main support – shopkeepers, bar proprietors, artisans; men with little knowledge of or much interest in national politics.

The MRP was reduced from 85 to 70 seats, the Socialists from 100 to 90, the classic Right from 125 to 95, and the Radicals, divided between 'Mendès' and 'Faure' candidates, dropped from 82 to 70 seats. In terms of the total vote, the Communists, with nearly 26 per cent, had emerged as by far the most widely supported party, followed by the classic Right (nearly 17 per cent), the Socialists (nearly 16 per cent), the Radicals (14.3 per cent) and the Poujadists (11.6 per cent). Unlike 1951, when the related lists system had ensured good fortune for the centre bloc, enabling it to withstand the challenge from Communists and Gaullists, this time the sparse use of such a system had favoured the extremists to right and left.

None of the commentators, the pollsters, the political would-be wizards had foreseen this outcome. This was not surprising. Never before in the course of four Republics had all the conventional parliamentary parties suffered such reverses, to the advantage of two parliamentary groupings which lay beyond the limits of the ordinarily accepted parliamentary spectrum. It appeared to make the prospect of finding a parliamentary majority which would exclude Communists and Poujadists a very difficult one. But the election result cut deeper than that. The successes of the two extremist parties showed that the call for renewal and change had evoked a response not primarily from Mendèsists, from all those whom the polls had shown wanting a clear-cut victory for a new Centre–Left coalition, but from a great body of discontented, alienated voters. Between them, they shared nothing in common save hostility towards the broad consensus which since the war, and despite deep ideological differences, had provided the country with a succession of roughly similar governments. In one sense, it had been a vote for change. But coming from the extreme Right and extreme Left it was not a defined and identifiable expression of opinion. It was more a disoriented and discordant howl of dissent. Barely nine and a half years after the birth of the Fourth Republic, France had shown itself – and in an impressively convincing manner, for over 80 per cent of the electorate had gone to the polls on 2 January – to be more divided and uncertain about the future than ever before.

CHAPTER 9

The Significance of Tomatoes

As is often the case after French elections, in January 1956 all the parties, with the exception of the Gaullists, claimed success. But this was a public pose. With the exception of the Communists and Poujadists, nobody was really satisfied. The Front Républicain, put together so hastily by Mendès-France, had won nearly 30 per cent of the popular vote but had only 150 seats. The Communists began agitating for a Popular Front. No one showed the least temptation to listen to them. The classic Right and the MRP tried to sell the idea of a 'national' government, to include Mendèsists and Socialists. That, too, got nowhere, being rejected by both Socialists and Radicals. In these circumstances, the elements of the Front Républicain, enjoying the largest share of electoral support, became the only basis on which to construct a majority. Within that grouping the role of the Socialists and their leader, Guy Mollet, was crucial. Despite Mendès' pre-eminence as a public and popular figure, Mollet and his men could justly claim to be the predominant force. They had ninety seats and 15.8 per cent of the vote.

It was therefore no great surprise when President Coty asked Mollet to form a government. There was more than mere arithmetic in his choice. If peace in Algeria was to be restored, as Mollet had promised to do by some as yet undefined method, he was better placed than Mendès, smeared as the latter was by right-wing allegations of having 'sold out' on Indochina and Tunisia. Besides, Mollet, a 'good European', had more chance of attracting support from the MRP and other 'good Europeans' from the Centre and Right, than Mendès, the 'murderer' of EDC.

There was not much love lost or ground shared in common between Mollet and Mendès, despite the support the Socialist party had given to Mendès during his premiership. Mollet, the

Lycée teacher of English, a rather dry and uncharismatic figure but a strict disciplinarian within the Socialist party, was made of very different clay to the heart-warming substance that had helped to form Léon Blum, the Socialist leader who, according to Mendès' own testimony, had had such a formative influence upon him. Also Mollet would have been less than human not to feel a pang – perhaps more than a pang – of envy and jealousy of the popular admiration evoked by Mendès, above all among younger Socialists, over whom he exerted an influence greater than he did over his own Radicals. Besides, there loomed between the two men the still undissipated cloud of the EDC. When Mendès, during the formation of the Mollet government, claimed the Quai d'Orsay for himself, Mollet, intent on having a 'good European' in that exalted post, demurred and offered him the Ministry of Finance instead. The MRP also objected to the idea of Mendès in charge of foreign affairs, and Mollet needed its support if he was to become Prime Minister. The EDC, though dead and buried, was still capable of exerting its influence even beyond the grave. This time it was Mendès' turn to refuse. He did not fancy becoming financially responsible for policies with which he already found himself out of tune. So he finished up with the senior position in the new government of Minister of State without departmental responsibilities.

The new team was made up of Socialists, Radicals and one prominent Gaullist, Chaban-Delmas. If this looked at first glance like a reflection of the Front Républicain, the impression was misleading. Though the balance within the new Assembly had shifted somewhat to the left compared with 1951, neither the Front nor the old, outgoing majority could by itself command a majority and form a government. The support of the Communists or the MRP or the Right would be needed. This was a long way away from Mendès' vision of a new and effective left-wing force in politics. Mollet quickly realised that the situation meant governing by means of shifting majorities, which would sometimes include the Communists, sometimes the others. His calculations immediately proved correct. The majority which carried him into power was widely – too widely – based. Four hundred and twenty votes were cast for the new government – most of the MRP, the surviving Gaullists, and all the Communists, the latter believing that the new Prime Minister would bring the Algerian war to an end. The minority which voted against or abstained was made up of Poujadists and some of the Right.

An outsider contemplating the election results might have mar-
velled at the ease with which Mollet cut through the difficulties and
won his massive victory. But this man from Mars would have been
mistaken in thinking that the 420 majority meant a broad measure
of agreement between the parties. On Algerian policy, for example,
the ostensible reason for which the election had been called, Mollet
in his investiture speech had had to resort to the usual ambiguities.
His government, he said, intended to 'maintain and reinforce the
indissoluble bond between Algeria and metropolitan France'. But he
also spoke of recognising and respecting 'the Algerian personality'
and of bringing about the complete political equality of all Algerians,
Muslim and European.

Mollet can scarcely be blamed for not having an instant formula
for Algeria. A few days before his investiture, he had told the
Socialist congress that there was no ready-made solution, certainly
no unilateral solution. 'We must take account of their [the Algerian
nationalists'] aspirations but they must, for their part, take account
of the French living in Algeria and of France's legitimate rights in
that country.' Up to that point, he seemed to be in broad agreement
with the advice proffered by Soustelle, the Governor-General, who
foresaw a greater part for Muslims in the administration of the
territory, the unification of the public services of Algeria and
metropolitan France, an equalisation, between Algeria and the
mainland, of Algerian wages and social security benefits, and much
bigger Algerian representation in the National Assembly in Paris.
This was certainly, on paper, a large measure of reform, but for
the Algerian nationalists there was nothing in it to presage an end
to French domination. Besides, Soustelle was on the way out. One
of the first acts of the new government was to announce his recall
and the appointment in his place of General Georges Catroux.

Jules Moch recalls in his memoirs being startled, on first seeing the
list of the ministerial appointments, to find Catroux's name.[1] This
seventy-nine-year-old General, a disciple of Lyautey in Morocco,
a senior Free French commander in the war, and an exponent
of liberal ideas about North Africa, was just the kind of man to
excite the suspicions of the Algerian *colons*. Soustelle's recall and
Catroux's nomination by Mollet seemed to them to foreshadow a
dangerous change in policy, an impression increased by an interview
given by Catroux to *Le Monde*. In it, while rejecting a purely
Muslim 'personality' for Algeria, he spoke of the possibility of a

single-college Algerian Assembly with executive power, and of his intention to make contact with any Algerian (i.e. Muslim) representatives whom he might consider valid, excluding those 'who had risen against France'. Worse still, from the *colon* viewpoint, was the welcome given to the news of his appointment by a representative Muslim group, who expressed confidence in his ability to find a solution 'inspired by Muslim national aspirations'. The French press in Algiers reacted unfavourably, and leaflets began to appear calling on the *colon* population to demonstrate against the new Governor-General on his arrival.

There is no doubt that at this point Mollet, though understandably without any very clear-cut ideas about the final form of a solution for Algeria, was in a liberal frame of mind. His choice of Catroux was proof of that. So was his preferred order of priorities: cease-fire (which meant of course contacts with the FLN), followed by elections and negotiations. He had moreover taken up an idea first advanced by Mendès in the course of the electoral campaign, namely that the new prime minister, whoever he might be, should go as soon as possible to Algiers to assert his authority. The comparison with Mendès' dramatic flight to Tunis on 31 July 1954 was obvious, but Mollet, unlike Mendès, was not made of the stuff for theatrical gestures or the administration of psychological shocks. A more prosaic and less imaginative personality, he made the bad mistake of announcing in advance the date of his visit to Algiers: 6 February. Once more, the French obsession with dates and anniversaries could be freely indulged: on the same day in 1934, violent clashes in the streets of Paris between Right and Left had seemed to many to be the prelude to civil war. The *colon* population in Algiers went to work to ensure his hostile reception. For the first time, an alliance which was to have fateful consequences for the Fourth Republic began to form between the *colons* and the extreme right wing in France.

Poujade had already made himself the champion of *Algérie française*, and Poujadists on the ground eagerly cooperated in preparations for the Prime Minister's arrival on the 6th. Poujade himself, who had no wish to see his movement perpetually tarred with the brush of extreme rightism, advised his followers to stay away from the demonstrations: 'A trap is being laid for us,' he said, a few days after the events of 6 February. But some of his local supporters in Algiers, notably Joseph Ortiz, bar-owner and demagogue, played a leading role in organising the mob. Where Poujadist influence made itself especially felt was among the ex-servicemen's associations, old comrades of the French expeditionary corps in the Italian campaign, of the First French Army, of the Armée d'Afrique.

One of the ringleaders here was a veteran of the Indochinese war, now a Poujadist deputy, who had earlier had a part in whipping up ex-servicemen's feelings at the Arc de Triomphe demonstrations in 1954. Another was Jean-Marie Le Pen, also a Poujadist deputy, destined to play a populist, extreme right-wing role under the Fifth Republic. A third figure was a Corsican lawyer, Jean-Baptiste Biaggi, a devout and excitable right-wing Gaullist with a distinguished Resistance record. He told the ex-servicemen: 'We must raise the temperature and bring down the régime . . . The Fifth Republic must arise from the street . . . The Fourth has had it.'[2] These *petits gens*, manual workers, ex-servicemen, clerks, shopkeepers, junior officials, closely mirrored their own background. Many had voted, after the Liberation, for the Socialist or Communist party. Except in one particular, they were as far away as it is possible to be from the rich and powerful French–Algerian industrialists and landowners who exercised so strong an influence in ministerial offices and parliamentary corridors in Paris. But that one particular was primordial: for them, *Algérie française* was not just a right-wing slogan, a blunderbuss pointed at the heart of Mendès and other 'traitors' in Paris, but a *cri de coeur*, a fervent and unaffected expression of the will to stand fast. A comparison would be with Carson's Ulster: 'Ulster will fight and Ulster will be right.'

The Prime Minister and his party (Catroux stayed behind in Paris) landed at Algiers at 2 o'clock on the afternoon of the 6th, a bitterly cold day. From there they drove into the city along deserted roads lined by a double rank of armed and helmeted troops, flown in for the occasion from other parts of Algeria and from France itself. This show of strength was later condemned by the Poujadists as a provocation: 'Were these soldiers there to protect the Prime Minister against a [rebel] attack? No; merely against the booing of honest Frenchmen who were unwilling to see the destiny of Algeria handed over to a professional liquidator.'[3]

It was the Poujadist claim that the ensuing disorders were the result of this alleged provocation, without which the crowds would have confined themselves to a 'contemptuous silence'. That is not credible. A lot of time and trouble had been spent whipping up

European feelings, so that an outburst of violence was inevitable and intended. At 3.15 Mollet's car drew up before the war memorial in central Algiers and the attendant band struck up the 'Marseillaise'. Its sound was entirely drowned by the booing and shouting of the huge crowd gathered in the square. A bombardment of the official party followed, the missiles consisting of oranges, rotten tomatoes (one of which was only deflected from Mollet's forehead by an accompanying officer) and lumps of lawn torn from the public garden in front of the memorial. Amidst increasing pandemonium, the Prime Minister climbed up the steps of the memorial to lay his wreath and then, protected by troops using tear-gar against the menacing crowds, hurriedly made off in his car to the Summer Palace. Immediately he had gone, the crowds broke through the barriers, seized the wreath and tore it to pieces. By this time numbering about 50,000, they surged through the streets, the police supine against the onrush, shouting 'Hang Catroux' and '*Algérie française*' towards the Summer Palace, whose precincts they managed to invade. Order was only restored in the evening when General Massu's parachute troops were called out to break up the crowds.

Inside the Summer Palace, the shaken Mollet was informed by the Prefect of Algiers and other officials that Catroux's safety could not be assured were he to show his face in the city. Putting a call through to Coty in the Elysée, Mollet learnt that Catroux had already proffered his resignation, which was promptly accepted. The next morning, receiving an ex-servicemen's delegation, Mollet said to them (according to the Poujadist paper's account): 'I came, I saw, I understood.' Whether or not he actually uttered these words (the 'understood' part anticipated General de Gaulle's cunning assurances two and a half years later), it was clear that he had yielded to the clamour of the mob. If another remark attributed to Mollet was really made – 'I should not have given in' – he would seem to have appreciated the enormity of what had happened. A few days later, François Mauriac, in *L'Express*, fired a broadside that was fierce even by his vituperative standards. He described Mollet as 'this supine schoolmaster, sitting there in his chair and allowing himself to be pelted by an unruly class with inky balls of paper.' The article, not surprisingly, caused a stir. Mollet accused Mendès of having inspired it, an allegation denied by the latter and by Mauriac.

In the Assembly the Prime Minister, ten days after his disagreeable experience in Algiers, spoke of the mob's behaviour as 'this distressing outburst', which seemed a distinctly mild description of a highly organised political riot. But Mollet was no coward; his wartime Resistance record had shown that. He really had been moved and impressed by the intensity of the emotions displayed that day and the fact that the jeering crowds were not composed of *grands colons* or middle-class families in easy circumstances, but workers, small shopkeepers, minor officials who felt their way of life, their very existence, to be under threat. 'It has to be said,' he told the Chamber, 'most of the demonstrators were completely in good faith', and he went on to assure the *colon* community that 'France will in no case abandon them, she will never abandon Algeria, she cannot abandon Algeria.' At the same time, he inveighed against the 'extremist propaganda' which had inspired the uprising, and referred to the upsurge in Algerian (Muslim) nationalism. In other words, like any decent, fair-minded man he tried to put into context the two opposing forces in Algeria. But to his critics in France, Mendès chief among them, and to foreign observers, it was clear that he had yielded to *colon* pressure.

The situation was admittedly nearly impossible. It was all very well for Mauriac to hurl his thunderbolts from the calm and safety of his study in Paris. On the ground in Algiers things looked different. Had Mollet insisted on Catroux arriving to take up his post, the Army would have had to ensure the security and freedom of movement of the new Governor-General. This could, and probably would, have led to a major clash with the European population, with dire consequences. It can thus be argued that Mollet had no real choice but to do as he did. Moreover in doing so and in subsequently preaching and practising a qualified form of an *Algérie française* policy, Mollet was only reflecting the feelings of the majority of his own compatriots. The Mendès-Frances and the Mauriacs were at this stage still only a minority voice. The polls showed that in February 1956 49 per cent of those questioned thought that Algeria should remain a department of metropolitan France as against 25 per cent who opted for a looser connection and 26 per cent who did not reply. Nevertheless, what the events of 6 February had shown was that from then on French policy for Algeria would be dictated in the last resort by Algiers, just as Catroux's resignation had been forced by Algiers. Although at the time it was inaudible to all save those with the most acute political hearing, in fact the ticking of the clock which measured the remaining lifespan of the Fourth Republic had already begun.

In place of Catroux, Mollet appointed Robert Lacoste as Minister-Resident in Algiers. A tough, right-wing Socialist – another Jules Moch or even Ernest Bevin – he had entered politics via the trade unions and the Resistance, of which he had been an active member. While he professed sympathy with Muslim claims for reforms and a better way of life and undertook to reduce the privileges and economic grip of the *grands colons*, he made it clear that his first task was to put down the rebellion and ensure that Algeria remained French. In the Assembly debate in March which resulted in the grant to the government, by an overwhelming majority, of special powers for its Algerian policy, he summed up his thinking in words which were a reminder that French colonialism, at least in its modern phase, was inspired by Jacobin sentiments of the benefits which France could and should confer on lesser breeds without the law: 'We can have our differences about the solutions [for Algeria], but there is not a French person who would accept the spectacle of France driven from a land which she settled by the indisputable power of armed force but which she conquered by the indisputable right of a civilising mission marked with generosity.'

In the same debate, although the Socialist rapporteur went through the motions of recalling that the job to be done consisted in bringing about conditions in which free elections could be held, most of the other speakers put the emphasis on the need for vigorous repressive action. Soustelle, by now a complete *Algérie française* man, said that the loss of Algeria would be a disaster comparable to Sedan (the French defeat in the Franco-Prussian war) and June 1940: 'France would cease to be a power.' These and similar arguments assumed all the greater significance in that both Tunisian and Moroccan independence became internationally established facts in March. The need to show that the way chosen for these protectorates should not and would not be followed by Algeria was, in the minds of most people, greater than ever.

From now on there was not much more public talk of recognising the Algerian personality, or whatever other code words may have been previously employed to signify the need to go some way towards meeting the claims of Algerian nationalism. Instead, the Mollet government proceeded to recall 70,000 reservists to the colours. Within six months, the level of forces in Algeria was

increased from 200,000 to 400,000, the greatest overseas operation undertaken by France since 1830. The despatch of young
conscripts involved the whole nation in a way that had never
occurred over Indochina. There was some resistance, encouraged
by the Communists, to these mobilisation orders, with women lying
on railway lines to prevent troop trains from leaving. But it did not
last long or amount to much. On the whole the nation accepted,
in some cases with enthusiasm, in others with resignation, being
locked into a war which was increasingly presented as the work
of evil Communist fanatics, fuelled by other fanatics in Cairo and
possibly, to the minds of the *Nous sommes trahis* lobby – always an
element in French attitudes towards the outer world – by intriguers
in Washington and London.

It does not call for the gifts of a seer to guess what this hardening
public opinion, let alone *colon* interests in Algeria or the French
Army in the field, would have thought had it known that the Mollet
government had been in touch between April and September 1956
with FLN emissaries. A series of meetings took place in Italy and
Yugoslavia between French officials and FLN representatives in an
attempt to work out a plan for a cease-fire, followed by elections and
negotiations for the future status of Algeria. The results were not
entirely negative, though major and predictable differences arose
over the connection between a cease-fire – Paris' precondition for
the whole process – and the FLN's desire for the establishment of
a provisional government at the same time as the cease-fire. These
differences would in the end probably have proved insurmountable,
but the matter was never put to the final test. The meetings were
abruptly cut short when in October a Moroccan plane with a French
flight crew transporting five of the main FLN leaders from Rabat
to Tunis was diverted on orders from Algiers and landed at Algiers
airport, where the Algerians were arrested. They spent five and
half years in French gaols but were never brought to trial. One
of them was Mohammed Ben Bella, later to be the first President
of independent Algeria. The initiative for this piratical act came
from the military in Algiers. In Paris, the (Socialist) Secretary of
State for War authorised it without referring to Mollet or any other
minister.

Apart from putting an end to the secret Franco-Algerian talks,
the repercussions were serious, the more so because, as the Prime
Minister and the few of his colleagues in the know appreciated

very well, the Suez operation was about to be mounted. This was no moment to be making gratuitous enemies among Arab factions, above all those with strong French connections. Both the King of Morocco and Bourguiba, the Tunisian leader, who could have contributed towards a solution of the Algerian problem, were furious, and Mollet's Minister for Tunisian Affairs and the French Ambassador in Tunis, to their honour, resigned in protest. But the harm could not be undone. In the eyes of the generals and colonels and majors and captains fighting in Algeria to repress the rebellion, the pursuit of the war was becoming an end in itself, justifying anything that could be done in its furtherance. There was a simple logic in this attitude. Why risk their own lives and those of the men they commanded if the end of the affair was to be a political negotiation with the nationalists which was more than likely to lead, at the least, to a weakening in the links between France and Algeria?

Soustelle, in one of his last reports to Paris before leaving Algiers, had put it succinctly: 'The morale of the army . . . is at rock bottom. . . . The general feeling is that we are going to "do a deal" and that, consequently, present sacrifices are to no purpose.'[4] This had been the dilemma in Indochina, where a war heavy in human and material losses had been fought with the original aim of re-establishing French ascendancy but later, as the political winds shifted, to sustain the newly granted independence of Vietnam. The same contradiction was, in Army opinion, unthinkable in Algeria. This was the place and the time to make it clear to the world that while France must be generous and understanding towards the depressed Muslim masses, the first priority was to ensure that there would be no more retreat and humiliation.

The ostensible aims of government policy remained those of pacification, elections and negotiations (though these were to exclude any idea of Algerian independence). But it was perfectly plain that after 6 February Mollet was more preoccupied in courting *colon* goodwill than in trying to win the hearts of the Muslims. In these circumstances, some ministers found no difficulty in accepting the Army's viewpoint about the nature of the war. Lacoste appears to have had an untroubled conscience, even in the face of increasing evidence that the police and some sections of the Army were using torture as a means of extracting information from Muslim suspects.

The Minister of Defence, Bourgès-Maunoury, took the same robust line. He interpreted an article written in the left-wing *France-Observateur* by Claude Bourdet, a distinguished non-Communist critic of government policy, as an incitement to disobedience among men called up. The offices of the magazine were raided and Bourdet briefly arrested. This would never have happened to critics of the Indochinese war. Over Algeria, by contrast, 'defeatism' was not to be tolerated. When a Sorbonne professor, Henri Marrou, wrote in *Le Monde* that he could not see how Algerian elections could ever lead to a peaceful settlement if, in the meantime, France used concentration camps, tortures and collective reprisals as her three principal weapons, police were sent to search his house. While daily life in France ran its normal course, the psychosis of war was beginning to take a hold and, at this stage, not many people were ready to resist it.

One notable member of the government who was not prepared to adopt this my-country-right-or-wrong stance was Mendès-France. Since the events of 6 February in Algiers, he had felt increasing concern about Mollet's and Lacoste's policies, arguing that sweeping reforms should be introduced simultaneously with the pacification process. He produced his own seven-point programme, which included the release of uncharged political prisoners, a free Muslim press, the expropriation of large landed estates and the enactment of a new municipal law to give a better standing to Muslim representatives. This programme, its author declared, was designed 'to promote native confidence and hope in France, without which, sooner or later, we French will be evicted from Algeria and from all of North Africa'. It appeared in the first issue of a new publication emanating from Radical party headquarters in Paris, and was embedded in an article which was comparable to Mendès' Cassandra-like speeches about the Indochinese war.[5] The article was hard-hitting and remarkably prophetic. The cost of the Algerian war would increase, it argued, and would mean the postponement of economic and social reforms at home. Government policy was wrong to think it could pacify first and hold free elections after that – 'the men of 6 February' would oppose any genuine election or genuine reforms and before long terrorism would flare up once more. Since 6 February and the dropping of Catroux, the article went on, Mollet's speeches had become more and more vague, while the fanaticism, hatred and despair of the Muslim population had increased.

If adoption of this programme was the price of Mendès remaining in the government, it was not one that Mollet was ready to pay. For the Algerian *colons* and for much of French opinion, application of the seven points would mean the end of most French interests in Algeria, so what would be the point of spending blood and money to achieve such a result? (Provided his reforms were introduced, Mendès approved of the intensified pacification process.) Here was the same, insoluble dilemma of the contradiction between what was supposed to be government policy in Paris and what was actually happening on the ground in Algeria. Having got no satisfaction from Mollet, or indeed from an important section of his own Radical party, thirty of whose deputies signed a statement condemning all forms of 'defeatism', Mendès resigned from the government at the end of May. Just as he had stepped down from de Gaulle's government in 1945 because he could not win acceptance for his economic and financial plans, so now the failure to get his seven points across made him decide to take to the wilderness. In both instances he had misjudged the mood of the country. He was never to hold office again.

Le Monde, commenting on Mendès' resignation, wrote that he 'is not an accommodating man, or at his best except as first violin'. That was true, but did not diminish the fact that his departure marked the end of what had been by far the most fascinating experiment in trying to persuade the Fourth Republic to cure its own ills. With de Gaulle brooding silently at Colombey, both of the most radical and inspiring figures in France were now absent from a stage on which an increasingly tense drama was being played. The difference between them was that de Gaulle was still in the wings, whereas Mendès had left the theatre altogether.

Though Mendès was out of the government, his message about Algeria was not forgotten. At the Socialist congress at Lille at the end of June, a section of the delegates was highly critical of the Lacoste policy and succeeded in forcing through a motion of a markedly anti-*Algérie française* nature. It called on the government to do everything to bring about a cease-fire 'with those against whom we are fighting'. This showed that the voice of the articulate Left was capable of making itself heard and helps to explain why Mollet continued at that stage to maintain secret contacts with FLN representatives. Possibly these left-wing pressures might have had more effect if the whole situation had not been transformed by

Nasser's nationalisation of the Suez Canal at the end of July. But a much more representative picture of popular opinion than that provided by the Socialist motion at Lille was given by the reaction to a book published later in the year: *Les Taxis de la Marne* by Jean Dutourd.[6]

The author, a well-known novelist, later to become a member of the French Academy, was twenty in 1940 when, after having been a soldier for only a fortnight, he was taken prisoner. His book – its title refers to the episode in September 1914 when a fleet of Paris taxis transported military reinforcements to the Marne battlefield where the German thrust towards the capital was held – took the form of an angry essay, or rather a series of essays, on what had happened to French honour, French moral fibre, the past greatness of France. If this sounds like the sour ruminations of some old retired officer full of right-wing prejudices, the French equivalent of Disgusted, Tunbridge Wells, it was nothing of the sort. Dutourd, by his own testimony, had flirted with Communism during the Resistance and at the Liberation and before that, in his youth, having discovered Anatole France and *Le Canard enchaîné*, had been filled with a 'horror of war, nationalism, the middle-class order of things, priests, etc.'. He gave an eloquent and important description of what the Communists felt in 1943 and what he felt about them:

> Patriotism and Communist doctrine marched side by side and I have never seen the Communists so happy as they were during the German occupation. . . . They were being tracked down, they were being shot but . . . their clandestine papers resounded with songs to the glory of France . . . How exalting this *communard* patriotism was. I was caught up in it just as they were . . . Here at last was the patriotism of the people, not the patriotism of the rich.

Compared with that spirit, and with the France of 1935, when she was a lion, 'with her institutions, her Cabinet ministers, her soldiers, her severe courts of justice, her sparkling navy, her strict prefects, her pacific empire, her cruel *colons* and her State patriotism', the France of 1956, wrote Dutourd, was 'a weak and divided country' and he himself had a heart 'bleeding from a thousand wounds, calling with all its will for a little seriousness and glory, hating with all its force the frivolous anarchy of its country and its times'. The description of the Thirties in France as a golden age was wildly inappropriate, but this did not seem to bother Dutourd, whose invective knew no bounds: 'Today, France has turned into a dying carcass on which her maggot-ministers prosper.'

Dutourd was especially indignant at what he called the 'glorification of failure', exemplified in the bestowal of the name of Dien Bien Phu upon a passing-out class of St Cyr cadets; indignant, too, at the assertion that the French parliament represented the country perfectly – 'too revolting to be believed right away', but 'nevertheless true'. He compared France to a pauper, to whose rags were still attached the tattered fineries of the past: 'the frayed fleurs-de-lis, the tarnished eagles, the plucked cock'. This pauper 'is being kicked out of Africa and Asia – spat on in the face by the guttersnipes of Cairo'. For Dutourd, the only bright spot in the landscape was de Gaulle, in whose speeches the word honour constantly recurred and whose only crime 'was to have believed too much in France – he wanted to lead his people on to new heights, but the people did not follow him'. The book ended with an admiring and wistful reference to its title, *Les Taxis de la Marne* – 'the name of the most glorious and least miraculous feat of the twentieth century'.

This extraordinary gallimaufry, as full of inconsistency as of passion, made an immediate impression, and for months the book was the most talked of, for and against, in Paris. Literary and intellectual circles tended to be disdainful about it as being too popular, but François Mauriac wrote of it as important 'perhaps less for what it clearly tells us than for what it represents . . . It is an outcry, at least someone has raised his voice.' Strictly speaking, the book was non-political in any party context, but as the Catholic philosopher Charles Péguy had put it fifty years earlier (he himself had died in action in 1914, leading his company in the very battle to which the famous taxis brought up reinforcements), everything starts in mysticism and ends in politics. Dutourd had his own brand of mysticism. His confused threnody on the death of patriotism accurately echoed the yearning for a nationalist revival which marked the closing years of the Fourth Republic, a national and collective consciousness expressed equally through such contrasting outlets as Mendès' calls for renewal, Poujade's championing of the cause of *Algérie française* and Mollet and Lacoste's tough line on Algeria. The shame of the defeat in 1940, synthesised so well in Dutourd's pages, was being experienced again sixteen years later, in the form of doubt and anguish, felt by Right and Left alike, at the thought of further mortification for France's position in the world.

Nasser's nationalisation of the Suez Canal in July 1956, and the almost universal condemnation of it by French non-Communist opinion, should have helped to heal these old wounds and foster a new sense of unity. Up to a point, it did. 'Aside from the Communist press, all the papers you read, which ordinarily feature dissenting convictions, and all the French people you see, whom you have formerly listened to for their differing opinions, have been printing or saying essentially the same thing, in an impressive sincere chorus of extreme national sentiment – there has been no moderate note, no voice of opposition.'[7] Just as, in London, Anthony Eden chose to see Nasser in the light of another Hitler whose predatory ambitions had to be stopped before it was too late, so in Paris a Munich complex prevailed. For Mollet, Nasser's book *The Philosophy of the Revolution* was comparable to *Mein Kampf*. The seizure of the Canal reminded the Minister of Justice, François Mitterrand, of the rape of Czechoslovakia in 1939. For the Foreign Minister, Christian Pineau, what had happened was especially galling, for earlier in the year he had been to Cairo and received reassurances from Nasser. In a speech to the National Assembly on his return, he had argued that Nasser was not Hitler, and that pointless flag-waving – 'rattling a wooden sword' was the expression he used – could bring no benefit. Even Gaston Defferre, the Minister for Overseas France, one of the principal Socialist supporters of the idea of negotiations with the FLN, favoured a military operation against Egypt.

The main reason why this new-found sense of unity in France contrasted so strongly with the divisions over Suez opening up in British politics lay in Algeria. Pineau's remarks about Nasser in the National Assembly had gone down very badly, for the mass of French opinion had allowed itself to be persuaded that without Egyptian support, the Algerian rebellion would quickly be mastered. Even before Suez, a large number of people considered either that Egypt was at war with France or that France ought to be at war with Egypt. Lacoste, once Nasser had nationalised the Canal, put it concisely and forcefully: 'One French division in Egypt is worth four divisions in Algeria.' This belief that Nasser was the main supplier of the FLN was a greatly oversimplified view of the situation, but in addition to the anti-French tone of the broadcasts from Cairo it had received apparent confirmation when in October a yacht carrying arms loaded in Alexandria was stopped and searched.

Mollet and the restricted number of his ministers who were privy to the secret had no hesitation in agreeing to the British–French–Israeli plan, hatched during the autumn of 1956, for a pre-emptive attack by Israel on Egypt; British and French forces would then intervene to 'separate the belligerents'. The links of sympathy with Israel were strong. The Mollet government had earlier stepped up the supply of arms to Tel Aviv and, after Nasser's move over the Canal, had authorised the transfer of nuclear technology which would in time enable Israel to establish her first atomic pile at Dimona.[8] As a further spur to action, there was growing impatience in France, as the early autumn days were consumed in complicated negotiations in London and New York for a peaceful solution to the crisis. Most parties and opinions were disappointed that force was not used, rapidly and effectively, in the early days and weeks of the Suez affair. The test of effectiveness, in French eyes, would be not just to teach Nasser a lesson but to overthrow him completely.

The reaction in the Assembly was predictably different from that in the House of Commons to the issue at the end of October of the Franco-British ultimatum to Cairo and Tel Aviv. Following on the planned Israeli attack on 29 October, this called upon both sides to cease hostilities, on pain of Franco-British intervention. With a few exceptions, the only dissenting voices came from the Communists on the extreme left and the Poujadists on the extreme right. Poujade himself, who not being a deputy led his own party from outside the Palais Bourbon, telephoned in with the bizarre instruction to his men 'not to vote for a war to help the Queen of England'. (A third of them disobeyed him, and a few of the ultra-nationalists broke with him for good.) It was noticeable that Mendès not only abstained from voting but failed to applaud Guy Mollet. But for the rest, the promise of attack against Egypt satisfied the deepest cravings of the collective French soul at that moment: to strike directly at the rabble-rouser and arms supplier in Cairo, to express disillusion with the ditherings in Washington and the United Nations, above all to reassert by martial means the claims of French patriotism and the position of France in the world. The fact that this aggression (few saw it as such) was to be carried out by a Socialist-led government did not enter into the scale of things. 'National Molletism', however curious a hybrid, suited the public mood very well.

That at least is how it seemed on the evening of 29 October. It was only when the Franco-British attack against Egypt had been abruptly brought to a halt by US and United Nations pressures, and the full measure of the fiasco realised, that the doubts and fears about Suez and the future in Algeria began to surface. Considering that it was the British who took the initiative for stopping the operation, while the French wanted to continue, there was surprisingly little anti-British recrimination. There was even some satisfaction in the fact that France, its government and its parliament had stood firm and unwavering behind the decision to intervene in Egypt, while the United Kingdom, having started off just as firmly, then began to behave as the French parliament and government usually behaved when, faced with the need for decision and action, all that happened was a clash of opinions and factions.[9] In fact, as petrol rationing, the result of the Canal being blocked, began to take hold, as the sales of petrol-saving minute 'bubble' cars soared, as housewives began to hoard sugar and salt (rumours circulated that it had protective qualities against radiation), so an air of confused resignation rather than anger prevailed. 'Suez was no more than a small break in the general bewilderment and discouragement of the French people, faced with painful international realities and the war in Algeria.'[10]

Guy Mollet, in an attempt to put the best possible face on things, even called in aid the Soviet suppression of Hungarian liberties to show that *Algérie française* was the only possible policy: events in Budapest, he told the Assembly, should cause the free world to understand better what France was doing in North Africa and what her withdrawal would mean. It was the old Indochinese argument: France was defending the interests and values of Western democracy, and thus deserved the support and understanding of her allies. This line guaranteed Mollet a large majority in the Assembly debate held just before Christmas 1956. Apart from the Communists, only two speakers – Mendès-France and Edgar Faure – were outspokenly critical of the Suez policy, and they got a very cool reception from the Chamber.

There was one further fall-out from Suez, not instantly discernible, but contributing powerfully to military sentiments about politics and politicians, especially among the parachute troops involved in the Suez operation. Pierre Leulliette, a young para officer who later wrote about his experiences,[11] described returning from Suez, feeling 'the shame, ridicule and ignominy of a winner who has to run away like a pathetic loser . . . Even in Indochina . . . where you were betrayed daily by everyone, they [the politicians] wouldn't have dared to do anything like that.' For the paras, humiliation at Suez reinforced the resolve not to suffer the same fate in Algeria.

The Soviet repression in Hungary, coinciding as it did with Suez, had a profound effect in France, as elsewhere in the Western world. On the night of 7 November, after the Red Army's tanks had brutally crushed the Budapest uprising, thousands of people mounted a violent demonstration outside Communist party headquarters and tried to sack the offices of *L'Humanité*. There were clashes with the police and with Communist counter-demonstrators, and although extreme right-wing agitators were certainly involved in exploiting the situation as much as they could, there was no doubt about the genuine depth of popular indignation. At the Hôtel de Ville, the Tricolour flew at half-mast in honour of the victims of Soviet oppression. For the Communist party itself, events in Hungary were a disaster. Already, earlier in the year, Thorez and the leadership had had to meet the embarrassing challenge of Khrushchev's criticisms of Stalin to the Twentieth Congress in Moscow, which they did by asserting that while mistakes might have been made under Stalin's régime, nothing could be allowed to detract from his achievements or from his status as a Soviet hero. This failed to please all the faithful, but the doubts and divisions were as nothing compared to the aftermath of Budapest.

In the weeks and months that followed, an important number of intellectuals broke with the party, thus finally ending the post-Liberation convention, indeed necessity, that a genuine intellectual had to be a Communist or at least share Communist or fellow-travelling beliefs. None made a more discussed and influential recantation than the arch-priest Sartre himself. In a 10,000-word analysis published in *L'Express*, he declared that Marxist Socialism, considered as 'merchandise exported by the USSR', was a failure, that friendship could no longer be felt for the Soviet leadership, and that the crime of Budapest was not just the use of tanks, but that they had been necessary 'after twelve years of terror and imbecility'. While still recommending the Left as the only political path to take, he announced his resignation from the Peace Movement in which he had played so prominent a part. Others followed his example. At the end of November, a number of Communist or

Communist-sympathising intellectuals, including Picasso, addressed a letter to the central committee full of complaints about the 'burning problems of conscience' which neither the central committee nor *L'Humanité* had helped to resolve.

The central direction of the party remained obdurate in its Stalinist thinking, and by the beginning of 1957 perhaps one-fifth of paid-up members failed to renew their cards. Since its exclusion from government in 1947, the Communist party had been in the political wilderness, but at least it had the satisfaction of knowing that it still commanded the support of over a quarter of the electorate. After Budapest its hopes, never realistic, of forming a new Popular Front faded away altogether, and its hold over popular opinion began to weaken. In a by-election in Paris in early 1957, the Communist share of the vote dropped from 26 per cent at the general election a year previously to 20 per cent, a significant decline even if it was rather less than had been expected, given the impact of Budapest.

At the beginning of 1957, though no one at the time could have known it, the Fourth Republic had only eighteen months of life left. That period was increasingly dominated by the war in Algeria and its economic, political, social and psychological effects. But there were developments and achievements in other fields, some of them highly creditable to the régime, that provided de Gaulle's Fifth Republic with welcome legacies which, like most oppositions who find themselves in power, it never properly acknowledged. Many of them were the work of the Mollet government. It was easy, and in some cases justified, to deride Mollet's broken promises, as the review *La Nef* did. Edited by Edgar Faure's intellectual and fashionable left-wing wife, its February issue remarked that 'the ordinary Frenchman sees in Mollet the reflection of his own self, just as he saw it in Pinay a few years ago'. Despite the lack of the promised peace in Algeria, despite the failure of Suez, despite the petrol shortage, 'We muddle through all the same . . . [Mollet] calls himself a Socialist, but puts France's national requirements first – in short, an honest man, who's doing what he can.' The tone was satirical and mocking, but in fact accurately summed up the sentiments of millions, probably the majority, of French people at the time.

Algerian affairs apart, it was not for nothing however that a Socialist-led government was in power. In late February, a third week of paid holidays – originally one of the lasting accomplishments of the pre-war Popular Front – was introduced. A little later came the National Solidarity Fund, a State-run scheme to provide a much-needed measure of welfare for the old; it was financed by an increase in income-tax, levied on stock exchange dealings and the introduction of road licences for cars. The classic Right fought so hard against it in parliament that the government had to resort no less than seven times to the procedure of confidence. Other reforms and projects which emerged from the ministries in Paris included provisions for low-cost housing, for agricultural cooperatives for farm machinery, a scheme for the development of Brittany, which became a forerunner of later policies of regional development, and encouragement for technical training in schools and colleges.

Along with these internal measures, all designed to help the country along the path of economic modernisation and greater social justice, went other reforms affecting France's position in the world. In June, Defferre, the Minister for Overseas France, promulgated an 'outline law' for the French Union, granting direct universal suffrage and a single electoral college in colonial territories in Africa and elsewhere, thus laying the foundations for independence for these countries upon which the Fifth Republic was to build. It was a measure of the problems posed by a large *colon* presence, unparalleled in such proportions elsewhere in Africa, that these liberal and realistic policies were not applied in Algeria.

Mollet and his Foreign Minister, both 'good Europeans', pressed on, in conjunction with their other European partners, with the construction of a wider Europe that seemed to have received such a setback when EDC collapsed. At the end of March 1957 the treaties instituting Euratom and the European Economic Community (EEC) were signed in Rome. They were ratified in the National Assembly in the summer – after the fall of the Mollet government, it is true, but the credit for having brought the treaties to parliament can fairly be placed to the latter's credit. In the debate, the Under-Secretary for Foreign Affairs, Maurice Faure (who had held the same post in the Mollet government), showed how far some French thinking had moved away from the post-war Gaullist conception of France as a great power which if necessary must go its own way. (Similar delusions lingered on at Westminster and not only in Conservative circles.) 'We are still living', he said, 'on the fiction of the four great powers [US, USSR, UK and France]. In reality, there are only two . . . Tomorrow there will be three – China. It depends on you whether there is a fourth – Europe. If you fail to make this choice, you condemn yourselves to walking backwards towards the future.'

The remaining Gaullists in the Chamber voted against the treaties, and so did Mendès-France, on the grounds of the weakness of the French economy. But the size of the majority – 342 to 239 – showed that despite the refusal of Britain, regretted by the Socialists and others, to make six-nation Europe a seven-nation affair, France was now committed to a European policy so deeply that de Gaulle, returning to power the following year, chose to accept the *fait accompli* and turn it to France's advantage, rather than seek to reverse steam. As with the making of the Coal and Steel Community seven years earlier, the resolve and leadership of Fourth Republican governments, however deficient in other respects, once more contributed in a major degree to the making of modern Europe.

But despite the favourable aspects of this balance-sheet, everything in the end came back to the Algerian war and the burden it imposed. Military reinforcements there, involving national servicemen, had the effect of withdrawing from the labour force about 200,000 men, as well as costing the budget an extra 300 million francs in military expenditures – and this at a time when the government's social policies had to be paid for. The result was that the budget deficit increased alarmingly, while the rising pressure of consumer and military demand could be satisfied only by imports. The unprecedentedly cold winter of 1955/56, when the rivers froze and there were three feet of snow in the streets of St Tropez, wrought havoc on crops, and made extra food imports inevitable. Reserves of foreign exchange dwindled and the Governor of the Bank of France warned that it would soon be necessary to put the economy on a war footing. This is just what the right wing, despite its vociferous support for *Algérie française*, was unwilling to do if it meant agreeing to higher taxes. Throughout the first half of 1957 right-wing discontent grew to keep pace with the dramatic increase in the commercial deficit. Finally, on 21 May 1957, the Mollet government fell when its financial measures were rejected in the Assembly by the usual ill-assorted mixture of malcontents – Communists, Poujadists, and seventy-five right-wingers and Radicals. It had lasted for nearly fourteen months, a record for the Fourth Republic.

With the usual delay and difficulty – the crisis lasted three weeks –

a successor government was formed under Bourgès-Maunoury, the forty-three-year-old Radical who, as Mollet's Defence Minister, had played a leading part in the Suez enterprise. Mollet, though holding no portfolio, continued as Socialist leader to dominate the political situation. As he and everyone else well knew, no government was possible without the support and votes of the Socialist party. If his position in Paris was unassailable, so was Lacoste's in Algeria. His policies for prosecuting the war remained unchanged, though some aspects of them encountered growing opposition within his own Socialist party, notably from Defferre, who along with Mitterrand was dropped from the new government. The resolve to keep Algeria French had indeed been reinforced by a new factor, made much of by Mollet before his fall. The oil and mineral riches, real or supposed, of the Sahara came to be seen as making it more essential than ever that Algeria should remain under French control, free from the predatory ambitions of the Americans, the Russians and, of course, the FLN.

Ideas about a workable solution for Algeria, let alone a parliamentary majority for such a solution, were as muddled and contradictory as ever. A good example of confused thinking was given by Alain Savary, Mollet's Minister for Tunisian and Moroccan Affairs, who had resigned over the affair of the arrest of the FLN leaders. Imbued with liberal ideas, he nonetheless could not accept that the Moroccan and Tunisian formula – i.e. internal autonomy leading to independence – was suitable for Algeria. On the other hand, the 'Algerian nation was in the process of establishing itself', although this did not, in Savary's opinion, run counter to the concept of 'indissoluble links' with France.

This blurred if well-meaning attempt to reconcile the irreconcilable found further expression in the 'outline law' for Algeria which the Bourgès-Maunoury government laid before parliament. Based upon ideas put forward by the previous government, it was supposed to provide Algeria with a new political statute, involving a degree of autonomy and dividing the country into a number of self-governing territories, each with a parliament and government, to be headed by a French official. The structure would be capped, in Algiers, by a 'federative parliament', from which would emanate a federative executive, also presided over by a French official. Paris would remain responsible for Algeria's foreign relations, justice, defence, education, shared financial questions and mining operations. If this mishmash predictably failed to appeal to the FLN, it equally attracted the fire of the *Algérie française* men. Soustelle declared that the project would very quickly lead to secession. In Algeria itself, Lacoste, normally popular with the *colons*, saw his stock suddenly falling. There was in the event no need for this alarm. At the end of September the Assembly rejected the outline law, and Bourgès-Maunoury resigned after only two and a half months in office. If there had been a chance, however slender, for a political settlement, it had now gone. All that the Bourgès-Maunoury government had managed to do during its short life was to get the European treaties (EEC and Euratom) ratified and to secure the Assembly's agreement to higher taxes to help to pay for the war, an agreement it had not been willing to give to the Mollet government. As Jacques Fauvet has written, 'Crises [i.e. the fall of a government and its replacement by another] are an expensive way of solving difficulties.'[12]

'Pacification' was thus left as the only identifiable policy for Algeria and it began to assume new and harsh proportions. Early in January 1957, faced by a mounting and expertly organised campaign of FLN terrorism in Algiers, culminating in the assassination of a leading *colon* 'ultra', Lacoste delegated responsibility for restoring law and order in the city to General Jacques Massu and his 10th Parachute Division, recently returned from Suez. It was a momentous step to take. The civil power had in effect handed over to the military. Even if Massu, a professional soldier with outstanding gifts of leadership and proficiency, was supposed to be a non-political general (unlike some of the obsessed colonels under his command), the seed had been sown from which before long would grow the tree of rebellion against the authority of Paris and the politicians. The 'battle of Algiers', ruthlessly fought by Massu and his men for the next nine months, ushered in a new phase of the war, in which success for the French forces was counterbalanced by an increasing awareness and anxiety in France itself about what was being done in France's name.*

With great thoroughness, Massu set about patrolling the city,

---

* In 1966 Gillo Pontecorvo made a film, *La Battaglia di Algeri*, which gives a remarkably authentic account of the 'battle of Algiers', despite its FLN slant. One of the chief FLN organisers of violence, who escaped the death penalty three times, was co-producer and played himself in the film.

dividing it into squares, checking all movement, searching houses and rounding up suspects, especially in the teeming Casbah, where the FLN bomb squads had their headquarters. Suspects were then interrogated by the parachutists, using methods which by any conceivable definition came under the heading of torture. The military theory, as old as warfare itself, was that any means are justified in preventing further violence and loss of life. If a suspect could be forced to reveal the names and whereabouts of the bombers and those who worked for them, then their evil work could be frustrated.

There is no doubt about the pattern and indiscriminate brutality of FLN terrorism. Using a team of Muslim girls to plant the bombs, the FLN chiefs struck at civilian targets such as bars and cafés, often full of innocent members of the public. One such incident left five killed and sixty wounded, another, where two bombs were placed in crowded sports stadiums, ten dead and forty-five injured. That these outrages were the FLN response to the excesses of European 'ultras' (one of which killed seventy Muslims, including women and children) was simply another tragic proof that violence begets violence. Whether they, or anything, justified the use of torture by regular, highly disciplined, soldiers, depends upon who is answering the question. Massù seems to have had no doubts about justification; he and some of his officers even tried the most frequently used treatment on themselves – the use of a magneto from which electrodes could be attached to the body of the victim, especially the penis.[13] What made this experiment futile was that, in contrast with what happened in a real interrogation, the self-inflicted sufferer could cause the current to be turned off when he had had enough.

The regular use by the 10th Parachute Division of these methods meant, in the words of one scrupulously fair non-French commentator, that 'torture became institutionalised in the army in Algeria'.[14] It meant also that as news of these interrogations spread so Frenchmen just as patriotic as Massu and his men, and a great deal more conscious of the values expected of a civilised nation, began to react. In March, Pierre-Henri Simon, a Catholic writer who had spent almost five years in German prisoner-of-war camps, published his book *Contre la torture*,[15] and a few days later the editor of *Le Monde*, Beuve-Méry, wrote that 'From now on, French people must realise that they no longer have the full right to condemn in the same terms as a decade ago the atrocities of Oradour [where in June 1944 the German SS massacred in reprisal the population of an entire village] and the torturers of the Gestapo.' A highly decorated general, Jacques de Bollardière, who was involved in the battle of Algiers, so much disapproved of what was going on that he asked to be posted back to France. Once there, he wrote a letter to *L'Express* in which, as well as approving the book by the editor, Jean-Jacques Servan-Schreiber, who had just served for six months as a parachutist in Algeria, he underlined 'the terrible danger there would be for us to lose sight, under the fallacious pretext of immediate expediency, of the moral values which alone have hitherto created the grandeur of our civilisation and of our army'. For this act of military indiscipline, he was sentenced to sixty days' 'fortress arrest'. Before beginning his punishment, this hero of the Second World War went to see de Gaulle, who said to him: 'You have done well, you have marked out the path of honour.'[16]

Another general who had served with great distinction in the Free French Forces, Pierre Billotte, wrote later in the year that there could be no question of obeying orders which were manifestly contrary to the laws of war: 'Although it would be a cruel duty to fulfil, [a military commander] should not hesitate, rather than agreeing to carry on a dishonourable practice, to expose his own troops, and even the civil population that he is protecting to the gravest dangers.' The examples set and principles expressed by these scrupulous men need to be balanced, when it comes to imputations about the French Army, against the practices of some of Massu's parachutists.

Such affirmations by senior officers who by no manner of means could be called left-wing had their counterpart among civilian officials. The Secretary-General at the Algiers Prefecture, Paul Teitgen, himself a Resistance hero and survivor of torture in Dachau, whose duties included overseeing police activities, found it impossible by March 1957 to reconcile his conscience with what was going on. In his letter of resignation to Lacoste, he wrote that on visiting the premises where suspects were held, he had 'recognised on certain detainees profound traces of the cruelties and tortures that I personally suffered fourteen years ago in the Gestapo cellars'. Lacoste persuaded him to withdraw his resignation, but by September he could stand it no longer. By that time, he calculated that 3,000 suspects, victims of the parachutists' attentions, had 'disappeared'. One of them was a young Algerian FLN lawyer, well known and liked at the Paris Bar, who was said by the authorities to have committed suicide 'to escape interrogation'. His former law tutor in Paris, René Capitant, Professor of Public Law at the University of Paris, and an ardent Gaullist, was so indignant that he informed the Ministry of Education that he was cancelling his lecture course. Numerous French Catholics were also troubled in their consciences.

But it was not until the following year, 1958, when the life of the Fourth Republic was moving towards its close, that large numbers of French people learnt, or were in a position to learn, of the full horrors of the parachutists' interrogation sessions in Algiers. Henri Alleg's book *La Question*[17] sold 60,000 copies in its first two weeks. In *L'Express*, Jean-Paul Sartre devoted a long article to the book. The entire issue was confiscated by the Paris police, on orders of the Minister of the Interior, and an issue of *France-Observateur* containing extracts from the book was also seized. Finally *La Question* itself was confiscated, the first time that a book had received such treatment for political reasons since the eighteenth century. The government enforcing these orders was the successor to Bourgès-Maunoury's, the penultimate before the Republic collapsed; in it Bourgès-Maunoury was the Interior Minister.

Alleg, a European Jew whose family had been in Algeria since the Second World War, was a Communist and the editor of *Alger Républicain*. He was an avowed sympathiser with the FLN, and for a month in the summer of 1957 was held and interrogated intermittently by the parachutists. They wanted to know who had sheltered him after he left his home and went into hiding. The descriptions of his sufferings are as horrific to read today as when they were published. He was subjected to the electric shock treatment, to half-drowning by water tortures, to body burns, to frequent batterings with fists. Through it all, he refused to give anything or anyone away, even withstanding the effects of the truth drug Pentothal. His courage won him the grudging admiration of some of his torturers. He survived and at the end of his book he wrote: 'I want [Frenchmen] to know that the Algerians do not confuse their torturers with the great people of France, from which they have learnt so much and whose friendship is so dear to them . . . But they must know what is done IN THEIR NAME.'

Sartre, in his *Express* article, said that the soldiers carrying out the tortures were 'frequently young men from France who have lived twenty years of their life without ever having troubled themselves about the Algerian problem . . . But hate is a magnetic field; it has crossed over to them, corroded them and enslaved them.' He claimed that although everyone knew that torture was being practised systematically in Algeria, 'Almost no one talks of it . . . France is almost as mute as during the Occupation [about Gestapo tortures] but then she had the excuse of being gagged.' This was not so. Among many signs of disagreement with the practice of torture, none was more striking than the reaction to *La Question* of four of France's leading writers: Jean-Paul Sartre himself, Roger Martin du Gard, André Malraux and François Mauriac. They all signed a protest. Mauriac and Sartre's names were not surprising, but the decision of the other two to add theirs was significant.

Even before publication of *La Question*, public disquiet had become so widespread that the Mollet government was led in 1957 to establish a commission for the protection of human rights and freedom. It did something to investigate past horrors and help to prevent future ones. Its highly critical report, sat on by the government, was published by *Le Monde* in December 1957, but it could not eradicate the use of torture. If such use was unacceptable to liberal and humanitarian consciences in France, it had become accepted in Algeria as a necessary means of quelling rebellion. Nor was it the parachutists who began it. As early as March 1955, a report by the Inspector-General of Administration confirmed its existence and even argued that the water torture and the electric shocks were, if carefully controlled, permissible methods of interrogation, 'no more brutal than deprivation of food, drink and tobacco'.[18] The then Governor-General, Soustelle, refused to accept these recommendations, but that did not mean that the procedures were abandoned. At the end of 1955, the Director-General of the Sûreté warned the Mendès-France government of 'excesses' on the part of both the Army and the police. He added that he found it 'intolerable' that the conduct of French police officers should recall the Gestapo, or that French soldiers should be compared to the German SS. Perhaps the most pregnant and prophetic observation of all was made by a member of the Protection Commission, Robert Delavignette, who in its report wrote that 'The most serious problem is not the atrocities themselves, but that as a result of them the

State is engaged in a process of self-destruction . . . What we are witnessing in Algeria is nothing short of the disintegration of the State; it is a gangrene which threatens France itself . . .'

The fall of the Bourgès-Maunoury government, brought about by the rejection of the Algerian outline law, was followed by the longest crisis in the history of the Fourth Republic. Thirty-five days passed in vain attempts by familiar figures – Pleven, Pinay, Mollet, Schuman – to scrape together a majority. Meanwhile the financial situation deteriorated further. Once more France was in the grip of inflation, with an increase of more than 10 per cent in the price index in 1957. Heavy borrowings from the Bank of France became necessary and the continuing drain on foreign reserves meant recourse to American bank loans and a disguised 20 per cent devaluation of the franc. As the cost of living soared, so labour troubles proliferated. In 'agitation week' in late October, there was a spate of strikes for higher wages – public transport workers, civil service members, teachers. Though the unrest was supported principally, and predictably, by the Communist-dominated CGT, the Catholic trade union movement was also vociferous in its claims, inviting its followers to withstand rising prices and social regression.

Yet the paradox was that this economic crisis, for all its gravity, was a crisis of prosperity. Never before in her history had France worked so hard, had so many people employed or produced so much. In Paris, the very physiognomy of the city was beginning gradually and barely perceptibly to change from the familiar nineteenth-century characteristics portrayed, say, by the painter Gustave Caillebotte – austere apartment blocks of stone-fronted façades and ornate arched entrances – to more modern creations of concrete and glass. In this autumn of 1957, with only six months life left to it, the Fourth Republic's achievements were dramatically symbolised by the huge structure, the Palais des Congrès, being built on the western outskirts of the capital, at the beginning of the great vista which, culminating in the Arc de Triomphe, greets the traveller from Rouen. This was the exhibition centre for industrial, technical and trade shows, the effort of a scientific and research organisation with the backing of many French industrialists and the blessing of the government. In the city itself, in the Marché St Honoré, where Fouché and Robespierre once harangued the Jacobin club, a multi-storeyed car-park, with an atomic air-raid shelter beneath, was going up. After having lingered for so long in the climate of the nineteenth century, France was now advancing with impressive speed into the twentieth. In balance of payments terms she was living beyond her means, but the feeling prevailed that in her extravagance there was some purpose, some sign of confidence in the future which transcended even the agonising complexities of the Algerian situation.

The search for a new government finally came to an end in early November 1957 when Félix Gaillard, at thirty-eight the youngest Prime Minister of the Fourth Republic, managed to assemble a majority which was a throwback to the Third Force ministries of earlier years. The MRP returned to office, the Socialists remained in place (which meant that Lacoste stayed at his post in Algiers), and were joined by representatives of the classic Right. In theory, this comprehensive majority should have provided a Ministry of All the Talents. In fact, as had happened so often before, it was composed of familiar old faces and agreed on very little. Between the Right and the Socialists there was hardly any common ground, above all when it came to *dirigisme* versus free market forces. (Shortly before his government's defeat in the summer, an exasperated Mollet had coined the phrase 'the stupidest Right in the world'.) As for Algerian policy there was a repeat performance of the Indochinese impasse: 'A majority neither for victory at any price nor for peace by negotiation but only for ineffective compromise solutions'.[19] The most that the new government could do was to persuade the Assembly to pass the outline law which had brought its predecessors down. But the right-wing support necessary for this result was secured only at the price of amendments which made the new legislation less likely than ever to be the means of weaning away Muslim opinion from the FLN.

The chaos of the parliamentary situation, the result of the 1956 general election, was complicated further by what had been happening within Poujadist ranks. Poujade's men – he himself was not a parliamentary candidate – had, against all expectation, won fifty-three seats. The first thing the Assembly did was to invalidate the elections of eleven of them, redistributing their seats among the other centre parties. Whatever the legal grounds for these invalidations, it looked like a nasty example of dirty politics and added to the general contempt with which Parliament was regarded by public opinion. From the start, Poujade had difficulty in maintaining control over the remaining forty-two, even though they had all taken an oath to observe discipline under pain of death. His instruction to them to vote against the Suez operation (see p. 275) shook the unity of the group, and Poujade himself suffered a personal setback when, in a by-election in Paris where he at last decided to try his parliamentary chances he was soundly defeated. Meanwhile in parliament, the Poujadist deputies, an undistinguished lot to say the least, were failing to make any significant impression or win any sympathies. Their movement was comparable to, but in fact very unlike, the by now moribund RPF, whose electoral successes in 1951 had helped both to threaten and reinforce the bulwarks of the Third Force. By contrast, the Poujadists, because of their lack of programme and parliamentary skills, appeared to threaten no one, despite the wave of protest which had swept them into parliament.

Nor did the cause of *Algérie française*, in which Poujade had invested so much of his energy and oratory, do much to further their fortunes. Poujade's fulminations in the Poujadist paper *Fraternité française* against foreign countries and trusts who, according to him, were planning to get their hands on the oil of the Sahara, were typically xenophobic and rumbustious. But the real note of the extreme Right was sounded by men like Jean-Marie Le Pen and J.M. Demarquet, both of them Poujadist renegades who had signed on to serve in Algeria, and Dides, the ex-police officer of the '*fuites*' affair. These three founded their own group, the Front National des Combattants, which was destined to play a role in the sequence of events which led to the demise of the Fourth Republic. Poujadism, for all its authoritarian nature, was never an extreme right-wing movement in the tradition of such factions in French history. It was what it had been from the beginning, the articulation of the 'little man's' fears and dislikes vis-à-vis the Establishment, the politicians, foreign competition and the rich. It was also the antithesis of the Mendèsian urge to modernise and change the way of life for millions of people. Its success may have been short-lived, but it stood nonetheless for an important tendency in French society in the 1950s, a tendency which could claim to represent the party to which all French people at some time belong or have intermittent urgings to belong: the party of *mécontentement national*.

If Poujade never became a convincing political figure on a national scale, and was certainly not seen as someone to turn to in time of trouble, he nevertheless felt himself sufficiently important to seek a meeting with a more substantial saviour-in-waiting. Those Paris politicians and commentators not on holiday in August 1957 were intrigued to learn that General de Gaulle, on one of his regular visits to Paris, had received Poujade, presumably at the latter's request. What they had to say to one another remained guesswork. Poujade's earthy vocabulary must have made a strange contrast with the General's lofty turn of speech (though de Gaulle could also resort on occasion to some distinctly picturesque forms of regimental slang). Whatever passed between them, the occasion lent strength to the rumours that, conscious of the Algerian cancer that was eating away the life of France, de Gaulle was planning a political come-back.

It was now more than two years since the General had last made a public appearance at one of his famous press conferences in Paris. The Gaullist offices in the Rue de Solférino, where he conducted his weekly audiences, had gone noticeably quiet. Sometimes his tiny and faithful staff had, in order to keep him busy and informed, to coax people to come and see him.[20] Yet through much of 1957, as the Algerian clouds darkened and France's sense of isolation and anxiety increased, above all as the government crisis in the autumn dragged on for weeks, de Gaulle's name had been invoked by newspapers and in political conversations as the person whose time might be at hand. It was the old phenomenon: when things were going well for the Fourth Republic, de Gaulle's stock sagged; when they were not, it rose. The French Institute of Public Opinion's polls showed a steady increase in those who wanted to see him back in power: 1 per cent in 1955, 5 per cent in April 1956, 11 per cent in September 1957. By January 1958, the figure had reached 13 per cent, still only a small minority, but a larger one than the support expressed for any other political figure.

The rumours and expressions of approval for de Gaulle's return to power were certainly not fuelled by the General himself. His visitors reported finding him in a mood of Spenglerian gloom and resignation. To the British Ambassador Sir Gladwyn Jebb he said, in March 1958 (only two months before the march of events swept him onwards to power), that before the régime collapsed, thus clearing the way for his return, all the chances were that he would be dead. He then, uncharacteristically, burst into tears.[21] He was careful to avoid any public stance over Algeria, though in his private conversations (which most of his visitors freely repeated) he seemed, while in no way abating his scorn for the existing régime, to be contemplating Algeria's inevitable emancipation, under one form or another. His mind had been moving privately in that direction for some time. In February 1955, talking to Geoffroi de Courcel, one of his earliest and most faithful supporters, later, under the Fifth Republic, to be French Ambassador in London and Secretary-General at the Elysée, he praised Mendès-France's policies of preparing to grant Tunisia internal autonomy, and said that both Tunisia and Morocco would soon have their independence 'and so will Algeria'. Courcel was amazed; this was going much further than ever Mendès, 'the prisoner of the Assembly' (Courcel's words), had dared to go.[22]

Two years later (autumn 1957) the General said much the same thing to Christian Pineau, Mollet's Foreign Minister, namely that sooner or later Algerian independence was ineluctable. Then why didn't he say so, asked Pineau. 'It's too soon,' was the reply. 'There is no question of my saying something while I lack the means to bring it about.'[23]* Still more surprising was the fact that such *Algérie française* and impeccably Gaullist men as Soustelle and Michel Debré could convince themselves, or be convinced, that the General shared their views. Was he saying different things to different people or did his visitors, reporting afterwards upon their conversations, put the gloss upon his words that suited them best? That some were certainly doing this is proved by a statement which de Gaulle's staff, clearly at his direction, found it necessary to issue in the summer of 1957. Those who purported to repeat what he said, this pointed out, did so on their own responsibility: 'When General de Gaulle thinks it useful to let public opinion know what he thinks, he will do so publicly – this applies specially to Algeria.'

What is sure is that once back in power, with all the authority that the new, Fifth Republican, Constitution conferred upon him, the General's ambiguities over Algeria persisted and were an important element in the early years of the new Gaullist régime. But these were

---

* Examples can be multiplied of de Gaulle talking privately like this about Algeria but refusing to speak out. P.-O. Lapie describes meeting a Free French friend who had worked with de Gaulle on his memoirs and who revealed (early 1958) that the General was saying in private: *'L'Algérie n'est pas la France.'* 'Let him say it in public' was Lapie's comment, to which his friend replied that de Gaulle would not do so because of his belief that 'There is nothing to be done within "the System".' See Lapie, *De Léon Blum à de Gaulle* (Paris, Fayard, 1971), p. 766.

tactical, the keeping open of options and not the result of muddled thought. *The Times'* Paris correspondent felt able to report, in June 1957, that the General was thinking in terms of internal autonomy for Algeria, based upon a general association between France and the three North African territories (Tunisia, Algeria, Morocco), and that were he to return to power he would 'open negotiations . . . with the FLN . . . and would ruthlessly oblige the Europeans in Algeria to accept the outcome.' Unlike many journalistic prophecies, this one proved to be reasonably accurate.

One significant and involved section of society which in no way considered that the Algerian war was comparable to a terminal cancer was the Army. Their views were not without foundation. By the end of 1957, the military situation had changed markedly in France's favour. Massu's success in the battle of Algiers, the uncovering of FLN arms dumps, systematic patrolling, and the creation of *harkis*, or auxiliary anti-FLN Muslim forces, had all contributed towards this improvement. So had the construction of barriers along the frontiers with Morocco and Tunisia designed to prevent the FLN from receiving arms and reinforcements and having recourse to safe base-camps. The Tunisian line in particular, called by the name (Morice) of the Defence Minister in the Bourgès-Maunoury government, was a formidable affair, an eight-foot electric fence running 200 miles southwards from the coast into the Sahara, and backed up with searchlights, watchtowers and minefields. It was highly effective in tying down or destroying FLN forces.

Along with these military efforts went the heroic work of the Sections Administratives Spécialisées (SAS), hundreds of detachments, each under an Arab-speaking French officer, who functioned as sympathetic administrators in the country villages and outlying districts where the Muslim populations were often under the double pressures of the French Army and the FLN. Created initially by Soustelle when he was Governor-General, and known as *képis bleus*, these groups of men did much to win over Muslim sympathies. Here was a practical expression of the *présence française* which was at once humane and effective, even though it was partly offset by another, negative, aspect of French policy, namely *regroupement*, or the uprooting and resettlement in barbed-wire encampments of peasant communities so as to isolate them from contacts with the FLN.

From the generals down to the captains and the lieutenants, and beyond them to the NCOs and ordinary soldiers, the Army therefore had good reason, on the whole, to think it was winning the war. What it was less sure of was the attitude of the politicians in Paris. Though the spokesman for the right wing had declared, during the debate which led to Gaillard's installation as Prime Minister, that 'It is at the moment when victory is near that no weakening can be tolerated', Gaillard himself had said that his government would be ready 'at any time to make the necessary contact with those with whom we are fighting'. This was supposed to be no more than a restatement of the well-worn formula (triptych, in the political jargon of the period) of cease-fire/elections/negotiations. But it was not encouraging to the men in the field. Nor was a joint initiative, in October 1957, by Bourguiba and the King of Morocco to lend their good offices in a search for a solution. Gaillard turned it down with the assertion that France would 'never' accept Algerian independence, but the fact that the offer had been made at all suggested that while the French Army might be winning the war on the ground, it could still lose it on the diplomatic and international front. A French officer, now retired, who in 1957 was a colonel commanding a unit in the Constantine area of Algeria, recalls making a report about his area in which he affirmed that the pacification programme there was 'very nearly achieved'. In his view, it was possible to think in terms simultaneously of peace and the *présence française*: 'A great many soldiers thought that the *dernier quart d'heure* had come.'[24]

Military suspicions that the battle won in Algeria would be lost in Paris were strengthened by the evolution of ideas in France. Though no political party other than the Communists chose to come out openly in favour of the principle of eventual independence, individual politicians such as André Philip, a Socialist intellectual and ex-minister, publicly urged acceptance of the idea of an Algerian national State. The Socialist party as a whole remained loyal to the policies of Mollet and Lacoste (even after Mollet had ceased to be Prime Minister), but some of its members were ready to mount a challenge. They included some student groups led by the young Michel Rocard, a future Socialist Prime Minister under Mitterrand in the Fifth Republic, and a number of dissident deputies who established a Socialist committee for study and action for peace in Algeria.

This did not cut much ice, but in June 1957 came a sensation from a different quarter. Raymond Aron, who besides being a professor at the Sorbonne wrote a column for the conservative *Figaro* and was not normally associated with any specifically political viewpoint, published a pamphlet called *La Tragédie algérienne*.[25] Beginning with a quotation from Montesquieu – 'Every citizen is obliged to die for his country, but not to live for it' – he went on to argue that 'Algeria's vocation for independence' had better be recognised. It was only false pride, he wrote, that led people to believe that France would be less great if she lost Algeria. It would be in the best interests of France to negotiate with the FLN for a gradual transfer of power and then to spend on repatriating several hundred thousand French citizens the money that would otherwise be devoted to prolonging a useless war. With the coming of Moroccan and Tunisian independence, it was 'senseless' to send an army of 400,000 into Algeria. As for Saharan oil, 'The richer the Sahara, the more necessary it is to come to an understanding with the Algerians.' Aron ended with the words: 'The nationalist demands . . . are a fact that cannot be ignored without a catastrophe. . . . The grandeur of power is something that France no longer possesses, can no longer possess.'

However unwelcome and shocking these arguments were at the time to much of French opinion, they were not entirely peculiar to Aron. Bourgès-Maunoury and Lacoste might scoff at left-wing journalists, magazines and intellectuals who wrote and campaigned against the use of torture and the pursuit of a war policy. But the coldly analytical Aron could not be lumped in with these, and nor could men of right-wing leanings such as Pinay or Paul Reynaud, who were beginning to question, albeit not publicly, whether in terms of political and economic advantage the Algerian war was worth it. This reappraisal in such unquestionably orthodox circles of French overseas policies had found expression a year earlier in a remarkable series of articles published in the weekly magazine *Paris-Match*. They were the work of Raymond Cartier, an able journalist who certainly could not be accused of left-wing sympathies. He argued, in essence, that the price of empire was too high: the cost to the taxpayer of maintaining France's hold over her African territories was out of all proportion to the benefits she derived from them. Instead of constructing hospitals and schools in Africa, would it not be more worthwhile to build them in France? Switzerland, Cartier pointed out, was the richest and most stable country in Europe and had never had a square metre of overseas territory. His reasoning recalled the arguments of eighty years earlier, when right-wing opinion, intent on winning back Alsace-Lorraine, inveighed against the diversionary imperial designs of Jules Ferry.

Cartier was writing explicitly about French black Africa, not Algeria. But when in 1957 Aron came to launch his pamphlet, which he followed up with another one the following year,[26] he kept to the same line of thought, from which all ideological or sentimental bias had been excluded in favour of what was reasonable and possible. The same could not be said exactly of another work published in 1957, *Présence française et abandon*, by François Mitterrand.[27] This expounded the theory that the surest way to put an end to the *présence française* overseas was to follow a policy of repression and refusal to listen to nationalist aspirations. Instead, evolution and negotiation was the right course. This was not the same argument as Aron's, but the latter would have been just as entitled, when accused of appeasement, to echo Mitterrand's question: 'Where are the real patriots?'

These various signs of what the *jusq'au-boutistes* considered 'defeatism', though indicative of the degree to which French opinion was beginning to be fragmented by the Algerian war, scarcely amounted to a protest movement. Though all sorts of weird ideas were floated about, such as a partition of Algeria leaving the central coastal plain in French hands, or the establishment of a Muslim Republic centred on Constantine, *Algérie française* was still the preferred watchword. Nonetheless, as the mists of autumn 1957 crept up the Seine and the golden and russet leaves fluttered from the trees in the great forests of Chantilly or Compiègne, conversations at private dinner tables dwelt increasingly on the theme that things could not go on as they were going, that even without the war the prospect of an increasing Muslim population dependent upon French financial support could not be looked on with any satisfaction. Thus far had the Cartier thesis taken root. But these remained private fears, not for public distribution. A surer guide to French feelings was the apoplectic and general reaction to the American and British decision in November to sell a limited quantity of arms to Tunisia, France having refused to do so. It seemed at the time, and still seems today, an extraordinary thing to have done.

Ostensibly the reason was that Bourguiba would otherwise have gone shopping in Cairo or Moscow. 'I think we made a serious error, at a critical moment when France was nervous and uncertain,' wrote Harold Macmillan in his memoirs,[28] adding that he did not fully realise the true situation in France. The French reaction was entirely predictable. Here were France's NATO allies selling arms to a country which was giving aid and comfort to France's enemies in Algeria. *Le Figaro* called it 'an odious blow', *L'Aurore* claimed to see the hand of the oil companies reaching out for the riches of the Sahara, even *Le Monde* wrote of 'the entente without cordiality'. Raymond Aron, not a man to give way to passions, thought it 'a deplorably clumsy method of expressing no confidence in France's Algerian policy'. Anti-British slogans were chalked on Paris walls; in the cinemas whenever a newsreel showed President Eisenhower or the Queen a wave of booing followed. There had been a similar response during the thirty-five-day government crisis to any appearance of a member of the National Assembly on the screen. An American observer of the Paris scene was by no means overstating things when she wrote in a letter in November: 'The French are in a vile humor.'[29] Their humour was destined to be put to yet severer tests in the climacteric year that was approaching.

CHAPTER 10

Plots and Plotters

The rebellion (French governments never called it a war, because Algeria was legally part of France) which erupted in Algeria on 1 November 1954, principally in the Aurès mountains and Kabylia, two traditional strongholds of banditry, was the work of the military section of the main nationalist movement, the Front de Libération Nationale (FLN). This had recently been founded by a group of Algerian nationalists who, despairing of the quarrels and animosities hitherto dividing and distracting the various segments of nationalist opinion, resolved to mount a revolutionary war aimed at nothing less than total independence. Nationalist aspirations had existed in one form or another in Algeria and among Algerians in metropolitan France since the Twenties. The previous major outburst of violence had been nine years earlier on VE day 1945 (8 May). Then, at Sétif,* eighty miles from Constantine in the eastern part of the country, large numbers of Muslims, driven apparently by a mixture of political discontent and economic privation, as well as by indignation at the exiling of the nationalist leader Messali Hadj, first clashed with the police and then embarked on a ferocious slaughter of Europeans, more than 100 of whom were done to death with the utmost brutality. The repression that followed was still more frightful. French defence forces, using aerial and naval bombardment, took a heavy toll of the local population, but nothing like as heavy as that inflicted by the frightened and angry Europeans.

The events of Sétif, though they were hardly remarked upon at the time in France and the world, were to be crucial. Firstly, they stiffened *colon* resolve to resist any attempt to recognise, or go some way to accommodate, Algerian nationalism. Secondly, with a mirror

* See p. 133.

effect, they encouraged even moderate nationalists to think that the only way forward for them was, in the last resort, through armed struggle. Mohammed Ben Bella, a much-decorated sergeant who had just returned from fighting with the French Army in Europe, and was later to emerge as one of the FLN leaders and the first President of the newly independent Algeria, wrote that 'the horrors of the Constantine area in May 1945 succeeded in persuading me of the only path; Algeria for the Algerians.'[1]

By 1954, large numbers of enlightened French people were willing to admit that past vacillation over a policy for Algeria, caused by die-hard *colon* interests and pressures, had cost dear. The 1936 Popular Front reforms, based on integration of the Muslim population with France, were effectively set on one side, while the 1947 statute, which really might have pointed the way towards a brighter future, was either not applied or, worse still, deliberately misapplied (see pp. 134 and 239). This sorry record gave the FLN what was, at minimum valuation, a good talking point: namely that to stand out for anything less than independence would be to invite the French once more to break their promises. Yet any prospect in Paris of a realistic approach to the Algerian problem was blocked by the permanent obstacle so often indicated in these pages: lack of a stable parliamentary majority in Paris for any adequately forward-looking policy for Algeria, be it the suppression of the rebellion by a combination of military means and genuine social reforms, or by some attempt to meet nationalist demands.

At first, French reaction to the 1954 uprising was limited. Mendès-France's government despatched reinforcements and asserted time and again, without any effective sign of contradiction, that Algeria was France and must for ever remain so. Mendès himself was as forthright as anyone. 'One does not compromise', he told the National Assembly, 'when it comes to defending peace at home and the unity and integrity of the Republic.' Mitterrand, the Minister of the Interior, was just as assertive of French rights and duties (see pp. 37–8). But it was not until after Mollet's fateful visit to Algiers in February 1956 that massive military reinforcements began to arrive from metropolitan France. It was later still that the realisation came that while the military problem obviously needed attention, this was also a social, political and psychological struggle, involving an unceasing battle for the control of men's minds.

The organisers of the rebellion had grasped this point long before.

Beginning as a series of terrorist actions, the rebellion, under the guidance of its organising committee in Cairo, became a politico-military movement. At this early stage, it had a good deal of support among the more politically conscious parts of Muslim opinion. Where this support was not voluntarily forthcoming, propaganda, intimidation and violence were freely used to evoke it. By the beginning of 1956, the soldiers and activists of the ALN (Armée de Libération, the military arm of the FLN) numbered probably no more than about 60,000. But they and the political influence of the FLN had spread over the whole of the country, achieving the proportions, and employing the methods, of a subversive and revolutionary war. As this situation developed, so effective power within the nationalist movement, itself riven with internal quarrels and schisms, tended to pass into the hands of the extremists.

At an FLN 'summit' conference daringly held in August and September 1956 on Algerian soil, under the noses of the French, future strategy and military organisation was decided upon, as well as war aims and the establishment of a 'National Council of the Algerian Revolution', a conscious copy of clandestine Resistance procedures in wartime France. Once Ben Bella and his four colleagues, who were among the original architects of the rebellion, had been captured by the French (p. 268) the actual control of operations on the ground was exerted by the military *maquisards*. Within the nine-member body set up by the summit conference under the name of Comité de Coordination et d'Exécution (CCE), which was supposed to be responsible for the political and military conduct of the struggle, the influence of the military clan was balanced against that of the politicians.

The FLN's war aims were extremely simple, as clear as crystal – unlike the confused and contradictory noises emanating from Paris – and totally unacceptable (at that stage) to no matter what government in France. It wanted French recognition of the Algerian nation (even though no such thing had ever existed) and of its territories, including the Sahara, followed by the cessation of hostilities and the recognition by France of a provisional Algerian government which would negotiate peace and organise elections. In return, this new Algeria would respect French cultural and economic interests, while those French who decided to stay on could choose between protected foreign status or Algerian nationality. There was to be no possibility of double citizenship privileges for the *colons*. Today, these terms

seem not unreasonable. They were indeed similar to the outcome of
the Evian negotiations which in 1962, under de Gaulle's presidency,
brought the war to an end. In 1956–7 however the men who put
them forward were very far from being seen, by French eyes, as
the 'valid interlocutors' for lack of whom there seemed to be no
other course but to continue the war.

The FLN military leaders, as time went on, resorted more and
more to terrorism and to brutal methods, both in Algeria and
France, towards Muslims who would not play their game. This gave
the French the chance to make their belated bid to win Muslim hearts
and minds. By early 1958, the situation in Algeria could be summed
up in three categories: one of them covered a tiny proportion of
the native population who had taken up arms to fight a war of
independence; a second indicated the French Army, administration
and civilian European population, all resolved, though in differing
frames of mind, to seal off the rebellion and maintain French
sovereign domination; while thirdly, in between, floated a great
mass of Muslims, many of whom had had enough both of the
exactions of the FLN and of the repressive efforts of the French.

Whatever conscience-stricken souls in France might think or infer,
these efforts were not confined to killing and torturing. Though the
aims of the Army and of the *colons* were in the last resort identical
– i.e. to keep Algeria French – there was no automatic sympathy
between the two. The Army did not, for the most part, consider
that it was there to protect and enhance the privileged position of
the *colons*, above all the rich and mighty among them. The policy
of 'pacification' meant that, after years of inaction, at last an attempt
was made to bring about something not far short of a social and
administrative solution. Up till then, it had been a question, over
much of the country, not so much of misrule as of no rule at
all. By the end of 1956, the regions which did not form part of
the large, urbanised and more or less European conglomerations
began to benefit, for the first time for 130 years, from the social
and economic advantages that had hitherto been denied them.
More than a thousand new *communes* (roughly equivalent to rural
district councils) were created, with new-built town halls, schools
and offices. The Army's role as a social welfare agency was greatly
expanded.

All this work (though it should have been done years before),
and the dedicated men who did it, deserved the highest praise.

What the Muslim masses thought of it all is hard to say. Early in 1958, a special correspondent of *The Times* made a tour of Algeria and asked the members of an all-Muslim council (no Frenchman was present) for their view of the new outline law recently passed by parliament in Paris. Their response was minimal. 'One might as well have sought their opinion of the late Beethoven quartets,' he reported.[2] But these men, and millions like them, would have been less than human if they had not reflected that all this admirable expenditure of money and effort would never have occurred if the rebellion had not stung the French into action. They would also have found confirmation of any scepticism they might have felt about real French intentions had they heard what a European vineyard foreman, of French citizenship and Spanish origins, told the *Times* man: 'You don't want to give the Muslim political power or equality of status, all he wants is to be administered justly by the French.' This is the way in which, years later in Rhodesia, white supremacists used to delude themselves and seek to delude others.

A further factor in 1957–8 was that, despite Massu's victory in the battle for Algiers and other French military successes, the war showed no sign of withering away. The ALN was as strong on the ground as ever, apparently able always to recruit more men, either as volunteers or by more forceful methods. This army contrived to remain essentially a guerrilla movement of the military–political type, eschewing pitched battles, lying up by day and moving at night, infiltrating the civilian population with a mixture of nationalist arguments and threats. In Tunis, where the FLN maintained its main propaganda offices, they claimed that although they could never bring the French Army in Algeria to its knees, they were militarily stronger than ever, they could never be beaten, they could keep it up for years. In Algiers, French Army spokesmen said much the same thing, but in the inverse sense. It might take years to master the rebellion, but it could and should be done – always assuming that the will was there, and by that the soldiers meant the will of Paris. Officers returning to the homeland in the spring of 1958, either on leave or at the end of their tour of duty, would freely assert their belief that if Algeria were to be lost, it would be lost in Paris. It was the same deep-seated lack of trust in the politicians that became so strong a feature among the members of the expeditionary corps in Indochina.

An integral part of this military thinking concerned Algeria's borders. If only the Tunisian border could be sealed off, the argument went, the war would come speedily to a halt. This was a greatly oversimplified view of things, but there was no doubt that the Tunisians did give a significant amount of help and comfort to the FLN. The French frontier fence, the Morice line, had done much, since its construction, to reduce the traffic, but still quantities of arms from Libya and points east flowed across the frontier and ALN men continued to cross in large numbers into Tunisia, to rest and recuperate before returning to continue the struggle. In Tunisian government circles there was no attempt to deny these facts. 'The government cannot and the population will not' stop the help that, directly or indirectly, fed the Algerian nationalist movement: this was the Tunisian formula, convenient for home and foreign consumption, but an open invitation to the French military in Algiers to do something fierce and retributive.

An occasion soon presented itself. In early January 1958, close to the village of Sakiet near the Tunisian–Algerian frontier, a detachment of the ALN crossed the frontier, killed fifteen French soldiers on patrol and took four more back into Tunisia as prisoners. A few days after this ambush, a French military aircraft was shot down by gunfire coming from the Tunisian side of the frontier. The French military authorities were disturbed and angry and urged the Gaillard government to act. At the end of January, it did so, granting the 'right of pursuit', though without specifying what form that should take. Early on the morning of 8 February, another French plane was shot at as it was flying over Sakiet. Two hours later came the French reprisal: eleven B-26 bombers and six fighter-bombers, escorted by eight fighters, bombed and machine-gunned Sakiet. It was a Saturday, and market day. A lot of the bombs fell on innocent victims – sixty-nine in all, including many women and children. Some hit the village school. A Red Cross vehicle, carrying Swiss and Swedish nationals, was also hit. There have been, in this book, various references to incidents presaging the death of the Fourth Republic. The Sakiet raid, and its consequences, was beyond doubt the most significant of these.

It is not completely clear, even after this lapse of time, where the responsibility lay for the Sakiet raid. Neither the Prime Minister nor the Defence Minister nor, most importantly of all, Lacoste were informed beforehand. If M. Edgar Faure's memoirs are to be believed, Gaillard, the Prime Minister, was left unaware of what had happened until hours after the raid.[3] Even then, in the belief that Sakiet was an Algerian village, he paid no special attention. It was not until Monday 10 February that he learnt the real truth. Lacoste, when he did get to hear of it, burst out 'They really are idiots.'[4] The High Command in Algeria, which authorised the operation, could invoke the principle of pursuit as already agreed by the government. But what had happened was aerial pursuit, and the bombing, either by intention or lack of precision, had been indiscriminate.

Later, in Paris, the government tried to extricate itself, as best it might, from the fiasco. Gaillard said that there was no international law which obliged a country permanently to put up with attacks from a neighbouring territory. Chaban-Delmas, the Defence Minister, asserted that Tunisia had become an important and highly developed base for the ALN. Predictably the Right approved the raid, the Left did not. Some more far-seeing members of the Establishment, such as Paul Reynaud and Edgar Faure, had severe misgivings as to the consequences. They were right. Sakiet not only took several steps further the process whereby decisions were taken in Algiers rather than in Paris, to the detriment of the authority of the régime; it also internationalised the Algerian war in a way which French diplomacy had been doing its utmost to prevent.

Bourguiba was outraged, ordering the evacuation of French garrisons still in Tunisia, recalling his Ambassador from Paris (significantly, the Ambassador, before leaving, went to Colombey to see de Gaulle, whom he later described as 'incarnating the real French conscience),[5] and taking the matter to the Security Council. The French government also lodged a complaint against Tunisia. This put France's British and American allies on the spot. If they were to maintain desirable relations with the Arab world, they could not side unreservedly with the French. On the other hand, there was the importance of NATO unity. The difficulty seemed to be solved, for the moment, by Washington, London and Paris agreeing to a 'good offices' Anglo-American mission. Headed by two diplomats, Robert Murphy for the Americans and Harold Beeley for the British, its task was to patch up relations between France and Tunisia and devise better arrangements for supervising the frontier, so that there need be no more Sakiets. In fact, not only did this mission fail to achieve anything, especially over the frontier question, but its very existence fuelled the resentment of those in France who considered that foreign powers, even friendly ones, had no business to be concerning themselves with what should be an exclusively French interest.

French reactions, a few months earlier, to the Anglo-American decision to sell arms to Tunisia were a sure pointer to what was likely to be the public response to the Anglo-American mission. Admittedly the mission, in its negotiations, refused to include in its scope anything to do with the political future of Algeria. But to suspicious French eyes, the principle of foreign intervention seemed to be making headway. For the FLN, the good offices affair was a kind of victory. For the *Algérie française* faithfuls, it boded ill. Already, in such circles, there was talk of a 'Government of Public Safety' to save Algeria. And already, as previously described, the name of de Gaulle was beginning to be heard, in private as well as in public. 'Rather the good offices of Charles de Gaulle than of the American Murphy,' declaimed Michel Debré, in the Council of the Republic.* In this thickening atmosphere of virulent anti-Americanism (with a fair measure of anti-British feeling too), the level-headed Gaillard could make little impression with his references to 'automatic xenophobia' and his civilised regrets about the tendency to blame the allies for anything disagreeable that happened to France.

Debré, later to be the first Prime Minister of the Fifth Republic, had been Senator from a department in central France since 1948. Given to extravagant language in defence of deeply held convictions, he had made valuable contributions, in the post-Liberation era, to national reconstruction, most notably in helping to establish the Ecole Nationale d'Administration (see p. 12). But once de Gaulle had gone from the scene this vehement patriot, Gaullist from the top of his head to the soles of his feet, became one of the régime's fiercest critics. Long before Sakiet and the death-throes of the Republic, he had been continuously and vociferously prominent in Paris, as an opponent of EDC, as an *Algérie française* fanatic, and as a fervent promoter of de Gaulle's return to power. One of the most prominent of the Gaullist old hands, or 'barons', he

* De Gaulle and the Gaullists had special reasons to distrust Robert Murphy. It was he who, at the time of the Allied landings in French North Africa in 1942, sought, in accordance with what was then his country's underlying hostility towards Free France, to promote the cause of de Gaulle's chief military rival, General Giraud.

helped to keep the flame alight when the fire of Gaullism was at its lowest, attending a lunch every Wednesday in Paris with other 'barons'. From 1956 onwards, he seldom moved out of the rarefied air of quasi-conspiracy. There were few meetings or movements of enthusiasts hoping and planning for the downfall of the Republic with which he was not connected. His activities, about which he made no secret, had won him the distinction of having his Paris front door watched over permanently by plain-clothes police. In 1957, in his pamphlet *Ces Princes qui nous gouvernent*, he mounted a ferocious attack against the leaders of the Fourth Republic, and in the same year he founded a political review, the *Courrier de la Colère*, which became the regular channel for his fulminations.

In all this work, Debré was inevitably brought into contact with all manner of dissidents and malcontents, not all of whom shared his loyalty to de Gaulle. One of these, General Jacques Faure, who as a young officer had come to know Debré through their common hostility to EDC, was a born intriguer, and had plenty of opportunity in Algiers, where he was serving, to make contact with extreme right-wing elements. At the end of December 1956, he was cocksure or naïve enough to reveal his fanciful plans for a military putsch to the Secretary-General of the Prefecture in Algiers (Teitgen, who felt so strongly about torture). The plan envisaged overthrowing the civilian administration in Algiers and replacing it with a military régime, while in Paris a political operation would be mounted to topple the government and the Republic. His ill-conceived act in talking to Teitgen cost Faure thirty days' fortress arrest, in the circumstances a surprisingly light punishment.

There was no proof, but a good deal of suspicion, that Debré could be connected with another, slightly later, piece of mayhem in Algiers. This took the form of an attack with two anti-tank projectiles on the offices of the Commander-in-Chief, Salan, thought by the hard-liners, possibly because he had been in charge in Indochina at the time of the cease-fire in 1954, to be 'unsound' on *Algérie française*. He was not at his desk at the time of the attack, but the explosion killed his military secretary, who was. The affair was, typically, never completely cleared up, despite the later trial of European 'ultras' suspected of being its authors. But it, and the Faure so-called 'plot', served to emphasise that the Algerian war, and the passions it aroused in Algiers and in some anti-régime quarters in Paris, was a permanent encouragement to those given to fishing in troubled waters to bait their lines and prepare for some sport.*

Prominent among these anglers were the ex-servicemen's associations, whose demonstrations and pressures at the Arc de Triomphe in April 1954 and in the streets of Algiers on 6 February 1956 have already been noted. Later grouped under the umbrella of the newly founded Comité d'Action Nationale des Anciens Combattants (CANAC), these associations and their leaders, though they might differ about the form the future should assume in Algeria, were all agreed on one thing: that the Fourth Republic's politicians were incapable of ensuring that Algeria remained French. For some – the minority, including especially those who served with the Free French Forces – the remedy was to bring back General de Gaulle. Most of the rest, some with a Pétainist past, had no time for him at all. But whatever their differences, the Algerian associations found no difficulty in subscribing to the oath which one of their leaders made public in Algiers, 'to oppose by every method any measure which could threaten the integrity of the territory [i.e. Algeria] and national unity'.

The establishment of CANAC had been preceded by that of another similar organisation, known conspiratorially as the 'Grand O', and composed principally of those who had fought in the Indochina campaigns. The head of this was General Cherrière, a former Commander-in-Chief in Algeria, and a Bonapartist by belief, as befitted someone whose great-grandfather had served in the Imperial Guard. He busied himself building up relations with ex-cadets of the military academies such as St Cyr, and paying visits to garrisons in Morocco and Algeria. He was also in touch with General Roger Miquel, commanding the Fifth military region in France and responsible for the twelve departments in southern France where most of the parachute battalions, whose role would be potentially vital in the event of a putsch, were stationed. How far

---

* Debré, in a conversation with the author in December 1989, vigorously denied being involved in any plotting, taking strong exception to the word. But he recalled warning de Gaulle, in February 1958, to 'be ready', and on 2 December 1957 he had written in the *Echo d'Alger*, the main right-wing European paper there, that 'as long as Algeria is French territory, the fight for *Algérie française* is a legal fight; insurrection for *Algérie française* is legitimate insurrection.' If this was not plotting, it had every appearance of encouragement to defy the established order.

the demonstrations and statements of these ex-servicemen's associations were truly representative is open to question. Though *Algérie française* was a trumpet call to which all could rally, the real activity came not from the two million or so who nominally made up the associations, but from a comparatively small number of hotheads, some of them with distinguished war and Resistance records. But though they may have been few in number, they had both the willingness and the power to foster a mood of subversion.

Well before Sakiet, in fact, a tendency was developing for some sections of the Army and the *anciens combattants* to make common cause, in the interests of *Algérie française* and in opposition to an increasingly impotent régime in Paris, with representatives of the political Right and the extreme Right, the latter the heirs to the pre-war fascist-type leagues. The situation made for some strange bed-fellows, some of whom did not even know they were bed-fellows: Gaullists, men of the Resistance, serving and retired officers, Pétainists, corporatists, adventurers. The personalities in this seditious mix also provided some interesting contrasts: Debré and Soustelle, parliamentarians and men of distinction with a record of achievement; Biaggi, the excitable Corsican lawyer and Gaullist, one of the ring-leaders in the anti-Mollet demonstrations in Algiers on 6 February 1956; Alexandre Sanguinetti, the Secretary-General of CANAC, another Gaullist and former commando sergeant; Bernard Lefèvre, an Algerian Poujadist who thought that Salazar's rule in Portugal was the best form of government; Pierre Lagaillarde, leader of the Algerian students, an extremist demagogue with nothing but contempt for Gaullist ambitions; Alain de Sérigny, the Pétainist editor of the *Echo d'Alger*; Georges Sauge, a Communist converted to Catholicism who made himself a kind of link man between extreme right-wing Catholic circles in France and the Fifth bureau of the Army concerned with psychological warfare.

Among the middle ranks of the officer corps, many of them Indochinese veterans, this notion of psychological war, calling for a fight against the enemy with his own weapons such as subversion and counter-revolutionary tactics, had become highly fashionable.* (It was not only the middle ranks who were interested. A correspondent

---

* They openly acknowledged their debt to Mao Tse-tung, whose 'war among the masses' theory of warfare had been so successfully used against them in Indochina.

of the Catholic paper *La Croix*, interviewing Massu in his Algiers headquarters in December 1957, found the only book on his desk was one called *Counter-Revolution, Strategy and Tactics*. By an anonymous author, it was published in Belgium and banned in France. The book laid out a plan for the seizure of power by the Army in Algeria, followed, according to the Franco precedent, by the establishment of a fascist-type régime in Paris.)[6]

As the army assumed more and more responsibility for civil administration in country districts, so its politicisation became more marked. Nowhere was this truer than among the elite parachute forces and their commanders, the renowned para colonels of Algeria. It would be an insult to the bravery of these outstanding officers, some of them heroes of the Resistance and of Indochina, to write them off as mere appendages of the lunatic Right in Algiers. But their scorn for the politicians in Paris, their devotion to *Algérie française* as a supposed bastion against Communism, and their easy popularity among the *colons*, made them and the ideas for which they stood an essential element in the pressures building up against the Fourth Republic and its leaders.

Compared with their military prowess, most of these men, despite their increasing involvement with the politics of *Algérie française*, were politically naïve, unwilling or unable to see further than the limits of their own obsessions. One such officer, destined to take a major part in the events of May 1958, was Colonel Jean Thomazo, a vigorous and guileless intriguer familiarly known as Nez-de-Cuir (leather nose), because of the leather strap he wore across his face to hide injuries sustained on the Italian battlefields of the Second World War. A Bonapartist like Cherrière, whose representative in Algiers he later became, he commanded an auxiliary military force composed of *colon* militiamen, whose feelings he shared completely. He was well known and liked among extremist circles in Algiers, where his simple belief that the Army should assume power was predictably popular.

Of all the activists with their different affiliations and backgrounds, among the most determined was Soustelle. In Algeria itself, his name was quasi-sacred to the *colon* population, infinitely more so than that of General de Gaulle. In France, he was able to win the support of a much wider and more respectable milieu than that represented by such desperadoes as General Faure or Maître Biaggi. Early in 1957, he helped to found the Union pour le Salut et le Renouveau de l'Algérie Française (USRAF), and to recruit to it such eminent and non-right-wing figures as Saliège, the Cardinal-Archbishop of Toulouse, the symbol of Church resistance under the occupation, Robert Schuman, the former Prime Minister and Foreign Minister, several former Governors-General of Algeria, including the aged Maurice Viollette, with his consistently liberal views, writers, academics, intellectuals.

This broadly based platform notwithstanding, USRAF and its leadership was characterised principally by wartime and Resistance traditions, its tone predominantly Gaullist. Via Soustelle himself, it maintained a close liaison with the General's entourage. From the beginning of 1958, it began to organise 'Committees of Public Safety' in many towns in France, whose activities (rather like the pattern of the defunct RPF) sometimes outran the plans and wishes of the leaders in Paris. As USRAF's attacks on the existing régime became increasingly shrill, so some of those who had originally signed its manifesto withdrew their names. Under the impulsion of Soustelle, USRAF was also the umbrella for a 'shadow Cabinet' designed to lead a future 'Government of Public Safety' and pave the way for de Gaulle. It was a curious embryo team. Apart from Soustelle himself, it included Bidault, no Gaullist despite his Resistance record, André Morice, a right-wing Radical dissident and even less of a Gaullist, and Roger Duchet, leader of the classic Right, who had never been a member of USRAF.

Someone of a different order was Jacques Chaban-Delmas, who contrived to preach the gospel for the return of General de Gaulle at the same time as he held the senior office of Minister of Defence in the Gaillard government. Leader of the Social Republicans (Gaullists) in the Assembly, a Resistance hero, rugby international and Mayor of Bordeaux, a post to which he was perpetually re-elected, he was still only forty-three in 1958, with years of active politics ahead of him. As Defence Minister in the Gaillard government, appointed to accelerate the programme for the construction of France's first atom bomb, he commissioned another Gaullist militant, Léon Delbecque, to establish a liaison post in Algiers. Its ostensible purpose was to supply the Minister with information and ideas about the progress of the campaign, in particular the development of psychological warfare against the FLN. In fact, Delbecque conceived his primary duty as seeking to canalise the *Algérie française* sentiments of the *colons* and the Army in the direction of a movement for the return of de Gaulle. Chaban-Delmas, asked in December 1989 whether during these months he was playing a double game, said first that it was 'understood' that he should be able to speak out in favour of de Gaulle's return while serving in the governments of the Fourth Republic; and second that while he received information from Delbecque about military and associated matters in Algeria, Delbecque 'told me nothing' about his political activities and preparations. Other contemporary witnesses, notably Maurice Faure, a Radical member of governments in the later years of the Fourth Republic, put it rather differently: 'Chaban shut his eyes.'[7] Despite Chaban's denials, the general assumption must be that he knew about, condoned, and sympathised with Delbecque's activities.

Delbecque's task, whether self-appointed or not, was not going to be easy. With some notable exceptions (Massu was one of them), the officer class in Algeria was not in the mass pro-Gaullist, the Algerian civilian population even less so. In the war, Pétain, not de Gaulle, had commanded its loyalties. Nonetheless Delbecque, helped by three other devoted Gaullists and a renowned parachute major, went energetically to work, making nearly thirty journeys between Paris and Algiers in the six months leading up to May 1958. Thomazo, initially frosty, was worked upon by Biaggi and ended by giving the Delbecque mission full support in preparing what was then intended to be a peaceful military coup in metropolitan France, carried out to the accompaniment of civilian demonstrations, which would lead to the collapse of the régime in Paris and an appeal for de Gaulle's return. The plan was timed for August, the height of the holiday season in France, when the Communists would find it difficult to mobilise their forces of resistance.[8]

Any attempt to describe and analyse this tangled web of conspiracy soon leads to the most fascinating and relevant question of all: how much did de Gaulle know and what did he think of it all? In his memoirs he wrote of the years leading up to May 1958 as ones when 'I was completely retired, living at La Boisserie [his house at Colombey], whose door only opened to my family and people from the village' – he would receive only 'two or three people, going increasingly rarely to Paris, where I agreed to see very infrequent visitors'.[9] This was disingenuous, to say the least. It may have been true of life at Colombey, but during his weekly visits to Paris in the months before May 1958 he was receiving a large number of visitors, including senior officers, and representatives of the Right and extreme Right, the Left and extreme Left. It is impossible that he was unaware of what some of these people, including some distinctly unsavoury specimens, were up to. As a soldier – and one out of seven of his visitors at the Rue de Solférino was an officer – he was certainly well informed about the state of opinion in the Army.

Where the machinations of Delbecque and his team – known as the 'antenna' – were concerned, from the beginning of March onwards Delbecque had meetings with Soustelle, Debré and the other Gaullist 'barons' each time he returned to Paris. Something of all this must have come to de Gaulle's knowledge. 'We did not tell him everything,' said Olivier Guichard, one of the younger 'barons' and a part-time member of de Gaulle's personal staff. 'We told him all that it was necessary for him to know.'* But though he always said that he had complete confidence in Debré, to most people the General contrived to be enigmatic about the likely and desirable future of Algeria and positively dismissive as to the prospects of his own return to power. Yet even this description needs qualifying. To some, he was more forthcoming than to others.

Of the conversations that people reported having had with the General at this time (spring 1958), one of the most revealing is that with the left-wing Socialist André Philip, who had worked with de Gaulle in Algiers before the Liberation:

DE GAULLE: 'The only outcome is via the independence of Algeria by stages, if possible in association with France.'
PHILIP: 'Yes, but I'm worried. An Army revolt is in preparation over there, in favour of *Algérie française* . . . You can't stop people from using your name.'
DE GAULLE: 'If there is a government, it will govern and the Army will obey. The Army only rebels when it is frustrated in its natural instinct to obey. If there is no government, the Army will assume power in Algiers. And as for me, seeing that there is no longer a State, I will assume power in Paris, in order to save the Republic.'

---

* Conversation with the author in Paris, December 1989. Like Debré, Guichard took exception to the word 'plotting', and was reticent about his role in the period prior to May 1958. Both men emphasised the leading part played by Delbecque.

PHILIP: But then you will never be able to proclaim the independence of Algeria.'
DE GAULLE: 'Come on, Philip, don't be naïve. You have lived in Algiers as I have. They are all noisy people. The only thing to do is to let them make a noise. As for the military, I shall remain calm while their leaders destroy each other. With what remains, I shall do what I want, with promotions and decorations.'[10]

This remarkably prophetic vision has to be balanced against what the General said to another of his interlocutors, the left-wing MRP deputy Robert Buron. He pressed de Gaulle to make a public statement about decolonisation, to which the General replied: 'It is too late . . . The situation cannot be stabilised for several years and I shall then be too old. The French must first plumb the depths before they can regain the heights.'[11] His pessimism and detachment were even more forcibly expressed to a delegation of CANAC, who went to see him at the end of March. 'This situation could go on for thirty or forty years,' [he told them.] 'De Gaulle, dead [he often spoke of himself in the third person] will perhaps be more useful to France in thirty or forty years than if he assumed power now. . . . Parliament will never recall me before the final catastrophe . . . The Fourth Republic is incapable of making war or peace . . .', and so on, in repetition of the tune he apparently played to nearly all his visitors. But then, talking to these ex-servicemen's representatives, came something rather different. Deploring the apathy of public opinion, he added: 'A slight awakening seems to have been occurring over the last two years. If this public awareness develops, if, under the pressure of events and the progressive paralysis of the régime, it becomes irresistible, I would face up to my responsibilities and would again gather up into my hands the national reins.'[12] Assuming that those present were correct in rendering this account of what the General had said, it would appear that he was showing something of a green light to a group of men – led by General Cherrière, he of the Grand O – who though not Gaullists were intent upon doing the Fourth Republic to death by one means or another.

Though more guarded towards Delbecque, who was received by him at the end of April, the General used similar language. Delbecque told him that Algiers was seething with extremist plots of every kind (this was no more than the truth). In all this confusion, he said, a lot of the Muslim population and a lot of the Army wanted to see him, de Gaulle, back in power. The General retorted, realistically, that he was not popular with the Army, and that in France itself Gaullist enthusiasts might go to work on public opinion, but they could not raise the temperature sufficiently to bring him back. Delbecque, the ever-faithful Gaullist, insisted. If, in really serious circumstances, the Army and the people turned towards him, what would his answer be? 'Delbecque,' intoned the General, 'I have always been in the habit of facing up to my responsibilities.'[13] If not a signal to go ahead, this was equally not a formula of discouragement for those wishing to carry on plotting.

At this stage, all the evidence suggests that de Gaulle did not foresee – and this could be said of most French people, including the conspirators themselves – the way in which events would unfold during May. Indeed, he charged his son-in-law, Alain de Boissieu, together with his brother-in-law, Jacques Vendroux, to organise his summer holidays, in the form of a lengthy journey through the French provinces.[14] Nonetheless, where his thoughts were concerned he kept his options open, knowing, like anyone who claims to be a statesman, the importance of not committing oneself too soon. Though the sense of impending upheaval made his position more delicate and relevant than it had been at any time since he threw in his hand twelve years previously, in a larger perspective he was what he had always been in relation to the Fourth Republic: the figure of the Commander in *Don Giovanni*, the stone statue in the background waiting, and destined, to step down from his plinth and settle the score for the folly and wrongdoing of the past.*

The Gaillard government did not long survive the shock of Sakiet and the Anglo-American 'good offices' mission. A former senior official, an expert on North Africa, summoned to the Hôtel Matignon to give advice, recalls his shock at hearing Gaillard say calmly, as he contemplated the situation, 'This will be the end of my government.'[15] Like someone very ill who has lost the wish to live, the government's will to survive was simply lacking, and there were real grounds for such pessimism. No more striking proof of this could have been given than the humiliating incident of 13 March when the Paris police force demonstrated in front of the

---

* In one important respect, this analogy fails to hold water. The stone statue ('*l'uomo di sasso*'), until finally it comes to life, never speaks. De Gaulle spoke, intermittently but always with passion, throughout the twelve years of the Fourth Republic's life.

Palais Bourbon, shouting anti-Semitic insults and threats. The police wanted payment of 'danger money', which they had been promised. Though their demonstration was supposed to be silent and orderly, it soon got out of hand. The participation of the ex-superintendent Dides, of Poujadist and extreme right-wing affiliations, helped to foster the disorder.

A month later, on 15 April, the government was overturned after a debate in the Assembly, convoked specially in the middle of the parliamentary recess, to discuss the sequel to the 'good offices' procedure. Soustelle administered the *coup de grâce*. As had happened so often in previous crises, the victorious majority was united by nothing save its eagerness to bring down the Ministry. The Communists, Poujadists and the Right voted together, linked, though for different reasons, in a common resistance to what they saw as foreign interference in French affairs. Their votes fell short of the constitutional majority, but just as the first government of the Fourth Republic (Ramadier's) had folded its tents and stolen away after an adverse vote which was less than the constitutional majority and therefore did not legally require its resignation, so now Gaillard, the head of the Republic's penultimate Ministry, did likewise. The Constitution certainly had its shortcomings, but repeated failure to adhere to it cannot justly be laid at its door.

It should have been fairly obvious, and was to some, that this collapse was not going to be just one more re-enactment of a familiar scenario. 'And if this crisis should be the last of the Fourth Republic?' asked Maurice Schumann after the Assembly had voted. Jeers and laughs were his only reply. In an atmosphere of increasing unreality, the stately ceremonial of consultation got under way to the derision of much of public opinion, by now more convinced than ever that the politicians in Paris, with their solemn rituals, were incapable of finding the answer to the Algerian or any other problem.

Not that this mood induced a recognisable wish for a change. What was remarkable about the spring of 1958 was that, while Algiers and some circles in Paris were hives of conspiratorial activity, while journalists and academics were writing in the national press that de Gaulle's hour had struck (notably Maurice Duverger, in a powerful article in *Le Monde* on 7 March), ordinary people went their ordinary ways, oblivious to the storm clouds rolling up, enjoying the prosperity which had come at last to France, clogging the approach roads of Paris on Friday and Sunday evenings as they made their way by car to or from the *résidences secondaires* which families of quite modest means were increasingly acquiring. There was of course concern about Algeria. With so many sons or brothers or boyfriends serving there, it was impossible there should not be. But it did not, in general, manifest itself in any tangible form. De Gaulle had noted this, and given it as a reason why his hour had *not* struck. The record of his conversation with the CANAC delegation has him explaining public apathy by the fact that 'opinion in general and each French person in particular is not yet really suffering as a result of the political, economic and social situation of the nation as a whole'.

Even the most fervent partisans of *Algérie française* had to admit to their relative insignificance. In mid-April, the chairman of the Society of former French residents in North Africa, a retired general, said at its first congress in Toulouse that 'Today we are one thousand French men and women, tomorrow we shall be 50,000 to 100,000, shouting in the streets and in front of Parliament.'[16] As for public feelings for, and interest in, the men and institutions of the Fourth Republic, a poll held in early 1958 with the question of what people would do in the event of a military uprising against the government yielded the answer that 90 per cent would wish to remain uninvolved. Only four in every hundred people asked said they would fight for the régime. A few months previously a group of 3,500 young men called up for national service were asked to name the Prime Minister and the winner of that year's Tour de France bicycle race. Only 15 per cent could answer the first question, as against 97 per cent for the second.

There were special reasons why this last (as it turned out to be) crisis of the Fourth Republic took so long to resolve. By the normal rules of the game, Coty should have sent for a representative of the party or group which had been most instrumental in finishing off Gaillard – Soustelle, for example. The President thought otherwise. He not only did not summon Soustelle, he did not summon anyone until five days had gone by. The reason was that the first round of voting all over the country for the cantonal elections – roughly equivalent to county council elections – was due on 20 April, and both Socialists and MRP feared that if Coty were to call upon a right-wing figure to form the government, this would give an electoral advantage to the right-wing parties. Not

before the evening of the 20th, therefore, did he send for Georges
Bidault.

His choice was determined by the expectation that Soustelle,
were he asked to form a government, would immediately call
for the return of General de Gaulle. There was no majority,
there was only a small minority in the Assembly in favour of
such an appeal. De Gaulle was realistic here in what he told his
visitors: the political parties would do their utmost to block his
path. The nomination of Bidault, on the other hand, presented
no such danger. There had never been much love lost between
him and the General, but at the same time he was an authentic
representative of the *Algérie française* school of thought which had
helped to bring down Gaillard. Ever since he had lost control of the
Quai d'Orsay, back in 1954, and suffered the humiliation of seeing
Mendès-France achieve an Indochinese settlement, this one-time
Professor of History and President of the National Council of the
Resistance had become identified more and more closely with the
nationalist Right. A remark he made some time previously to a
colleague, about his attitude over the Indochinese war, is significant:
'What has given unity to my philosophy and life is the struggle against
nationalism. I fight Indochinese nationalism and Arab nationalism
just as I fought against German nationalism.'[17] Nothing can tarnish
Bidault's wartime record, but he was among those many Frenchmen
under the Fourth Republic who considered that French nationalism
was right, proper and natural, whereas the nationalism of others,
particularly of territories subject to French control, was not.

Bidault jumped at the chance of forming a government which
would reflect those views and quickly put together a team which
included Soustelle, Duchet and Morice – the 'shadow Cabinet' established some months previously. Had the Assembly voted Bidault
and his colleagues into power, there would have been no explosion in Algiers and the history of modern France could have
read differently. In fact, there was never the slightest chance of
a parliamentary majority for such a government, which could be
sure of only about 150 right-wing votes. The Communists, who had
combined with this 150 to finish off Gaillard, were certainly not
going to repeat the performance in order to establish a right-wing,
Algérie française administration. Above all, Bidault's own MRP,
from which his extremist views increasingly isolated him, refused
to cooperate; the party chairman, Pierre Pflimlin, was instrumental

in the decision not to support Bidault, a fact duly noted by the men of Algiers.

Bidault having withdrawn, the next person to try his hand was René Pleven, a former Prime Minister and Defence Minister. Bidault, in his attempts to form a government, had acted like a showjumper rushing his fences. Pleven worked at a slower tempo. He first tried to get all the parties save the Communists to agree on a charter embodying Algerian policy. This approach ran into serious procedural difficulties. In addition to these, once again the electoral calendar intervened. The second round of voting in the cantonal elections was on 27 April, and Pleven had to wait until that was over to begin his serious consultations with the parties. The timetable was stretched still further by the need of the Socialist party, according to its statutes, to hold an Extraordinary National Council to decide whether or not to join a Pleven government. Because the newly elected county councils would be holding their first, important, meetings on 30 April, and because 1 May was Labour Day and a national holiday, the Socialists decided that the earliest date when they could meet was 2 May. When they finally did so, they voted by a large majority not to cooperate. The rank and file had for long been unhappy over Lacoste's policy in Algeria. Now was the time, they concluded, to rebuild party unity by declining all responsibility for policy-making.

This setback to Pleven, who finally decided to abandon his efforts when the Radicals also created difficulties, meant that the crisis was pushed into its fourth week. The succession of delays was fully accountable for, but the general impression given was deplorable. Nothing could have shown more painfully than this slow and futile minuet the inadequacy of the machinery of State in face of the challenges confronting it, and the preoccupation of the politicians, to the exclusion of apparently everything else, with their party games and subterfuges.

Meanwhile in Algiers, where rumours ran wild, tension was mounting. As the result of Delbecque's efforts, a 'vigilance com- mittee' had been established, bringing together all those repre- sentatives of political parties, trade unions, ex-servicemen's and *colon* organisations, determined to keep Algeria French. Within this committee ran different and opposing currents. For Delbecque and his Gaullist team, the main aim was to prepare the way for the return to power of General de Gaulle, using the cause of *Algérie française* to do so. Another faction, much more extreme in its aims and backgrounds, went by the name of the 'Group of Seven'. As well as Lagaillarde, the fiery student leader, who although he had completed his military service, continued to swagger about in the green and black camouflage uniform of the parachutists, it included two Poujadists and other 'ultras' who felt no enthusiasm for de Gaulle as a saviour figure. In their muddled and excitable thinking, the Seven had got no further than wishing to see the Army take over in Algiers, in order to throw off the yoke of the hated politicians in Paris, who would be forced to give way to a Government of Public Safety, whatever that meant. By the end of April, the differences between these two tendencies had not fully emerged. As Pleven continued with his leisurely efforts to form a government, the vigilance committee, under Delbecque's inspiration, had no difficulty in organising a mass demonstration in the streets for 26 April. Lacoste sought to ban it, but it took place all the same, without incident, although *colon* auxiliary units had to be restrained from taking matters into their own hands. At the end of it, the Prefect of Algiers received a delegation which gave him a petition to be forwarded to the President of the Republic. This asked for the formation of a Government of Public Safety, 'the only one capable of restoring national greatness and independence'. There was no mention of de Gaulle.

The effect of this demonstration in metropolitan France was minimal. Many people outside the inner circles of Gaullism had never heard of Delbecque. Even fewer knew he was the eyes and ears of the Minister of Defence. One of them was Lacoste, who objected to his intrigues and after much persistence had him recalled to Paris. Delbecque could afford to ignore such hostility. The demonstration of 26 April had shown that he and the vigilance committee could get the European crowds and the ex-servicemen onto the streets in impressive numbers, this time without the anti-Muslim excesses which had marked previous *colon* manifestations. It had been a successful dress rehearsal for the real thing. What that thing would be was spelt out by Lagaillarde when, on 26 April, he shouted to the mob: 'Today is a demonstration of silence and dignity, but if parliament does not want to understand, we will go through to the end.'

Pleven having failed to form a government, Coty turned next to Pflimlin, Chairman of the MRP. A fifty-year-old from Strasbourg,

Minister in various previous coalition governments, he formed part of the left-wing, liberal tendency within his party, to which Bidault had been so alien. His main preoccupation was with constitutional reform, for like many other thinking people he was dismayed at the deterioration of the institutions of the Fourth Republic. On Algeria he was no die-hard, but he certainly saw no quick solution. His views, set out in various articles and speeches, stopped well short of prescribing independence, but he had written recently of talking to 'the representatives of those who are fighting' (which could only mean the FLN), and had expressed the opinion that the only conceivable solution for Algeria was a political one. That he also had spoken and written of negotiating only from a position of strength mattered little to the *Algérie française* lobbies in Paris and Algiers. For them, he was a surrender man just as, in another context, Mendès had been a surrender man, someone to be resisted and undermined by every possible means.

These feelings received powerful encouragement from a very different quarter. Pflimlin having chosen another Minister for Algeria, a war hero of impeccably orthodox views, Lacoste was preparing to leave Algiers, despite pressing appeals from the Army and the Algiers lobbies to stay on as the head of a movement of resistance to Paris. In a farewell meeting with senior Army officers, he let fall a warning about 'a diplomatic Dien Bien Phu' in the making. Even though the phrase was not of his own invention – Bourguiba had previously made use of it – the effect of his uttering it at this moment was equivalent to dropping a lighted match into a box of fireworks. From now on, the plotters on both sides of the Mediterranean were convinced that a legally established Pflimlin government would be the prelude to an Algerian sell-out. The time for words had passed, the hour for action had arrived.

While French people went normally about their business and their pleasures, unaware of the quickening tempo of events, Pflimlin, who was nominated by Coty on 8 May 1958, lost no time in getting together a ministerial team. Very few people other than Pflimlin himself knew that the President, in asking him to form a government, had indicated that if he failed, he, Coty, would appeal to General de Gaulle.[18] The President was an honest, patriotic man of modest intelligence who had only been elected to the Elysée four and a half years earlier after twelve rounds of voting (see p. 184). As early as 1956, in view of the palpable malfunctioning of the machinery of State, he had begun to consider procedures under which he might make way for de Gaulle,[19] although he knew of parliament's opposition to such a prospect. Now eighteen months later, as the government crisis dragged on, he put out feelers. On 5 May General Ganeval, the head of the President's military household, went to see de Gaulle's staff officer, Colonel Bonneval, and Olivier Guichard to enquire on Coty's behalf what de Gaulle's conditions would be for a return to power. The answer was not encouraging. The word from Colombey, relayed four days later by Guichard, was that Coty would have to make his request in writing and the political parties would have to agree, before the investiture vote in the Assembly, upon a majority. When the vote did take place, it would be in the absence of de Gaulle.[20] True to the doctrine he had been preaching since 1946, if he could help it the squire of Colombey was having no truck with party politics.

On 9 May, two events of crucial importance contributed to the unfolding drama. First, the FLN press office in Tunis announced that three French soldiers, prisoners for more than eighteen months, had been executed, in reprisals for the French execution of two FLN captives. The news was greeted in Algiers with furious indignation. For the plotters, this was the alarm bell. Ideas of an uprising in August were overtaken by the need for swift reaction, in the form of a mass demonstration. 'The Seven', who saw things almost entirely in Algerian terms, wanted it on the 12th. Delbecque, never losing sight of the ultimate objective of de Gaulle's return, successfully argued for the 13th, a day on which the investiture debate on the Pflimlin government would be taking place in the National Assembly, when the pressures of Algiers could be applied (so it was calculated) with maximum effect.

Secondly, 9 May saw the formal entry of the Army into the political arena. Already, during Pleven's attempts to form a government, General Salan, the Commander-in-Chief in Algeria, an experienced and somewhat inscrutable officer with no visible leanings towards Gaullism and no known sympathy with plots and plotters of whatever inspiration, had been asked by Pleven for his advice and had flown to Paris with the message that the Army would not accept any cease-fire that was contrary to its honour. The only possible formula for a cease-fire, Salan told Pleven, was one which invited 'the Algerian rebels' to lay down their arms and guaranteed them, by means of a wide-reaching amnesty, their inclusion in the framework of a reconstituted Franco-Muslim community. Even if it had been by invitation, this was a direct invasion by the armed forces of the territory of political responsibility. From that moment on, the men in Paris, whether they were called Coty or Pleven or Pflimlin, knew or anyway ought to have known that, concerning Algeria, effective executive power no longer lay within their grasp. In fact, this had been true, even if not immediately evident, ever since Mollet's capitulation to the Algiers mob on 6 February 1956.

Now, on 9 May, this Rubicon was, so to speak, crossed for the second time. On the evening of that day, the four senior Generals in Algeria, plus the Admiral commanding the naval forces, handed to Lacoste, for transmission to General Ely, Chief of the General Staff in Paris, a telegram, signed by Salan and couched in uncompromising terms. No less than three times in its short text the word 'surrender' (*abandon*) was used. Press reports were suggesting, these service chiefs said, that diplomatic procedures were in the making which would lead to the abandonment of Algeria (the Dien Bien Phu formula of which Lacoste had warned). The telegram continued:

> The Army in Algeria is concerned with its sense of responsibility towards the men who are fighting and who are in danger of making a useless sacrifice if [parliament] is not resolved to keep Algeria French, and towards the indigenous population and those French Muslims who, more numerous every day, are renewing their confidence in France. . . . The French Army would, to a man, consider the surrender of this part of the national heritage to be an outrage. Its desperate reaction is unpredictable. I request you to draw the attention of the President of the Republic to our anguish, which can only be assuaged by a government firmly resolved to keep the French flag flying in Algeria.*

Neither this telegram, nor Salan's earlier advice to Pleven, referred directly or indirectly to de Gaulle or to the need for a government of public safety. Whatever plans Delbecque in Algiers or the Gaullist

---

* The Army's feeling at this time, and later, when in 1961 the 'Generals' revolt' mounted a direct challenge to de Gaulle's intentions over Algeria, was in part inspired by the pledges it had given in the name of France to Muslim anti-FLN auxiliaries and civilians. (Many of these were indeed tortured, and some killed, in acts of revenge after the French withdrawal.) Many people who disapproved of the military taking things into their own hands could feel some sympathy for those caught in this dilemma.

conspirators in Paris were cooking up, very few people at the end of April or the first two weeks in May rated the chances of a return of the General as more than a remote possibility. In France itself, despite impatience and derision over the lack of a properly constituted government, there were no signs of a popular Gaullist groundswell. Though Delbecque had hoped and intended that the successful demonstration in Algiers of 26 April would be matched by a show of strength in Paris on the part of the ex-servicemen's associations, it had not been forthcoming. Sanguinetti, their leader, said that if he managed to get 300 onto the streets, that would be good going. In the event, there was none. For the Gaullists, the problem was the same as it had ever been: how to link the civilian and military hostility in Algeria towards the régime in Paris with a movement for the return of de Gaulle. What was necessary was that the *colons*, the students, the ex-servicemen and large parts of the Army should be brought to accept that de Gaulle was the best person to ensure that Algeria remained French.

The first considerable sign that European opinion in Algeria could be recruited in support of the Gaullist cause came on 11 May. Alain de Sérigny, the editor of the *Echo d'Alger* and its Sunday companion *Dimanche-Matin*, had become convinced, under the influence of Soustelle, not only that a Pflimlin government would be disastrous and must be prevented, but that the surest way of doing this would be to involve de Gaulle. The issue of *Dimanche-Matin* of 11 May contained a leading article by Sérigny which took the form of an appeal to the General. He made no bones about his Pétainist past but argued that the situation in Algeria and in France itself had become 'positively dramatic'. He said he knew de Gaulle's reasons for not speaking out when unequipped with the means to act. Nevertheless, 'turning towards you, I cry "I implore you, speak, speak quickly, *mon Général*, your words will be [the sign for] action."' However belated and improbable, this was a notable addition to the nucleus of Gaullism in Algeria.

By 12 May, Pflimlin, having sought (unsuccessfully) to calm things down with assurances that his idea of an armistice in Algeria was inspired by the example of 11 November 1918, 'which restored Alsace to France', had picked his ministers and was ready to undergo the test of the Assembly. The political pundits did not rate his chances of success highly. His opening address dwelt at length on the need for institutional reform, including amendments to the Constitution of a kind to allow the proper functioning of a parliamentary system. Lack of this had 'destroyed the attachment of Frenchmen to the régime to a really dangerous degree of disaffection. . . . The degradation of our institutions menaces the very existence of the Republic.' De Gaulle could not have put it more energetically himself. On Algeria, Pflimlin pledged his government to continue and strengthen the war effort, adding that it was not resigned to a permanent war, but would seize on any opportunity to bring about peace. However, it would 'never permit the bonds which unite Algeria to France to be broken'.

In other words, Pflimlin's Algerian policy was, nuances apart, no different from Mollet's, which had been approved several times by the Assembly. Suspicions that he was contemplating a sell-out should have been without foundation. The reverse was the case. Even as he was speaking, those suspicions were being translated dramatically into action in Algiers. During the evening, news of the upheaval there reached the Palais Bourbon. In the Champs Elysées, a few hundred demonstrators sent up shouts of *'Algérie française'* and *'L'armée au pouvoir'*, and there were some clashes with police in the Place de la Concorde. But there was no real heart in these manifestations, which were supposed to be in sympathy with and support of the events in Algiers. The debate in the Assembly was adjourned more than once and not finally resumed until 1.15 a.m. on the 14th of May. France still had no properly established government, apart from the caretaker team led by Gaillard, the outgoing Prime Minister, who had resigned almost a month earlier.

What had happened in Algiers was that 'the Seven', rather than Delbecque and his Gaullists, had set the pace of events. The latter intended that the demonstration of 13 May, ostensibly a mark of respect for the three French soldiers executed by the FLN, should culminate in the establishment of a Committee of Public Safety, which in turn would call for a Government of Public Safety, in Paris, led by General de Gaulle. Everything was to be peaceable and orderly. Only the 'vigilance committee' would enter the government offices and at no time would the impression be created of a *coup d'état*. Soustelle, whose arrival from Paris was an essential part of the plan, would provide the necessary political leadership, installing himself in Lacoste's empty office and launching an appeal to de

Gaulle. Delbecque, although banished from Algeria by Lacoste
(who had himself by now returned to France), had found his way
back to Algiers, whence he was in frequent telephone contact with
Debré or Soustelle in Paris. 'The Seven' had other ideas. Under
the influence of Lagaillarde they resolved that 13 May should lead
to the 'capture' of the main government building (known as the
Government-General, or 'GG' for short) and the installation there
of a Committee of Public Safety which would remain in place until
there was a Government of Public Safety in Paris. The Army, they
calculated, would have to side with them, or shoot them, and there
was not much risk of the latter. De Gaulle figured nowhere in these
plans.

On the afternoon of the 13th, as huge crowds began to move
through the streets leading to the war memorial and the 'GG'
(sacking the American Culture Centre on the way), Lagaillarde, in
his (illegally worn) para uniform, urged them on to action.To shouts
of '*L'armée au pouvoir*' and '*Massu au pouvoir*', the Commander-
in-Chief, Salan, arrived at the war memorial, laid a wreath and
departed to the sound of boos; he was not popular with the *colon*
mob. This was Lagaillarde's moment. At the head of a crowd
of students and young people, he pressed on towards the 'GG,'
undeterred by the riot police's resort to tear-gas. Commandeering
a lorry (some accounts say it was a military vehicle whose use the
troops did nothing to prevent) as a battering ram, the students forced
the iron grilles, and within seconds the mob was within the building,
sacking offices, throwing papers and files out of the windows, to the
delight of the huge crowds below. The riot police withdrew and the
parachutists, who took their place, made no effort to impose order.
Salan, informed of what was happening, arrived at the 'GG' by a
subterranean passage and was soundly booed by the crowds when
he appeared on the balcony.

Massu, on the other hand, popular with the Europeans ever since
his victory in the battle for Algiers, was greeted enthusiastically.
Rather reluctantly, and in the interests of reasserting control, he
agreed to head a Committee of Public Safety, made up of an extraordinary collection of seventy-four people, ranging from serving
officers such as Thomazo, representatives of the Seven whose
ruthless determination had helped to create the situation, Sérigny,
some of the students, Delbecque and some of his faction, and at the
last moment, three dependable Muslims, supposedly representing

9 million of their co-religionists. In some ways, it had not been a good day for Delbecque. He had missed the storming of the 'GG' and seen the control of events pass into the hands of the 'ultras' and thence into those of the mob. But at least he and his Gaullists had the satisfaction, before night closed in, of knowing that the Army had, under the pressure of the day's disorders, finally committed itself. Salan agreed to send a message to the Elysée containing the words: 'The responsible military authorities consider it an imperative necessity to appeal to a national arbiter with a view to constituting a government of public safety . . . A call for calm by this senior authority is alone capable of re-establishing the situation.' Salan had stopped short of using de Gaulle's name, but nobody could be in any doubt about the meaning of the phrase 'national arbiter'. Even though Soustelle had failed to materialise, the Gaullist cause was gaining strength.

In Paris, the effect of all this upon the deputies debating Pflimlin's future was exactly the reverse of what the various plotters intended. Frantic consultations followed receipt of the news from Algiers, with a view to the formation of a national government, but in the end Pflimlin, assured of Socialist support – as usual the Socialists held the political balance – decided to persist. When the sitting of the National Assembly was resumed, in the early hours of 14 May, he described the attitude of the military in Algiers as 'insurrectionary' and told the packed benches that France was perhaps on the verge of civil war; the country must have a government. 274 votes were cast in his favour (most of the Socialists, MRP, Radicals, one quarter of the Right), 129 against (three-quarters of the Right, the Poujadists, two-thirds of the Gaullists). The Communists abstained. France again had a proper government and its most urgent task was to react to the situation in Algiers.

Three choices lay before it: to meet the revolt head-on in a trial of strength; to seek to assuage the rebels by coming out openly for *Algérie française*; or to appeal to de Gaulle. All three were unattractive. The first contained the seeds of civil war, with the Communists playing to the full their self-styled role of defenders of the Republic; the second, in so far as it meant adopting and approving the demands of the Algiers insurrection, was a straightforward caving-in to illegal pressures and as such distasteful to the majority of deputies and probably to the majority of public opinion; the third was, at that stage, almost universally unpopular with the political parties. Pflimlin and his Ministry did what most men not imbued with greatness would have done: they improvised as best they might. At their first Cabinet meeting, held at dawn on the 14th, they decided to confirm the orders issued a few hours earlier by Gaillard, in his capacity as acting Prime Minister; all powers in Algiers were to be delegated to Salan, all communications between France and Algeria suspended, the gendarmerie in Paris reinforced, and Coty, as Commander-in-Chief of all the armed forces, made a proclamation by radio, ordering the Army to obey the legal government.

To many people in France, it seemed on 14 May that the revolt in Algiers had been, or was in the process of being, nipped in the bud. The tone of the Paris press was scarcely encouraging towards the rebel cause. *Le Figaro*'s leading article was entitled 'Re-establishing legal authority'. The left-wing *Libération* headline read 'The Republic in danger'. The political bureau of the French Communist party, via the pages of *L'Humanité*, declared that a fascist *coup de force* had occurred in Algiers and appealed to all to 'defend the Republic and liberty'. Alone, *Le Parisien Libéré* carried the headline 'Only one recourse – de Gaulle'. Within the new government the Minister of the Interior, at its dawn meeting, had spoken of starving Algeria out. His colleague at Defence sent a telegram to all regional commanders in Algeria, ordering them to impose military discipline.

In Algiers, the situation looked somewhat different from the heady expectations of the previous day. Pflimlin's investiture had come as a nasty shock to the plotters and to the generals. 'We're done for' and 'We shall all be shot' were two of the reported reactions of the senior officers and officials who had spent much of the night of 13/14 May in the 'GG'.[21] Delbecque and the Gaullists, who had been expecting the arrival from Paris of Soustelle to give weight and authority to their position, were disconsolate at his failure to appear. They were also perturbed by the deafening silence from Colombey-les-Deux-Eglises. The 'ultras' of the Seven, though they cared nothing for de Gaulle, were equally discouraged, while still counting on the mob to carry the day. For the generals (the generals in Algiers that is; at that stage, the military commanders in the rest of the country remained, for the most part, unaffected by, or hostile to, the developments in Algiers) the prospect was particularly dismaying. Their choice was either to obey the legally constituted government in Paris, which would put them on collision course with the *colons*, the crowd and the Committee of Public Safety whose patrons they had just become, as well as with many of their own junior officers; or to join the rebellion against Paris, in which case they would be guilty of sedition. Their anxieties were well expressed by Massu at a press conference held at midday on the 14th, when he refrained from attacking the new government, denied being factious, and said that the Committee of Public Safety, of which he was now chairman, would be dissolved directly a new Minister for Algeria assumed his post.

Such a prospect was not at all to the liking of Delbecque or of the Seven and their supporters. The momentum which, in their different ways, they had helped to create appeared to be faltering. Salan, loath to break with Paris, remained a key but still a hesitant figure, while in Paris Pflimlin seemed to strengthen his authority by broadening the basis of his government with the inclusion of four Socialist ministers, among them Guy Mollet and Jules Moch, who found himself back at the Ministry of the Interior, whence he had directed with such skill and energy the battle against the Communists, nearly eleven years earlier. Meanwhile the biggest unknown quantity of all observed his usual routine. May 14 was a Wednesday, which was the day for General de Gaulle's weekly visit to Paris. He seemed unperturbed, replying to a question about how he saw the events in Algeria: 'What events?' His publisher, who had asked the question, was anxious about the third volume of the General's memoirs, still being written. His distinguished and best-selling author sought to reassure him: 'I have just finished the sixth chapter, I've only got the seventh and last to do. I will have completed it by 15 August. We can publish in October.'[22] In the event, the book was not published until the following year, 1959.

The only possible interpretation to put upon this example of studied indifference is that it was a deliberate attempt to mislead. The General knew perfectly well what was happening in Algiers, having been brought up to date by his staff at the Rue de Solférino. Moreover, in no more than twenty-four hours' time he was to give voice in the first of a series of carefully calculated and worded statements which formed, and were intended to form, the rungs of the ladder leading upwards to the cherished goal of power. Like the Duke of Wellington, whose presence at the Duchess of Richmond's ball just before Quatre-Bras and Waterloo was in the nature of a deception plan, designed to reassure doubters that nothing was untoward, so de Gaulle on the eve of his greatest adventure contrived to give the impression that the stone statue was as marmoreal as ever. It was a fine piece of play-acting by a master actor, recalling Richelieu's dictum: *'Savoir dissimuler, c'est le savoir des rois.'*

CHAPTER 11

Journeys of a Black Citroën

If 14 May marked an entr'acte in the drama, during which the principal players nervously watched one another and the end of the piece was still in doubt, the events of 15 May were decisive in determining the fate of the Fourth Republic. Firstly, Salan, from the balcony of the 'GG', shouted 'Vive de Gaulle' to the crowds massed below. He did it only after a certain amount of hesitation and, having done it, seemed surprised at himself. But he did it. The indefatigable Delbecque was the man who metaphorically pushed him over the edge, having first persuaded him to use the name of de Gaulle when addressing the Committee of Public Safety. Then, on the balcony outside, Delbecque reminded the Commander-in-Chief, as he was turning away from the microphone having completed his speech with the ritual words *'Vive l'Algérie française. Vive la France'*, that he had omitted the magic name. Salan turned back to face the crowd and added: *'Et vive de Gaulle'*. This was not only the most senior – and incidentally non-Gaullist – officer in Algeria talking, he was also, and simultaneously, the delegated representative of the newly elected government in Paris and someone expressly condemned by the head of that government for having assumed 'an attitude of insurrection against Republican law'. In this elaborate double game, it was hardly surprising if signs and symbols began to assume greater importance than realities. It can only be guesswork, but fascinating guesswork, to speculate what would have happened if Salan had not heard, or had disregarded, Delbecque's reminder on the balcony that morning. Possibly the revolt would have collapsed altogether. More likely, the extremists, both civilian and military, would have neutralised Salan and Massu and tried to export their revolt to metropolitan France. As it was, the appeal to de Gaulle was rapturously received by a city that up to then had shown little or no enthusiasm for him. The favourable reaction of the Muslim population was particularly significant.

Secondly, de Gaulle made the first of his moves. It is generally assumed that he did so in response to Salan's invocation of his name. That is what it looked like, but in fact he prepared his statement during the morning of the 15th, before he could have known about Salan, and handed it to Guichard, bidden to Colombey for lunch, to pass to the French press agency.[1] It was a meticulously composed affair, in which the word Algeria did not appear and the rebels in Algiers remained unrebuked, but which amounted first of all to a form of burial service for the régime and its government and secondly to an official notification that he, de Gaulle, was ready to take over:

> The degradation of the State inevitably involves the alienation of the associated peoples [coded language for, among others, Algerians of all races, but subtly indicative of a future there rather different from the simple formula of *Algérie française*], disquiet within the army at war, national disruption, the loss of independence. For twelve years France, at grips with problems too harsh for the party system, has been caught up in this disastrous process. In the past, the nation, from its heart of hearts, trusted me to lead it in unity to its salvation. Today, as it faces a grave new trial, may the country know that I hold myself ready to assume the powers of the Republic.

That evening, from a balcony in Algiers, transformed virtually into a tribune from which to harangue the crowds, a triumphant Delbecque read out the General's message. Its nuances went unnoticed, as ten thousand throats acclaimed it.

Ten years later, in his *Mémoires d'espoir*,[2] de Gaulle explained what prompted him to act as he did. Even allowing for the tendency of such memories, recollected long after the event, to provide convenient justification for actions taken and policies adopted, de Gaulle's go a long way towards putting into true perspective his feigned indifference to the events around him. Sometime in the period before and immediately after 13 May he became convinced, in his own words, that he would have 'to go into action'. The threat of a military dictatorship in France itself, with all its consequences, could lead to civil war 'unless a national authority could suddenly rally opinion, assume power, and rally the State. That authority could not be other than my own.' In the same passage he wrote of being kept abreast of events by his staff and his own contacts at the Rue de Solférino, of being made aware of the 'confusion which put my name on to the agenda of suggestions and calculations'. So he was convinced, and his statement of 15 May made this plain, that the Fourth Republic was dying and that, by some procedure as yet undefined, he must be responsible for its sequel. But there was still a long way to go before a legal basis for his return to power – the only one acceptable to him – could be laid.

The editor of *Le Monde* had some harsh but logical things to say about this thunderbolt from Colombey.[3] In talking about 'the powers of the Republic', he wrote, the General had deliberately ignored the men (i.e. the Pflimlin government) who had been regularly entrusted with those powers. The effect was to make it seem as though de Gaulle had by implication approved the Algerian revolt. The government now had two choices, *Le Monde*'s article continued: either to hearken to de Gaulle and to the Algerian plotters whom he had implicitly covered with his moral authority (for that is how his words would be interpreted, wrote Beuve-Méry), or face up to an illegal and revolutionary situation.

Many people, in and out of parliament, agreed with this analysis. Why had the General not breathed a word of condemnation of the rebels, military and civilian, above all the former? In talking, in his grandiose way, about 'assuming the powers of the Republic' what powers did he mean? Was he not drawing up a blueprint of his own dictatorship? In view of the reactions of the press to this first initiative by the General, very few people would the following day have estimated his chances of a return to power as anything but remote. Yet little more than a fortnight later, the National Assembly welcomed him back by a comfortable, if not overwhelming, majority. Developments during that fortnight were crucial in bringing about this extraordinary somersault. The first of these developments was, as its author intended it to be, the statement from Colombey of 15 May.

Pflimlin and his team, though sounding off with some bellicose noises, were unwilling, or felt unable, to accept the stark choices set out by *Le Monde*'s editor. Although he was ready, as de Gaulle was not, to stigmatise the Algiers revolt, Pflimlin remained in constant telephonic touch with Salan, himself the recipient of the special powers delegated to him by Paris. It was a tactic comparable to fighting a fire not by resort to hosepipes and foam but by being careful not to fan the flames, in the hope that it will go out by itself.

Looking back with hindsight, one can feel sympathy with Pflimlin in his dilemma. He was the leader of a constitutionally elected government, but his first concern was to preserve French unity and avoid civil war, which meant refraining from a public break with the semi-disaffected Army. That in turn meant not alienating its leaders. In other words, the myth of the Army's loyalty had to be maintained, even if Pflimlin himself knew it to be a myth. At the same time, with the Communists enjoying their self-appointed role as defenders of Republican liberty, he had to guard against any possibility of a new Popular Front, which would almost certainly bring on another sort of civil war. On the evening of 16 May, the Assembly approved a state of emergency by 462 votes against 112. The Communists voted with the majority, and Pflimlin made it clear, as Mendès-France had done in June 1954, that he was going to subtract their contribution from the total. Once again, the situation had arisen whereby the elected representatives of one quarter of the electorate were treated, for parliamentary purposes, as though they did not exist.

In the extraordinary situation of divided power now prevailing – Salan, the officially recognised rebel in Algiers, and the legal but increasingly impotent government in Paris – there was a third element, represented by the crafty recluse of Colombey. Pflimlin chose, publicly at least, to ignore him, making no public reference to de Gaulle's statement of 15 May, which left the latter in possession of the initiative. He could, for example, have said something to the effect that vaguely worded claims to national leadership had no relevance when there already existed a constitutional government whose defence of Republican values called for the support, not the hostility, of all patriots (that sort of thing sounds very well in French). As it was, it was left to Guy Mollet, the Socialist leader, by now the deputy Prime Minister, to respond, which he did in the lobbies of the National Assembly during the debate on a state of emergency. There he made it known to journalists and others that he would like to have the General's answer to three questions: did he recognise the legitimacy of the present government, did he disavow those who had set up Committees of Public Safety in Algeria, and was he ready, if called upon to form a government, to appear personally before the National Assembly with a programme, and if this failed to gain approval, to withdraw again?

There was nothing wrong with these questions; they were entirely apposite. But inevitably, and despite Mollet's indignant assertions to the contrary, it looked as though for the first time a leading non-Gaullist politician was publicly contemplating the General's return, was moreover opening up a channel for dialogue between the régime and Colombey. In the cat-and-mouse game which he had started, the General had caught another mouse. He was quick to realise his advantage, announcing that he would hold a press conference in Paris on the 19th, the first he had given for three years. He was risking nothing. In the unlikely event that by then the government had got the better of the men in Algiers, he had only to point to the mistakes and inadequacies which had led to the crisis in the first place. If on the other hand the situation was still out of control, his claim to 'the powers of the Republic' would look all the more realistic.

The 17th and 18th of May, an interval which could be described as waiting for the General, were marked with developments boding ill for Pflimlin's authority. Soustelle gave the slip to the police guard on his Paris apartment and turned up in Algiers, where Salan accorded him the coolest of receptions but where the news, once disseminated, was greeted enthusiastically by the public. From the inevitable balcony, he shouted to the enraptured crowds the inevitable words: '*Vive la République. Vive l'Algérie française. Vive la France. Vive de Gaulle.*' He had come in the nick of time. According to one source,[4] Delbecque and his Gaullists, as well as other leading members of the Committee of Public Safety, were in imminent danger of being arrested on the authority of Salan and as part of the arrangements between him and Pflimlin for a return to normality. If this reality were the case, then Pflimlin's double game would have been justified. But the possibility of such a denouement was never put to the test, for Soustelle's arrival changed everything. Now it was Salan's turn to fear arrest. The rebellion, and the movement for the return of de Gaulle, was back on course, the breach between Algiers and Paris extended to the point of being unbridgeable.

Particularly striking was the way in which the demonstrators in the streets of Algiers now included large numbers of Muslims. Salan, in his report to Paris – the lines of communication were still open

– wrote of an 'extraordinary revolution of feeling in the sense of a total spiritual fusion of the two communities [which] constitutes a determining factor in the situation'. It was indeed extraordinary. Some of it was certainly due to the pressures and persuasions of the French psychological warfare teams, manipulating Muslim opinion. But that opinion was also influenced quite independently by the respect and expectation it harboured for the name of de Gaulle.

As the day and hour of the General's press conference approached, he was kept informed by his immediate staff of plans, hatched in Algiers by Massu and Salan and coordinated with a number of generals and military commands in France, above all Miquel at Toulouse, for a military operation in Paris and metropolitan France, involving parachutists from Algeria, Miquel's forces from his Toulouse command, and tank units from Rambouillet, outside the capital. Its purpose would have been to bring pressure to bear on parliament and government to make way for de Gaulle. That at least was the general idea of 'Operation Resurrection', although some of the more excitable elements, under the influence of the loud-mouthed Lagaillarde, saw it more as a chance to repeat in Paris the achievements of 13 May in Algiers, including an assault on the Palais Bourbon. Those involved in the plan had a certain success in spreading news about their intentions throughout the ministries in Paris, in the hope that fears of such an operation would have the effect of making its actual launching unnecessary. Coty was sufficiently impressed to talk about creating a form of fortress around the Elysée to which ministers and their staffs could withdraw. He could have been joking, but even jokes can have a deeper meaning.

De Gaulle and his men, while not above using the threat for their own advantage, were however opposed to any project which would make it appear as though he was planning to return to power as the result of a Latin-American type *pronunciamento*. This had never been his intention. In the end, the military operation and its accompanying civilian demonstrations in Paris were cancelled or at least postponed, at the urging of the Gaullist barons and of Pflimlin's own staff, authorised by him to try to prevent a *coup de force*.[5] De Gaulle himself kept his distance, but the outcome showed that both the Pflimlin government and the chief Gaullists shared a common interest in averting what might have been the beginning of civil war. The existence of the plan, with its far-reaching ramifications throughout the country, served nonetheless to show how far and fast authority was slipping away from the government's hands, in particular how disaffection within the higher command had enlarged the gap between the Army and the politicians.

This tendency received further significant confirmation with the resignation, on 17 May, of General Ely, the much-respected Chief of the General Staff. And as though to drive the point home, the French air force began flying its planes in the formation of a cross of Lorraine. There was as well, on the day of the press conference, a convincing proof of apathy on the part of the working class. The CGT called for a general strike but the order was poorly followed. In Paris, the Métro came to a halt, but the buses ran as usual, and only a handful of men came out at the Renault factories and the mines. The French workman, though he might be opposed to Gaullism and its chief, was not going to put himself to any trouble to defend the Republic from whatever threats might be facing it.

This indeed was the prevailing feeling, 'People are in no mood for violent change', *The Times* reported on 18 May, 'and want to be left in peace.' There was, it is true, along with the apathy, a sense of apprehension and expectancy. The dissemination campaign of the military plotters had some effect. Were parachutists really going to drop from the skies at any moment? Sales of newspapers doubled. Housewives began laying in extra stocks of food (as they did at the time of Suez) and supplies of rice, sugar and pasta were temporarily exhausted in the Paris groceries. But if, these precautions apart, there were open signs of jumpiness, they came not from French people but from foreigners. As is often the case, the greater the distance from the scene of action, the wilder and more inaccurate the rumours from without. From all over the world flowed reports that civil war was imminent in France. A party of sixty-eight American farmers, making a European tour, refused to leave their plane when it made a service stop at Orly. They had been told in Geneva and Rome, they said, that a revolution was going on in France, and that their lives would be in danger if they put so much as a foot on French soil.[6] In London, a daily paper reported – it was the work of a member of its London staff, sent specially to cover the situation and unversed in French ways – that thousands of civilian refugees, fearful of civil war, were quitting Paris for the open country, their cars piled high with perambulators and mattresses, a repeat, in fact, of the exodus of 1940. This innocent had failed to realise that what he had seen was the customary weekend rush from the capital. The Quai d'Orsay gave proof of the importance of normality by issuing a strong protest to the British Embassy.

Promptly at 3 p.m. on 19 May, General de Gaulle entered the huge ballroom of the Palais d'Orsay, a former railway station transformed into a hotel,* close to his headquarters in the Rue de Solférino. As was the case with so many of his so-called press conferences in the past, some of those present were not journalists at all. They included old Gaullist faithfuls such as Chaban-Delmas and Debré, less identifiable supporters making up a Gaullist claque, and writers and intellectuals; François Mauriac had Graham Greene in tow. There were, as well, of course, hundreds of real French and foreign journalists. In the streets outside, the Minister of the Interior, Jules Moch, had deployed an enormous number of riot police and *gardes républicains*, by his own calculation the biggest mobilisation of police ever to be seen in Paris.[7] He was determined that neither the extreme Left nor *Algérie française* enthusiasts were going to disturb the peace.

Since his last public appearance, nearly three years previously, the General had aged visibly and put on weight. But there was no trace of weariness about his performance. Speaking, as he usually did, without notes, his voice, mostly firm and authoritative, occasionally rising almost to a falsetto when he wished to signify irony or scorn, he parried with great skill and effectiveness the questions put to him, some of them repeating precisely Guy Mollet's three points. Beginning with the confident, indeed immodest, claim that 'I am the man who belongs to no one and who belongs to everyone', he at once clarified his earlier reference to assuming the 'powers of the Republic'. It meant, he said, those powers that the Republic had delegated – in other words, there was no question of stealing authority or possessing it by force. The procedure by which such delegation could take place could not be the normal one that had become 'so habitual that everyone is tired of [it]' – a dig at the ponderous ritual of installing a new Prime Minister after the collapse of the previous one. An exceptional procedure would have to be adopted for investiture by the National Assembly.

Already de Gaulle was building bridges – though he was not going to specify in advance their size and shape or the materials

---

* Now the Musée d'Orsay.

from which they would be made – between the existing régime and the successor which he proposed to provide. For a man so consistently caustic about the role of political parties, he showed an acute awareness of the importance of the Socialists, who, it was plain, held the key to parliamentary approval for his return to power. Unfortunately, in his desire to say nice things about Guy Mollet, he made a serious error, asserting that in 1945 Mollet, then a promising young Socialist, had stood at his side on the balcony of the town hall of Arras when he, de Gaulle, as head of the provisional government, visited northern districts soon after the Liberation – 'These are things one never forgets.' On the contrary, here was something which it would have been best not to remember, for Mollet was not only not on the balcony that day, he was serving as an officer with the French forces in Normandy. He and de Gaulle had never met. A compliment is nonetheless a compliment, and the falsity of this one was not immediately spotted by the audience at the Palais d'Orsay.

One particular question from the floor aroused the General's indignation. It concerned his attitude towards basic public liberties. His voice rising an octave, his long arms gesticulating in such a way as to indicate his incredulity that such a notion could be entertained, he replied: 'Did I ever make any assault on basic public liberties? On the contrary, I restored them . . . Why should I, at the age of sixty-seven, begin a career as a dictator?' It was a genuine and effective reminder of his wartime and Liberation role, when he led and embodied the effort to rid the country of its occupiers and restore freedom.

On Algeria, he chose to skate on some very thin ice. Recalling Lacoste's Dien Bien Phu remark, he asked: 'How could [Algerians] not revolt in the long run? [They] are now seeking a remedy for [their] misfortunes outside parliamentary coalitions . . . it is absolutely normal and natural . . . The best proof that the French of Algeria do not want . . . to break away from metropolitan France is precisely the fact that they say "Vive de Gaulle."' The only thing to do was to prevent Algeria from drawing away from France. 'Algeria must remain with us' – the nearest (but how significantly far it was) the General got to saying *Algérie française*. There was no condemnation of the plotters and the activisits in Algiers, nor indeed of those in Paris. Pressed on this point, de Gaulle said, enigmatically: 'I wish to give courage and strength to those French people who want to re-create national unity, whether they are on one side of the Mediterranean or the other.' He was able to turn Pflimlin's double-faced policy to good account by recalling that 'At present generals [in Algiers] are being called seditious persons, while up to now, as far as I know, no penalty has been inflicted on them by the public authorities [i.e. the Pflimlin government], who have even delegated more authority to them. In that case, I who have no public authority – why do you want me to call them seditious persons?' On the broader matter of the Army's role in the Algerian rebellion he was explicit: 'I understood full well the attitude and action of the military command in Algeria . . . [The Army] is normally an instrument of State, providing of course, there is a State.'

Then, having burnt no boats, having left undefined his ideas about the future of Algeria, as well as about the method by which he could 'assume the powers of the Republic', but having firmly placed his feet upon the second rung of the ladder to power, the General left Paris and went back to Colombey; or, to put it in his own special language, 'Now I shall return to my village and remain there at the disposal of the country.'

The effect of his words on the political parties was mixed. The all-important Socialists remained for the most part hostile, while Mendès-France, speaking in the debate on constitutional reform which the government, in a desperate eleventh-hour attempt to disarm the critics of the régime was trying to put through parliament, was emphatic in his censure of de Gaulle for having failed to condemn sedition. He was scarcely less critical of the government for its equivocal attitude, and called upon Pflimlin to 'condemn without reservation or compromise the agitators of all sorts, the carpet-bag politicians over there and the spokesmen of minor interests who are exploiting patriotic emotions for their own fraudulent schemes'. Pflimlin remained undeflected in his efforts to achieve a settlement with Algiers without bringing de Gaulle into the equation. The government, he declared, considered that the military commanders exercising authority in Algeria 'have obeyed our wishes to defend national unity, public order and Republican integrity'.

The Prime Minister was not alone in trying to have the best, or anyway the least bad, of both worlds. The Assembly proceeded to adopt unanimously a Socialist-inspired motion which, without containing a specific reference to the Army's role in Algeria, expressed 'to the soldiers and their commanders the nation's deep gratitude for the services already rendered to the unity of the country and the flag of the Republic'. This was a world which would have been familiar to Alice in her adventures through the looking glass, where things were upside-down and back-to-front, where demands that the Algiers rebels be condemned as the enemies of democracy could be accompanied by effusive praise for the military commanders who were covering, and in some degrees leading, the activities of those self-same rebels.

In the days following his press conference, de Gaulle began to receive important political visitors who thought it worthwhile to undertake the long drive to Colombey. (As one wag put it, it was just as well that the General had not chosen to live in Perpignan.) Antoine Pinay, the prototype 'average Frenchman', who in 1952 had been more responsible than anyone for breaking up the RPF by seducing some of its deputies, returned impressed by what the General had said about the need for national unity. Georges Boris, Mendès' friend and adviser, who as a member of Mendès' Cabinet in 1954 had come under heavy fire from the Right and some of the MRP for his alleged softness towards Moscow, took the road to Colombey, where he was treated to assurances that the Left had nothing to fear or suspect in the General's return to power. De Gaulle knew that if he was to return legally, he must win over the Left, or at least some part of it. Boris had been with him in wartime London, so was a natural left-wing figure to be thus cajoled.

On the other side of the Mediterranean, events were moving at a sharper pace. On 24 May, French people setting off on the long Whitsun weekend were astonished to learn that Corsica had seceded to the rebel camp without a shot being fired in anger. The operation had been planned mostly in Algiers, notably by Massu, covered by Salan, and was made easy by the fact that in Corsica the police, the gendarmerie and most of the prefectorial administrators put up no resistance. The island was garrisoned by parachutists, and Corsicans figured largely among the *colon* population of Algiers. It was not difficult for local conspirators, using the paras and reinforced by a group from Algiers carrying Salan's orders, to mount an operation which quickly secured the Prefecture in Ajaccio, the capital, and established Committees of Public Safety according to the Algerian pattern. Salan appointed Thomazo military governor. This was the most seditious challenge yet to the Pflimlin government and a further proof that its authority was disintegrating. Plenty of people were capable of remembering that, fifteen years earlier, Corsica had been the first area of French territory to be liberated. It was not as though the government in Paris could be alleged, even by the most excitable minds, to be about to 'surrender' Corsica, as it was suspected of wishing to do with Algeria. Was this bold new move by Algiers the prelude to an invasion of the mainland?

Salan, by this time used to crossing Rubicons, had crossed another. For the Commander-in-Chief in Algiers, possessing the delegated powers of the central government, to encourage a part of metropolitan France to secede from the rest could not be other than a seditious act. Jules Moch, the Minister of the Interior, despatched riot police from Nice, using Air France planes because military pilots were not to be trusted. They were met by paratroops and promptly joined the rebels. Undaunted, he planned to land 600 troops at Bastia, in northern Corsica, where the Socialist mayor remained loyal. But both the Army and Navy general staffs in Paris were dubious about the prospect and over many ministers' minds, Pflimlin's especially, hovered the spectre of civil war if the paras and the Corsicans resisted. Mollet wanted to know if the operation's success could be guaranteed. At a Cabinet meeting during the evening of 25 May, Moch was overruled and the operation cancelled. He later described this decision as 'disastrous, taken against my wish, on 25 May at 7.00 p.m., and which tolled the passing bell for the legal government.'[8] He himself tried to resign, but Coty persuaded him not to.

Notwithstanding its unshakeable observance of the Whitsun bank holiday weekend, the French public quickly realised the significance of developments in Corsica. Rumours of an impending invasion spread swiftly. *L'Humanité* brought out a special Sunday edition which the Ministry of the Interior promptly ordered confiscated. The press the next day expressed, across a wide range, a degree of national concern not previously registered. *Le Populaire*, the Socialist paper, was surprised that de Gaulle remained silent. *Le Figaro*'s columnist, André François-Poncet, an authentic pillar of the Establishment, wrote that the General would be 'untrue to himself if he allowed it to be thought that he is with the rebels and those engaged in sedition'. Other illustrious voices, some of them Socialist, joined the chorus demanding a sign of disapproval from the General. Vincent Auriol, the former President of the

Republic, wrote to him about 'a rebellion against the institutions and laws which France had freely chosen'. Guy Mollet, who had been planning a meeting with the General which the Corsican operation made impolitic, also wrote to Colombey, regretting in strong terms that de Gaulle had not seen fit to condemn 'the madmen who have embarked upon an attempted *pronunciamento*', which would mean that France ran the danger of being the only country in Europe to 'undergo a putsch, whose authors claim to use your name, and you keep quiet.'

But despite the uncompromising tone of Mollet's letter (he was writing in his own name, but that did not alter the fact that he was leader of the Socialist party and Deputy Prime Minister), despite the fact that in it he said he considered the General's return to power would be a mistake, it also contained implicit approval of some of the General's ideas and intentions, notably on Algeria, on resisting any thought of becoming a dictator and on refusing to contemplate a foreign policy which would isolate France from her allies. Unlike most of the rest of his party, Mollet was already halfway down the road which was to lead him in the end to accepting, even to welcoming, the General. No wonder that de Gaulle, in his reply, showed that he was satisfied with the progress of his plan for a legal return to power. 'We are indeed', he wrote, 'nearly agreed on matters that are basic.' As for Auriol's letter, it went much further in foreseeing how, once the General had disavowed the Corsican operation, he could again become leader of the nation equipped with special powers. This attitude was notably selfless on Auriol's part. In his years as President, he had had to suffer insult and calumny at the hands of Gaullist supporters and the RPF, much of it directed against his own family.

But no word of disavowal came from Colombey. De Gaulle's attitude was what it had been from the beginning: his desire not to be restored to power on the back of a military putsch was genuine, but to his thinking the only way he could prevent it and the civil war which would be likely to follow would be if he were head of the government. Without any authority, he could not even stop people from using his name. For him, the Corsican secession was just one more example of how the government of the country was falling to pieces.

After all these years it is clear, in a way it was not in May 1958, how far events played into de Gaulle's hands. And those events were not fortuitous. Even if some things did not turn out as planned – the storming of the 'GG' by Lagaillarde's students, for example – the movement to kill off the Fourth Republic was the result of months of preparation and planning by Gaullist and other disaffected networks. The General was not automatically a party to every move, every decision, but by biding his time, avoiding committing himself and letting developments take their course, he handled his ship in such a way that it could scarcely avoid finishing up in a position where the wind would blow it into harbour.

There were occasions however when de Gaulle had to exert special pressures on the helm. This was true notably over the question of a meeting with Pflimlin. In his usual lofty way, he had let it be understood, at the press conference on the 19th, that it was for 'the authorities' to approach him. ('I would . . . make it known to an authorised person what sort of procedure [for the legal transfer of power] seemed adequate to me' . . . 'I shall remain [at Colombey] at the disposal of the country'). The trouble was that despite his stream of visitors and his impressive postbag, despite Guy Mollet's letter (of which Pflimlin knew nothing at the time), no properly 'authorised person' had yet made the expected approach. Time was slipping by. He decided therefore to take the initiative himself. In his memoirs[9] he says he learnt 'from an official source'* that following the Corsican operation, military moves in France itself were planned for the night of 27/28 May. He therefore sent a message to Pflimlin saying that if the situation was not to deteriorate further, they needed to meet and that he was ready to talk to him in Paris that night. The message ended with something not far short of an ultimatum, to the effect that if Pflimlin did not agree to this, he, de Gaulle, would make public such a refusal. Through his staff, he suggested – always with an eye on the crucial factor of Socialist support – that Pflimlin should be accompanied at the meeting by Guy Mollet and Jules Moch. The latter refused to attend, and Guy Mollet, for reasons of Socialist solidarity, felt compelled to stay away also. The Prime Minister and the General were therefore alone when they met secretly that night, 26 May,

---

* Jean Lacouture says that the source was the Ministry of the Interior. If true, this suggests that by this time there was a regular channel of communication between the authorities in Paris and Colombey. (*Le Politique, 1944–1959*, p. 475.)

at the home of a faithful Gaullist, the curator of the Château of St Cloud, on the western outskirts of Paris.

Though reasonably friendly, the encounter was not a success. Once more, it was a question of where de Gaulle stood vis-à-vis sedition in Algiers and Corsica. Later accounts of the conversation differ. De Gaulle's own memoirs are particularly selective, recording that when they parted he was convinced that Pflimlin would soon step down in favour of himself.[10] According to what the Prime Minister told his staff and colleagues, he had given no such impression. On the contrary, he had made it plain to the General that no government resignation could be contemplated until the latter had publicly disavowed the events in Algeria and Corsica. Jules Moch, having been told by Guy Mollet, who had it from Pflimlin himself, wrote in his book that the General's answer to this was to voice his disapproval and scorn for the Corsican rebels, at the same time reaffirming the impossibility of saying this openly except as someone called upon by the régime to act as arbiter – i.e., the government must first resign and make way for him.[11] Pflimlin replied that it was not possible for him, who had received a legal mandate from the National Assembly, to do as the General asked. The most he could offer was a round-table meeting of national parties – i.e. excluding the Communists – to try to agree upon a formula for the legal assumption of power by de Gaulle. The latter seemed interested in this notion, but again the opposing ideas of the two men about when and in what circumstances the General should come out against the Algerian and Corsican rebels created an apparently insuperable obstacle. It was a real *dialogue des sourds* – an exchange between two deaf men. When after two and a half hours it came to an end, it was settled between them that, if it seemed necessary, a communiqué should be issued to the effect that no agreement had *yet* been reached. The General was driven back, through the dawn light, to Colombey; an exhausted Pflimlin returned to the Hôtel Matignon.

What happened next is straightforward enough to describe, less so the reasons. Unless he cat-napped in the car, the General could have had very little sleep that night. Once back in Colombey, he set to work to draft a statement which had little to do with, which indeed largely misreported, the meeting at St Cloud. It was delivered to a member of Pflimlin's staff just before noon on 27 May and made public soon after that. (Pflimlin himself, like a doctor frantically in search of a last-minute remedy for a dying patient, was at the Council of the Republic, the upper house of parliament, discussing with its Speaker the arrangements for a debate on constitutional reform.) The statement read:

> I began yesterday the regular process necessary to the establishment of a Republican government capable of assuring the unity and independence of the country. I am relying on this process to continue and on the country to show, through its calm and dignity, that it wishes to see it end successfully. In these conditions any action which affects public order, from whatever side it might come, carries the risk of serious consequences. Even in making allowances for circumstances I could not approve such actions. I expect the ground, naval and air forces now in Algeria to continue their exemplary conduct under the orders of their superior officers – to those officers I express my confidence and my intention to establish contact with them immediately.

Like most of the General's effusions, this was a skilfully drafted, multi-purpose affair. For the politicians, there was the assurance that his objective was a Republican government. For the armed forces, there was something akin to an order to observe discipline. For hotheads and adventurers, there was a clear mark of disapproval.

There are at least three possible explanations why de Gaulle acted as he did. The first and most sinister is that having got no satisfaction out of Pflimlin, and seeing the increasingly promising path to power still blocked, he decided to take matters into his own hands, even to the point of lying to France and the world. By no possible stretch of the imagination could the abortive meeting at St Cloud be said to have amounted to a 'regular process' for changing the government in his favour. If correct, this version of events would give the picture of a power-hungry man, ready in order to achieve his ambitions to resort to deceit and falsehood. Against it must be set the second explanation, which is that sometime between leaving St Cloud and drafting his statement at Colombey, he received information that Operation Resurrection – the plan coordinated between Algiers and some of the regional military commanders in France for a military operation to force the government out and bring de Gaulle in – was imminent. For two good reasons, de Gaulle wished to prevent this from happening: he had no interest or desire to accede to power in this way, and he was as conscious and apprehensive as Pflimlin and many other responsible people of the dangers, if such an operation were to be launched, of civil war, with French people killing one another.

The third and most plausible explanation why de Gaulle issued his hair-raising statement lies in a combination of the two others. As his biographer puts it, 'He was operating at a strategic level where no one could emulate him, making use of threats to overcome resistance to his assumption of power, announcing that assumption to get rid of the threats.'[12] Or, in the words of another commentator, 'He gathered into his own hands all the strings of the intrigue, those of Paris and Algiers. [He was going to] gamble with the threats which were taking shape to hasten his arrival in power, he was going to gamble with his approaching arrival in power in order to delay the threats.'[13]

Whether or not fresh information about Resurrection reached Colombey on the morning of 27 May (in de Gaulle's memoirs he claims, as already noted, that he got wind of it on 26 May), it is certain that the rumours of the previous ten days, many of them sedulously spread by the plotters themselves, of an imminent parachute drop on Paris were growing stronger. Nor were they mere rumours. A detailed timetable existed, approved by Miquel, the general at Toulouse who was to be the commander in France of Resurrection.[14] The purpose of the operation, which was to be confined to the Paris area, was defined as 'the establishment of a Republican Government of Public Safety, under the Presidency of General de Gaulle'. It provided for such details as the occupation of the airfields at Le Bourget and Villacoublay by tank units, the seizure of the Eiffel Tower, the Prefecture, the Hôtel de Ville, the Quai d'Orsay, the Palais Bourbon and the broadcasting studios, the use of paratroop reservists and ex-servicemen of the Indochinese campaign and the support of riot police and ordinary police, whose disaffection would make it impossible for the government to use them to oppose a coup. Posters and radio bulletins were to explain that this was not a military coup, but a process designed to restore General de Gaulle to power.

At 10 a.m. on 27 May, Jules Moch learnt, from a message passed from the US Consul-General in Algiers to the Quai d'Orsay, that Resurrection was due to be launched that night. Were the military plotters really preparing to move, and/or was the General using the scare to further his own designs? The answer is almost certainly yes to both questions. Jules Moch, in an article published a month later, said that 'serious troubles' were expected on the night of the 27th, and that he remained convinced that the General's 'regular process' statement had avoided the worst, and had been made for exactly that purpose and not as a trick to force the pace.[15] Mollet, writing a year later,[16] probably put it best when he said that de Gaulle was the recipient, as were government ministers, of a number of alarming reports about the state of mind of the Army and the intentions of some of its leaders, and that his desire to see the worst averted led him to take the initiative.

In any event, his 'regular process' declaration got a mixed reception in Paris. Pflimlin was understandably surprised and annoyed. This was not at all his reading of the situation as it stood when he parted from the General in the small hours of the 27th. De Gaulle had put him in an impossible position: he, the Prime Minister, had not even reported to the President of the Republic the details of the St Cloud meeting. Coty however dissuaded him from issuing a denial. After all, de Gaulle's statement, however unexpected and inaccurate, did express disapproval of military adventures and enjoined discipline in the armed services. As Jules Moch was reported as saying, 'Speaking as a militant [Socialist], I am scandalised, speaking as a Minister of the Interior, I am reassured.'[17] His colleagues in the Socialist parliamentary party were in agreement with only the first of his reactions. At a special meeting held later in the day, they voted by 111 to 3 in favour of a manifesto requiring the 'regularly invested, legal, government' to stand fast and refusing Socialist support for de Gaulle, whose action in putting himself forward 'remains by any estimation a defiance of Republican legality'. Their indignation was directed not only against de Gaulle, but against Mollet, for the lone and (so it seemed to many) devious hand he had been playing.

When the National Assembly met late that night, Pflimlin told the deputies about the St Cloud meeting, thanked de Gaulle for his disapproval of any action threatening public order, and said that the government's future was in the hands of the Chamber. He received an enormous vote of confidence on the issue of constitutional reform – 405 (including the Communists) to 165. On paper it could be argued that the Fourth Republic and its twenty-fourth government were impregnable. In fact, nothing could have been further from the truth. On a technical point, the two-thirds majority needed for constitutional reform had not, given the rite of subtracting the Communist votes, been achieved. But above and beyond that, by now there were few so deaf as not to hear, whether they liked the sound or not, the measured tread of the stone statue as it stepped down from its pedestal and began to make its fearsome way forwards. As Georges Bidault was reported as saying in the lobbies after the vote to any deputies within earshot, 'Between the Seine and you, there is only de Gaulle.'

At 2 a.m. on 28 May, after the Assembly had risen, the ministers met at the Hôtel Matignon and embarked on a fierce discussion about what the government should do next: stand firm or resign. Already the right-wing members of Pflimlin's team had decided to drop out. Some ministers, the Socialists especially, argued that, after the Assembly's vote of confidence, it would be completely irresponsible for Pflimlin to resign. There was some talk about mobilising public opinion, up to that moment so slow to react. But the drawback to that strategy was something for all to fear: it meant in the last, more probably in the first, resort cooperating with the Communists, and apart from other objections, given the attitude of the Army in Algeria and in France itself, this in turn meant running the risk of civil war. The most telling argument was developed by René Pleven, the Foreign Minister. In his quiet, unemotional way, he reminded everyone that while it was correct to say that the government was the only legal source of authority, of what did that authority consist? The Minister for Algeria could not go there, just as the Minister of the Sahara could not visit his territory. The Minister of National Defence was no longer obeyed by the Army, the Minister of the Interior had lost control of the police. 'We claim to exert power, but we do not have it.'[18]

Faced with such home truths, and by now himself convinced that as de Gaulle's return was desirable it was vital to ensure that he came in legally, Pflimlin wound up the meeting and went to the Elysée to present his resignation to Coty. The latter, and even more his staff, had been waiting and hoping for such a move, so that de Gaulle could forthwith be called upon to end the growing nightmare. But Pflimlin's resignation was not unqualified. He did not, he said, want the President to accept it until the way was clear for de Gaulle to succeed him. That would not be so until there was a clear majority in the Assembly ready to accept and approve. So the resignation was only conditional. Given the government's impotence, given the persisting threat of a military *coup de force*, this emphasis on due and proper constitutional forms might seem so much posturing. In fact, there was something admirable about the insistence of Pflimlin and others, Coty in particular, on the importance of observing legal procedures. Thé Fourth Republic may have expired because of its humiliating inability to make its limbs obey its head, but its demise was not without a certain dignity.

The 28th of May – already marked, almost before it began, by Pflimlin's effective resignation – was to be another crucial day in these protracted death-throes. Only a few hours after the Prime Minister had been closeted with the President, de Gaulle at Colombey received some military visitors from Algiers. He himself, wishing to be better informed about what was going on, had asked Salan to send someone qualified to impart such information. Nothing could have demonstrated more plainly the effective passing of power from Paris to Colombey than this request, amounting almost to an order, from de Gaulle. He even ensured that the dying government knew. about this message, and the dying government not only did nothing to impede it but sped it on its way.

General André Dulac, accompanied by three other officers, was the man Salan chose to go to Colombey. According to the book Dulac published eleven years later,[19] de Gaulle asked him what Algiers would do if the Socialists in the Assembly continued to block the way to his legal assumption of power. Dulac unfolded the details of the plan for 'Resurrection' (of whose existence de Gaulle was of course aware). De Gaulle explained that he did not wish to be the subject of such an operation, to appear as the champion of one side in the struggle. He would prefer, after a few days, to be called in by popular demand, as an arbiter, to assume leadership so as to spare the nation pointless divisions. If this account is correct, it amounts to a qualified approval by de Gaulle for Resurrection, even though he wished to play no part in it. The same approval is implicit in the message to Salan with which Dulac says the General entrusted him: 'Tell Salan that what he has done, and is going to do, is for the good of France.' Dulac and his companions flew back to Algiers, where their account of the meeting with de Gaulle was regarded by Salan as a green light for Resurrection. Delbecque, usually ready to envisage any means for achieving a Gaullist restoration, was surprised that the

General had apparently chosen to associate himself with these military threats.

The question of de Gaulle's attitude towards Operation Resurrection leads straight back to the larger one, which has already occupied some space in these pages, of how far he connived at or made use of the military and civilian conspirators. He often resorted to ambiguity as a way to avoid committing himself, but in this case there cannot be much doubt attaching to such phrases (assuming he uttered them) as he used in his message to Salan. Another account had him saying to his visitors: 'If they [i.e. the National Assembly, especially the Socialists] don't want de Gaulle, then do what is necessary.' The most plausible interpretation is that while his resolve not to be borne to power on the back of a military coup remained as strong as ever, his frustration at the continuing opposition of parliament caused him to contemplate at least the bluff, and perhaps as a last resort the reality, of a military operation, as the result of which he would emerge as a national saviour, a *deus ex machina* who would bestow upon the impending tragedy a (more or less) happy ending.

For those with long memories, his words of more than eight years earlier, when in October 1949 he addressed the National Council of the RPF, should have served as a reminder of what, in certain circumstances, de Gaulle was prepared to do:

> We shall not man the barricades to get rid of the system by force. . . . It could happen however – we have already seen it happen – that a cataclysm occurs and sweeps away what remains of public authority, just as some people were annihilated by the events of 1940. In that case – I am weighing my words – we would be the only recourse and in the general deficiency would assume all the responsibilities necessary to assure the safety of the country.[20]

Despite the intervening years of self-exile and apparent despair, this pledge still stood. The 1949 speech was made in terms of the threat then existing of a third world war and the disruption it would cause. But for de Gaulle, the same argument held good in 1958, when the threat came not from without but within. Here, amidst all the intrigues, plots and double games, lay the elemental rationale with which he was inspired as he approached the moment of decision in 1958. So far as he was concerned, this was to be no *coup d'état* but an essential act of service to his country.

Meanwhile in Paris, on the afternoon of the 28th, a giant demonstration march wound its way from the Place de la Nation to the Place de la République, the traditional itinerary of Republican, as compared with military or official, manifestations. It was organised by a largely Socialist-inspired group called the Comité d'Action et de Défense Républicain and the Communists were not invited to take part. The demonstrators marched by professions and trades – lawyers, professors, Renault workers – and among them the most striking section was composed of former prisoners in German concentration camps, wearing their pyjama-like striped garments. Predictably, the Communists refused to be kept out. Along with Mendès-France, Mitterrand, André Philip, Albert Gazier (a Socialist minister in the Pflimlin government), the leaders of the CGT and the Christian trade unions, as well as some MRP and Radical deputies and a host of other left-wing figures, walked the leading lights of the People's Party – the Communists. *L'Humanité* and *Le Populaire* claimed next day that half a million people turned out; *Le Figaro* put the figure at 150,000. Whatever the truth, it was to all appearances an impressive show of resistance to the intriguers in Algiers and Paris. 'Soustelle to the scaffold' and '*Le fascisme ne passera pas*', the crowds shouted, and '*De Gaulle au musée*', although it was noticeable that this came mostly from Communist throats. Given the traditional reputation of the Paris mob for violence of expression and action, it was a strikingly mild slogan.

But behind the façade of Republican unity there lay profound disagreements. Few of the non-Communist marchers wanted to make common cause with the Communists, isolated as they had been for the last eleven years from the mainstream of political life by the Cold War and by their own conduct. The demonstrators of 28 May may have been united in their opposition to a military *coup d'état*, but that was the only issue on which they did agree. Above all, there was no sign that ordinary French people were ready, in the popular phrase, to *descendre dans la rue* – to fight to defend their cause. The demonstration, in the words of one observer, 'turned out to be as disciplined and unexciting as a Sunday school picnic'.[21] Increasing prosperity and decreasing respect for Republican institutions as exemplified by the men and *mores* of the Fourth Republic had done much to defuse the passions of the past. For the Left, the barricades of the Commune were a cherished historical memory, not, in 1958, a realistic model.

The last episode of this fateful day took place late at night, once more at the Château of St Cloud, where forty-eight hours earlier Pflimlin and de Gaulle had met. This time the company consisted of the General, persuaded earlier by Coty to return to Paris, André Le Troquer, President (Speaker) of the National Assembly, and Gaston Monnerville, President of the Council of the Republic. It was Coty's original wish that the two parliamentarians should be accompanied by Vincent Auriol, his predecessor at the Elysée. But the latter, still without an answer to his earlier letter to the General, declined, and it was left to the other two to conduct the discussion with de Gaulle about the procedure for his legal assumption of power. No more than the earlier meeting was the occasion a successful one.

The Speaker of the Assembly, Le Troquer, a Socialist, was very conscious of his hierarchical position as the second person in France after the President. Vain, pompous and of questionable morals – his name was later to be linked with a sexual scandal involving young girls – he chose to play to the full his role as guardian of the Constitution, refusing to envisage the General's terms which were: no personal appearance in the National Assembly when it proceeded to approve or disapprove his nomination as Prime Minister; prorogation of the Assembly for a year, during which the country would be governed by special decree; and preparation of a new Constitution, to be submitted to a national referendum. Le Troquer rejected all this as smacking of a plebiscite. Although Monnerville, an agreeable native of the French West Indies, was more conciliatory, the discussion was clearly deadlocked, and de Gaulle left for Colombey, saying to Le Troquer, as he went, that 'If parliament agrees with you I will have no alternative but to leave you to have things out with the parachutists and go back into retirement, with grief as my companion.'

De Gaulle's conditions were indeed out of tune with both the spirit and the letter of the Constitution. Nor is this surprising. Not only did he despise that Constitution, he had a genuine horror of the National Assembly. Le Troquer was therefore technically on good ground when he objected. He was suspected however of harbouring other thoughts. According to Jules Moch,[22] Le Troquer had in mind the possibility that, faced with the continuing impasse, Coty would resign, whereupon he, Le Troquer, would automatically become President *ad interim* and would set about choosing a new prime minister.

For the moment, the two emissaries could do no more than report to Coty, at the Elysée, the failure of the mission, which they did at about 1 a.m. on the 29th. The President decided to make one last desperate throw. Using the right bestowed upon him by the Constitution, he dispensed with most of his night's sleep to work upon the draft of a statement which could then be read to the National Assembly. In this dramatic and unprecedented communication, made, as the President put it, 'on the verge of civil war', he announced that he had 'turned to the most illustrious of Frenchmen, to him who, in the darkest hours of our history, was our leader for the reconquest of liberty and who, having created national unity around him, refused dictatorship in order to establish the Republic'.

Conscious that the legality of what he was going to do might be challenged, Coty explained that while normally after the fall of a government, the President designated a prime minister for the Assembly to approve or disapprove, there could now be 'clearly no question of my multiplying designations' – i.e. continuing to put forward names until, as had so often happened in the past, the Assembly, largely through lassitude, finally pronounced in favour of the President's latest choice. 'There can no longer be a question of parties settling the destiny of our country behind closed doors.' Referring to the previous night's meeting at St Cloud, Coty admitted that there remained 'considerable difficulties' over his appeal to de Gaulle. 'Should I then abandon calling on the man whose incomparable moral authority would ensure the salvation of the country and the Republic?' He proceeded to give his own answer: 'I ask General de Gaulle to agree to come and confer with [me] and examine . . . what, in the framework of Republican legality, is necessary immediately for a government of national safety . . . I will then take upon my soul and conscience the decision which rests upon me.'

And if all this should come to nothing, if the path for de Gaulle's instatement remained blocked, then, said Coty's message, he himself would step down and hand over to Le Troquer, as laid down by the Constitution. The unexpressed but implicit thought was that

the choice was between de Gaulle and a new Popular Front; with
the latter prospect Coty refused to associate himself.*

This message was read at 3 p.m. on 29 May by the President of the
Assembly, Le Troquer, to a packed house, its members standing as
a mark of respect. It was said, at the time and after, that Le Troquer
sought to show his own disapproval of its contents by reading it
very fast. But he always rattled through any announcements from
his presidential chair, so that proved nothing. What was obvious
within the Chamber was that tempers were running high. At the
point where Coty spoke of his 'soul and conscience', the 140 or
so Communists ostentatiously sat down, followed by some of the
Socialists. '*Goujats*' ('boors') screamed a voice from the centre.
As the reading came to an end, chaos ensued. The Communists
hammered on their desks with their fists, and shook those same
fists at the deputies on the right, shouting at the tops of their voices:
'*Le fascisme ne passera pas.*' Then they burst into the 'Marseillaise',
which evoked in return a shower of insults from the Centre and
Right. From the national anthem, the Communists moved on to the
'Chant de Départ', the revolutionary hymn composed to mark the
fifth anniversary of the fall of the Bastille. When they came to the
resounding line '*Tremblez, ennemis de la France*', they gesticulated
furiously towards the right-hand half of the hemicycle. The past
twelve years had seen many an angry scene in the Chamber, but
nothing to equal this. For the onlooker, even one who had noted
the lack of cohesion or pugnacity in the afternoon's left-wing march,
it seemed to presage the possibility of violence and fratricidal strife
in the streets.

In Algiers meanwhile, on this 29th of May, preparations were
going ahead for the launching of Resurrection. A new factor had
come into play, in the shape of what, according to one version of
events, amounted to de Gaulle's explicit approval of the operation.
In a book published nearly a quarter of a century later by General
Jouhaud, in 1958 Army Commander in Algeria, the story is told

---

* According to one account (*Le Monde*, 29 May 1958), Coty considered that if
the parties continued to impede de Gaulle's return, the only option remaining
would be to call on Mitterrand to form a Popular Front government. This
Coty could not bring himself to do. Another name of a potential Popular
Front prime minister which went the round of the parliamentary lobbies was
that of Marcel-Edmond Naegelen, a Socialist former Governor-General of
Algeria.

of how a General Nicot of the Air Staff in Paris, enquired of the Gaullist team at the Rue de Solférino what de Gaulle's views were. One of them, Pierre Lefranc, telephoned to Colombey, explaining the reluctance of the General Staff to embark on Resurrection without de Gaulle's explicit approval. By this account, de Gaulle, at the other end of the line, expressed himself in such a way that Lefranc was able to turn to the others in the room and say that the General had given his complete agreement. This news was conveyed, first by a telephone call and then, when that was cut off, by a cable, to Jouhaud in Algiers, for him to inform Salan and Massu. A second telegram from Paris, despatched after it was known that de Gaulle was en route to the Elysée to be received by Coty, cancelled the operation.[23]

One of the difficulties in arriving at the truth about such stories, as well as about the degree of de Gaulle's complicity in the military conspiracy, is that many of them emerged in the 1962 trials of the rebellious generals, notably Salan and Jouhaud. Naturally it was in the interests of these men, on trial for their lives, to make de Gaulle, by now the President of the Fifth Republic, look as double-faced and conspiratorial as possible. Thus in the Salan trial, the Corsican deputy Arrighi, who had played a leading role in bringing the island over to the side of Algiers in May 1958, alleged that de Gaulle had sent instructions from Colombey to Algiers to prepare for the adhesion of Corsica to the rebel movement – i.e. had initiated and backed the Corsican breakaway. At the same trial Miquel, the Toulouse general who was to direct Resurrection, testified that his soundings about de Gaulle's views had evoked the response that while he, de Gaulle, did not want a parachute landing on Paris, he would accept whatever situation presented itself.[24]

As for Nicot's story, after the publication of Jouhaud's book Lefranc, who was supposed to have made the telephone call to Colombey, denied ever having made it[25] – a denial which brought a counter-denial from Nicot. These claims and counter-claims throw no light on the telegram from Paris to Jouhaud, sent after communication by cable had broken down, which purported to signal de Gaulle's 'complete agreement' with Resurrection.

Resurrection was timed to begin at 1 a.m. on 30 May. Coty was kept informed – it was in this shadow of a military coup and its possible sequel of civil war that he decided to send his message to parliament – and Jules Moch urged the prefects in the provinces not to cooperate with or accept orders from seditious elements, and if necessary to abandon their posts and go into hiding, from where they should seek to organise resistance to the coup. The government (Pflimlin's resignation was still not legally an accomplished fact) would carry on the struggle from northern France. Whether or not these precautions would have been effective, the authorities were right to take Resurrection seriously. The generals were not bluffing. They were ready to move if the way was not rapidly cleared for de Gaulle, or if the Communists went on the war-path. 'If the political parties had failed to agree on the legal return to power of General de Gaulle, then the parachutists would certainly have arrived.'[26] Nor was Coty bluffing when he threatened to resign. He really intended, if his plan to call on de Gaulle should be thwarted, to leave the Elysée, and instructed his staff to reserve a room for him at a Paris hotel for the night; his valet packed a suitcase for him.[27] It was surprising, given the nearness of the military threat, that the atmosphere in Paris and elsewhere was not more tense than it was.

The key to the situation remained where it had always been – in the hands of the parliamentary Socialists. Coty's message had done little or nothing to reassure the majority of them. Their opposition to de Gaulle was founded partly upon recent memories: had not the parties of the Fourth Republic, the Socialists foremost among them, had to withstand, over a period of years, his bruising attacks, and those of the RPF before its disintegration? But there was as well something almost visceral in their feelings about the General. The very fact that he was a military man was enough, according to the old traditions of the French Left, to condemn him. The end of the Dreyfus affair, after all, was not much more than half a century old, and that is not long in French political memory. Though there had never been any valid comparison between de Gaulle and Boulanger, the force of association was too strong to resist for many a Socialist mind, imbued with the shining notion of '*défense républicaine*'. Pierre-Olivier Lapie, whose memoirs have been quoted in the earlier chapters of this book, gives a graphic description of the meeting of the Socialist parliamentary group which followed de Gaulle's 'regular process' statement:

The comrades were besides themselves, hearing nothing, wishing to understand nothing, all talking at once. For most of them, the unilateral decision of a man [de Gaulle's statement] wounded parliamentary honour, awakened the Republican feelings concealed in their hearts, recalled the *coup d'état* of December 2 [1851, by Louis Napoleon] or, nearer at hand, the memory of 10 July 1940 [Pétain's assumption of power]. . . . Finally, the old Socialist reflex against the *képi* was felt at full strength.[28]

The first break in this Socialist wall of anti-Gaullist hostility came on the evening of the 29th with the publication of de Gaulle's reply to Auriol's earlier letter to him. The troubles in Algiers, he wrote, had been provoked by the chronic impotence of the public authorities – i.e. successive governments. Although they had spread by making use of his name, he, de Gaulle, was in no way involved. Given the situation, he had suggested forming a government, by legal means, which would restore authority and promote the adoption of a new Constitution. But, the letter went on, he had run into determined opposition from parliament. As he was not ready to accept power except from the hands of the people or their representatives, 'I fear that we are moving towards anarchy and civil war . . . In that case those who through a sectarian bias which is incomprehensible to me [he meant the Socialists] are going to prevent me from once more getting the Republic out of trouble . . . will bear a heavy responsibility. As for me, I shall have no more to do, until my death, save to live with my grief' – another form of the Corneille-like words he had used to Le Troquer after the disastrous meeting at St Cloud.

The Socialists at the Palais Bourbon considered this reply, heavy though it was with reproach for their attitude, sufficient grounds to provide a basis for negotiation. Then came the news that de Gaulle, once more making the three-hour journey between Colombey and Paris in his old black Citroën, was at the Elysée, where he was greeted by an emotional Coty. The ensuing conversation between the French President and 'the most illustrious of Frenchmen' led to the latter agreeing to form a government. The General made some concessions, notably that he would appear before the Assembly and make a short statement (though he refused to sit out the ensuing debate), and that the period during which he wanted to be granted full powers, free from parliamentary interference, would be six months rather than a year. He was probably always ready to make these concessions as a last resort, but not before, in his usual cunning way, he had won the maximum number of points for his cause. He also consented to follow the hated procedures of the Fourth Republic to the point where he would confer with the representatives of the different parties, though they would have to come all together and not one by one.

Later that night, the General's office issued a statement setting out the conditions under which he would be ready to form a government. 'I could only undertake the task of leading the State and the nation,' it read, 'if these indispensable conditions were granted to me with the frank and wide-sweeping confidence required for the salvation of France, of the State and of the Republic.' Significantly, the statement contained no direct reference to Algeria. All it did was to promise changes 'in the relationships between the French Republic and the peoples associated with it'. This was not what the *Algérie française* men were waiting to hear. As the Citroën set out on the return journey to Colombey, excitable Gaullist groups, some of them earmarked to reinforce Operation Resurrection, if it ever came, rampaged down the Champs Elysées sounding the horns of their cars and shouting '*Vive de Gaulle.*' Though the verdict of the Assembly was still an unknown factor, *The Times* correspondent felt able to tell his readers as the long day ended that 'with luck and a little good will, the French nightmare looks like drawing . . . to a close.'

The next day, 30 May, was spent by the General in wooing the Socialists, upon whom the vote in the Assembly depended. It was an effort of blandishment quite at variance with his earlier scornful refusal to have anything to do with the party system. First Auriol, then Guy Mollet, accompanied by the leader of the parliamentary party, Maurice Deixonne, went to Colombey-les-Deux-Eglises (the latter, like Mollet, a schoolteacher and confirmed anti-clerical, complained that two churches were a bit much for him). There they were treated to a fine display of sweet reasonableness. It included assurances that in the new régime the government would remain responsible to the National Assembly, that he, de Gaulle, did not intend to be the representative of the Committees of Public Safety, or govern in the name of a lot of turbulent generals and colonels, and that as concerned the component parts of the French Union, they would be given the choice between independence and inclusion within the French Community. For

Algeria, he foresaw some form of federal or confederal links with France.

The Socialist visitors returned to Paris completely won over and reported their enthusiasm to the parliamentary group. Guy Mollet, speaking at a Socialist party conference some weeks later, justified his attitude by explaining that though the General was not a Republican by origin, he knew that France was Republican and democratic. 'He had become a Republican by the light of reason.' Many of the Socialist deputies on 30 May, however, remained doubtful. Ramadier, the first Prime Minister of the Fourth Republic, spoke for them when he objected to the pressures brought to bear on parliament by the insurrectionaries in Algiers. A degree of international Socialist support for these doubters came from Mr Michael Foot, future leader of the British Labour party, in Paris to report on events for the *Daily Herald*. In one of his pieces for that paper he was disparaging about President Coty, who was, he asserted, 'the great nothing of the Fourth Republic . . . All he has in his power to bestow is the flimsy camouflage of legality.' The Minister of the Interior, rendered partly impotent by the disaffection of the police, still enjoyed enough authority to order Mr Foot's expulsion from the country.

The game, in fact, was not yet played out. In Algiers, the spectacle of de Gaulle receiving the Socialist leaders did not go down well with either the military or the civilian hotheads. This was not the death and burial of 'the system' on which they were counting. At Toulouse, General Miquel, designated the commander-in-chief in France of Operation Resurrection, was also unhappy at the turn of events. He nonetheless hesitated to give the order to launch, and came under pressure from extremists who wanted to shoot the prefect and the mayor. Private and secondary airfields all over France remained closed, by government order, their airstrips blocked by barriers.

Meanwhile de Gaulle, this time accompanied by Mme de Gaulle, returned once more to Paris in readiness for his meeting the next day (Saturday 31 May) with the leaders of the parliamentary groups. Despite his earlier insistence on 'exceptional procedure', and his scornful rejection of the ritual accompanying the fall of one government and its replacement by another, the consultations and contacts of these days began increasingly to resemble these traditional methods, so reviled by de Gaulle himself. When at the Hôtel Lapérouse, his habitual Paris address, he received the leaders of twenty-six parties and groups (the Communists were absent, though accounts differ on whether that was their own choice or because they were uninvited) and explained to them his plans and intentions, the effect was remarkable. No one knew better than he the art of seduction, when he chose to exercise it. Even old Ramadier was converted, though Mitterrand remained hostile. The General's acceptance the following day by the Assembly seemed a foregone conclusion. What was still in doubt was the size of the majority. While he set about choosing his government, the Socialist deputies and senators (i.e. members of the Council of the Republic), meeting together, voted by the narrowest of majorities – 77 to 74 – in favour of approving de Gaulle's premiership. Once again, as was the case over the European Defence Community, the Socialist party was split down the middle.

On Sunday 1 June, more than twelve years after voluntarily relinquishing the reins of government, Charles de Gaulle was voted back into power by the elected representatives of the French people. The figures were 320 for, 224 against, with thirty-five abstentions. It was scarcely the sweeping vote of confidence which the General had said he was looking for. Only forty-two Socialists were in the majority, compared with forty-nine who voted against. Like them, the Radicals were also split: twenty-four for, eighteen against. The opponents included Mendès-France. Mitterrand, within his small group, also rejected the General. Nearly all the MRP, including Bidault, voted for, as did the Poujadists and of course the Gaullist rump. The Communists and their fellow-travelling friends were solidly against.

In July 1940, only eighty deputies had stood out against Pétain's take-over of a defeated France. Now nearly three times that number sought to bar the way to him whom the President of the Republic had described as the most illustrious of Frenchmen. While there was no valid comparison between the two occasions, it was not the happiest of events, even if the 'democratic' opposition, once the Communist votes had been subtracted, numbered only eighty-three. The thought that two weeks earlier the General would have won no more than a handful of votes was not much consolation, for it simply underlined the fact that the change of hearts and minds had been brought about by military threats. Nearly thirty years later, Maurice Faure, in 1958 a rising young Radical deputy who had already held ministerial office, explained that while on that Sunday in June he had voted for de Gaulle as the only man able to avert the worst, he did so in the knowledge that the Assembly was not being given a free choice; the threat of Resurrection, and the prospect of the paras' arrival had seen to that.[29] The vast difference between the votes of 1940 and 1958 is marked by the fact that the eighty anti-Pétainists had long since achieved a kind of immortality, while the 224 anti-Gaullists were never to win a similar respect, however sincere their motives and passionate their feelings. At least the presence among the majority of nearly half the Socialist deputies meant that the unrewarding and rigid division of French political opinion into Right and Left had been partially avoided.

Despite the General's strenuous efforts to charm the political parties into accepting him, uncertainty prevailed until the last moment. His appearance before the Assembly was first announced for 10 a.m., then for an hour later. Rumours began to circulate that he would not appear at all unless he could be sure of 400 votes. During the morning, according to the evidence given by Salan at his trial for insurgency in 1962, Guichard telephoned to him in Algiers with the warning to stand by – i.e. to be ready to launch Resurrection – as things were going badly. Finally however, at 3 p.m., the General arrived at the Palais Bourbon, whose precincts were surrounded by large forces of police and security troops. He entered the Chamber together with a crowd of deputies making a late arrival and at first was hardly noticed. When his tall figure was spotted there was applause from the Centre and Right. He sat alone on the empty ministerial benches until called to speak and then, from the rostrum, delivered his short speech – most of which, contrary to his usual unaided oratory, he read in unemotional tones. He was heard in silence, even the Communists remaining quiet.

Cast along the broadest lines, the speech nonetheless gave a fair summary of what de Gaulle proposed to do. If elected, he said, he would ask for full powers for six months, at the end of which 'the public powers will be able to resume the normal course of their functioning' – i.e. parliamentary government would begin a new life. His plans for constitutional reform were to be based on the three principles of universal suffrage, a proper division of powers, and the responsibility of government to parliament. On Algeria, he said very little, contenting himself with the pledge to 'organise the relations between the French Republic (under its new Constitution) and the peoples associated with it'. Then, with only the slightest of rhetorical flourishes about the 'unity, integrity and independence of France', he left the Chamber and returned to his hotel to await the Assembly's vote.

His choice of ministers had already been announced. Far from sweeping away all the relics of the past, the General had included many of the old familiar faces in this team: Guy Mollet and Pflimlin as Ministers of State, Pinay at the Ministry of Finance, a Radical at Education, and MRP at Labour. Much of the rest of the team was made up of non-political figures, senior officials such as Couve de Murville, an Ambassador, who was created Foreign Minister. If the Fourth Republic were not so obviously on its death-bed, one could have thought it was being given a powerful life-restorative. This display of continuity between the past and the future moved de Gaulle to the sardonic comment that 'We only need MM. Poujade, Maurice Thorez and Ferhat Abbas [a prominent FLN leader] and we would all be here.'[30] No wonder that Algiers was in a state of consternation: apart from Michel Debré, who was given the Ministry of Justice, where preparing the new Constitution would keep him fully occupied, the prospective government contained none of the well-known representatives of the *Algérie française* school of thought. Was it conceivable that de Gaulle, once in power, was going to betray the hopes and interests of those who had helped to put him there?

The answer to that question was in time to be yes, but on 1 June 1958, and in the debates which followed and resulted in the General being granted all his conditions, that as yet unknown factor played no part. What did concern many deputies – and here they were reflecting a large measure of public opinion – was precisely the opposite consideration: that de Gaulle was being swept into power as the result of plots and plotters. Mitterrand made the point dramatically when he said that while in 1944, appearing before the first Consultative Assembly, the General had honour and the nation as companions, his companions now, whom no doubt he had not chosen, were 'a *coup de force* and sedition'. Mendès-France felt just as strongly. He could not vote for de Gaulle, he said, because it would be a vote taken under the constraint of insurrection and the threat of a military coup. He referred to individual threats made against certain deputies, to blackmail by threat of civil war, and concluded that the government was being imposed upon the Assembly 'by the same men' (he was thinking of his experiences as

Prime Minister when his Tunisian policies were undermined by the North African lobby) 'who in the past have destroyed all attempts at a reasonable and humane solution in North Africa'.

There is no question that large numbers of people, while greatly preferring de Gaulle to the parachutists and the wild men of Algiers, while cherishing no affection or respect for the existing system, also felt that the country had been duped and outmanoeuvred by sections of the Army and by the Algerian *colons*. But there was also, in this attitude, a degree of having it both ways which the editor of *Le Monde* was quick in the case of doubting deputies to identify.[31] They were resorting once more, he wrote, to 'one of the wretched tricks which degraded and finally lost the Fourth Republic'. This consisted of the argument that if the General failed (to get the situation under control) they would be comparable to the eighty heroes of 1940. If he succeeded, they could join in the victory and share its fruits. Beuve-Méry, whose attitude towards de Gaulle, though fluctuating, had more often than not been one of reluctant admiration, concluded that he, de Gaulle, now had a right to 'the loyal cooperation of his fellow citizens'.

This is what he quickly got. A public opinion poll carried out later in June showed that of those questioned 83 per cent (against 4 per cent) had confidence in de Gaulle to restore obedience in the Army, 70 per cent (as against 8 per cent) believed he could reform the Constitution, 68 per cent (as against 14 per cent) saw him as the restorer of national unity. (Significantly, only 44 per cent as against 18 per cent felt he could solve economic questions, the field in which most of the governments of the Fourth Republic, including de Gaulle's own post-Liberation administration, had shown themselves, in differing degrees, to be incompetent.)

But before the days of the Fourth Republic could be effectively numbered, it was necessary to make arrangements for the birth of its successor. Here de Gaulle ran into serious difficulties with the Assembly. He had asked to be granted special powers in three respects: Algeria, executive power to govern by decree for a period of six months, and constitutional reform. The bill affecting Algeria went through both the Assembly and the Council of the Republic without difficulty (the same sort of power had been accorded to the Mollet government in March 1956). The second bill also passed, although not so easily. But it was over the third, involving constitutional reform, that the real battle was joined. For the General, who had spent many of the last twelve years excoriating the inadequacies of the 1946 Constitution, this was crucial. He did not share the widely held view that the problems of decolonisation, above all in Algiers, had led to paralysis. For him, it was the other way round: the paralysis of the system had led to disastrous colonial wars. It followed that the most urgent task was to change the system, enabling it to resolve problems and conflicts.

The bill embodying the germ of this constitutional reform seemed, on its first appearance, to give de Gaulle's government constituent powers which did not require reference back to the Assembly. Although it was ridiculous to compare de Gaulle with Pétain, to fail to recognise the differences in the situation of 1940, when enemy forces occupied half France, and that of 1958, the shadow of the vote of 10 July 1940 by which the Assembly handed over power to Pétain lay darkly over the Palais Bourbon. It had been precisely this memory which had led a majority of the 1946 Constituent Assembly to opt for a system which left the Assembly with sovereign power and the President of the Republic with severely limited authority. The relevant universal suffrage committee of the Assembly therefore amended the bill in a way to restore to parliament the control, if not the initiative, over constitutional reform. At that point in the evening of 2 June, the General came down to the Palais Bourbon to try to salvage the bill.

For someone on record with his dislike of the Assembly and its ways, he seemed remarkably relaxed and easy, joking and talking with his colleagues on the ministerial bench as though he had been in parliament for a lifetime and liked it. But his tone was serious when he rose to warn the deputies that were they to accept their committee's redraft of the bill, his government would resign. No one in the Assembly, he asserted, had suggested that the existing system should be maintained. He also claimed that there was total agreement that the Assembly as constituted was incapable of effecting a real reform of institutions. In a moving passage about some of his opponents – he was surely thinking, among others, of Mendès, his one-time Minister and member of the Free French Forces – he said that among them were certain men to whom he remained 'profoundly attached for all sorts of reasons which have to do with the past and which I hope may hold good also for the future'. But these amiabilities did not deflect him from his main purpose, which was to ensure that parliament gave him the mandate and the means to effect an efficient reform of the Constitution. There can be little doubt that even as he spoke, so eloquently and reasonably – at one moment he raised a laugh all round the Chamber by referring to 'the pleasure that I have this evening at finding myself among you' – memories must have been running through his mind of the situation twelve years previously, when as head of the provisional government he had had to sit on the sidelines and watch the parties in the Constituent Assembly prepare a Constitution that promised and proved to be disastrously unworkable.

In the end, a compromise was sought and found. De Gaulle gave two assurances – that constitutional reform presupposed the existence of a National Assembly elected by universal suffrage, and that the powers of the President of the Republic and of the Prime Minister would remain distinct – and the Assembly voted for a bill which, according to a concession by the government, allowed a parliamentary consultative committee a role in the process of constitutional reform. The majority – 356 for, 161 against, with 73 abstentions – was not only larger than the General had secured for his investiture and included some of the previously hostile Socialists, but fulfilled the constitutional requirement of a two-thirds majority, thus obviating the need for an immediate referendum. The next morning, 3 June, the General, enlarging his unlikely career as a parliamentarian, went to speak for his bill to the Council of the Republic. There things went more smoothly and the bill was carried by a huge majority.

At last de Gaulle and his government, having secured all the powers he had asked for, were firmly in the saddle. Officially, the Fourth Republic was still in existence, with de Gaulle as Prime Minister, operating from the Hôtel Matignon, and Coty still the tenant of the Elysée. But no one had the least doubt about the real position: with parliament prorogued and a government equipped with far-reaching powers, the Fourth Republic had been put to sleep until, six months later, it could be replaced by its successor, whose clothes would be tailored by hand to fit the lofty figure of the General. No wonder he said to the hall porter at the Hôtel Lapérouse, on returning there late at night after the final session of the Assembly, '*Albert, j'ai gagné.*'[32] Even more revealing were his reported words to Delbecque, who had hastened from Algiers to see the conquering hero. 'Bravo, Delbecque,' he said. 'You played well.' Then he added: 'But you have to admit that I played well also.'[33]

His claim is borne out by the facts; he had played very well indeed. But whether he was always entirely scrupulous as to the rules of the game remains an open question. It is one which many French people still tend to shy away from. Nearly twenty-seven years after the events described in this chapter, a television programme about the *'treize mai'* 1958 and its consequences, transmitted on 19 January 1985, gave the results of an opinion poll organised especially for the programme. To the question 'Do you think that the return of General de Gaulle was the result of a plot?', 33 per cent of those questioned replied Yes, 25 per cent No, and 42 per cent had no answer.[34]

CHAPTER 12

Epilogue: 'Au revoir, Monsieur Coty'

More than thirty years after the events described in the last chapter, Michel Debré, one of the architects of the Fifth Republic and a man who for a long time before 1958 had worked single-mindedly for the return of General de Gaulle, replied with a scornful negative to the question of whether the Fourth Republic could have been saved: 'Of course not, it was unsavable.'[1]

To men of his convictions, the collapse of the hated régime, with its malfunctioning institutions and lack of authority, was inevitable sooner or later, and the sooner the better. That collapse duly came, but *pace* Debré, there was little predetermined about it. This book has recorded the various mishaps and breakdowns which, like milestones, marked out the path leading to the burial ground of the unloved and discredited system, but this kind of treatment is greatly helped by hindsight, indeed would be impossible without it. Although at the time more and more people, apart from Debré and his friends, were coming increasingly to feel, with each successive government crisis, that the *crise de régime* was at hand, very few were expecting or hoping for the return of the General. At the end, the attitude of the public was one not so much of indifference as of reluctance to back either the status quo or the designs of the wild men in Algiers. One French historian has attributed the final disintegration to 'a sort of Gaullist gas, to begin with at very low pressure, [which] was able to spread everywhere because there was no resistance to it.'[2]

What happened in May 1958 was not a revolution but a change of régime, brought about by a relatively few determined men who knew how to manipulate the state of discontent prevailing in civil and military circles, first and foremost in Algeria. Parliamentary government finally reached a point where its authority became so paralysed that a special form of *coup d'état* could be organised and carried forward until in the end the sovereign power, as vested in parliament and president, was glad to welcome and legalise it, in preference to the other, dreaded, alternative of civil war. Though historical analogies are rarely exact, there are a number of approximate precedents in recent French history for what occurred in 1958. In each case, the majority of people, alarmed or bewildered by the turbulent waters threatening to engulf them, turned almost instinctively to a known saviour figure. Thiers in 1871, Clemenceau in 1917, Poincaré in 1926, Pétain in 1940: all these men shared with de Gaulle the same experience of having at one moment played a leading role, subsequently abandoning it, voluntarily or otherwise, and later being summoned back by popular acclaim, which in its turn derived from a feeling of confidence in a leader already tested and proven.

Parliamentary democracy is a difficult piece of machinery to operate in any country. The French, caught since the Revolution in a love–hate relationship between freedom and authority, seem to find it especially difficult, with the result that after living with its imperfections for a time, they periodically reveal a tendency to have recourse to a famous name or figure who will provide the strong government they think they need. (This is not to suggest that the Fifth Republic, with or without de Gaulle, is a form of elected dictatorship. Parliament exists, elections are held regularly, individual liberty is assured. But anyone with personal experience of parliamentary life under the Fourth Republic, with its recurrent crises and shifting majorities, will probably admit that the National Assembly of those days provided a more exciting stage to act upon than does its successor. In these times (1991) the semicircular Chamber in the Palais Bourbon often has only a sparse attendance and no longer echoes, as it once did, to the clash of party rhetoric and passion. Stability has been achieved at the price of tedium.)

There are many interwoven strands in the tapestry depicting the Fourth Republic's unsuccessful attempts to combine freedom with discipline. Some of them can be traced back to the very issues to which the revolutionaries of 1789 and after failed to find a satisfactory answer. They include the reluctance of most of the electorate in the post-war period, heavy with the memories of Vichy, to countenance strong government; the sharp divorce between the French citizen as a man or woman and that person as an elector; the *esprit frondeur* which dwells in the mind of every normal French man or woman and causes them to rail against and mock those who are trying to rule them; and, most important of all where the Fourth Republic's capacity to survive was concerned, a generalised unwillingness to face up to the issue of decolonisation. Many people in London (or The Hague) found it difficult to accept, after the war, that the days of European colonial empires were numbered. But they were less numerous and influential than those in France, who allowed their hearts to overrule their heads by subscribing to the theory that for overseas territories which owed their creation or development to French genius, time had stood still, that there was no reason to make any important adjustments to the pre-war status quo. Indeed, an important extension to the theory was that not making such changes would help to ensure that France remained a great power, with a leading role to play in the world.

One factor contributing to this last trend was the words and doctrines supplied by General de Gaulle and his followers. He did not confine himself to an unchanging barrage of scorn for the system he sought to replace. He also exerted an influence on thinking about colonial questions, the rock upon which the Fourth Republic foundered. Despite his display of apparent liberalism at the Brazzaville conference (p. 35), despite his private acceptance, long before 1958, of the inevitability of a change in the status of Algeria, de Gaulle's views in 1946, when the Constitution was in the making, were inflexibly orthodox. In the Epinal speech of September 1946, he declared it to be essential 'that the French Union be French – i.e. that France maintains its control over the Union's foreign policy, defence policy, communications and economic affairs.'[3] The belief, inherent in these words, that French greatness depended upon the untrammelled retention of her empire, was shared, among others, by Bidault, who imposed it upon the Constitution-making process in such a way as to get the French Union off to an unhappy start. But de Gaulle's words, and the subsequent emphasis of Gaullist propaganda upon the iniquity of giving anything away to the nationalists in overseas France,* had a marked effect upon the rest of the MRP, a party whose natural

---

* In 1947 de Gaulle threatened, once he regained power, to impeach anyone responsible for the loss of any French territory: see J. Lacouture, *Ho Chi Minh* (Paris, Seuil, 1967), p. 15.

instincts would otherwise have inclined it to liberal and generous ideas on colonial matters.

Once the RPF had been created, it and the MRP found themselves bidding for much the same votes. It was inevitable but not conducive to forward thinking that the MRP should be constantly aware of the need to give proof of its imperial virility. This ultimately proved to be the party's nemesis. As it emerged from the Resistance, the MRP was perhaps the most promising new phenomenon in post-war French politics. Centre or Centre–Left in outlook, the embodiment of the will for reconciliation between Church and State, it should have provided an exemplar for other parties and politicians of like mind to follow and associate with. It did indeed play a key role in almost every coalition government, and to its credit took the lead in moving in the direction of European integration. But its colonial ideas, and the responsibilities its leaders assumed over the Indochinese war, caused it to become hopelessly enmeshed in an unpopular and unsuccessful enterprise. The result, so harmful to itself and to the pattern of politics, was that the promise and hopes of earlier times were replaced by disillusion and discredit.

The special problem for France of decolonisation could not be better defined than by Professor Alfred Grosser: 'To accord freedom to the overseas populations, the only parliamentary majority was one including the Communists; to defend the freedom which Communism would destroy, the only majority was one which included those who would refuse to grant freedom in Africa and Asia.'[4] In other words, the forces of the Right were needed to combat the Communist threat, while the Communists were a necessary (but suspect to the point of being unusable) part of any majority capable of supporting a policy of decolonisation.

Grosser adds that 'Italy without colonies and Britain without a Communist electorate were better placed.' Both points are apposite, that about Italy especially so. Since the foundation of the Italian Republic, its record of governmental instability has been just as bad, and for some of the same reasons, as that of the Fourth Republic in France. Yet there has been no upheaval there comparable to that set in motion by the events of 13 May 1958 in Algiers. Parliamentary democracy has continued to function, however erratically and whatever the degree of alienation of most Italians from their political system. It could of course be maintained that Italy exists as a modern State despite, and not because of, her government and institutions. The near-chaos of her régime of political parties is no doubt one of the reasons why, notwithstanding the strength of her economy and the skills of her people, Italy fails to occupy, as post-1958 France does, a prominent place on the international stage. But these arguments do not alter the fact that Italy, with the largest Communist party in Western Europe and a gravely defective political machine, was never called upon to face the colonial challenge that confronted and baffled governments in Paris.

A powerful Communist party, confined by its allegiances and the pressures of the Cold War to the political wilderness, was one of the impediments to the effective operation of the system. Another, just as influential, was the post-Liberation acceptance by the major political groupings of the party machine as the mainspring of doctrine and management. This had the effect of making individuals less important than their party programmes. Brought about by the belief that excessive individualism had contributed largely to the decadence of the Third Republic, this evolution was at once the cause and result of the new electoral law, another bad fairy's gift at the cradle of the Fourth Republic. It substituted for the old constituency vote (the majority system) the *scrutin de liste* involving proportional representation. With considerable but not fundamental alterations (e.g. the *apparentements* of 1951), this electoral arrangement lasted throughout the period, with the consequence that the party system, whose impact upon the Third Republic had been greatly softened by the personal links existing between elector and candidate – voting for a man rather than an idea – remained one of the monoliths of the Fourth Republic. Vincent Auriol, in a letter written in 1958, expressed the view that proportional representation was the principal cause of the disease that ate away the régime.[5]

At a very early stage, de Gaulle had warned against these dangers. The State, he said, cannot be built or made to function on the basis of the many and profound divisions among French people, whom the parties represented. Since no single party had sufficient authority to govern the country, there could, he rightly foresaw, be only a series of coalitions in which the inter-party differences would prevent any consistent policy-making. The final result would be that the State 'becomes a sort of territory to be conquered and divided among the parties, while other forces [e.g. the Communists] try to dominate it by taking advantage of its weakness and confusion.'

This analysis, read today, has the truth and simplicity of a Euclidean proposition. But at the time (1946), such an attack on the party system, coming from one who had himself exercised from a lonely eminence the highest powers, looked like a bid for personal power (see chapter 2). As such, it served only to encourage the parties, especially those of the Left, to exaggerate their sense of 'Republicanism'. The result was a Constitution which placed all effective power in the hands of the National Assembly and its committees, making the government responsible to the Chamber, and the Chamber, for the five years of its mandate, responsible in effect to no one. Though there was a provision for the dissolution in certain circumstances of parliament, only one Prime Minister in twelve years ever made use of it (see chapter 8), with unforeseen and unfortunate results.

The Constitution, approved with the narrowest of margins by a lukewarm electorate, was so full of faults that its revision ought to have been an obvious and urgent need. Many attempts were indeed made to revise it. Of its 106 articles, only two were not the object of suggested reform.[6] But the conditions laid down for revision were difficult of fulfilment: for the final reading of a revision measure, majorities consisting of two-thirds of the Assembly and three-fifths of the two Houses voting together were needed. And apart from this numerical obstacle, any significant amendment would have had to call for a limitation upon the sovereign powers of the Assembly. The required majority could never be found for that. With much difficulty, the two Houses agreed in 1954 to some minor revisions. But at least until Pflimlin's eleventh-hour, fifty-ninth-minute efforts, it was a more or less accepted fact that the régime, though it had few friends or defenders, was incapable of reforming itself. It was precisely because of this that de Gaulle, in June 1958, fought and won the battle to keep responsibility for drawing up the new Constitution as far away from parliament as possible.

Whether it was men or institutions who were most to blame for the failure of the Fourth Republic is still a point of contention in France. Mendès-France, the only politician who managed, for a brief period in 1954–5, to rise above the thrust and pull of the parties, the lobbies and pressure groups, always considered that it was men, and their abuse of institutions, who were most at fault.[7] They did not, he thought, rise to the levels of the problems confronting them. It is undeniable that the defects of the Constitution were made worse by the way in which it was so often disregarded – by the habit, for example, of prime ministers handing in their resignation when a confidence vote against them in the Chamber, while negative, fell short of the constitutional majority which made resignation mandatory.

Moreover, as Mendès himself had every reason to remember, the shortcomings of men and institutions alike were aggravated by the unruly methods of work in parliament and government: long night sittings in the Chamber, inadequate control by the executive over the French parliamentary equivalent of 'government business', ministerial and Cabinet meetings at all hours of the day and night, protracted wrangles between political parties over the distribution of government jobs. In his diary for 1948, Auriol gives a description, at once amusing and deplorable, of himself and his staff walking about in the Elysée gardens reciting poetry at three o'clock of a summer morning, while they waited for news of whether the squabbling between the Socialists and MRP over who was to have which ministerial post was going to allow André Marie, the Prime Minister-designate, to form the new government. (No one was more critical than Auriol himself of the way in which the system functioned, or rather failed to function. His diaries are full of passionate denunciations, which de Gaulle himself could not have improved upon, of men, parties and institutions alike. At the same time, Auriol was continually conscious of his responsibility as protector of the Constitution, whatever its blemishes.)

These bad habits imposed a formidable strain on ministers, above all the Prime Minister. For the forty-five days in 1952 when he held that office, Edgar Faure lost more than four kilos in weight, and as he said afterwards was saved from physical collapse only by 'the perennial instability of governments'. His two experiences as Prime Minister led him to make a positive case not only for the frequent fall of governments but for nocturnal sittings of the Assembly: 'The need for crises in certain circumstances', he wrote, long after the Fourth Republic was dead and buried, 'is of the same order as night sessions. Both make it possible, under the effect of lassitude, to approve of indispensable but difficult decisions which would otherwise have been indefinitely refused or postponed.'[8]

A good deal of supporting proof can be summoned up for Mendès' point about the inadequacy of the Fourth Republic's leaders. Previous chapters have recounted how some of these men, many of them of real worth and ability, repeatedly looked truth in the face and then turned away from it. Armchair criticism is all too easy, but it is tempting to speculate on what would have happened had national servicemen (the *contingent*) been sent to Indochina; the end of the war there might not have been so inglorious for France, the regular Army might not have been so alienated from and hostile to the political régime in Paris. The General Staff were always urging it; the politicians, with an eye to public opinion and their electoral prospects, hung back, failing to give a lead. If the authors and supporters of the European Defence Community had followed up their original bold impulse with more initiative and resolve, they might have got it through parliament and thus avoided the long hiatus, so damaging to France's international standing as well as to the cause of effective coalition government at home. If the men in power had felt able, as the cost and burden of the Algerian war mounted, to say in public what many of them began to think and say in private about the myth of pretending that Algeria was an integral and inalienable part of metropolitan France, perhaps the events of May 1958 would never have occurred. All these decisions and actions would at the time have been difficult and unpopular, evoking strong reactions from those who opposed them. But as Mendès had pointed out, to govern is to choose, and in all these cases there was a signal failure to make the choice.

The Fourth Republic, like most other régimes the world over, had its fair share of mediocre and pusillanimous ministers (some of whom kept reappearing on the ministerial merry-go-round each time a government fell and was replaced by another). But the principal reason for lack of firm leadership and bold decisions was not so much moral cowardice as the stark facts of parliamentary arithmetic. Previous chapters have described how once the exclusion of the Communists had shattered the shaky and artificial structure of the post-war tripartite coalition, there were as many majorities as there were problems. The government of the day could hope to find among its potential supporters a majority (but not of course the same one) for or against *dirigisme*, for State subsidies for Church schools or against them, in favour of EDC or of its rejection, for continuing the war in Indochina or for a negotiated peace. Agreement on all these points – in other words, on a statesmanlike programme designed to serve the national interest – was rarely if ever possible. Only when an advanced state of weariness or alarm prevailed among the deputies, who on such occasions were presumably reflecting the feelings of their constituents, was a satisfactory consensus obtainable. Even that did not last, once the immediate needs of the moment had been met. Mendès' own experience was a case in point. He won massive support for his negotiations to end the Indochinese war but six months later found himself as much a victim of the Chamber's relentless scoreboard, itself the mirror of what de Gaulle had called 'the profound divisions among French people', as his predecessors and successors.

Without absolving either men or institutions for having helped to bring the State to the edge of the abyss, a case can be made out that the governments and parliament of the Fourth Republic, often accused of being isolated from public opinion and distracted by arcane rites and rituals, in fact reflected faithfully – all too faithfully – the opinions, or lack of them, of the electorate: indifference to the war in Indochina, divided views over EDC, inability or unwillingness to face up to the realities of the Algerian situation. 'The faults of the Fourth Republic arose from its being too responsive . . . Its weaknesses . . . were the weaknesses of the nation it represented too well.'[9]

The arguments about the responsibility of men as against institutions can be prolonged *ad nauseam*. Blame probably needs to be distributed evenly between the two. In 1954, just at the moment when Mendès became Prime Minister, *Le Figaro* ran a series of articles reporting the answers of five prominent politicians to the question, 'How can the political authority of France be restored?' Apart from Mendès himself, the five included René Mayer, a former Prime Minister, Lecourt, leader of the MRP in the Chamber, Chaban-Delmas. the Gaullist leader, and the Socialist Naegelen, a former Minister and former Governor-General of Algeria. Their replies reveal, at a time when the French Republic was eight years into its life, a forthright recognition that the system was not working, combined with a sense of hopelessness about any possible remedies. Mayer and Lecourt both deplored the unlimited powers of the Assembly. Chaban-Delmas voiced the conventional Gaullist doubts about 'the Mandarin system being abolished by the Mandarins themselves'. Naegelen and Mendès were more inclined to blame policies – or the lack of them – than institutions. The articles were summed up by André Siegfried, who struck the most depressing note of all when he asked whether 'these experienced and vigorous leaders', were they to find themselves in the seat of power (as Mendès was on the point of doing), would 'do better than their predecessors – better than they themselves did – when they were in power'.

What is beyond dispute is that the French people, by their decision of 28 September 1958 in the referendum on the Fifth Republic's Constitution, convincingly rejected the theory and practices of the Fourth. The new draft, the work not of a Constituent Assembly but of de Gaulle's government and a restricted group of experts and parliamentarians, embodied the ideas of the Bayeux speech of twelve years earlier: a stronger executive, in the shape of greatly enhanced powers for the President of the Republic, correspondingly diminished powers for parliament, and new arrangements for the relationship between executive and legislature. According to these, it became the responsibility of the opposition, should it wish to challenge the government, to show that it could provide a governing majority, instead of the government having constantly to seek the confidence of the Chamber. In a record 85 per cent turn-out, four out of every five of those voting approved the new Constitution. In metropolitan France, 17,669,000 said Yes (79.25 per cent), 4,624,000 said No (20.75 per cent).

Less than three years earlier, in the general elections of 1956, the Communist Party alone had garnered more than 5 million votes. Nothing could have shown more clearly the earthquake effect of the events of May 1958. Not only did about 30 per cent of Communist electors, hitherto the most consistently stable body of opinion, desert the party, but both the Communists and those sections of the non-Communist Left who voted No had made it plain during the referendum campaign that their vote would not be one in favour of the spurned Fourth Republic but for a method of Constitution-making different from that laid down by de Gaulle.

The result of the vote on 28 September was a striking contrast with the 1946 referendum on the Fourth Republic's Constitution, which gained the approval of only one-third of those voting. Just as the first of the post-war referenda – on whether to reinstate the Third Republic or draw up a blueprint for its successor – resulted in a massively backed decision to break with the past, so in 1958 the mass of opinion, forgetting or disregarding the intrigues and blackmail of only four months earlier which had helped to bring de Gaulle back to power, expressed its confidence in him and his ideas of how France should be governed.

In fact, the so-called break with the past was not as abrupt or complete as it seemed. The men and institutions of the Fourth Republic might be discredited in popular imagination, but the government of the Fifth remained, as before, responsible to the Assembly. The President of the Republic and the Prime Minister continued to be two separate persons with separate functions. Whatever suspicions might have been entertained in the past about de Gaulle's supposed intentions, the new system was not a presidential one. As for men, the General expressly recognised the worth of leaders like Pflimlin, Mollet and Pinay by including them in his government, where they contributed towards the drafting of the Constitution. Nevertheless, that Constitution was the tangible expression of de Gaulle's long-held belief that, as he put it, 'the French nation will flower again or perish according to whether the State has or has not strength, constancy and prestige enough to guide it in the way it should go.'[10] The 1946 Constitution was made against de Gaulle, its 1958 successor for him. Those trying to operate the earlier model had to suffer his constant sniping; he laboured under no such disadvantage.

From a later perspective it is possible, as the preceding pages have already suggested, to present a rather more favourable view of the Fourth Republic's record than its many critics are ready to allow. Certainly the instability of governments and their frequent failure to manage the national finances often revealed a lamentable spectacle to French and world opinion. It was little consolation for French officials stationed abroad during this time to note, as the wife of one such representative in London recalled years later,[11] that the more frequently governments in Paris fell, the more sympathetic their English friends became. Those friends probably did not grasp fully the intractable nature of the French situation. The exclusion of the Communists from government, the coming of the Cold War and the foundation of de Gaulle's RPF imposed on the centre parties and majorities who had to govern the country strains unknown to British or American political life. The Third Force coalitions, so often accused of *immobilisme*, were nevertheless able to fight off the double challenge while ensuring that personal rights and liberties remained intact and the work of reconstructing the economy continued. Their leaders could without shame or exaggeration have re-echoed the reply given by the Abbé Sieyès to the question of what he had done during the Revolution: 'I survived.'

A good idea of the ardour of this battle on two fronts is conveyed in a passage from the Auriol diaries for 1951, written in the wake of the general election that made the Gaullists the largest party in the Assembly after the Communists. He is explaining his reluctance to turn to de Gaulle:

> I do not want to call on someone whose purpose is to overthrow a constitution of which I am guardian. He also makes a public show of his scorn for [other political parties] and relies only on his own party . . . which is a totalitarian party, grouped round his person . . . This is simply personal power . . . I know he is a true patriot . . . but we nearly lost the régime and our freedom to the Communists, and I am not going to hand over the Republic to adventure and the unknown.[12]

Accounts of normality make for uninteresting reading; good news is no news. This probably explains why, apart from grumbles and criticisms, comparatively little mention is to be found in contemporary records of what life under the Fourth Republic was really like for the ordinary citizen. In the immediately post-war period, shortages, the black market, war damage and social unrest made it often a precarious affair, but that was true of most of the rest of Europe, victorious or vanquished. As time went on, as the Marshall Plan began to take effect and efforts at financial stability represented by the stewardship of Mayer or Petsche or Pinay or Faure achieved a measure of success, so daily existence resumed something of its normal tempo, with the quality of life steadily improving. The leader-writers and political pundits in the capital were ready at every government crisis with their prophecies of doom and disaster. Outside Paris, in the countryside and the provincial towns, most people went their way largely unconcerned about the dramas at the Hôtel Matignon or the Palais Bourbon, the greater part of them content to share in the boom of prosperity which, for the five years preceding May 1958, nothing had been able to stop. A journey through the provinces at any time between, say, 1950 and 1958 was a constant reminder of the gulf of feeling and attitude that habitually separates the intensity of the Paris atmosphere from the more phlegmatic approach of the people in the country towns and villages.

This refusal to get excited about large national issues was at best a valuable contribution to stability and continuity, a corrective to the antics of the politicians in Paris. At worst, it came close to apathy. The 1956 general election was a case in point. Provoked by Edgar Faure's bold dissolution of parliament, the election was supposed to indicate the general will about what should be done over Algeria. In fact, in the absence of any clear message from the party leaders and programmes, it indicated almost nothing at all. The new Chamber was even more divided than its predecessor. In terms of yielding any benefit from the democratic process, the elections had served no more purpose than, for example, an inquiry into the colour of the voters' eyes.

There was however nothing apathetic about another battle which was fought during these years all over France. It was one between the upholders of the commercial and social status quo and the protagonists of modernisation and economic reform, in general terms between Poujadism and the school of thought represented by Mendès and Monnet (though the two men held sharply opposing views on many points). By 1958, there was no question as to which trend was winning. Retailing, in the Fifties, saw its sales increase by 40 per cent, and the beneficiaries were not the small shop-holders championed by Poujade, or even the big Paris stores, but the multiple chain suppliers, such as Uniprix, and the cooperatives. Service industries were increasing all the time, the number of air passengers doubled, so did the telephone traffic. A consumer society was coming into being, bringing in its wake not just a remarkable display of economic growth – industrial output increased by more than 50 per cent in seven years, at an annual rate of about 6 per cent – but also a fundamental change in personal habits and attitudes. Even the notoriously backward agricultural sector was being transformed: by 1955, 10 per cent fewer farm workers were producing 25 per cent more than in 1938, even though the peasants were the largest sector of the population not to gain as much from the general expansion as other sectors did. But though the benefits of this continuous revolution were unevenly spread, there was no doubt that France was leaving the stagnation and Malthusianism of the past behind her and moving steadily into the modern age.

This rapid evolution of the Fifties was all the more remarkable in that the ideas and machinery of the Fourth Republic were in many respects not much more than a continuation of those of the Third. For all the post-Liberation hopes and intentions for a new start, the outcome was a system best suited to a country of small farmers, a large rural population, small businesses and strong regional contrasts. It was thus not particularly appropriate to the needs and pressures of a modern state. The Monnet Plan, the lead taken over Europe and the gradual creation of a consumer society were all achievements brought about despite rather than because of the institutions and political *mores* of the time.

They certainly were not the fruit of the party régime or of the chaotic debates in the National Assembly. Many of them were due to the far-sightedness and vigilance of highly competent civil servants and government-appointed boards and agencies, the excellence of whose staffs went far towards compensating for the weaknesses in the machinery of State. The quality of these administrators, many of them the products of the Ecole Nationale d'Administration ('Enarchs', as they are known), was the envy of other nations less well equipped in this respect. The system 'provided . . . senior civil servants with management and administrative training far superior to anything in Britain, where the job of a civil servant was still seen essentially as to advise his minister on policy. The omnicompetence of these . . . "Enarchs" was legendary.'[13] As a prime example of how to lay the foundations for the future, the Monnet Plan, though not without some shortcomings, was also outstanding.

But the politicians and the derided 'system' must be credited with some sensible and forward-looking actions and policies. In March 1950, for example, the Bidault government approved a plan for economic decentralisation, designed to remedy the situation where one-half of France, north-east of a line running from Le Havre to Grenoble, contained two-thirds of the population, three-quarters of the wealth, all the major industries and of course Paris itself, whereas the other half, to the south-west of the line, was the underprivileged *désert français*. This decision of 1950 led by stages to the approval, after prolonged debates in parliament, of an outline law embodying regional developments, town planning and construction. This, and other parallel measures, provided the vital stepping-stones which enabled the Fifth Republic to establish a separate government department for regional development.

Reference has already been made (see chapter 9) to another outline law, passed in June 1956, introducing far-reaching reforms into the territories of French black Africa. Although French overall control remained, as it was bound to do under the Constitution, with its emphasis on the 'Republic one and indivisible', universal suffrage was extended to all these territories, as well as a large measure of local autonomy. With skill and perseverance, Defferre, the Minister concerned, succeeded in winning acceptance for this bill against the usual unholy alliance between the die-hard Right and the Communists. Although it is correct to say that the problems created by decolonisation brought the Fourth Republic to its end, it is also right to remember that responsible ministers did wake up, albeit belatedly, to the fact that changes were needed, even if that realisation stopped short of facing up to the realities of the Algerian situation.

Politicians, of whatever persuasion or nationality, are notoriously slow to acknowledge the results achieved by their opponents and predecessors. The attitude of the men of the Fifth Republic, from de Gaulle downwards, towards the previous régime conformed with this rule. Yet without the planning and preparation of some of the leaders and officials operating in the years before 1958, France would have been ill-placed to meet the challenge of the Common Market when it came, or to continue her impressive march down the road of modern progress. Specifically, de Gaulle would have found it much more difficult to create his prized nuclear *force de frappe* if successive Fourth Republican governments had not taken crucial decisions on atomic development. Even as the Republic was expiring in 1958, preparations were going forward for the testing of France's first atomic bomb.

Despite the disastrous confusion of ideas over Indochina and North Africa, the field of foreign policy yielded the most notable crop sown by the Fourth Republic. Immediately after the war, it seemed as though a particularly tiresome form of French nationalism, watered and fed by de Gaulle and Bidault, would be the *leitmotiv* of the new régime. French diplomacy tried to perform an increasingly unconvincing balancing act between the USSR and the USA, while at the same time pursuing a hard line towards Germany. Then came the Marshall Plan, the entry of the Communists into opposition and the coming of the Cold War. Abandonment of the earlier stance was virtually inevitable, and despite de Gaulle's consistently unhelpful criticism, Bidault showed courage and realism in helping to steer France firmly into the Western camp and in shouldering responsibility for the London Agreements on a new status for Germany. His replacement at the Quai d'Orsay in the summer of 1948 by Robert Schuman marked a further turning-point in French policy. Now the movement for greater European unity, founded on reconciliation with Germany, began to gather pace. It received a major setback over EDC, but then regained momentum with the passage by the Assembly in 1957 of the Common Market and Euratom treaties. Unlike the fiasco of EDC, these achievements were the result of real leadership. There was plenty of opposition to these forward-looking ideas about Europe: the Communists, the nationalists in Gaullist and right-wing ranks, the Poujadists, the protectionists and representatives of small businesses all objected for different reasons. But their resistance was overcome or bypassed, so that the new Europe was branded with a French trade mark so indelibly that de Gaulle, restored to power, would have had great difficulty erasing it, even supposing he had wished to do so.

Two comparisons suggest themselves here. First, while in Paris imaginative European policies were being conceived and acted upon, in London a cold shower of scepticism about these initiatives was kept steadily running. British leaders of both parties, enjoying all the advantages of a stable and unchallenged political system, chose to beguile themselves in the Fifties with fantasies like the famous concentric circles – an imaginary balance of relationships between Britain and the US, the Commonwealth and continental Europe. British policy-makers may have seen further and acted more wisely than their French counterparts when it came to decolonisation. On Europe, on the other hand, the limpid light of the Ile de France picked out the shape of things to come with far greater definition than was possible in the murk and muddled thinking of London.

Secondly, there is the question of what French foreign and particularly European policy would have been had the General not thrown in his hand in 1946. The answer must inevitably be speculative, but if his Bayeux ideas had been embraced by the Constitution-makers, with the result that a strong executive power was entrusted to Gaullist hands, it seems more than likely that instead of moving towards a new concept of international relations, France might have had for years on end to suffer the dangers of a policy of nationalist grandeur and self-delusion. Had the Gaullist notion of *l'Europe des patries* taken hold in the late Forties, before the laying of the foundation stones of interdependent Europe, that Europe might never have been built.

So the profit-and-loss account of the Fourth Republican era needs in the interest of fairness to be readjusted. None can pretend that these were years of glory, a golden age to savour and become nostalgic over. But Beuve-Méry's epitaph[14] that the régime died 'much less from the blows it received than from its unfitness to live' seems today too sweeping a judgement. Admittedly the difficulties it had to contend with, some of its own making, some thrust upon it, were too great to give it the prospect of long life – though some of them it did overcome. Many of them remain today an endemic part of French politics, above all when it comes to deciding how to distribute the national income. Notwithstanding the depth and bitterness of the differences over EDC or decolonisation, this was the main and persistent cause of political dissension between Left and Right under the Fourth Republic, and explains why the Socialists brought down so many coalition governments. The institutions of the Fifth Republic do not allow for such gymnastics, but human nature changes little and the same grounds for disagreement are still there. Just because a new Constitution was introduced in 1958 it did not mean that the running sores of the past were healed overnight. The *bouilleurs de cru*, so resistant to reform under the Fourth Republic, were just as effective and powerful a lobby under its successor, successfully derailing a government proposal that the right to a licence to distil tax-free spirit should die with its holder. 'The country remained divided on social, economic, educational, foreign, colonial and constitutional questions, just as in the days of the System.'[15]

Though equipped after 1958 with all the powers he wanted, de Gaulle was unable to avoid running into severe trouble – with some of the Army and the *colons* over his plans for Algeria, with the students in 1968, with traditional pressure groups such as the farmers. Yet 1958 – or rather 1959, when the new Republic was officially born – was a time of almost boundless hope, comparable with the 1944–5 period. In the electoral campaign of the autumn of 1958, leading up to the first general election after the adoption of the new Constitution, the predominant sentiment all over the country was that General de Gaulle should be trusted absolutely to order French fortunes for the best, including an Algerian settlement on any terms that seemed suitable to him. A desire for change went hand in hand with immense confidence in the power and personality of the General.[16]

The hopes of 1958 had a very different basis compared with those of 1945. The post-Liberation dream of national unity, cherished in the Resistance and idealised in de Gaulle's speeches at the time, soon faded, as it was bound to do. It never had much reality, symbolising not much more than a general but vague wish for a fresh start which overlooked the divisions left over by the war. One of the founding fathers of the MRP, François de Menthon, wrote that the Republic 'was going to free itself on its own, purified by the sacrifices, the sufferings, the *camaraderies* of the Resistance'. This quasi-mystical vision disregarded the fact that those sufferings and sacrifices had been the experience of the minority of the French people. Far more numerous were those who accepted, with resignation or relative contentment, the rule of Vichy. Then, after the Liberation, came the equally divisive effect of the *épuration* process, when punishment was visited, too harshly in the view of some, not harshly enough in that of others, upon those who had pushed too far the idea of accepting the unavoidable.

Thus the French people, while outwardly professing, in the first flush of the Liberation, a longing for unity and a wish for change, were in fact full of fears and contradictory aims. In these circumstances, it was hardly to be wondered at if the politicians and the parties lost their way. They might have done better, in those early years, to have hearkened to General de Gaulle, who suffered no doubts about which road France should take. But there were ample reasons, already explained, why his message fell, for the most part, on deaf ears. So the men of the moment – many of them, like Bidault or Mollet, new to national politics – were left to do the best they could. As the years went on, they were joined in power by politicians of pre-war parties and generations, in whom the desire for change was not always apparent and was sometimes non-existent. So most of the leaders of the Fourth Republic were condemned, whether they liked it or not, to preside over a transitional stage in French history, instead of playing the role of pioneers of a brave new world. Without fully realising it, they became builders of bridges between the outmoded and complacent régime of the Third Republic and the modern era of the Fifth. It is to their lasting credit that some of the bridges are still standing today.

Compared with the background of frustrated expectation which marked the beginnings of the Fourth Republic, the Gaullist revival, signalled by the return of de Gaulle in 1958 and given substantial form in a new and widely approved Constitution, was no pipe-dream. That Constitution has already, at this moment of writing, endured longer than any of France's Republican Constitutions, with the exception of that of the Third Republic. As for de Gaulle's influence, it lasted well beyond his second retirement in 1969 and his death the following year and is still reflected in the far from still waters of French politics.* Time alone can tell whether the Fifth Republic will continue to be able to command the degree of respect and confidence for lack of which its predecessor expired. Meanwhile, for the student of French affairs, watching with fascination the interplay of forces within what French school textbooks call the Hexagon, de Gaulle's own description of his countrymen can never be far out of mind: 'the most fickle and unmanageable people on earth'. The leaders of the frequently beleaguered and derided Fourth Republic must often, in their moments of trial and perplexity, have arrived at that conclusion themselves.

The troubled life of their Republic, which had passed into a state of trance in June 1958, finally came to a close on 8 January 1959 at the Arc de Triomphe, which is where this book began. On that day, General de Gaulle, his new Constitution in force, his own election as President carried by 78.5 per cent of the 81,000 voters in a freshly established electoral college (parliamentarians, members of county councils, representatives of overseas bodies), arrived at the Elysée to take over from M. Coty. The latter, normally no great phrase-maker, outdid himself in verbal elegance and generosity of spirit by declaring that the General, *'le premier des français, est maintenant le premier en France'*. The two Presidents and their staffs then lunched together and afterwards drove up the Champs Elysées to lay a ceremonial wreath on the tomb of the Unknown Soldier. After this, the protocol was for the new President to escort the old to his car, to be driven away to his native town of Le Havre. Instead, the General plunged into the crowd to shake the outstretched hands of crowds of ex-servicemen, bestowing upon

---

* 1990, the twentieth anniversary of his death and the fiftieth of his first wartime broadcast from London, appealing to French people to continue the struggle, was a kind of Gaullist apotheosis, so fervent were the celebrations. President Mitterrand, who strongly opposed de Gaulle's return in 1958, played a prominent part in the ceremonies.

his predecessor no more than an '*Au revoir, Monsieur Coty.*' The outgoing President was left, with only his personal staff about him, a forlorn and disregarded figure standing on the pavement which surrounds the Arc.[17] Despite a well-attested vindictive streak, de Gaulle was normally well-mannered. His motive on this occasion can only be guessed at,* but the episode marked a symbolic and rather pathetic end to a régime for which, fairly or unfairly, none had ever felt much respect, still less affection.

* Pierre Viansson-Ponté, in *Histoire de la République Gaullienne*, vol. I (Paris, Fayard, 1971), p. 84, suggests that de Gaulle wanted to demonstrate that there had in effect been no true transfer of powers between him and Coty, because the latter, since May 1958, had no powers to transfer.

Chronology

1944	19–25 August	Liberation of Paris.
	9 September	De Gaulle forms first provisional government.
	23 October	Allies officially recognise provisional government.
1945	8 May	German surrender.
	15 August	Japanese surrender.
	21 October	Referendum on abolition of 1875 Constitution and general elections for Constituent Assembly.
	21 November	De Gaulle forms new government.
	21 December	General Commission of the Monnet Plan established.
1946	20 January	De Gaulle resigns.
	24 January	Tripartite agreement between MRP, Socialists and Communists.
	29 January	Félix Gouin forms new government.
	5 May	New draft Constitution rejected in referendum.
	2 June	General elections for second Constituent Assembly.
	16 June	De Gaulle's Bayeux speech.
	26 June	Georges Bidault forms new government.
	13 October	Second draft Constitution approved by referendum.
	10 November	General elections to National Assembly.
	16 December	Léon Blum forms new government.
	19 December	Beginning of Indochinese war.
1947	16 January	Vincent Auriol elected President of the Republic.
	28 January	Paul Ramadier forms new government.
	7 April	De Gaulle launches the *Rassemblement du Peuple Français* (RPF).

1947	4 May	Communist ministers dropped from Ramadier government.
	2 July	USSR refuses to participate in Marshall Plan.
	5 October	Creation of the Cominform.
	19 & 26 October	Gaullist successes at municipal elections.
	19 November	Resignation of Ramadier government.
	22 November	Robert Schuman forms new government.
1948	19 July	Resignation of Schuman government.
	27 July	André Marie forms new government.
	27 August	Resignation of Marie government.
	11 September	Henri Queuille forms new government.
1949	4 April	Atlantic Treaty, establishing NATO, signed in Washington.
	6 October	Resignation of Queuille government.
	29 October	Bidault forms new government.
1950	9 May	Schuman announces plan for European Coal and Steel Community (ECSC).
	24 June	Bidault government resigns.
	25 June	Outbreak of Korean war.
	13 July	René Pleven forms new government.
	26 October	Pleven announces plan for European army (EDC).
1951	7 January	Resignation of Pleven government.
	13 March	Queuille forms new government.
	17 June	General elections to the National Assembly.
	10 July	Resignation of Queuille government.
	8 August	Pleven forms new government.
	13 December	National Assembly ratifies Schuman plan.
1952	7 January	Resignation of Pleven government.
	22 January	Edgar Faure forms new government.
	29 February	Resignation of Faure government.
	6 March	Antoine Pinay forms new government.
	27 May	Six-power EDC Treaty signed in Paris.
	28 May	Anti-American demonstrations in Paris, Duclos arrested.
	29 December	Resignation of Pinay government.
1953	7 January	René Mayer forms new government.
	6 May	De Gaulle allows RPF deputies to go their own way.
	21 May	Resignation of Mayer government.
	26 June	Joseph Laniel forms new government.
	22 July	Pierre Poujade launches his movement.
	27 July	Armistice in Korea.
	20 August	Sultan of Morocco deposed.
	23 December	René Coty elected President of the Republic.

1954	4 April	Prime Minister and Minister of Defence booed at Arc de Triomphe.
	7 May	Fall of Dien Bien Phu.
	12 June	Resignation of Laniel government.
	18 June	Pierre Mendès-France forms new government.
	20 July	Geneva agreements on Indochina.
	30 July	Mendès-France announces internal autonomy for Tunisia.
	30 August	National Assembly rejects EDC.
	1 November	Beginning of Algerian rebellion.
	30 December	National Assembly approves plan for German rearmament (Paris agreements).
1955	26 January	Soustelle appointed Governor-General of Algeria.
	6 February	Resignation of Mendès-France government.
	25 February	Faure forms new government.
	2 April	State of emergency in Algeria.
	5 November	Sultan of Morocco restored to throne.
	29 November	Resignation of Faure government.
	2 December	Dissolution of National Assembly.
1956	2 January	General elections to National Assembly.
	5 February	Guy Mollet forms new government.
	6 February	Mollet pelted with tomatoes in Algiers.
	7 March	Independence for Morocco.
	20 March	Independence for Tunisia.
	26 July	Nasser nationalises Suez Canal.
	29 October	Israel invades the Sinai.
	30 October	Franco-British ultimatum to Nasser.
	5 November	Franco-British attack on Port Said and Canal.
	7 November	Franco-British action broken off.
	29 November	Petrol rationing.
1957	7 January	Massu made responsible for order in Algiers.
	25 March	Treaty of Rome (EEC) signed.
	21 May	Resignation of Mollet government.
	12 June	Maurice Bourgès-Maunoury forms new government.
	10 July	National Assembly ratifies Rome Treaty.
	30 September	Resignation of Bourgès-Maunoury government.
	5 November	Félix Gaillard forms new government.
1958	8 February	French air force bombs Sakhiet in Tunisia.
	13 March	Police demonstration outside National Assembly.
	15 April	Resignation of Gaillard government.

1958	26 April	Demonstration in Algiers for *Algérie française*.
	13 May	Government offices in Algiers invaded by mob; Pierre Pflimlin forms new government.
	15 May	De Gaulle: 'I am ready to assume the powers of the Republic.'
	19 May	De Gaulle holds press conference in Paris.
	24 May	Corsica taken over by Algiers rebels.
	28 May	Resignation of Pflimlin government.
	29 May	President Coty invites de Gaulle to form new government.
	1 June	De Gaulle forms new government.
	28 September	New Constitution for Fifth Republic approved by referendum.
	23 & 30 November	General elections to National Assembly.
	21 December	De Gaulle elected President of the Fifth Republic.

Notes

Prelude

1 Quoted in *L'Année politique 1954* (Paris, PUF, 1955), p. 20.
2 Edmond Jouve, *Le Général de Gaulle et la réconstruction de l'Europe* (Paris, Librairie de Droit et de Jurisprudence, 1967), p. 209.
3 François Mauriac, foreword to Jacques Dumaine's memoirs, *Quai d'Orsay* (Paris, 1955; abridged English edition, London, Chapman & Hall, 1960), pp. 3–4.

Chapter 1

1 Robert Aron, *Histoire de la Libération de la France* (Paris, Fayard, 1959), p. 445.
2 Quoted in Jean Lacouture, *De Gaulle*, vol. II, *Le Politique, 1944–1959* (Paris, Seuil, 1985), p. 13.
3 Charles de Gaulle, *Mémoires de guerre*, vol. III, *Le Salut, 1944–46* (Paris, Plon, 1959), p. 315.
4 Georgette Elgey, *Histoire de la IVe République*, vol. I, *La République des illusions* (Paris, Fayard, 1965), p. 40.
5 Claude Mauriac, *Aimer de Gaulle* (Paris, Grasset, 1978), p. 146. Mauriac, François Mauriac's son, was de Gaulle's private secretary immediately after the war.
6 Quoted in Bernard Ledwidge, *De Gaulle* (London, Weidenfeld & Nicolson, 1982), p. 180.
7 *Le Figaro*, 7 September 1944.
8 *Le Monde*, 25 October 1945.
9 Quoted in Elgey, op. cit., p. 32.
10 See article in *The Times*, 14 December 1948.
11 *Le Populaire*, 2 September 1946.
12 Raymond Aron, *Mémoires* (Paris, Julliard, 1983), p. 234.
13 Quoted in Jean-Pierre Rioux, *The Fourth Republic 1944–58* (translated from the French, London, CUP, 1987), p. 32.
14 See P. Novick, *The Resistance versus Vichy, the purge of collaborators in liberated France* (New York, Columbia University Press, 1968).

15 Rioux, op. cit., p. 38.
16 De Gaulle, op. cit., p. 107.
17 Rioux, op. cit., p. 42.
18 De Gaulle, op. cit., p. 236.
19 De Gaulle, *Discours et messages*, vol. I, *Pendant la guerre, juin 1940–janvier 1946* (Paris, Plon, 1970), p. 473.
20 Janet Flanner, *Paris Journal 1944–65* (New York, Atheneum, 1965). An American resident in Paris, Janet Flanner contributed a regular 'Paris letter' to the *New Yorker* under the pen-name of 'Genêt'.
21 Philip Williams, *Crisis and Compromise* (London, Longman, 1964), p. 97.
22 Quoted in Elgey, op. cit., p. 55.
23 Printed as an annexe to Jacques Fauvet, *La Quatrième République* (Paris, Fayard, 1959).
24 Quoted in Lacouture, op. cit., p. 124.
25 De Gaulle, *Le Salut*, p. 122.
26 François Goguel, *Aspects de la société française* (Paris, Librairie Générale de Droit et de Jurisprudence, 1977).
27 Information supplied by Maurice Schumann, to whom the remark was made.
28 Lacouture, op. cit., p. 223.
29 De Gaulle, *Le Salut*, p. 281.
30 Jacques Dumaine, *Quai d'Orsay* (London, Chapman & Hall, 1960), p. 36.
31 Flanner, op. cit., p. 52.
32 Jules Moch, *Une si longue vie* (Paris, Laffont, 1976), p. 198.
33 Dumaine, op. cit., p. 36.

Chapter 2

1 Charles de Gaulle, *Mémoires de guerre*, vol. III, *Le Salut, 1944–46* (Paris, Plon, 1970), p. 287.
2 Author's conversation with Maurice Schumann, Paris, December 1989.
3 *Combat*, 2 February 1946.
4 *Le Populaire*, 24 May 1946.
5 De Gaulle, *Discours et messages*, vol. II, *Dans l'attente, février 1946–avril 1958* (Paris, Plon, 1970), pp. 5–11.
6 ibid., vol. I, *Pendant la guerre, juin 1940–janvier 1946* (Paris, Plon, 1970), p. 370.
7 Jacques Juillard, *La IVe République* (Paris, Calmann-Lévy, 1968).
8 Quoted in Raoul Girardet, *L'Idée coloniale en France* (Paris, Table Ronde, 1972), p. 288.
9 *Combat*, 21 December 1945.
10 André Siegfried in *L'Année politique 1946* (Paris, PUF, 1947).
11 Paul Delouvrier & Roger Nathan, quoted in G. Elgey, *Histoire de la IVe République*, vol. I, *La République des illusions, 1945–51* (Paris, Fayard, 1965), p. 145.

12 Vincent Auriol, *Journal du Septennat* (7 vols, Paris, Armand Colin, 1970–, henceforward abbreviated as *JS*), vol. II, p. 307.

13 Claude Mauriac, *Aimer de Gaulle* (Paris, Grasset, 1978), p. 370.

14 Auriol, *JS*, vol. I, p. 20.

15 Dennis Duncanson, *Government and Revolution in Vietnam* (London, OUP, 1968), p. 155.

16 Jean Lacoutre & Philippe Devillers, *End of a War* (London, Pall Mall Press, 1969), p. 138.

17 Jean-Marie de la Gorce, *Naissance de la France moderne* vol. I, *L'Après-guerre, 1944–52* (Paris, Grasset, 1979), p. 247.

18 Jacques Dumaine, *Quai d'Orsay* (London, Chapman & Hall, 1958), p. 94.

19 Quoted in Bernard Fall, *The Two Vietnams* (London, Pall Mall Press, 1963), p. 72.

20 Jean Lacouture, *De Gaulle*, vol. II, *Le Politique, 1944–1959* (Paris, Seuil, 1985), pp. 165–6.

21 *Le Figaro*, 24 February 1946.

22 P. Devillers, *Histoire de Vietnam de 1940 à 1952* (Paris, Seuil, 1952), p. 242.

23 ibid., pp. 244–6

24 Letter first published in Elgey, op. cit., vol. I, p. 161; further information supplied by Maurice Schumann, Paris, December 1989.

25 Devillers, op. cit., p. 268.

26 Quoted in Gorce, op. cit., p. 267.

27 Thierry d'Argenlieu, statement to *France-Soir*, 2 January 1946.

28 Auriol, *JS*, vol. I, pp. 157–8.

29 Quoted in Joseph Buttinger, *Vietnam, a political history* (New York, Praeger, 1968), pp. 284–5.

30 Author's conversation with Maurice Schumann, Paris, December 1989.

31 Paul Rivet, *Le Drame franco-vietnamien* (Paris, Cahiers Internationaux No. 6, 1949).

32 Janet Flanner, *Paris Journal 1944–65* (New York, Atheneum, 1965), p. 78, entry for March 1947.

Chapter 3

1 Quoted in Jean-Marie de la Gorce, *Naissance de la France moderne*, vol. I, *L'Après-guerre, 1944–52* (Paris, Grasset, 1979), p. 88.

2 F.H. Hinsley & C.A.G. Simkins, *British Intelligence in the Second World War*, vol. IV (London, HMSO, 1990), p. 83.

3 Charles de Gaulle, *Mémoires de guerre*, vol. III, *Le Salut, 1944–46* (Paris, Plon, 1959), p. 99.

4 Quoted in G. Elgey, *Histoire de la IVe République*, vol. I, *La République des illusions* (Paris, Fayard, 1965), pp. 42–3.

5 Jacques Dumaine, *Quai d'Orsay* (London, Chapman & Hall, 1958), p. 38.

6 Quoted in Jean-Pierre Rioux, *The Fourth Republic 1944–58* (London, CUP, 1987), p. 55.

7 Dumaine, op. cit., diary entry for May 1946.

8 Alexander Werth, *France 1940–1955* (London, Robert Hale, 1956), p. 277.

9 Interview with *The Times*, 17 November 1946.

10 Quoted in Elgey, op. cit., p. 258.

11 Vincent Auriol, *JS*, vol. I, p. 210.

12 J.R. Tournoux, *Carnets secrets de la politique* (Paris, Plon, 1958).

13 Quoted in Elgey, op. cit., p. 292.

14 Dumaine, op. cit., p. 115.

15 Jean Lacouture, *De Gaulle*, vol. II, *Le Politique, 1944–1959* (Paris, Seuil, 1985), p. 296.

16 P.-O. Lapie, *De Léon Blum à de Gaulle* (Paris, Fayard, 1971), p. 78.

17 Auriol, *JS*, vol. I, p. 441.

18 Quoted in Rioux, op. cit., p. 127.

19 Quoted in Elgey, op. cit., pp. 330, 336.

20 *L'Humanité*, 3 October 1947.

21 Auriol, *JS*, vol. I, p. 529.

Chapter 4

1 Jean Monnet, *Mémoires* (Paris, Fayard, 1976), p. 271.

2 ibid., p. 270.

3 Published as Annexe 7 in Vincent Auriol, *JS*, vol. I, p. 695.

4 Auriol, *JS*, vol. II, p. 80.

5 Janet Flanner, *Paris Journal, 1944–65* (New York, Atheneum, 1965), p. 82.

6 Léon Noël, *La Traversée du désert* (Paris, Plon, 1973), p. 49.

7 Author's conversation in Paris, December 1989, with M. Jean Laloi, one of the officials present.

8 Auriol, *JS*, vol. II, p. 241.

9 Jacques Dumaine, *Quai d'Orsay* (London, Chapman & Hall, 1960), p. 183.

10 *The Times*, 4 October 1948.

11 Quoted in Alexander Werth, *France 1940–1955* (London, Robert Hale, 1956), p. 404.

12 Auriol, *JS*, vol. II, p. 574.

13 Flanner, op. cit., p. 99.

14 Georges Pompidou, *Pour rétablir une vérité* (Paris, Flammarion, 1982), p. 78.

15 Auriol, *JS*, vol. III, p. 49.

16 P.-O. Lapie, *De Léon Blum à de Gaulle* (Paris, Fayard, 1971).

17 Press conference of 14 May 1947. See *L'Année politique 1947* (Paris, PUF, 1948), p. 305.

18 Report of the parliamentary commission of inquiry into the affair (the Delahoutre Report), p. 1552.

19 ibid., p. 182.
20 Conversation with the author, Paris, February 1989.

Chapter 5

 1 Quoted in Jean-Marie de la Gorce, *Naissance de la France moderne*,
     vol. I, *L'Après-guerre 1944–52* (Paris, Grasset, 1979), p. 451.
 2 Jean Monnet, *Mémoires* (Paris, Fayard, 1976), p. 337.
 3 ibid., pp. 341–2.
 4 Georges Bidault, *D'une Résistance à l'autre* (Paris, Presses du Siècle,
     1965).
 5 Monnet, op. cit., 360.
 6 René Massigli, *Une comédie des erreurs, 1945–56* (Paris, Plon, 1978),
     p. 203.
 7 Edwin Plowden (Lord Plowden), *An Industrialist in the Treasury*
     (London, André Deutsch, 1989), p. 91.
 8 P.-O. Lapie, *De Léon Blum à de Gaulle* (Paris, Fayard, 1971),
     p. 408.
 9 *La Nef*, issue of March 1953, pp. 7–9.
10 See Raymond Aron and others, *Les Origines de la guerre d'Algérie*
     (Paris, Fayard, 1962).
11 Private conversation with the author, Paris, February 1989.
12 Quoted in Raoul Girardet, *L'Idée coloniale en France* (Paris, Table
     Ronde, 1972), p. 281.
13 Lapie, op. cit., p. 229.
14 Jean Planchais, *La Malaise de l'Armée* (Paris, Plon, 1958), p. 10.
15 G. Elgey, *Histoire de la IVe République*, vol. I, *La République des
     illusions, 1945–51* (Paris, Fayard, 1965), p. 500.
16 Henri Navarre, *Agonie de l'Indochine* (Paris, Plon, 1957), p. 320. For
     the same views expressed twenty years later, see also Navarre, *Le
     Temps des vérités* (Paris, Plon, 1979).
17 Jean-Pierre Rioux, *The Fourth Republic 1944–58* (London, CUP,
     1987), p. 215.
18 Planchais, op. cit., pp. 17–18; John Steward Ambler, *The French Army
     in Politics, 1945–62* (Ohio State University Press, 1966), p. 97.
19 ibid., p. 96.
20 Jean Lartéguy, *Les Centurions* (Paris, Presses de la Cité, 1960).
21 Jacques Dumaine, *Quai d'Orsay* (London, Chapman & Hall, 1960),
     p. 272.
22 Robert Buron, *Carnets politiques* (Paris, Plon, 1968).
23 Quoted in Elgey, op. cit., pp. 507–8.
24 Quoted in Jean Lacouture, *De Gaulle*, vol. II, *Le Politique, 1944–1959*
     (Paris, Seuil, 1985), p. 374.
25 Jacques Soustelle, *Vingt-huit ans de Gaullisme* (Paris, Table Ronde,
     1968).
26 Quoted in Gorce, op. cit., p. 208.
27 Jean-Paul Sartre, *Qu'est-ce que la littérature?* (Paris, Gallimard, 1948).

28 Jacques Fauvet, *Les Forces politiques de la France* (Paris, Fayard, 1951).
29 Herbert Lottman, *The Left Bank, Writers in Paris* (London, Heinemann, 1982), p. 251.
30 Dumaine, op. cit., p. 187.
31 Françoise Sagan, *Un certain sourire* (Paris, Julliard, 1957), p. 42.

Chapter 6

1 Interview in *Paris-Presse*, 18 April 1952.
2 Quoted in G. Elgey, *Histoire de la IVe République*, vol. II, *La République des contradictions, 1951–54* (Paris, Fayard, 1968), p. 63.
3 See Alexander Werth, *France 1940–1955* (London, Robert Hale, 1956), pp. 577–80.
4 Quoted in Jean-Marie de la Gorce, *Naissance de la France moderne*, vol. II, *Apogée et mort de la IVe République 1952–58* (Paris, Grasset, 1979), p. 15.
5 Jean Lacouture, *De Gaulle*, vol. II, *Le Politique, 1944–1959* (Paris, Plon, 1978), p. 284.
6 Jean Monnet, *Mémoires* (Paris, Fayard, 1976), p. 397.
7 René Massigli, *Une comédie des erreurs, 1945–56* (Paris, Plon, 1978), p. 284.
8 Dean Acheson, *Present at the Creation* (New York, W.W. Norton, 1969), pp. 443–4.
9 ibid., p. 444.
10 ibid.
11 Monnet, op. cit., p. 459.
12 Massigli, op. cit., p. 257.
13 Acheson, op. cit., p. 459.
14 *Documents on British Policy Overseas*, Series 2, vol. I (London, HMSO, 1986), p. 342.
15 Acheson, op. cit., p. 552.
16 Account given in Monnet, op. cit., pp. 420–1.
17 See essay by Lord Normanbrook in Sir John Wheeler-Bennett (ed.), *Action This Day, Working with Churchill* (London, Macmillan, 1968), p. 41.
18 Acheson, op. cit., p. 647.
19 ibid., p. 650.
20 Press conference, November 1953 (see also p. 182).
21 Raymond Aron & Daniel Lerner, *La Querelle de la CED* (Paris, Armand Colin, 1957; English edition, London, Thames & Hudson, 1957), p. 10.
22 Quoted in Massigli, op. cit., p. 362.
23 Aron & Lerner, op. cit., p. 10.
24 Hervé Alphand, *L'Etonnement d'être, Journal 1939–1973* (Paris, Fayard, 1977), pp. 242–3.

25 *Foreign Relations of the US* (henceforward referred to as *FRUS*) for 1951 (Washington DC, US Government Printing Office), vol. VI, part 2, 19 March 1953.
26 Quoted in Jacques Fauvet, *La IVe République* (Paris, Fayard, 1959), p. 244.
27 *FRUS*, vol. VI, part 2, p. 1398.
28 Full account of the speech in *FRUS*, vol. V, part 2, pp. 1779–82.
29 *FRUS* 1952–4, vol. V, part 1, p. 469.
30 Quoted in Werth, op. cit., p. 569.
31 Story told in Elgey, op. cit., p. 416.
32 Printed as Annexe X in Vincent Auriol, *JS*, vol. VII.
33 Georges Bidault, *D'une Résistance à l'autre* (Paris, Presses du Siècle, 1965).
34 Janet Flanner, *Paris Journal, 1944–65* (New York, Atheneum, 1965), pp. 214–15.
35 Private conversation with author, Paris, February 1989.
36 Auriol, *JS*, vol. VII, pp. 381, 384.

Chapter 7

1 Henri Navarre, *Agonie de l'Indochine* (Paris, Plon, 1957), p. 3.
2 Mondon Report on the piastre traffic (Paris, Imprimerie de l'Assemblée Nationale, 1954). The report, which was never debated, contained evidence about Bao Dai's involvement in the traffic.
3 Anthony Eden, *Full Circle* (London, Cassell, 1960), p. 89.
4 Vincent Auriol, *JS*, vol. VII, p. 485.
5 *Le Monde*, 1 December 1953.
6 Navarre, op. cit., p. 255.
7 Findings of the Catroux Commission, and details of the Navarre plan, published in G. Elgey, *Histoire de la IVe République*, vol. II, *La République des contradictions, 1951–54* (Paris, Fayard, 1968), pp. 553ff.
8 Eden, op. cit., p. 101.
9 ibid.
10 *FRUS*, vol. XIII, part 1, p. 1371.
11 Information supplied by M. Maurice Schumann, who acted as interpreter between Dulles and Bidault.
12 McGeorge Bundy, *Danger and Survival* (New York, Random House, 1988), pp. 260–70.
13 Gladwyn Jebb, *The Memoirs of Lord Gladwyn* (London, Weidenfeld & Nicolson, 1972), p. 270.
14 Edgar Faure, *Mémoires*, vol. I (Paris, Plon, 1982), p. 586.
15 Quoted in Jean Lacouture, *De Gaulle*, vol. II, *Le Politique, 1944–1959* (Paris, Seuil, 1985), p. 409.
16 *FRUS*, vol. V, part 2, p. 1426.
17 Claude Nicolet, *Pierre Mendès-France ou le métier de Cassandre* (Paris, Julliard, 1959).

18 Private conversation with the author, September 1988.
19 See especially, for the witness of two senior pro-EDC French ambassadors, Jean Chauvel, *Commentaire* (Paris, Fayard, 1972); Hervé Alphand, *L'Etonnement d'être* (Paris, Fayard, 1977).
20 *FRUS*, vol. V, part 1, pp. 1018ff.
21 ibid., p. 1024.
22 ibid., p. 1031.
23 ibid., p. 1029.
24 ibid., p. 1037.
25 Information supplied by M. Robert Rothschild, London, April 1989. He was Spaak's *directeur de cabinet* at the time.
26 Pierre Rouanet, *Mendès-France au pouvoir* (Paris, Laffont, 1965), p. 270.
27 *FRUS*, vol. V, part 1, p. 1059.
28 *Documents diplomatiques français 1954* (Paris, Imprimerie Nationale, 1955). These minutes of the Brussels conference were recorded by Belgian officials. A detailed account of this stormy meeting was also reported to Washington by Tomlinson (*FRUS*, vol. V, part 1, pp. 1054–6).
29 Paul-Henri Spaak, *The Continuing Battle* (London, Weidenfeld & Nicolson, 1971), pp. 167–8.
30 *FRUS*, vol. V, part 1, p. 1062.
31 Spaak, op. cit., p. 157.
32 For the account of the Chartwell meeting, see British Cabinet document WU/1197/783 G, of 23 August 1954. The French account is as cited in note 28 above, p. 135.
33 Jacques Fauvet, *La IVe République* (Paris, Fayard, 1959), p. 277.
34 *Documents diplomatiques français*, op. cit., p. 137.

Chapter 8

1 Jean-Pierre Rioux, *The Fourth Republic* (London, CUP, 1987), p. 338.
2 ibid., p. 321.
3 ibid., p. 379.
4 See P. Thibaud & B. Cacérès, *Regards neufs sur les budgets familiaux* (Paris, Seuil, 1958).
5 Philip Williams, *Crisis and Compromise* (London, Longman, 1964), p. 348.
6 Robert Buron, *Carnets politiques* (Paris, Plon, 1968).
7 See Alexander Werth, *France, 1940–1955* (London, Robert Hale, 1956), pp. 204–8.
8 Janet Flanner, *Paris Journal, 1944–65* (New York, Atheneum, 1965), p. 299.
9 Werth, op. cit., p. 264.
10 See two articles in *The Times*, 21 and 22 April 1955.

Chapter 9

1 Jules Moch, *Une si longue vie* (Paris, Laffont, 1976).
2 Alistair Horne, *A Savage War of Peace* (revised ed., London, Macmillan, 1987), p. 149.
3 The Poujadist newspaper *Fraternité française*, issue of 11 February 1956.
4 Horne, op. cit., p. 152.
5 See Alexander Werth, *The Strange History of Pierre Mendès-France* (London, Barrie, 1957), pp. 306–8.
6 Jean Dutourd, *Les Taxis de la Marne* (Paris, Gallimard, 1956).
7 Janet Flanner, *Paris Journal, 1944–65* (New York, Atheneum, 1965), entry for 5 September 1956.
8 Jean-Marie de la Gorce, *Naissance de la France moderne*, vol. II, *Apogée et mort de la IVe République* (Paris, Grasset, 1979), p. 370.
9 See *The Times* article of 3 December 1956.
10 J.-P. Rioux, *The Fourth Republic 1944–58* (London, CUP, 1987), p. 275.
11 Pierre Leulliette, *St Michel et le dragon* (Paris, 1961).
12 Jacques Fauvet, *La IVe République* (Paris, Fayard, 1959), p. 333.
13 See Jacques Massu, *La vraie bataille d'Alger* (Paris, Plon, 1971).
14 Horne, op. cit., p. 199.
15 Pierre-Henri Simon, *Contre la torture* (Paris, Seuil, 1957).
16 Léon Noël, *La Traversée du désert* (Paris, Plon, 1973), p. 49. Despite de Gaulle's tribute, he did not, on his return to power the following year, restore this man of honour to a command befitting his record.
17 Henri Alleg, *La Question* (Paris, Minuit, 1958).
18 Quoted in Horne, op. cit., p. 197.
19 Philip Williams, *Crisis and Compromise* (London, Longman, 1964), p. 52.
20 See Jean Lacouture, *De Gaulle*, vol. II, *Le Politique, 1944–1959* (Paris, Seuil, 1985), p. 419.
21 Author's conversation with Lord Gladwyn, London, March 1989.
22 Author's conversation with M. de Courcel, Paris, March 1989.
23 Conversation between Pineau and Lacouture, July 1984, quoted in Lacouture, op. cit., p. 431.
24 Conversation with the author, Paris, February 1989.
25 Raymond Aron, *La Tragédie algérienne* (Paris, Plon, 1957).
26 Raymond Aron, *L'Algérie et la République* (Paris, Plon, 1958).
27 François Mitterrand, *Présence française et abandon* (Paris, Plon, 1957).
28 Harold Macmillan, *Riding the Storm* (London, Macmillan, 1971), p. 331.
29 Susan Mary Alsop, *To Marietta from Paris, 1945–1960* (London, Weidenfeld & Nicolson, 1976), p. 310.

Chapter 10

1 Quoted in Alistair Horne, *A Savage War of Peace* (revised ed., London, Macmillan, 1987), p. 28.

2 *The Times*, 5 March 1958.

3 Edgar Faure, *Mémoires*, vol. I (Paris, Plon, 1982), pp. 668–9.

4 Horne, op. cit., p. 267.

5 Jean Ferniot, *De Gaulle et le 13 mai* (Paris, Plon, 1965), p. 154.

6 *The 13th of May, the Advent of de Gaulle's Republic, a documentary collection* (London, OUP, 1968), p. 247.

7 Conversations with the author, Paris, December 1989.

8 See M. & S. Bromberger, *Les 13 complots du 13 mai* (Paris, Fayard, 1959), p. 46.

9 Charles de Gaulle, *Mémoires d'espoir*, vol. I, *Le Renouveau, 1958–62* (Paris, Plon, 1971), p. 19.

10 Quoted in J.R. Tournoux, *La Tragédie du Général* (Paris, Plon, 1967), p. 284.

11 Robert Buron, *Carnets de la guerre d'Algérie* (Paris, Plon, 1965).

12 Quoted in J.R. Tournoux, *Secrets d'Etat*, vol. I (Paris, Plon, 1960), p. 231.

13 Jean Lacouture, *De Gaulle*, vol. II, *Le Politique, 1944–1959* (Paris, Seuil, 1985), p. 446.

14 ibid., p. 451.

15 Conversations with the author, Paris, March 1989.

16 See *The Times*, 15 April 1958.

17 Quoted in an obituary notice in *Le Monde*, 28 January 1983.

18 Ferniot, op. cit., pp. 243–4.

19 Léon Noël, *La Traversée du désert* (Paris, Plon, 1973), pp. 135–6. He recounts how some young deputies, including Giscard d'Estaing, a future President of the Fifth Republic, made a *démarche* to Coty in December 1956, urging him to appeal to de Gaulle when the next government crisis occurred.

20 Olivier Guichard, *Mon Général* (Paris, Grasset, 1980), pp. 355–6.

21 Tournoux, op. cit., p. 289; Lacouture, op. cit., p. 464.

22 Story recounted in Ferniot, op. cit., p. 303.

Chapter 11

1 Jean Lacouture, *De Gaulle*, vol. II, *Le Politique, 1944–1959* (Paris, Seuil, 1985), p. 468.

2 Charles de Gaulle, *Mémoires d'espoir*, vol. I, *Le Renouveau, 1958–62* (Paris, Plon, 1970), p. 22.

3 *Le Monde*, 17 May 1958.

4 J.R. Tournoux, *Secrets d'Etat*, vol. I (Paris, Plon, 1960), p. 294.

5 M. & S. Bromberger, *Les 13 complots du 13 mai* (Paris, Fayard, 1959), pp. 315–16.

6 Story told in Tournoux, op. cit., p. 340.

7 Jules Moch, *Une si longue vie* (Paris, Laffont, 1976), p. 524.

8 Moch, writing in *Le Midi libre*, May 1959.

9 De Gaulle, op. cit., p. 28.

10 ibid., p. 29.

11 Moch, *Une si longue vie*, p. 534.
12 Lacouture, op. cit., p. 476.
13 Jean Ferniot, *De Gaulle et le 13 mai* (Paris, Plon, 1965), p. 434.
14 ibid., pp. 398–401.
15 Moch, writing in *Le Midi libre*, June 1958.
16 Guy Mollet, writing in the *Revue socialiste*, May 1959.
17 Quoted in Ferniot, op. cit., p. 435.
18 ibid., p. 448.
19 André Dulac, *Nos guerres perdues* (Paris, Fayard, 1969), pp. 87–8.
20 De Gaulle's address published in *Rassemblement*, the RPF organ, 8 October 1949.
21 Susan Mary Alsop, *To Marietta from Paris, 1945–1960* (London, Weidenfeld & Nicolson, 1976), p. 318.
22 Moch, *Une si longue vie*, p. 538.
23 Edmond Jouhaud, *Serons-nous enfin compris?* (Paris, Albin Michel, 1984), p. 62.
24 See *Le procès de Raoul Salan*, in the series *Les Grands Procès Contemporains* (Paris, Albin Michel).
25 See *Le Monde*, 18 June 1984.
26 Author's conversation with Michel Debré, Paris, December 1989. He added that the parachutists would have been welcomed 'with open arms'. There is no doubt that Debré favoured Resurrection.
27 M. & S. Bromberger, op. cit., p. 422.
28 P.-O. Lapie, *De Léon Blum à de Gaulle* (Paris, Fayard, 1971), p. 807.
29 Conversation with the author, Paris, December 1989.
30 Quoted in Ferniot, op. cit., p. 482. In fact, de Gaulle seems to have made the remark later on, when in July he gave Soustelle a post in the government.
31 *Le Monde*, 3 June 1958.
32 Quoted in Olivier Guichard, *Mon Général* (Paris, Grasset, 1980), p. 362.
33 Quoted in Ferniot, op. cit., p. 484.
34 Quoted in Lacouture, op. cit., p. 487.

Chapter 12

1 Conversation with the author, Paris, December 1989.
2 François Goguel (ed.), *Actes du Colloque de Nice* (conference held in 1977 on the birth, life and death of the Fourth Republic) (Paris, Librairie de Droit et de Jurisprudence), p. 215.
3 *Le Monde*, 1 October 1946.
4 Alfred Grosser, *La Quatrième République et sa politique extérieure* (Paris, Armand Colin, 1967), p. 398.
5 See *Le Monde* for 24, 25 and 27 February 1979 for reports of a symposium on the Fourth Republic. The conference had its attention drawn to this letter by René Massigli.

6 Goguel (ed.), op. cit., p. 95.
7 See *Le Monde*'s reports on the symposium mentioned in note 5 above, which Mendès addressed.
8 Edgar Faure, *Mémoires*, vol. I (Paris, Plon, 1982), p. 257.
9 W.G. Andrews, *French Policy and Algeria* (New York, 1962), quoted in Philip Williams, *Crisis and Compromise* (London, Longman, 1964), p. 45.
10 *L'Année politique 1958* (Paris, PUF, 1959), p. 558.
11 Conversation with the author, Paris, February 1989.
12 Vincent Auriol, *JS*, vol. V, p. 493.
13 Denis Healey, *The Time of My Life* (London, Michael Joseph, 1989), p. 405.
14 In *Le Monde*, 29 May 1958.
15 Philip Williams & Martin Harrison, *De Gaulle's Republic* (London, Longman, 1960), p. 164.
16 See *The Times* file for November 1958 for reports from the provinces.
17 Account given in Jean Lacouture, *De Gaulle*, vol. II, *Le Politique, 1944–1959* (Paris, Seuil, 1985), pp. 687–8.

Bibliography

Dean Acheson, *Present at the Creation* (New York, W.W. Norton, 1969)

Henri Alleg, *La Question* (Paris, Minuit, 1958)

Hervé Alphand, *L'Etonnement d'être, Journal 1939–1973* (Paris, Fayard, 1977)

Susan Mary Alsop, *To Marietta from Paris, 1945–1960* (London, Weidenfeld & Nicolson, 1976)

John Steward Ambler, *The French Army in Politics, 1945–62* (Ohio State University Press, 196)

Raymond Aron, *La Tragédie algérienne* (Paris, Plon, 1957)
   L'Algérie et la République (Paris, Plon, 1958)
   Mémoires (Paris, Julliard, 1983)

Raymond Aron & Daniel Lerner, *La Querelle de la CED* (Paris, Armand Colin, 1957; English edition, *France Defeats the EDC*, London, Thames & Hudson, 1957)

Raymond Aron and others, *Les Origines de la guerre d'Algérie* (Paris, Fayard, 1962)

Robert Aron, *Histoire de la Libération de la France* (Paris, Fayard, 1959)

Vincent Auriol, *Journal du Septennat, 1947–1954* (7 vols, Paris, Armand Colin, 1970–71)

Georges Bidault, *D'une Résistance à l'autre* (Paris, Presses du Siècle, 1965)

Merry & Serge Bromberger, *Les 13 complots du 13 mai* (Paris, Fayard, 1959)

McGeorge Bundy, *Danger and Survival* (New York, Random House, 1988)

Robert Buron, *Carnets de la guerre d'Algérie* (Paris, Plon, 1965)
   Carnets politiques (Paris, Plon, 1968)

Joseph Buttinger, *Vietnam, a political history* (New York, Praeger, 1968)

Jean Chauvel, *Commentaire, d'Alger à Berne* (Paris, Fayard, 1972)

Philippe Devillers, *Histoire de Vietnam de 1940 à 1952* (Paris, Seuil, 1952)

André Dulac, *Nos guerres perdues* (Paris, Fayard, 1969)

Jacques Dumaine, *Quai d'Orsay* (abridged English edition, London, Chapman & Hall, 1960)

Dennis Duncanson, *Government and Revolution in Vietnam* (London, OUP, 1968)

Jean Dutourd, *Les Taxis de la Marne* (Paris, Gallimard, 1956)

Anthony Eden (Lord Avon), *Full Circle* (London, Cassell, 1960)

Georgette Elgey, *Histoire de la IVe République*, vol. I, *La République des illusions, 1945–51* (Paris, Fayard, 1965); vol. II, *La République des contradictions, 1951–54* (Paris, Fayard, 1968)

Bernard Fall, *The Two Vietnams* (London, Pall Mall Press, 1963)

Edgar Faure, *Mémoires* (2 vols, Paris, Plon, 1982)

Jacques Fauvet, *Les Force politiques de la France* (Paris, Fayard, 1951)
La IVe République (Paris, Fayard, 1959)

Jean Ferniot, *De Gaulle et le 13 mai* (Paris, Plon, 1965)

Janet Flanner, *Paris Journal, 1944–65* (New York, Atheneum, 1965)

Charles de Gaulle, *Mémoires de guerre*, vol. III, *Le Salut, 1944–46* (Paris, Plon, 1959)
Mémoires d'espoir, vol. I, *Le Renouveau, 1958–62* (Paris, Plon, 1970)
Discours et messages, vol. I, *Pendant la guerre, juin 1940–janvier 1946*; vol. II, *Dans l'attente, février 1946–avril 1958*; vol. III, *Avec le renouveau, mai 1958–juillet 1962* (all Paris, Plon, 1970)

Raoul Girardet, *L'Idée coloniale en France* (Paris, Table Ronde, 1972)

François Goguel, *Aspects de la société française* (Paris, Librairie Générale de Droit et de Jurisprudence)
(ed.), *Actes du colloque de Nice* (Paris, Librairie Générale de Droit et de Jurisprudence, 1977)

Paul-Marie de la Gorce, *Naissance de la France moderne*, vol. I, *L'Après-guerre 1944–52*; vol. II, *Apogée et mort de la IVe Republique 1952–58* (Paris, Grasset, 1979)

Alfred Grosser, *La Quatrième République et sa politique extérieure* (Paris, Armand Colin, 1967)

Olivier Guichard, *Mon Général* (Paris, Grasset, 1980)

Denis Healey, *The Time of My Life* (London, Michael Joseph, 1989)

F.H. Hinsley & C.A.G. Simkins, *British Intelligence in the Second World War*, vol. IV (London, HMSO, 1990)

Stanley Hoffman, *Le Mouvement Poujade* (Paris, Armand Colin, 1956)

Alistair Horne, *A Savage War of Peace* (revised ed. London, Macmillan, 1987)

Ronald E.M. Irving, *The First Indochina War* (London, Croom Helm, 1975)

Gladwyn Jebb (Lord Gladwyn), *The Memoirs of Lord Gladwyn* (London, Weidenfeld & Nicolson, 1972)

Edmond Jouhaud, *Serons-nous enfin compris?* (Paris, Albin Michel, 1984)

Edmond Jouve, *Le Général de Gaulle et la réconstruction de l'Europe* (Paris, Librairie de Droit et de Jurisprudence, 1967)

Jacques Juillard, *La IVe République* (Paris, Calmann-Lévy, 1968)

Jean Lacouture, *De Gaulle*, vol. II, *Le Politique, 1944–1959* (Paris, Seuil, 1985)
   Ho Chi Minh (Paris, Seuil, 1985)

Jean Lacouture & Philippe Devillers, *La fin d'une guerre, Indochine 1954* (Paris, Seuil, 1960); English trans., *End of a War* (London, Pall Mall Press, 1969)

Pierre-Olivier Lapie, *De Léon Blum à de Gaulle* (Paris, Fayard, 1971)

Jean Lartéguy, *Les Centurions* (Paris, Presses de la Cité, 1960)

Bernard Ledwidge, *De Gaulle* (London, Weidenfeld & Nicolson, 1982)

Pierre Leulliette, *St Michel et le dragon* (Paris, 1961)

Herbert Lottman, *The Left Bank, Writers in Paris* (London, Heinemann, 1982)

Herbert Luthy, *The State of France* (London, Secker & Warburg, 1955)

Harold Macmillan, *Riding the Storm, 1956–59* (London, Macmillan, 1971)

Donald Macrae, *Parliament, Parties and Society in France, 1946–1958* (London, Macmillan, 1967)

René Massigli, *Une comédie des erreurs, 1945–56* (Paris, Plon, 1978)

Jacques Massu, *La vraie bataille d'Alger* (Paris, Plon, 1971)

Claude Mauriac, *Aimer de Gaulle* (Paris, Grasset, 1978)

François Mitterrand, *Présence française et abandon* (Paris, Plon, 1957)

Jules Moch, *Une si longue vie* (Paris, Laffont, 1976)

Jean Monnet, *Mémoires* (Paris, Fayard, 1976)

Henri Navarre, *Agonie de l'Indochine* (Paris, Plon, 1957)
   Le Temps des vérités (Paris, Plon, 1979)

Claude Nicolet, *Pierre Mendès-France ou le métier de Cassandre* (Paris, Julliard, 1959)

Léon Noël, *La Traversée du désert* (Paris, Plon, 1973)

P. Novick, *The Resistance versus Vichy, the purge of collaborators in liberated France* (New York, Columbia University Press, 1968)

Jean Planchais, *La Malaise de l'Armée* (Paris, Plon, 1958)

Edwin Plowden (Lord Plowden), *An Industrialist in the Treasury* (London, André Deutsch, 1989)

Georges Pompidou, *Pour rétablir une vérité* (Paris, Flammarion, 1982)

René Rémond, *Le Retour de de Gaulle* (Paris, Editions Complexe, 1984)
   Les Droits en France (Paris, Editions Aubier Montaigne, 1984)

Jean-Pierre Rioux, *La France de la quatrième République, 1944–58* (2 vols, Paris, Seuil, 1980 & 1983); English edition, *The Fourth Republic 1944–58* (London, CUP, 1987)

Paul Rivet, *Le Drame franco-vietnamien* (Paris, Cahiers Internationaux No. 6, 1949)

Pierre Rouanet, *Mendès-France au pouvoir* (Paris, Laffont, 1965)

Françoise Sagan, *Un certain sourire* (Paris, Julliard, 1957)

Jean-Paul Sartre, *Qu'est-ce que la littérature?* (Paris, Gallimard, 1948)

André Siegfried, *De la IVe à la Ve République* (Paris, Grasset, 1958)

Pierre-Henri Simon, *Contre la torture* (Paris, Seuil, 1957)

Jacques-Soustelle, *Vingt-huit ans de Gaullisme* (Paris, Table Ronde, 1968)

Paul-Henri Spaak, *The Continuing Battle* (London, Weidenfeld & Nicolson, 1971); abridged English edition of *Combats inachevés* (2 vols, Paris, Fayard, 1969)

J.R. Tournoux, *Secrets d'Etat*, vol. I (Paris, Plon, 1960)
   Carnets secrets de la politique (Paris, Plon, 1958)
   La Tragédie du Général (Paris, Plon, 1967)

Pierre Viansson-Ponté, *Histoire de la République Gaullienne*, vol. I, *La fin d'une époque, 1958–1962* (Paris, Fayard, 1971)

Alexander Werth, *France, 1940–1955* (London, Robert Hale, 1956)
   The Strange History of Pierre Mendès-France (London, Barrie, 1957)

Sir John Wheeler-Bennett (ed.), *Action this Day, Working with Churchill* (London, Macmillan, 1968)

Philip Williams, *Crisis and Compromise* (London, Longman, 1964)
   Wars, Plots and Scandals in Post-War France (London, CUP, 1970)

Philip Williams & Martin Harrison, *De Gaulle's Republic* (London, Longman, 1960)

Documents, Newspapers etc.

Documents diplomatiques français, 1954–56, including Annexes (Paris, Imprimerie Nationale, 1955–59)

Documents on British Policy Overseas, Series 2, vol. I (London, HMSO, 1986)

Foreign Relations of the United States, vols V, VI, XIII (Washington, DC, US Government Printing Office, various dates)

Journal Officiel (Paris, Imprimerie Nationale, 1945 onwards)

Le Procès de Raoul Salan, in the series *Les Grands Procès Contemporains* (Paris, Albin Michel)

P. Thibaud and B. Cacérès, *Regards neufs sur les budgets familiaux* (Paris, Seuil, 1958)

The 13th of May, the Advent of de Gaulle's Republic, a documentary collection (London, OUP, 1968)

Files of *The Times, Le Monde*, and other French papers and magazines, many of them now extinct.

Index

Acheson, Dean, 126, 169–70, 172, 174, 176
Action Française (movement), 157
Action française (newspaper), 73n
Adenauer, Konrad, 123, 125, 128, 172, 222, 226
affaire des fuites, 236–7
alcoholism, 233–4, 256, 382
Algeria: and French colonialism, 37, 135–6; nationalist riots, 63, 133; status, 129, 239; Assembly established and reforms in, 134–5, 249; war (rebellion) in, 237–9, 267–70, 293–5, 297–301; Soustelle appointed Governor-General, 239; police and army torture in, 242, 269, 283–7; rebel violence and reprisals in, 248–9; as 1956 election issue, 252–3, 256–7; French intransigence over (*Algérie française*), 253–4, 263–8, 281–2, 295, 305–8, 319, 323; de Gaulle and, 254; Mollet's policy on, 261–2, 265–6; Catroux's Governor-Generalship, 262–3, 266; Lacoste in, 267, 269–70,

273, 281; French forces in, 267–9, 280; and Suez crisis, 269, 274–6; Mendès-France's 7-point programme for, 270–1; and Defferre's 'outline law', 279; economic effect of war, 280; 1957 'outline law' for, 281–2, 287, 301; 'pacification' and repression in, 282–7, 292, 300; de Gaulle's views on, 291–2; renewed French demands for independence, 293–5; socio-economic reforms, 300–1; French military-political intrigues and alliances over, 305–8, 320–2; and movement to recall de Gaulle, 321–6, 337; European revolt in, 323–5; and Corsican secession, 339–40
Algiers: de Gaulle's wartime government established in, 6–7; European anti-Mollet demonstrations in, 264–5, 298; 'battle of', 282, 292, 301; May 1958 demonstration and revolt, 323–6; Muslim demonstrators in, 333–4; and de Gaulle's government, 361
Alleg, Henri: *La Question*, 285–6